LEARNING RESOURCE
WILKES COMMUNITY COLLEGE 28667

D0025254

CHILDREN AND DEATH

Edited by

Danai Papadatou
University of Athens

Costas Papadatos
University of Athens

⬤HEMISPHERE PUBLISHING CORPORATION
A member of the Taylor & Francis Group

New York   Washington   Philadelphia   London

CHILDREN AND DEATH

Copyright © 1991 by Hemisphere Publishing Corporation. All rights reserved. Printed in the United States of America. Except as permitted under the United States Copyright Act of 1976, no part of this publication may be reproduced or distributed in any form or by any means, or stored in a data base or retrieval system, without the prior written permission of the publisher.

Copyright for cover art is held by Yiorgos Polos. All rights reserved.

Copyright for Chapter 11 is held by Elisabeth Kübler-Ross. All rights reserved.

Copyright for Chapter 26 is held by Sandra L. Bertman. All rights reserved.

Chapter 16 was previously published in *The Journal of Palliative Care* (Spring 1990). 6: 1. Reprinted by permission.

1 2 3 4 5 6 7 8 9 0   B R B R   9 8 7 6 5 4 3 2 1

This book was set in Times Roman by Hemisphere Publishing Corporation. The editors were Lys Ann Shore and Deena Williams Newman; the production supervisor was Peggy M. Rote; and the typesetters were Anahid Alvandian, Deborah S. Hamblen, and Darrell D. Larson, Jr.
Cover design by Sharon M. DePass.
Printing and binding by Braun-Brumfield, Inc.

A CIP catalog record for this book is available from the British Library.

Library of Congress Cataloging-in-Publication Data

Children and Death / edited by Danai Papadatou, Costas Papadatos.

    p. cm—(Series in death education, aging, and health care)
   Outgrowth of the International Conference on Children and Death,
held in Athens, in Oct. 1989.
   Includes bibliographical references and index.
   1. Terminally ill children—Psychology.   2. Children and death.
3. Children—Death—Psychological aspects.   4. Grief.
I. Papadatou, Danai,   II. Papadatos, Constantine J.
III. International Conference on Children and Death (1989: Athens,
Greece)   IV. Series.
RJ249.C487 1991   90-20331
155.9′57—dc20   CIP

ISBN 1-56032-043-5
ISSN 0275-3510

Contents

PART TWO: GRIEVING CHILDREN AND FAMILIES

PART THREE: DYING CHILDREN, FAMILIES, AND PROFESSIONALS

PART SIX: STRESS, COPING, AND NEEDS
OF PROFESSIONALS

CONCLUSION

EPILOGUE

Contributors

Ann Armstrong-Dailey, Children's Hospice International, Alexandria, Virginia, USA

Ofra Ayalon, Ph.D., University of Haifa, Israel

Sheryle R. Baker, M.A., The Life Center of the Suncoast, Inc., Tampa, Florida, USA

Leslie Balmer, M.A., York University, Toranto, Ontario, Canada

Sandra L. Bertman, Ph.D., University of Massachusetts Medical Center, Worcester, Massachusetts, USA

Stavroula Beratis, M.D., University of Patras, Medical School, Patras, Greece

Dora Black, M.B., FRCPsych, D.P.M., The Royal Free Hospital, London, England

C. M. J. Boon, M.A., Pediatric Oncology Center, Groningen, The Netherlands

Mina Bouras, Ph.D., Athens, Greece

Elisabeth Budd, R.N., Hospital for Sick Children, Toronto, Ontario, Canada

Lisa Caufield, R.N., Hospital for Sick Children, Toronto, Ontario, Canada

Charles A. Corr, Ph.D., Southern Illinois University at Edwardsville, Edwardsville, Illinois, USA

Betty Davies, R.N., Ph.D., University of British Columbia, Vancouver, British Columbia, Canada

Ciarán M. Duffy, M.B., B.Ch., F.R.C.P.C., Montreal Children's Hospital, Quebec, Canada

Janna A. Excell, M.Ed., Evergreen Mortuary and Cemetery, Tucson, Arizona, USA

Fran Zappia Farrell, R.N., M.S.W., University of Arizona, Health Sciences Center, Tucson, Arizona, USA

Stephen Fleming, Ph.D., York University, Toronto, Ontario, Canada

Laurie Gottlieb, R.N., Ph.D., McGill University, Montreal, Canada

Earl A. Grollman, D.D., Belmont, Massachusetts, USA

J.E.H.M. Hoekstra-Weebers, M.A., Pediatric Oncology Center, Groningen, The Netherlands

G.B. Humphrey, M.D., Ph.D., Pediatric Oncology Center, Groningen, The Netherlands

John J. Hutter, Jr., M.D., University of Arizona, Health Sciences Center, Tucson, Arizona, USA

Sue Jennings, Ph.D., London Hospital Medical College, London, England

W.A. Kamps, M.D., Pediatric Oncology Center, Groningen, The Netherlands

Gideon Koren, M.D., A.B.M.T., Hospital for Sick Children, Toronto, Ontario, Canada

Elisabeth Kübler-Ross, M.D., The Elisabeth Kübler-Ross Center, Headwaters, Virginia, USA

Mooli Lahad, Ph.D., Community Stress Prevention Centre, Kiryat, Shmona, Israel

Ariella Lang, R.N., M.Sc., Jewish General Hospital, Montreal, Canada

Marcia Lattanzi-Licht, R.N., M.A., Comprehensive Psychological Services Group, Boulder, Colorado, USA

Maurice Levy, M.D., Hospital for Sick Children, Toronto, Ontario, Canada

J. L. Littlewood, B.Sc., Ph.D., Loughborough University of Technology, England

Ida M. Martinson, R.N., Ph.D., University of California, San Francisco, California, USA

Paul S. Meltzer, M.D., Ph.D., University of Arizona, Health Sciences Center, Tucson, Arizona, USA

Danai Papadatou, Ph.D., University of Athens, Athens, Greece

Pamela Pollock, R.N., B.Sc.N., Hospital for Sick Children, Toronto, Ontario, Canada

Ginette Raimbault, M.D., Hospital for Sick Children, Paris, France

Therese A. Rando, Ph.D., Therese A. Rando Associates, Ltd., Warwick, Rhode Island, USA

Byron Samios, M.D., National Drug Organization, Athens, Greece

Stephen P. Spielberg, M.D., Ph.D., F.R.C.P.C., Hospital for Sick Children, Toronto, Ontario, Canada

Derek Steinberg, M.D., B.S., M.Phil., F.R.C.Psych., Bethlem Royal Hospital, and the Maudsley Hospital, Beckenham, Kent, England

Nassia Varveri-Sofra, National Drug Organization, Athens, Greece

Hannelore Wass, Ph.D., University of Florida, Gainesville, Florida, USA

Robert L. Wrenn, Ph.D., University of Arizona, Tucson, Arizona, USA

Preface

The idea of this book grew out of the International Conference on Children and Death, held in Athens in October 1989. Internationally known guest speakers, expert participants, and students attended and contributed to the richness and success of this conference. It was a unique experience that provided all of us— gathered from different countries around the world—with the opportunity to share knowledge, insight, and support. It also strengthened our sense of community in promoting the philosophy of death education, hospice care, and bereavement support for children and families in need. This meeting reaffirmed the conviction that exploring the issue of death may help each of us identify our values, priorities, and goals in life and enhance the quality of our everyday living by giving it deeper meaning.

We hope this volume will be useful to health professionals, educators, caregivers, and all those who interact with children and families confronting death, dying, and bereavement. Some of the questions that guided our efforts in editing this book have been the following:

How can we educate children about death?

What is the quality of care we can provide to families of children who are dying?

How can we best understand the bereavement process experienced by family members when a child dies?

We hope readers will be stimulated to explore these issues further and to develop the skills needed for caring effectively for grieving or dying children and their families.

This book is unique in that it brings together the knowledge and expertise of experienced professionals who come from different cultures, backgrounds, theoretical perspectives, and clinical settings. Several chapters provide clinical insight and expertise, others address theoretical issues, and some refer to research projects that help advance knowledge in the field of thanatology and improve the quality of care provided to those in need.

In an introductory chapter, *Earl Grollman* provides a sensitive and caring approach, enriched by useful guidelines, to explain death to children and to ourselves. The remainder of the book is divided into six parts, each addressing a significant topic from different perspectives.

Part One describes how children, adolescents, and young adults are affected by death in our contemporary societies.

Hannelore Wass, applying Jean Piaget's theory of cognitive development and her own research findings, describes the development of death-related concepts, ideas, concerns, and feelings in early childhood, later childhood, and adolescence. She offers valuable suggestions for providing death education and grief support to healthy children at these developmental levels.

Charles A. Corr addresses the characteristics of adolescence and focuses on societal, cultural, and contemporary issues that have a direct bearing on how teenagers relate to death. In addition, he provides helpful guidelines to assist adolescents who struggle with the difficult realities of dying, bereavement, and suicide.

In his chapter, *Robert Wrenn* examines how colleges and universities handle the death of a student and how they provide support to all parties concerned. This interesting topic, investigated here for the first time, offers a challenge for further study.

Wass, Corr, and Wrenn all refer to death attitudes and related behaviors as they occur in western societies, although Wrenn compares his findings to Japanese culture.

Mooli Lahad and *Ofra Ayalon* provide another perspective, describing not only a different culture, but also a society in which children and adolescents grow up under the reality or threat of war. They discuss the distress and possible long-term effects of living under war conditions and describe a stress inoculation program that assists children to enhance their coping abilities during highly stressful periods of their lives.

In the last chapter of Part One, *Stavroula Beratis* describes some of the cultural factors that possibly lead Greek adolescents to suicidal behavior. Adolescent suicidal behavior is a growing concern in contemporary societies. Suicide ranks as the second leading cause of death among persons aged 15–19 in the United States. The incidence of attempted suicide among adolescents, although underreported and difficult to determine, has increased at a disturbing rate not only in the United States, but in Europe and other countries of the world. In contrast, the low adolescent suicide rate in Greece constitutes a phenomenon of interest.

Part Two addresses clinical and research issues related to the grieving process experienced by bereaved children and families.

Janna Excell presents, through the illustration of a case study, the counseling objectives, skills, and techniques used to inform a child about the death of a loved one and to prepare him or her for the experience of mourning.

In the following chapter, *Stephen Fleming* and *Leslie Balmer* describe a group intervention approach with bereaved children. They present useful information about the framework, structure, and content of such groups, as well as the facilitation strategies used in the exploration and expression of children's reactions to the death of a parent or sibling. Their chapter emphasizes the unique features of support that bereaved children may find within a group setting, during a highly traumatic period of their lives.

In the following chapter, *Betty Davies* discusses the research conducted on the long-term effects of sibling loss on surviving children. The author presents the findings of four studies, which indicate that responses of these children can be profound, and long lasting, and may be affected by factors such as the family environment.

In the last chapter of Part Two, *Dora Black* presents the benefits of a family-oriented approach used with bereaved or about-to-be-bereaved families in England.

Part Three addresses issues related to the care of dying children and their families.

Elisabeth Kübler-Ross, a leading figure in the field of thanatology, presents her model for understanding human development, and describes how development is affected when a child is confronted with a life-threatening illness. She illustrates, through several examples, the richness of the symbolic communication used by dying children and urges professionals to work on their own unfinished business, and to develop their spiritual quadrant in order to help these children and families most effectively. The author not only shares her professional experience but also confides some aspects of her personal development through her unique and challenging work.

From the same theoretical perspective, *Sheryle Baker* introduces a number of creative therapeutic strategies involving art and imagery. She uses these to understand and help children face and work through their feelings, fears, and concerns when dying or grieving. Like Kübler-Ross, Baker stresses the child's inner awareness of illness, dying, and death, which the child often communicates nonverbally.

As the majority of terminally ill children die in a hospital setting, *Ginette Raimbault,* a prominent psychoanalyst, presents the special issues confronted by staff members who care for these children and their families. She describes the interventions applied at the Institut Gustave Roussy (an oncology center) in France. Also from a psychoanalytic perspective, *Mina Bouras* presents a case study that brings to light some of the ethical issues referring to the decision-making process of managing the care of a seriously ill child. She stresses the role of the unconscious in the communication and interaction among child, family, and professionals.

The focus of Part Four is on the circumstances surrounding the dying child and the programs providing care at home or in the hospital.

John Hutter, Fran Farrell, and *Paul Meltzer,* who work in Arizona with pediatric oncology patients of various ethnic backgrounds, present the innovative application of a family-network model to deal with the crisis of diagnosis and the ongoing management of the family's needs through the terminal phase. The authors identify factors affecting the decision of whether to provide care in the hospital setting or the home setting.

The home care alternative is feasible and desirable when the needs of the child and the family are carefully identified and assessed. The chapter by *Ciaran Duffy* and his colleagues illustrates the assessment of the necessity and feasibility of introducing a home-based palliative care program for terminally ill children who were admitted to the Neurosurgical Unit of the Hospital for Sick Children in Toronto, Canada.

Few research projects have been carried out on issues related to the psychosocial needs of terminally ill children and family members during the terminal phase. *G. B. Humphrey* and his colleagues introduce readers to the findings of four studies addressing these issues as well as the role played by the child in decisions regarding the care provided to him or her.

The founding director of Children's Hospice International, *Ann Armstrong Dailey,* in her chapter discusses the philosophy of the hospice movement and describes the services provided by this active international organization to children, families, and caregivers confronting life-threatening conditions and/or bereavement.

In Part Five, emphasis is given to understanding parental bereavement and to providing help in the process of adjustment to loss. No other bereavement is as long-lasting, intense, and painful as the one experienced by parents who lose a child. *Therese A. Rando* presents an interesting framework for understanding and working through parental bereavement. *Ida Martinson* confirms the long-lasting effects of such bereavement through the presentation of her research findings on parents' adjustment seven to nine years after the death of a child with cancer.

Ariella Lang and *Laurie Gottlieb,* through their own research on marital intimacy, dispel the myth that the loss of a child leads to divorce or family break-up. They contribute to a deeper understanding of how bereaved husbands and wives perceive their marital relationship and how the death of an infant affects the bereaved couple's intimacy when compared to nonbereaved couples.

In the final chapter of Part Five, *Sue Jennings* emphasizes how in western societies the bereavement experienced by couples who are unable to conceive a child remains unrecognized. She discusses an innovative program that introduces dramatherapy as an approach and method in dealing with infertility at the Academic Unit of Obstetrics and Gynaecology at London Hospital, in Great Britain.

Part Six explores the stress reactions, feelings, and needs of professionals involved in the care of children and families who are confronted with death, dying, and bereavement.

The testimony of a psychologist who has been working with dying children for several years is given by *Danai Papadatou,* who reflects on the difficulties and rewards of accompanying dying children in their journey through life to death. *Marcia Lattanzi-Licht* provides a framework for understanding the distress experienced when caring for these children and suggests guidelines for effective coping. Finally, *Derek Steinberg* in his chapter—which was the result of a creative workshop conducted during the conference—challenges professionals to acknowledge and work through some intense feelings experienced when they confront dying and bereavement in their work.

In the Conclusion *Sandra L. Bertman* uses the arts and the world of popular culture to address themes of death, dying, and bereavement as they relate to children and families. She illustrates how the arts can be used creatively in death education and death counseling.

In the Epilogue, *Byron Samios* and *Nassia Varveri-Sofra* report that *thanatos* in Ancient Greece was perceived as an integral part of life, although it remained incomprehensible and a senseless reality when it concerned the death of a child.

We hope this book will provide readers with comprehensive information of professional and personal value, and will promote a deeper understanding and a more caring and insightful approach in working with children and families who are dealing with dying, loss, and bereavement. What is shared through this book is what these children and their families have taught us.

Danai Papadatou, Ph.D.
Costas Papadatos, M.D.

Acknowledgments

We would like to extend our appreciation to several people for their involvement in the preparation of this book. First, we express our heartfelt thanks to the authors who contributed chapters. With their clinical, teaching, and research experience, their insight and expertise, all of them have added significantly to the value and uniqueness of this volume.

We are particularly grateful to Professor Charles Corr who willingly took the time to review the manuscript, made helpful suggestions, and generously shared his expertise in editing books related to the field of thanatology. He has been a guiding force both throughout the organization of the International Conference on Children and Death and during the preparation of this book.

We are also deeply thankful to Professor Robert Wrenn, who not only has been our mentor, friend, and adviser, but also has helped us in many ways to transform a dream into reality.

Four people deserve particular mention for their direct influence on this work: Myrto Nielsen, psychologist, colleague, and close friend, who has spent hours working on the manuscript and offered valuable advice and unparalleled support in our pursuits; Andrée Metaxa, who contributed with enthusiasm and persistent dedication to the editing of the volume; Lambrini Tzoufra for her excellent secretarial assistance, always offered so willingly; and Maria Koutsoumbelis for her availability to help and to offer useful comments whenever needed.

We are also grateful to Hemisphere Publishing Corporation, and particularly to acquisitions editor Ron Wilder, for the supportive, calm, and confident manner in which he worked with us.

It has been an enriching and unique experience for us both—father and daughter—to have worked so smoothly and well together toward a common goal, through a process of learning from each other and of discovering how much more we have yet to learn. In our efforts we received the unfailing, love, care, and support of Clea, Yiorgos, and Daphne, our family members, to whom we owe a debt of gratitude.

To all these people, who have so generously offered their invaluable support, energy, and enthusiasm, we extend our warmest thanks.

Introduction

Chapter 1

Explaining Death to Children and to Ourselves

Earl A. Grollman

To everything there is a season, and a time for every purpose under the heavens:
A time to be born, and a time to die.
Ecclesiastes 3:1–2

Sorrow makes us all children again.
Ralph Waldo Emerson

It was more than two decades ago when I wrote my book *Explaining Death to Children*. At that time, the subject was taboo. Somehow, many people believed that if death was not discussed, it would magically disappear. Since that time we have learned that just as we cannot protect ourselves from life, so we cannot protect our youngsters from death. Traumatic experiences belong to both adulthood and childhood.

   Where can one turn in tragedy if no one will admit that there is a tragedy? If loss can be acknowledged, we find comfort in what we mean to each other—even in the midst of lingering pain and loneliness. Death is a universal and inevitable process that must be faced by people of all ages. Children who are able to participate with their families, after the death of someone they love, will be better equipped to understand and manage the emotions of their grief. It is in that spirit that I present the following guidelines for helping explain death to children.

Do Not Avoid the Subject of Death in the Home, the School, the Church or Synagogue.

One of the most difficult tasks following the loss of a loved one is discussing death with children. The problem is intensified when adults are in the midst of coming to terms with their own grief. The feelings and perspectives of youngsters are often overlooked because of the false assumption that young people are just too sensitive and cannot possibly cope with this difficult subject. Yet in reality they are confronted with it: in word and song, in the natural world of plants and animals, as well as among their families and friends, and in the daily news.

Good mental health is not the denial of tragedy, but the frank acknowledgement of painful separation. One of the worst difficulties is youngsters' lack of understanding because of adult secrecy. Remember, a person is a person, no matter how small.

Do Not Discourage the Emotions of Grief.

Many times we overlook the fact that grief comes to all of us. Children, too, know sorrow. Grief enables people of all ages to come to grips with the reality of change in their lives and to establish new patterns of existence.

Grief is an emotion, not a disease. It is as natural as crying when one is hurt, eating when hungry, sleeping when weary. Grief is nature's way of healing a broken heart. Children undergo many of the same emotional reactions to death that mature adults experience. They have needs that must not be overlooked and feelings that require full expression. Repressed emotions can be dangerous and lead to further distress and even mental illness. It is vital that children be allowed to express painful sentiments when they first experience them.

Do Not Tell Youngsters Something They Will Later Need to Unlearn.

Death cannot be swept under the rug, shut in a closet, or explained through fairy tales and half-truths. Trust and truth are children's needs. For example, adults often suggest that the dead person is "sleeping" and will someday, magically, return during the child's lifetime. However, when the realization of the loss sets in, the child may take his or her parents to task for not having told the truth of the death. Adults may avoid explaining death, or try to explain it with fantasies because they wish to appear to know all the answers. Mature people do not have to profess infinite knowledge.

Use words like *die*, or *dead*, not *went away on a long journey*, *left*, *lost*, or *passed away*. Distortions of reality create lasting harm. It is far healthier to share with children the quest for wisdom than to appease their immediate curiosity with fairy tales in the guise of fact.

Do Not Alter the Role of the Child.

The living youngster does not replace a dead sibling. When a parent dies, the child does not suddenly become the "man" or the "woman" of the home. Children should be encouraged to be with their own friends and become involved once again in their usual activities. No child (or adult) should be told to "be brave." Having to put on a false front makes grieving that much more difficult.

It is preferable for the conversations about death to take place in a familiar setting—at home if possible. Talk in a quiet, honest, and straightforward manner. Gently explain what happened, and why there is so much sorrow. Try to encourage further dialogue. When adults lend a sympathetic ear, they are, in the best sense, catalysts for a child's understanding and healing.

Do Not Speak Beyond a Child's Level of Comprehension.

Since so much depends upon each youngster's stage of development, the grieving process in children is highly complex. For instance, a 3-year-old's understanding of death (and the mourning process) will be different from that of a 6-year-old.

Psychologist Maria Nagy explored the meaning of death to children of various ages. She found that at age 3–5, children deny that death is final. To them it is like going to sleep, or like a parent's going to work or away on a brief vacation. Between 5 and 9, youngsters accept the idea that someone else has died, but usually not until the age of 10 do they understand that they themselves will die.

Don't rush with explanations that children cannot understand, or plan one big "tell it all." Thought must be translated into the comprehension of each child. Avoid abstractions by using simple and direct language.

Do Allow Children to Go Through Their Own Individual Stages of Grief.

Youngsters, as adults, act out their emotions in a variety of contexts. Experts have determined that grieving children may express varied feelings, which could include the following.

Shock and Denial *"It can't be true."* Children at first may not accept the fact that the death has really occurred, and may act as though it did not happen. Thoughts of loss can be so overwhelming! Youngsters are not unfeeling or hard-hearted even if, initially, they seem to take the death lightly. They simply need time to cushion themselves against the impact of the tragedy.

Physical Symptoms   *"I feel sick."* Children may express various complaints, such as stomachaches or headaches. Anxiety is often expressed in bodily distress.

Anger   *"Why did God let it happen?"* Being mostly concerned with their own needs, youngsters may be furious with the person who died, thus causing them and their family much grief. Hostility may be directed toward God because a "miracle" did not keep the person alive. Feelings of rage are a normal response to death. Children should know that "nice" people sometimes become angry.

Guilt   *"Why did I . . . ?"* *"Why didn't I . . . ?"* Children may believe that they caused the death by having been naughty. They may feel responsible for not having been "better" in some way. Perhaps they had angry thoughts about the person, or were not quiet enough in the house. Reassure them again and again that they did not in any way cause the death.

Jealousy   *"How come Peter's father is still alive?"* It is difficult to witness families that are still intact. Envy is as old as Cain and Abel, Joseph and his brothers, David and Saul.

Anxiety and Fear   *"If you die too, who will take care of me?"* Children may fear that another member of the family will also die. They may panic at the thought that they could become ill with the same sickness that caused the death of the person. They may cling to those who play an important role in their life and ask them, "Do you really love me?" If the death was a sudden one, explain how rare this is and assure the youngster that you and they can expect to live a long, long time.

Sadness and Loneliness   *"Can't my brother come back? I miss him, and I want to play with him."* It is natural to want to talk, touch, and share with the deceased. It is normal to feel empty and alone because it is difficult to adjust to a new situation in life. Allow for crying. Tears—wet and warm—help to wash away feelings of frustration, sorrow, and anger. But be aware that tears are not the only measure of a child's grief. Unfortunately the crying, boisterous child receives the most sympathy. Less demonstrative youngsters also need adult attention and support.

There is no single way for children to grieve. Just provide the environment in which emotions can be shared freely. If more than one child is involved, spend undistracted time with each one alone.

Do Make Referrals to Other Supportive People.

There are many times when even the best intentions of an adult are simply inadequate. You should consider seeking professional help if, after many months, children continue to display one of the following behaviors:

- Look sad all the time with prolonged depression
- Keep a fast pace and are unable to relax the way they used to, with you and their friends
- Do not care about how they dress and look
- Seem tired or unable to sleep, with their health suffering markedly
- Avoid social activities and wish more and more to be alone
- Are indifferent to school and hobbies they once enjoyed
- Feel worthless, with bitter self-incrimination
- Rely on drugs and/or alcohol
- Allow their moods to control them instead of controlling their moods.

Seeking further help from a guidance counselor, a school psychologist, or a mental health facility is not an admission of weakness. On the contrary, it is a demonstration of courageous resolve to seek assistance during difficult times.

Do Notify the Child's School or Day Care Center About the Death.

Often children who are grieving regress, do less well, or seem "out of it." Inform the school so that teachers may understand the child's possible change in behavior. Staff can offer extra support and understanding only when they are notified of the crisis in the child's life.

Also consider suggesting that the school make death education part of the curriculum. Clifton Fadiman wrote in his afterword to an edition of Louisa May Alcott's *Little Men* the following passage: "The most moving episode has to do with John Brooke's death and funeral. As I read it, I find myself wondering why most books for children are afraid to mention death." It is not a question of whether children will receive death education, since they witness so much violence on television. The challenge is to provide death education that is helpful and informative.

Do Encourage Children to Participate in the Family Sorrow.

Children, too, need to express their emotions through the ceremonies of death—the visitation, the funeral, the "Shivah," the burial. They should be told that a funeral is a significant occasion, a chance to say good-bye to the one who died. Explain the funeral arrangements, and if possible include the children in the discussion. Let them know what to expect, and give them permission to attend.

Some children worry about the dead person suffocating in the grave. Reassure them that the deceased does not need to breathe, and that the person no longer suffers or feels pain.

Allow children to participate in the rituals as they wish. If they are reluctant to attend the service, do not force them or make them feel ashamed. Be sensitive to the age and level of understanding of each child.

Do Consider Grief Support Groups for Children.

Youngsters may wish to join a group of others who are grieving. Learning about the experiences of peers can offer invaluable insights into their own feelings. Many times children have difficulty in speaking to significant adults. They say: "I was afraid to cry in front of my parents because I didn't want to upset them anymore than they were." Or: "People ask me how my parents are doing, but never ask how I am"; "I thought I should be over my pain after the first week."

After attending peer support groups, they report: "I understand now that I'm not alone." "My feelings are okay." "I could hear others saying things I was afraid to admit to myself." Children need support, encouragement and friendship just as adults do.

Do Give Continued Assurance of Love and Support.

The greatest gift that adults can give a child is *themselves*. Their caring and concern over the next months and years will be of inestimable value in assisting the child's recovery. Be willing to listen for minutes, hours, even days. Youngsters need to talk, not just to be talked to. Many children have an almost insatiable need to pour out their feelings.

Try to recall the wonderfully happy times shared with the loved one who has died, not just the sad moment of death. Remind youngsters that the loss of one important relationship does not necessarily mean the loss of others—including the relationship they have with you.

Finally, when words fail, touch! Attitude can be more important than words. Physical demonstrations of love and support are vital to a grieving child. As adults walk the long and difficult path of separation, they can find, with their children, new dimensions in their capacity for caring and understanding.

In truth, for people of all ages, healing is a process, recovery is a choice!

Part One

Death in the World
of Children
and Adolescents

Chapter 2

Helping Children Cope with Death

Hannelore Wass

One of our problems as adults is that we forget our own childhood. As a consequence, we tend to underestimate our children. We underestimate their tremendous need to know and to make sense of the world and objects, events, and people in it—including themselves—and their relationship to this world. We question their intelligence, and often sorely underestimate the depth of feelings they experience. This is true particularly in respect to difficult issues such as death and dying. When it comes to death, we tend to think the child is incurious, thoughtless, and unfeeling. In fact, children—even young children—are very curious about death, especially when they first encounter it. They want to know what happened, how it happened, why it happened, and what happens next. These basic questions, as much as questions regarding birth ("where do babies come from?"), are a sign of healthy, normal development, and deserve to be valued and dealt with. They are too important to be ignored, deflected, or left for other sources to answer.

We often also erroneously assume that children are emotionally fragile. We fear that death is so horrible, so catastrophic that they will be shattered by it. In truth, most children are hardy and resilient. They have remarkable inner strength and determination to grow and to go forward.

It is natural for children to develop concerns, fears, and anxieties about death. They become most deeply concerned about how death affects them, their own well-being, and that of those who care for them. They also develop altruistic concerns, learning to fear for others as well as themselves.

All human beings experience fear. It is alright to have fears. We cannot hope to protect children entirely. We can, however, help by acknowledging this reality, by making sure children gain proper perspectives on their fears, and by providing our unfailing love and reassurance.

Children also experience the pain of loss and other reactions—physical, emotional, behavioral—not unlike adults. Learning to deal with and to transcend many small and some not-so-small losses is part of development throughout life. It is very important to learn, in childhood, healthy coping strategies. For this learning, children need our assistance, understanding, and care.

In this chapter, I will discuss some research findings and thoughts about the development of death-related understandings, ideas, and what we think are related concerns, fears, and anxieties at three developmental levels: in early childhood (i.e., the preschool ages), in later childhood (i.e., the pre-adolescent ages), and in adolescence. I will also briefly describe some of the types of deaths that children may confront and how these deaths affect them at these developmental levels. Finally, I will suggest some ways in which parents, counselors, teachers, and other professionals might be helpful to healthy children at these levels. Comments that are applicable to older children as well as to adolescents will be addressed together, while themes that seem unique at each level will be discussed separately.

Any time we think of aspects of human behavior as evolving in stages, perhaps in three, we can also think of transitions from one stage to the next. We then have five stages. Where there are progressions, there can also be regressions. At any rate there are always fluctuations. When we formulate stages in cognitive or affective development, we make broad generalizations that are necessarily oversimplifications. Nevertheless, they can be useful as overviews, as points of departure for further explorations, or as outlines for understanding children's behavior in regard to death—the focus of this chapter.

As with any aspect of development, there are large individual differences in the ages at which children reach a more mature understanding of death. Individual differences are a function of maturation, life circumstances, experience, adult-child interactions, and a host of other factors. This point is important when comparing healthy to dying children. Dying children's life circumstances and experiences are certainly extreme and may have a profound impact on their perceptions and cognitions. For example, a 5-year-old child suffering from leukemia who has been in four remissions and is now back in the hospital, knows much more about death than a healthy child does. This child may not know exactly what happens when one dies, but the child knows and understands that he or she is in deep trouble (Bluebond-Langner, 1978).

In the early 1980s, in collaboration with Dr. Claes-Goran Wenestam at the University of Goteborg, Sweden, I carried out research concerning children's concepts of death (Wenestam and Wass, 1987, 1986). Over 400 children, ages 5–18, participated in these studies. Essentially they were comparisons of children's thoughts about death. This qualitative study primarily involved Swedish and U.S. children, as well as a smaller sample of 55 children, ages 12–16, from Athens, Greece. We asked children to make a picture of what came to their mind when they heard the word *death* or *dead* and to explain what they had drawn, on the back of the picture or orally. We then did a content analysis of the pictures and explanations. At the time we were interested in possible differences among the three cultures, and we found some. However, I was very impressed with some basic similarities related to the children's age (developmental status). Indeed, children's understandings of death seems to evolve in a stage-based progression from less to more mature, which is generally consistent with Jean Piaget's theory of cognitive growth (Piaget, 1929; Wass 1984b, 1989).

YOUNG CHILDREN

Understandings of Death

Young children, up to approximately age 5, have an immature understanding of death. They do not yet grasp the essential components of the concept 'death', its irreversibility, and its universality. They view death as sleep, loss of mobility, a temporary malfunction, a restorable condition. This is so because the reasoning they use to understand and explain happenings in the world is immature—"preconceptual" or "preoperational," in Piaget's (1929) terms.

Four kinds of causal thinking the child uses are relevant to our discussion. One is *anamistic*, the belief that everything is alive—clouds, flowers, mountains, the sun, tricycles, cars, and airplanes. Another kind is *magic thinking*, the notion that some things and people have power over others. This kind of thinking prevails in fairy tales in which a prince can turn into a frog and wishes come true. This may be one of the reasons why young children are so fond of fairy tales. But magic also has its negative aspects. Children who think they can "will" things to happen may be frightened by this sense of omnipotence. What young child hasn't, at times, been frustrated and angry with his or her parents, for instance, and wished them ill or dead? When a parent actually dies, the child may believe that he or she is responsible for the death.

A third kind of thinking is termed *psychological causality*. It refers to the tendency in young children to perceive a psychological motive as the cause for everything (Wass & Cason, 1984). For instance, children may not understand that their parents took them to the hospital because they were sick. The children may think it is because their parents are angry. They may not understand the cause-effect relationship between a medical condition and its treatment, and may think a doctor or nurse gives the painful shot or other medical treatments because the children were naughty.

A fourth kind of thinking is *artificialistic reasoning*, the belief that everything is manufactured for the benefit of people. For example, babies are made in factories, where they have noses and ears put on and tongues put in. People can also be repaired like broken toys. It is easy to see that in this perceptual world there is no room for death, and consequently when the child is confronted with it, careful explanations are needed.

Fears

Young children have a variety of fears. They fear punishment, which represents their parents' displeasure with naughty behavior; they are afraid of wild animals, of monsters, of the dark. They may have anxieties about being left alone and about being abandoned (Wass & Cason, 1984). Not knowing what death is,

Figure 1 *Teacher:* "What is *dead?*" *Student:* "People lay down." *Teacher:* "What happened?" *Student:* "He shot him." (boy, age 5).

they cannot very well be afraid of it. Or can they? I think most healthy young children probably feel safe and protected most of the time. But they do know *some* things about death, early on. When we asked young children, "What is *dead*? What comes to your mind when you hear the word?", they commonly told us of causes, of external, violent causes of death: People get stabbed or shot, die in a fire, get run over by a truck, or get eaten by lions, tigers, or sharks (Wenestam & Wass, 1987; Wass, 1984b).

Where do young people get this information? The major source is probably the mass media, especially television, videos, and films. Most deaths on prime-time television are violent. Children's cartoons are even more violent than adult dramatic programs, containing about five times as many violent episodes (Wass & Stillion, 1988). Of course, cartoon characters are indestructible. No matter how much they get bashed, smashed, or exploded, they always come out alive and, apparently, unharmed. This may take some of the sting out of the violence, but it also reinforces the child's immature thinking patterns. In addition, it conveys a terrible message: Violence has no adverse consequences for the victim or the perpetrator. Children's exposure to television is massive; it is estimated that in the United States 3- and 4-year-olds spend an average of 4 hours a day in front of a TV set, while older children are believed to spend more time watching television than they spend in school (Wass & Stillion, 1988).

I think young children do fear for their safety. Fortunately, they learn to manage these fears. One way they achieve this is by believing they are invincible. When you ask young children, "When will you die?" most will answer quickly and firmly, "I don't die" or "Never." When asked to explain, they say, "Because I don't have to" or "Because I don't want to." These children know that death is bad and unpleasant, something they don't want to have happen to them, and they rely on magic and on significant adults in their lives to protect them from it. But even if death were to happen, they think it is not too bad, since there are things you can do to bring the dead back to life. These are some of the actions young children have suggested to reverse death: "help them get up," "put them to bed," "take them to the hospital," "give them hot milk and an oatmeal cookie," "the doctor can make them better." Sometimes children believe you do not have to do anything to the dead since they do it themselves: they "wake up," "get up," or "eat pizza."

Encounters with Death

There comes a time when the child is confronted with death and needs to revise his or her thinking and perception. Hopefully this happens with "small deaths," such as those of bugs, worms, caterpillars, or frogs. We are most helpful in answering the child's questions when our replies are simple, clear, and truthful, and when these are given in a low-key and calm manner.

The child's first encounter with death may happen when parents are not present. Three-year-old Kevin was playing with his friend Sheila in the yard when they discovered a lizard that didn't run off. Something was wrong. It just lay there. It looked strange. They poked it, but it didn't move. "It's sick," Kevin offered. "Nah," said Sheila, "it's dead." She gave it a kick and ran off. Kevin headed straight for his mother, and demanded, "Mommy, what is *dead*?" "What do *you* think, Kevin?" his mother responded. This question gave her time to catch her breath. It also helped her discover the context from which the question arose and indicated what the child was thinking. Kevin answered: "The lizard didn't run away, maybe it hurt its foot." The mother wanted to see the lizard, so they both had a look. Then she said: "Kevin, this lizard is dead. It cannot move. It is not breathing any more. It is dead."

Perhaps parents should *create occasions* for the child to experience small deaths and losses. I do not mean that they should go out and kill animals, but why not keep goldfish, gerbils, or other small animals as pets? What better way to help a child to learn, firsthand, about the facts of life than with pets (especially a small pet with a short lifespan)? What better opportunity to teach the child to love, tend, and grieve for another creature?

We can also create opportunities for a child's vicarious experience with death through children's literature. Writers have an uncanny gift for putting into words the various emotions death evokes in us. There are many outstanding books on the market in the United States (Wass, 1984a). These include *Charlotte's Web*, the wonderful story of a spider who died; *The Tenth Good Thing About Barney*, which is about the death of a pet cat; *When Violet Died*, the story of a pet bird; *My Grandpa Died Today*, a sensitive account of the loss of a grandfather; and *Nana Upstairs and Nana Downstairs*, a simple and caring story about the deaths of two grandmothers. Such books are excellent sources of information. Reading about the behavior of others is strikingly powerful in changing or developing attitudes (Bandura, 1977). Books can be therapeutic and comforting as well. They may also serve as vehicles for starting a conversation about death with the child, when parents find it difficult or do not know how to broach the subject.

When a Parent Dies

Sometimes, the child's first encounter with death is a major loss, such as the loss of a parent. There is no diplomatic way of telling a child that his or her daddy has died. Following is the reconstructed and compressed dialogue between 4-year-old Bobby and his Aunt Ruth, which took place over a period of two days after his father's sudden death.

Aunt Ruth: Bobby, I have some very sad news. Your daddy died in the hospital last night.

Bobby: He was sleeping yesterday.

AR: He is not sleeping anymore; he is dead, honey.

B: Is he dead in the hospital?

AR: No, he is in the funeral home . . . .

B: What's a funeral home?

AR: That is where the body is put when a person dies.

B: (Strong signs of beginning anxiety) Why didn't he come to our house? That's where he lives.

AR: He doesn't live anymore, Bobby. He is dead. He can't walk. He can't move. He can't breathe. That's what *dead* means.

B: Will he be back on Saturday?

AR: Your daddy can't ever come back. Your daddy is dead. We are all very sad. We will be sad for a long time. We will always remember him.

B: (Now crying) But he promised to take me to the puppet show on Saturday. Who will take me?

AR: Uncle Jack and I will take you to the puppet show.

B: Goodie! Will my daddy be back for Christmas?

AR: No, Bobby, your daddy is dead. He cannot come back again.

B: (Crying) But why isn't he coming back?

AR: Because he is dead.

B: Who made him dead?

AR: Nobody. He died.

B: Where did he go?

AR: Your daddy is with God.

B: Why does God want my daddy?

AR: Only God knows that.

B: I want my daddy.

AR: Yes, Bobby, of course you want your daddy, but he is dead. But your mommy loves you very much, and I do too, as well as Uncle Jack, Aunt Mary, Grandpa William, Grandma Laura, Susan, Kevin, Bill, Sandy, and Lisa, and lots of people. And God loves you, too.

B: I hate God. He is mean.

AR: It's all right to be mad at God. He understands.

Such a dialogue is difficult and frustrating because it makes us feel helpless and anxious. Nevertheless, it helps the child. What does not help the child is to tell him or her that Daddy is in a "deep sleep" or "went on a long trip." Although such statements are credible to the child, they suggest that the death is temporary, and that Daddy will eventually wake up or return from his trip. With such lies, we merely postpone confrontation with the facts. Lies also erode children's trust in us and cause feelings of loneliness and isolation. Whatever we tell young children, we need to make certain that they come to the following understandings:

• The father did not die on purpose. He could not help it. Dying is something no one can help.

- The death was no one's fault. In particular, it was not the child's fault.
- The father did not want to die.
- The father was not angry with the child.
- The father loved the child.
- The father can never come back.
- The child will be loved, cherished, and cared for.
- It's all right for the child to cry when he feels sad, and to get angry.
- It's all right to laugh and play and to have fun, too.

We need to give these explanations over and over, patiently, together with much comforting, hugging, and holding. Bobby, like other young bereaved children, may experience a variety of other reactions to his father's death. He may regress to earlier modes of behavior and wet his bed (that happens even among older children), suck his thumb, revert to baby talk, have temper tantrums, and act out or withdraw. We need to be alert to these symptoms as well as understanding and sympathetic toward the child. It is easy for adults to become wrapped up in their own shock and pain, to rally around the bereft adults, or to become immersed in the rituals following the death. Family members or others need to tend to the child's needs as well. It would probably be a worse mistake to send the child away "until it's over." If funerals and memorials serve a therapeutic function—as most professionals believe—then isn't the child entitled to participate in these rites and benefit from them?

Helping Young Children in School

Teachers in school also should help the young child deal with death. They need to be informed when a child is bereaved, so they can respond to the child in a sensitive manner in the classroom.

I will recount here an incident reported to me by parents, involving their surviving daughter Susie, which took place some weeks after their son Jamie died. Susie was in first grade. One morning she stood before her classmates during "Show and Tell" and told them quietly, "My brother Jamie died." The teacher was totally unprepared, and her response was silence. She pretended she had not heard and motioned to another child to come forward. But Susie was determined and repeated in a louder tone, "My brother Jamie died." Now, all the children had heard, and the teacher could no longer pretend. They looked expectantly at the teacher, then at Susie, then back at the teacher who was petrified. Susie demanded to be heard. She shouted the statement at her teacher who promptly came to life, for she was on familiar ground again, took the child by the hand, and said, "We do not shout in this classroom." She then walked Susie out of the room.

There may be times when teachers have to face the issue of death when they least expect it. At such times the best pedagogy may fail, and the only thing they can do is simply to respond as human beings. Any mistakes we make in such cases are probably not as bad as trying to ignore the issue. When we do nothing, we teach powerful lessons by default, such as that it is too terrible to talk about death, that adults can't handle it, that when grown-ups have problems they forget about children, or that children are not important.

A dramatic incident exemplifying how teachers may have to discuss death with children was the explosion of the U.S. space shuttle *Challenger* in 1986. This mission was of special significance to American schoolchildren, because among the seven astronauts killed was Christa McAuliffe, a teacher who was to broadcast lessons from space right into their classrooms. Thousands of schools had planned to participate in these lessons. Several million children in the United States and Canada witnessed the explosion in live broadcasts or rebroadcasts. There were 40 million children attending public schools in the United States in 1986, and hundreds of children in mid-Florida watched the lift-off and explosion from their schoolyards. What sort of teacher could ignore such a happening, turn off the TV set, and go on to other lessons? From what I heard, most teachers stopped their regular activities and dealt with the event *in some way*. Most teachers tried to find out what had happened. Some prayed. Some cried. Most shared their shock, anger, sorrow, and feelings of loss, and encouraged their pupils to talk and express themselves (Blume et al., 1986). Thousands of schoolchildren, with their teachers' directions, wrote letters of condolence, drew pictures, and even sent gifts to Christa's own children, to her pupils, even to the president of the United States.

OLDER CHILDREN AND ADOLESCENTS

Understandings of Death

Older children are very much the scientists in their cognitive development. They are interested in objective observation, in concrete physical and mechanical aspects of things and processes, and in the laws describing them. By this age, they clearly understand death as the cessation of functions. When the researcher asks them, "What happens when people die?" they answer, "When people die they stop living. The heart stops beating, the brain and everything stops working." They are interested in the distasteful details of death and the postmortem physical changes that adults don't like to think about. They want to know why people die with their eyes open, what is *rigor mortis* and *livor mortis*? They wonder if it is true that fingernails and beards still grow after one has died, and if the body still moves. They want to know if people are ever buried alive. They know that, in a burial, the body is put in a casket, which is then placed in the ground at the cemetery. They are aware that there is a funeral. Then the body starts rotting until only bones remain, which gradually rot into the ground. Death processes and funerals are very much on their minds.

Figure 2 "The word *dead* [Gk. *thanatos*] makes me think of graves and the cemetery" (girl, 12 years old).

Older children know that death is universal: What lives, dies; and no magic tricks can keep us alive.

Concerns and Fears

At this stage everything about death can be frightening: the fact that it happens, its processes, its relentlessness, and also its apparent capriciousness. Older children are preoccupied by corpses, funerals, and decay, not because they are morbid but because they really want to know what goes on. I believe that with knowledge they gain a measure of control over their fears and anxieties. It is therefore important that we answer children's questions. If we have no answers we should find sources containing the information, such as books or knowledgeable people such as health professionals. Otherwise, children will look for answers elsewhere.

Recently some unrated videotapes have appeared in the video rental shops in the United States, often marketed as "documentaries." In fact, these videos contain very offensive footage of close-ups of various forms of violent death, murder, execution, war, mutilation, and cannibalism. They are very popular among older children and adolescents who often meet in groups at someone's house and have "viewing parties." The idea is to see how much one can take before being "grossed out" by these videos. These viewing sessions again may be attempts by young people to gain some sense of mastery over their fears.

The same dynamic may also explain why older children and adolescents seem to enjoy gruesome jokes they share among themselves. Gallows humor seems to help adults who work with the dying and dead. It may help children, too. Each generation seems to have its own tradition of deadly humor. My peers recite this rhyme from their childhood: "The worms crawl out, the worms crawl in, they crawl all over your mouth and chin." Immediately following the explosion of the space shuttle *Challenger*, some horrible jokes relating to the disaster were circulated among older children and adolescents. An example is: "Where did the Challenger astronauts go for their vacation?" "All over Florida." These jokes apparently help to alleviate or ward off anxieties (Wass & Stillion, 1988). We should be tolerant of them. They are certainly not products of sick juvenile minds, and they do not indicate that our young people are calloused.

At times, older children still engage in magic thinking and rituals to help manage their fears. For example, they believe that when you pass a cemetery you must hold your breath, or that when you see a black cat crossing the street in front of you, you have to quickly count to 10 and back, or that you should avoid stepping on the cracks in the sidewalk so as not to "break your mother's back." Even adults have their superstitions, such as crossing themselves or knocking on wood to avert ill consequences. Older children may still be afraid at night. A 9-year-old boy I know places all his toy weapons—water pistol, knives, tanks, laser guns—strategically around his bed at night, to protect him from ghosts, werewolves, and other demons while he sleeps. We should be understanding of—and we should certainly avoid making fun of children because of—such behaviors.

In addition, older children imagine what it is like to be dying. Such thoughts can bring on fears. In our studies, older children often shared their fears as they explained their thinking: death is "horrible," "frightening," "the worst thing that can happen in your life." One 10-year-old put it this way: "I think when people know they are going to die they get very scared and just lie there. I hope I never die." Another said, "I try not to worry about it. I hope it won't happen until I am very old" (Wass, 1984b). The hope of a long life is perhaps the most comforting thought that children have about death. After all, in modern developed countries, old age is considered the proper time for dying. For a 10-year-old that is far in the future.

By and large, older children accept their parents' beliefs about life after death, heaven, hell, God, and the devil; they view these in concrete terms and do not seem to give too much thought to them. Some express doubts about how much fun it would be in Heaven ("You probably couldn't play baseball: God wouldn't allow it"). Children at this level generally seem comforted by believing in some form of existence after death, whether "heaven," the "happy hunting ground," or reincarnation ("You may come back within a year").

Death in the Media

Meanwhile, on this earth, there is no lack of death in young people's lives. They are bombarded with death, on television, in videos, and in feature films. This kind of death may be impersonal and indirect, but it is vivid and spectacular. Consider the daily news: Except for famous personalities, ordinary natural deaths are not considered newsworthy. To make the news, death must be high drama. On the news people get shot or stabbed; they die in fires, train, bus, or plane accidents; they perish in earthquakes, floods, or hurricanes. Then there are fiction, documentaries, and "docudramas." Eighty percent of the deaths depicted on prime-time drama programs are violent (Wass & Stillion, 1988). Geoffrey Gorer (1965) has long ago pointed at the attraction to violence and perverse forms of death in American popular culture. He calls it "pornographic death." This trend seems more pronounced today than ever before. In addition, death scenarios presented in the visual media seldom permit viewers to empathize with the victims and seldom are pain, suffering, or other grief reactions of survivors shown in these media. What do children learn from such portrayals?

We already have strong evidence of television's power and influence on behavior. In an analysis of research on the effects of television viewing on children, scientists concluded that watching televised and filmed aggression leads to increased aggression among child viewers (National Institute of Mental Health, 1982). Psychologists have also begun to focus on the effects of television viewing on young persons' perceptions of the real world (Hawkins & Pingree, 1982). In one of our studies, for example, we found that children vastly overestimate the number of murders committed in the United States each year. Nearly 1/3 of the 12- to 18-year-olds thought more than 5 million people were murdered annually. Some suggested 50 million or more. The actual figure is approximately 24,000 out of a population of 240 million (Wass, Raup & Sisler, 1989).

Most television programs are mellow and tame compared to the grossly violent feature films that have appeared on the American market, such as the Rambo series. They, in turn, seem almost innocent in comparison to the grosser "slasher" films that specifically cater to children and adolescents. This summer the fifth in the "Nightmare" series was released, subtitled cynically "The Dream Child." The series hero, Freddy Krueger, is a razor-clawed stalker, killer, and mutilator of teenagers. Videotapes for home viewing are even more offensive than feature films because they are largely unrated.

It is very important that we recognize this distorted depiction of death, especially in our era, when personal encounters with death have become less common. The distortion is all the more powerful when it is not balanced and muted by more natural and gentler deaths. Parents, who are the most significant persons in children's lives, need to monitor and mediate between their children and the bewildering onslaught of death-related stimuli in the electronic media. Professionals can also be helpful. The formation of vocal advocacy groups in America, such as those of pediatricians, teachers, and parents, can help increase public awareness of this issue and use pressure to bring about changes in the entertainment industry.

Concerns about Large-Scale Destruction

Towards the end of childhood and in adolescence, children become deeply concerned about the welfare of others as well as their own. While accidents and individual violence are still on their minds, they are also aware of organized and large-scale death. They worry about war, the nuclear threat, the effects of pollution, acid rain, and other threats to global survival. These concerns are evident in our studies and seem to be especially prominent among the older European children and adolescents.

These same concerns also surface in rock music. Rock music is, of course, the young generation's public forum for asserting its independence and its own ideological position. In addition, I think rock music is also a sounding board for and mirror of most of their anxieties. Reading the lyrics of rock music is quite instructive. Death themes, both literal and metaphoric, are surprisingly common. Among the themes of protest, we find songs that speak out against starvation, war, and global nuclear destruction. One of the most popular songs, "Bloody, Bloody Sunday," sung by the rock group U-2 (1983) in the album *War*, is a good example. It includes the following lines:

> I can't believe the news today
> I can't close my eyes and make it go away
> How long, how long must we sing this song?
> Broken bottles under children's feet,
> Bodies strewn across a dead end street,
> And today the millions cry,
> We eat and drink while tomorrow they die.

Young people often overreact. Parents should encourage their children to express their worries and anxieties. They should provide them with relevant information leading to a more hopeful perspective, which may lessen anxieties. The best kind of help they can give is to share quality time with their children in wholesome family-oriented interactions. At all times, parents should provide an atmosphere of mutual trust and acceptance with an open system of communica-

Figure 3   "Re-armament will lead us to death" (boy, 15 years old).

tion in which joyful and distressing events as well as important, difficult, and controversial issues are discussed. Most children, even adolescents, want, need, and appreciate their parents' guidance and expressions of care.

Adolescents' Thinking and Beliefs

By the time children reach adolescence, their cognitive development is further advanced. They are now capable of propositional and hypodeductive thinking. They can take ideas apart and restructure and combine them in new configurations. These abilities are needed because at this stage the young person is

Figure 4 "I have drawn a burnt forest. After the death of the forest our own death will follow" (boy, 12 years old).

developing a new identity, new roles, and new relationships. During this period of transition, previously held perceptions and understandings must be reexamined, analyzed, and changed. Adolescence is a time for existential confrontations: Who am I? Who do I want to be? Where am I going? What is life, anyhow? In this context, questions about death are a natural, integral part of the attempt to reach a new understanding and create a new sense of purpose. At this stage, the adolescent is philosophical and often thinks of death in more abstract terms: What is the nature of death? of dying? of existence after death?

These are some examples of beliefs that adolescents hold:

Death is at first coal-black. Everything is black. Gradually it gets lighter. I don't believe you go to heaven. I think you are reborn as another being.

After we die our spirits enter another sphere more beautiful than anything on earth. It is filled with love and joy.

Figure 5   "Death is a gray lifeless wall followed by a big black hole down which you fall; but right at the end there is a yellow light; what is behind that, I don't know" (girl, 17 years old).

Other adolescents accept their parents' religious beliefs but on a deeper, more abstract level than they did earlier.

Fears

Adolescents can be quite fearful about death. At this stage they have a better idea of what it means to lose one's life and of the many possibilities that may remain unrealized. The anxieties this understanding creates can be profound, but generally more immediate issues take priority. There are intimate relationships, careers, jobs, and money to worry about, new bodies to adjust to, and new selves to define. When fears about death do surface, adolescents are not likely to admit them.

In our studies (Wass, 1984b) adolescents essentially said these things about death and their concerns:

Why dwell on it? There is nothing I can do about it.

Death for me is a long way down the road of life. Right now I worry more about what I'm going to do with my life than how I'm going to terminate it.

I plan to live a long, fruitful life and if I get worried about dying at all, it won't be until I'm old.

One way adolescents seem to cope with their death fears is by believing they are invincible. More than any other age group, adolescents tend to take risks, to act the daredevil, as if to defy death. Their apparent attraction to so-called slasher films and videos may well be an attempt to control death-related anxieties.

It is sad to note that adolescents feel they cannot discuss the subject of death with their parents (Wass, Raup & Sisler, 1989). It is even sadder that parents are uncomfortable with the subject and, if at all possible, avoid discussing it with their children (McNeil, 1986).

In a sense, the entire period of adolescence is about death and loss, the loss of childhood and of the protective warmth of the support coming with it. Transcending that loss and creating the new adult is an awesome task. Parents can be of great help to their teenage children by being tolerant and open. They are needed as listeners, sounding boards, and gentle guides in this time of transition.

Uncommon Losses

Fortunately, it is no longer common for children and adolescents to lose a member of their immediate family, such as a parent or sibling. One estimate is that fewer than 10% of children in the United States experience a parental loss. Because of the neonuclear structure of the family in Western developed coun-

Figure 6 "I believe in an eternal life after death without faults or sins. I believe all souls go to Heaven, Heaven being defined as true inner peace within yourself and God" (boy, 18 years old).

tries, high mobility, and increasing life expectancy, many children may not be directly affected by the loss of grandparents either. This lack of personal familiarity with death, however, has some important implications. For most children the grief over the loss of a close family member is more difficult to deal with *because* it is no longer the norm. Bereaved children and adolescents often feel "diminished," "ashamed," "lonely," or "like a freak." This perceived loss of peer status compounds their primary loss. Peers are less able to identify with the bereaved child because bereavement is not part of their own experiences. Lack of empathy, in turn, makes it more difficult for them to give comfort and support to bereaved peers.

Many adults are similarly inexperienced. I think that today the loss of one's child is more difficult to grieve over than before, because it is unexpected and uncommon. The question, "Why me?" is more salient. The fact that they are in a minority is one reason for people with similar tragedies to band together in mutual and self-help groups.

The parents' problems with grief can profoundly affect the bereaved child sibling. That sibling may experience an additional loss: that of the parents' caring comfort at a time when it is most needed. A 12-year-old boy who lost a brother said, "My dad can't talk about it, and my mom cries a lot. It's really hard on them. I pretend I'm O.K. I usually just stay in my room." It is sad to know there are children who must suffer their grief silently and alone, while most self-help groups are addressed to bereaved adults. Children have to rely on their parents for access to most resources for help. When we as professionals help parents, we are also helping children.

We have enough data from research and clinical observations to know that the loss of a parent or sibling brings on reactions in children and adolescents quite similar to those of adults, and that all the helpful things we do for bereaved adults also help the children. We know that each loss brings unique and special problems for the child. A *parent's death* is very threatening to children because they depend on their parents for primary care and support. The whole system is shaken when part of the foundation is gone. The *death of a sibling* is very threatening because it exposes children's own vulnerability. The shield of invincibility is broken. Parents are not the infallible protectors they were thought to be. These anxieties often go unspoken and unnoticed.

GRIEF SUPPORT AND DEATH EDUCATION IN THE SCHOOLS

Grief Support and Intervention

Because bereaved children and adolescents are in school for most of the day, teachers and school counselors should be informed of the loss. This is important not just for emotional assistance but also because bereaved children have difficulty concentrating on their work, lose motivation to learn, and lack energy, and as a result their school performance suffers. In addition, they may become disruptive and act out in class. When teachers are unaware of the underlying cause of this school behavior, they may discipline and punish children when what they need is understanding, patience, and support.

Sometimes a classmate, schoolmate, teacher, or other member of the school community dies. These deaths have to be dealt with and grieved for. Nearly 40,000 children and young adults died in the United States in 1986. Three-fourths of these were the result of accidents or violence. It is quite likely that a schoolmate will die some time during a child's school years. When a schoolmate dies—especially when the death is violent and unexpected, and most particularly when it is a suicide—children and adolescents may be deeply affected. They may react with a host of feelings ranging from agitation to rage. It is important for schools to be prepared to give immediate emotional assistance to bereaved students—individually and in groups—as long as it is needed.

It is up to the helping professionals to see that parents, schools, and the general public become more aware of the dynamics of grief and the needs of bereaved children. Some progress has been made in this direction, as indicated by a recent study that shows nearly 20% of the public schools in the United States have some sort of grief counseling and support program for individual students within the school setting (Wass, Miller & Thornton, in press).

Teaching Children about Death

We should help children learn about death in school. Along with the family, schools are the primary institutions for socializing and educating the young. Their role is to transmit their culture's knowledge, practices, skills, and values to the next generation. Death is part of that heritage. Ideally, discussions of death in school do not need special courses and curricula. Instead, they should be naturally but systematically integrated into existing studies wherever they fit. For example, in courses on life sciences, students learn about the life cycle of the bee or the butterfly; why could they not learn about the human life cycle as well? In courses or units on family planning or psychology, it would be appropriate to include the study of birth, growth, adulthood, aging, grief, and death. Children could also be taught about death in the health education curricula. Unfortunately, U.S. public schools offer very little systematic death education, despite efforts by leaders in thanatology and education who for two decades have articulated the need, rationale, and goals and have offered guidelines, suggestions, and resources for such education. Only about 1 in 10 schools offers any systematic death education (Wass, Miller & Thornton, 1990).

When we teach children about death and grief in various courses of study, when parents talk about it, when we have helped children with smaller losses such as that of a pet, they will be better able to cope with the major losses that will inevitably occur, and they will be better able to help friends and classmates who are experiencing one.

But there is more to it than that. Death education can be an impetus for appreciating the beauty life offers, for adopting healthy living habits, for enhancing the ability to cherish, for striving to improve the quality of life for oneself and for others, for deepening love and friendship, and for setting and focusing more sharply on one's goals. All these life-enhancing effects have been reported by adults and children who have been close to death or otherwise confronted it in a profound way. Why should it not work for all of us, including children?

REFERENCES

Bandura, A. (1977). *Social learning theory.* Englewood Cliffs, NJ: Prentice Hall.

Bluebond-Langner, M. (1978). *The private worlds of dying children* (pp. 192–199). Princeton, NJ: Princeton University Press.

Blume, D., Whitley, E., Stevenson, R. G., Buskirk, V. A., Morgan, M. A., & Myrick, R. D. (1986). Challenger 10 and our school children: Reflections on the catastrophe. *Death Studies, 10,* 95–118.

Gorer, G. (1965). The pornography of death. In G. Gorer (Ed.), *Death, grief, and mourning* (pp. 192–199). Garden City, NY: Doubleday.

Hawkins, R. P., & Pingree, S. (1982). Television's influence on social reality. In D. Pearl, L. Bouthilet, & J. Lazar (Eds.), *Television and behavior: Ten years of scientific progress and implications for the eighties* (pp. 224–247). Washington, DC: U.S. Government Printing Office.

McNeil, J. N. (1986). Talking about death: Adolescents, parents, and peers. In C. A. Corr & J. N. McNeil (Eds.), *Adolescence and death* (pp. 185–201). New York: Springer.

National Institute of Mental Health. (1982). *Television and behavior: Ten years of scientific progress and implications for the eighties, Vol. 2: Technical reviews.* Washington, DC: U.S. Government Printing Office.

Piaget, J. (1929). *The child's conception of the world.* London: Routledge and Kegan Paul.

U-2 (1983). Sunday, Bloody Sunday. In *War*, Island Records.

Wass, H. (1984a). Books for children: An annotated bibliography. In H. Wass and C. A. Corr (Eds.), *Helping children cope with death: Guidelines and resources.* (pp. 151–207) (2nd ed.). Washington, DC: Hemisphere Publishing.

Wass, H. (1984b). Concepts of death: A developmental perspective. In H. Wass and C. A. Corr (Eds.), *Childhood and death* (pp. 3–24). Washington, DC: Hemisphere Publishing.

Wass, H. (1989). Children and death. In R. Kastenbaum and B. Kastenbaum (Eds.), *Encyclopedia of death* (pp. 49–54). Phoenix, AZ: Oryx Press.

Wass, H., & Cason, L. (1984). Fears and anxieties about death. In H. Wass and C. A.

Corr (Eds.), *Childhood and death* (pp. 25–45). Washington, DC: Hemisphere Publishing.

Wass, H., Miller, M. D., & Thornton, G. (1990) Death education and grief/suicide intervention in the public schools. *Death Studies. 14,* 253–268.

Wass, H., Raup, J. L., & Sisler, H. H. (1989). Adolescents and television: A follow-up study. *Death Studies, 13,* 161–173.

Wass, H., & Stillion, J. M. (1988). Death in the lives of children and adolescents. In H. Wass, F. M. Berardo, and R. A. Neimeyer (Eds.), *Dying: Facing the facts* (pp. 201–228). Washington, DC: Hemisphere Publishing.

Wenestam, C., & Wass, H. (1986). Qualitative differences in thinking about death: Cross-cultural exploration of American, Greek, and Swedish adolescents. Paper read at the 8th International Congress of Cross-Cultural Psychology, Istanbul, Turkey, July 6–10, 1986.

Wenestam, C., & Wass, H. (1987). Swedish and U.S. children's thinking about death: A qualitative study and cross-cultural comparison. *Death Studies, 11,* 2, 99–121.

Chapter 3

Understanding Adolescents and Death

Charles A. Corr

Kohlberg and Gilligan (1971) have described adolescents as incipient philosophers gathering data about the broadened horizons of their lives and seeking to make sense of those data. In recent years, we have learned much about death, dying, and bereavement, with particular reference to the elderly, on the one hand, and to children, on the other. In my judgment, however, adult philosophers of adolescent life have much to learn about the scope and significance of adolescent involvement with death, dying, and bereavement. This chapter offers a sketch of those involvements, comments on their interconnections, and suggestions toward a preliminary assessment of their meaning.

Many people are not eager to think about actual or potential conjunctions between adolescents and death. We prefer to avoid associating these vibrant, growing young people with issues related to the end of life. At one level, this appears to represent a natural human tendency to turn away from unattractive thoughts and realities. At another level, this sort of aversion can become a matter of concern in its own right. For example, professionals specializing in the study of adolescents and adolescent development frequently neglect death-related dimensions of adolescent life. Well-known textbooks and reference sources on adolescent psychology (e.g., Adelson, 1980; Conger & Peterson, 1984) often have no discussion of death, dying, or bereavement. Similarly, standard reference sources in life span or developmental psychology (e.g., Field et al., 1982; Mussen et al., 1979) tend to confine discussion of death-related matters to a concluding chapter on old age and the elderly.

This is unacceptable and even foolish. Death is a reality that can be identified in many different forms in the lives of contemporary adolescents (Corr & McNeil, 1986). We distort our appreciation of adolescence as a distinctive era in the life span when we deliberately set aside some important dimensions of that period. Also, we handicap both our ability to empower adolescents to help themselves and our own capacity to intervene on their behalf in constructive ways, when we do not understand the special forms and textures of death-related experiences in adolescent life.

In order to redress the balance, we must draw attention to some of the salient ways in which death is made real for adolescents in contemporary society. Of necessity, this chapter primarily addresses adolescents in North America, for they are the adolescents that I, and the scholars I will cite, know best. Even though the adolescent experience is inevitably lived out differently in various parts of the world, I hope the content of this chapter will be relevant and useful to adolescents outside North America.

There is much we currently do not know about adolescents and death. Many opportunities—some of which will be identified here—are open to us for study and research.

There are many ways in which adults and adolescents can help each other in relation to death-related issues. An important part of that interaction depends on how adults can bring insight, experience, and maturity to the aid of adolescents. It is also worth noting how the fresh sensitivities and keen insights of adolescents can be of comfort and value to adults and to younger children. We share a common condition—mortality—and a common universe. There is in principle no reason why adolescents and adults cannot be of help to each other.

The first section of this chapter focuses on adolescence itself, its boundaries, and its interpretations. Then I present, in succession, issues related to death, dying, bereavement, and suicide. Finally, I offer some concluding thoughts about helping adolescents and about help to be obtained from adolescents.

ADOLESCENCE

A Recent Invention and Its Boundaries

For quite a long time in human history, children were thought of as no more than small adults. Not so very long ago, writers like Ariès (1962) helped to draw attention to the special qualities of childhood as a distinctive period in the life span. This opened the way for investigation into the specific needs and tasks of children. Eventually, it led to further distinctions within childhood, between infants, young children, preschoolers, and children of primary school age.

All of that is helpful; however, if it remains limited to these observations, then it might seem that when childhood ends, adulthood begins. In fact, some people do appear to act on the belief that adulthood follows childhood directly, and this may in fact be the case in some parts of the contemporary world. That is, around the beginning of the second decade of human life, family and social responsibilities may have increased, work may have come to occupy an increasing part of daily living, and a formal ritual may have marked a "coming of age" or transition into partnership with other adults.

In many societies around the world, however, adulthood is postponed. An intermediary period is interposed between childhood and full adulthood. This is *adolescence*, a period of some 6 to 12 years made possible by increased average life expectancy and enhanced living standards for the population as a whole. Like many interstitial periods, adolescence shares elements of what precedes and follows it. Adolescents are no longer merely children, but they are expected to retain many childish ways. At the same time, adolescents are not yet fully recognized as adults, but they are increasingly permitted to act in adult ways.

What are the boundaries of adolescence? Are they chronological, so as to begin at age 10 or 12 and end at age 18 or 20? Are they biological, with puberty serving as the initial defining marker? Are they social, starting with secondary school, on the one hand, and ending with leaving one's home and family of origin, on the other? Or do these boundaries fluctuate?

My daughter recently moved to another city to attend a new university. On some days, I found her to be a mature woman of the world who wished her father would allow her to be free to make all the important and not-so-important decisions in her life. On other days, she was a young girl seeking out daddy's guidance in dealing with the perplexities of life. Not long ago she called me to say that her car would not start. I suggested she could have the automobile fixed. She cried and told me she had the habit of talking to her car, as she would to a friend, and she just could not believe that, in return, it would treat her this way.

To ask about the definition and boundaries of adolescence is not merely to pose sterile, academic questions. Fleming and Adolph (1986, p. 98) have noted that a "subject of dispute in research on adolescents in general, is defining what one means by an 'adolescent'." The grief literature includes studies of young people ranging from 2 years of age to 16 or 17 (Caplan & Douglas, 1969; Van Eerdewegh et al., 1982), while others (e.g., Hardt, 1978) have looked at participants aged 13–26 years. How can we compare such studies, and what can we learn from them about that which is characteristic or distinctive of adolescence?

As we think of boundaries between childhood and adolescence or between adolescence and adulthood, two questions arise:

1 Would it not be better to conceive these boundaries as more or less extended periods in their own right, rather than as sharp lines of demarcation?
2 Should we not also think of internal horizons within the adolescent era, e.g., between early and late adolescence (Kagan & Coles, 1972)?

The possibility of extended outer boundaries originates in the observation that all individuals do not move from one period in the life span to another at precisely the same time or speed. The notion of inner boundaries reflects differences between adolescents in the early years of secondary school and their older counterparts in university or in the working world.

My purpose in raising these questions is not to settle them, but rather to encourage further thinking and additional precision about this interesting period of life.

Interpretations of Adolescence

Another aspect to be considered is how scholars have chosen to interpret adolescence as a period in the human life span. Two primary and contrasting models serve to illustrate this issue. The first, drawn from the psychoanalytic literature, emphasizes the stresses and difficulties in the adolescent period (e.g., Freud, 1958) and describes problems faced by adolescents in coping with developmental challenges and losses. Adolescence is seen as a stormy sea of transition, and adolescents are thought to long for—even mourn—the simpler, now-lost times of childhood. As a result, periods of depression are thought to be common, even characteristic, in adolescence.

Quite a different view has been put forward by Offer, Ostrov, and Howard (1981). Based on large-scale and cross-cultural research, this view suggests that adolescence is basically a time of happiness and self-satisfaction. Adolescents are said to face the present and the immediate future with little fear and with a reasonable amount of confidence.

These views seem to be diametrically opposed. Certainly, they describe quite different frameworks within which to think about adolescence. One might wonder if they can be integrated in any way, or if (as is often the case) they each describe different aspects of the adolescent experience?

Offer, Ostrov, and Howard (1981, p. 121) have remarked that adolescence is "the world's most perfect projective device for adults." This is an important caution. Do adults see adolescence through their own distorted lenses? And are those distortions, as Bandura (1980) has suggested, to some extent self-fulfilling prophecies? If a significant portion of adolescent life is lived out in relation or response to adult images and structures, then it would be very interesting to study how the adult side of the equation works to influence the adolescent side.

ADOLESCENCE AND DEATH

Four topics among several can serve to illustrate issues that have a direct bearing on how adolescents relate to death itself. These are (1) the social context and the primary death-related patterns, including the leading causes of death, within which adolescents live; (2) death-related concepts and their significance for adolescents; (3) the influence of nuclearism and the nuclear era on adolescents; and (4) death-related themes in adolescent music. I shall examine each of these in turn.

Death and the Societies in Which Adolescents Live

Death is not experienced in the same way at all times and in all places. The faces that death presents to adults and adolescents are different in different societies. Sometimes we do not notice this or pay much attention to its significance. In other words, we act as if our interactions with death have been true at all times and in all places. But as Kastenbaum (1972) has pointed out, each society has its own death system, and each of these sociophysical networks mediates and expresses the relationship to mortality in its own way. Even if we rebel against our own society, we will not understand ourselves accurately if we do not understand the death system within which we function.

In North America and in most other parts of the contemporary developed world, the death system is characterized by: (1) diminished contact with natural death experiences (lower mortality rates than in the past, increased average life expectancy, increased institutionalization of death and professionalization of death-related experiences; (2) increased contact with fantasized or surrogate death experiences (particularly through the media); and (3) significant changes in the character of human-induced death (Corr, 1979). In the ways in which their social systems permit or prevent involvement with death, today's adolescents in developed countries are inhabitants of a very special time and place. They do not have the same encounters with death as did their predecessors in the not-too-distant past or their contemporaries in developing countries.

In this regard, it is interesting to reflect on the leading causes of death among adolescents in North American society. These are accidents, suicide, and homicide. All are human-induced deaths, constituting a recent trend. Even by comparison with other age cohorts in our own society, adolescence is the only period in the human life span when natural causes are displaced by human-induced factors as the leading causes of death. In other words, when death comes to adolescents in North American society, it mostly presents itself in relatively sudden, unexpected, and even traumatic ways. The reason for this, in part, is that most adolescents are healthy young animals. They have escaped the dangers of natural death in childhood and have not lived long enough for the dominant degenerative diseases of adulthood to end their lives. Most adolescents will live on into adulthood if they or we do not cause their death.

Adolescents do encounter death in contemporary society. In recent years, the specter of acquired immune deficiency syndrome (AIDS) has added a new factor to these encounters. However, the pattern of these adolescent encounters with death is in many ways special, limited, and distorted. Just think of the media alone: lots of killing, very little grief, few deaths, and great selectivity in terms of both those who die and the manner of their demise.

Death-Related Concepts and Their Significance of Adolescents

It is generally accepted that by the beginning of the adolescent period individuals with normal cognitive development have the ability to understand death as final, universal, and inevitable. Agreement on this point does not seem to depend on the account that one accepts of children's abilities to understand and conceptualize death (Lonetto, 1980; Wass, 1984). However, it is one thing to have the capacity to form concepts and quite another to appreciate their significance. Consider two examples of how this might relate to adolescents.

Alexander and Adlerstein (1958) noted sharply discrepant responses to an empirical study that associated death-related stimulus words with decreased galvanic skin resistance. Scores from boys who were 5–8 years old and 13–16 years old contrasted with those 9–12 years old. Interpretation of these results centered not on the capacity to form concepts, but on the emotional significance of the concepts. This means that death was said to have "a greater emotional significance for people with less stable ego self-pictures" (Alexander & Adlerstein, 1958, p. 175). If so, research needs to focus on the *significance* of death-related concepts and attitudes of adolescents, not just on adult-like abilities to understand such concepts and issues (Maurer, 1964).

A second, similar conclusion can be drawn from a lesson that Tolstoy's creation Ivan Ilych had learned in college as an adolescent, but the truth of which was only brought home to him during the process of his dying. As Tolstoy (1884/1960, p. 131) wrote, "The syllogism he [Ivan] had learnt from Kiezewetter's Logic: 'Caius is a man, men are mortal, therefore Caius is mortal' had always seemed to him correct as applied to Caius, but certainly not as applied to himself." Like Ivan, many adolescents are adept at defending themselves from the personal import of that which they are intellectually capable of understanding about death. Even though adolescents may acknowledge the implications of mortality in some safer or more reflective moments, the intensity of present living often leads them to be reluctant to admit how vulnerable their own lives are. As Gordon (1986) has said, adolescents often manifest an illusion of invulnerability and shield themselves with a tattered cloak of immortality carried over from childhood.

Some factors that contribute to an unwillingness in many adolescents to recognize the personal implications of mortality have to do with the limits of adolescent experience and the patterns of mortality in our society. Breadth of experience is often associated with appreciation of dangers in everyday living, lethal potential in shared activities, and the implications of risk taking. If one sees oneself as immortal, or if one perceives death not to be of much relevance to one's current life, then danger, lethality, and risks all appear to be much more benign than they really are. Thus, adolescents might be expected to drive powerful automobiles in more reckless and risky ways than would older, slightly more experienced (and perhaps also more frightened) adult drivers. And, of course, evidence shows that adolescents do, in fact, behave in precisely this way (Jonah, 1986).

Adolescents and Nuclearism

Nuclearism has both military and civilian faces. For the first, the threat of nuclear war is the threat of mass death on a scale and in ways that were inconceivable before 1945. It may also be the threat of cataclysmic human-induced extinction. Hersey (1959) and Lifton (1967, 1979) sought in quite different ways to point out the implications of this new mode of death and its contribution to the definition of a new era in human life. Only in recent years have researchers begun to study what this means for adolescent life and development (e.g., Beardslee & Mack, 1982; Escalona, 1982; Goodman et al., 1983; Snow, 1984). Results are perhaps not yet sufficiently broad-based or definite to rely upon with full confidence, but it seems clear that at least some adolescents are concerned in important ways with the threat of nuclear war and its implications, and that such concerns may express themselves in cynicism and distrust regarding political leaders and the adult generation.

In the last few years, we have come to see that nuclearism also has a civilian face, experienced through "incidents" at the nuclear power plants at Three Mile Island in the United States and at Chernobyl in the Soviet Union. The meaning attributed by adolescents and others to these powerful events needs to be investigated.

Death and Adolescent Music

Death-related themes are prominent in adolescent music. Music, as Attig (1986) has noted, occupies a central place in the lives of many adolescents. It is an important aspect of their milieu and a common idiom shared across the national, political, and cultural boundaries of our world. Those who might wish to think that the everyday lives of adolescents are simply divorced from topics and issues related to death need only listen to the music of adolescents or talk about it with these young people, to discover their error.

Adolescents may prefer one or more musical forms or subtypes, but they usually know most of the music that is, or recently has been, popular among their peers as a part of their environment. Sometimes, they will say that they have not previously thought about this music from a death-related perspective. But this particular point of view can be intriguing to them, and will often stimulate them to recall other songs with similar topical associations.

As a popular cultural phenomenon, some of this music and its associated lyrics are imaginative and of high quality, while other examples are repulsive. Occasionally, popular music yields enduring melodies or poetry. More often, popular culture is gone in a brief flash or survives in musical form as "golden oldies" on radio stations specializing in pandering to the memories of those who are slightly older and, perhaps, more affluent than adolescents.

Adolescent music is a fast-changing phenomenon that has not been well studied or catalogued from a death-related standpoint. There are only two accounts of which I am aware (Attig, 1986; Thrush & Paulus, 1970), and even Attig leaves us nearly a full decade behind. Moreover, the variety of this music is staggering.

Consider, for example, three titles: "Die Young, Stay Pretty" by Blondie (1979); "But I Might Die Tonight" by Cat Stevens (1970); and "And When I Die" by Blood, Sweat, and Tears (1969). All three are connected with confronting aging and death, though in different ways. Should I favor fast living over the long, slow decline of aging? Can I anticipate a peaceful, natural, and satisfying death or not? Should I conform to, or resist, the cultural norms favored in my society?

Of course, these are not the only songs about death and aging. The Beatles wondered about being needed and cared for in old age in "When I'm Sixty-Four" (1967); Paul Simon reflected gently and respectfully about old friends in his song by that name (1968); and John Denver even asserted that "it turns me on to think of growing old" in "Poems, Prayers, and Promises" (1971).

The viewpoints in these and other songs are understandably different. Some voice the criticisms of youth who speak against life itself or in opposition to the apparent materialism of adults. Others speak in favor of quality in living, urging listeners to seize life, to live out their dreams now, or to seek to contribute to a better world. Some songs are merely self-indulgent and short-sighted. They parallel the voices of rebellious youth urging comrades not to trust anyone over 30. Some may help to lead individuals and societies to reexamine their values and to strive to become more sensitive and caring. Some reflect the voices of those who will become bitter and disillusioned, mired in middle age and selling life insurance.

The folk song "Will the Circle Be Unbroken?" (1969) sung by Joan Baez asks questions about life after death. Another song, "Stairway to Heaven" (1971) by Led Zeppelin, urges the importance of the transformation in one's being, in order to achieve salvation. And "Abraham, Martin and John" (1975) by Dion is a tribute to Abraham Lincoln, Martin Luther King, Jr., and John F. Kennedy. What does the prospect of death require of us in our living? What will death mean for us when it comes? How are we connected, if at all, to those who are now dead? These issues about what Lifton (1979) called meaningfulness in life, the concept of continuity, and modes of symbolic or literal immortality abound in adolescent and other kinds of music.

Loss, grief, and bereavement are also addressed in music familiar to adolescents. Two good examples are Paul Simon's "Bridge over Troubled Water" (1970), and Abba's "The Way Old Friends Do" (1981), which are classic themes of sharing sorrow, offering support, and finding comfort. Hospice programs and support groups offering mutual aid for the bereaved try to implement similar principles.

The advice in "Don't Cry Out Loud" (1978) by Melissa Manchester runs against these themes. However, both David Gates's "Everything I Own" (1973) and Mike and the Mechanics's "The Living Years" (1988) publicly mourn the death of fathers and lament what has been lost. Consequently, there is much that can be tender and even helpful in some popular music familiar to adolescents.

The subject of suicide is not neglected in this music, although it is treated in quite different ways. In "I Think I'm Gonna Kill Myself" (1972), Elton John sings about suicide as a means to draw attention to teenage troubles. And the advice from the Blue Oyster Cult is "Don't Fear the Reaper" (1976). Against this, Queen recommends "Don't Try Suicide" (1980), and Billy Joel counsels that we have patience with ourselves and our imperfections and keep on going, in "You're Only Human (Second Wind)" (1985).

Many adults who have admired or laughed over the past decade at the antics of the characters in the very popular movie and television series "M*A*S*H," are surprised to learn the words to its familiar theme song, "Suicide Is Painless" (1970). Is suicide painless? For whom? Protagonists or survivors? Is it an option to keep open in the face of life's sorrows? Should we be nonjudgmental when individuals exercise that option?

War and various catastrophes appear as themes that are slightly less salient in adolescent music at the present moment. But several very different titles and performers remind us of their prominence when disagreements about the war in Vietnam and about the nuclear arms race were at their height. These include: "I-Feel-Like-I'm-Fixin'-To-Die-Rag" by Country Joe and the Fish (1967); "The Wall" by Pink Floyd (1979); "We'll All Go Together When We Go" by Tom Lehrer (1966); "A Hard Rain's Gonna Fall" by Bob Dylan (1963);

"When All the Laughter Dies in Sorrow" by Chicago (1971); and "Before the Deluge" by Jackson Browne (1974).

There are also songs about drugs, hunger, violence, murder, alienation, and what some have called pornographic depictions of death.

It is important to note that most of this music was not written or performed by adolescents. The writers, performers, and producers of adolescent music are themselves almost exclusively adults, but the main public to which they market their wares consists of adolescents. Some argue that the lyrics, titles, and even in some cases the names of the performers do not count, since only the music— and perhaps just the beat—is significant to adolescent audiences. This view seems difficult to accept. Advertisers pay large amounts of money to associate favorite names, concepts, phrases, and lyrics with what are thought to be attractive melodies and visual images. In a similar way, lyrics that appear in popular adolescent music cannot be wholly separated from the attractiveness of the melodies. When adults have paid little attention to this music and have hardly even surveyed or catalogued its lyrical content, can we expect to know much about its significance?

Wass, Miller, and Stevenson (1989) and Wass and her colleagues (1989) have offered exploratory studies that suggest that some kinds of music are listened to more frequently by certain types of adolescents. We might be interested, for example, in correlations with music whose lyrics promote homicide, suicide, and satanic practices, and we might wonder what connections with such destructive lyrical themes tell us about their adolescent listeners. These are beginnings that deserve careful replication and development as we look more closely at this prominent facet of adolescent life.

ADOLESCENTS AND DYING

Sadly, dying is a part of the lives of some adolescents. Coping with dying is, of course, a task we will all face, unless our own death is sudden and unanticipated. But in the case of adolescents, the process of coping with dying has some special qualities since, as Papadatou (1989) has rightly noted, both dying and adolescence are transitional phases. On this ground, "it could be argued that seriously ill adolescents experience a double crisis owning to their imminent death and their developmental age" (p. 28).

Like others who cope with dying, adolescents face a need to find meaning and purpose both in their lives and in their deaths. In other words, "dying adolescents are fully involved in 'living experiences' " (Papadatou, 1989, p. 28). This is the fundamental premise of hospice care: dying patients are living human beings. Dying is not a psychiatric illness; it is a normal and natural part of life. Our task is to discover what is central for adolescents, both as individuals and as members of that age-group, in the living time that remains to them, and to identify what we can do to help them satisfy their needs.

Those who have worked with dying adolescents speak of their needs in different but not dissimilar ways. Adams and Deveau (1986) have reported that dying adolescents need to maintain a sense of identity, to be treated with honesty, to pursue independence, to control what is happening to them, to have opportunities for privacy, to pursue an orientation to the future, and to experience love, comfort, reassurance, and freedom from pain. Waechter (1984) put this another way when she spoke of the following concerns of dying adolescents: isolation, my body, the future, and threat. Papadatou (1989) has emphasized that dying adolescents desire to strive for independence, need to control some aspects of their lives, and struggle to maintain a sense of identity, dignity, and pride.

What becomes obvious is the very great importance for dying adolescents of living in the present and of being oriented towards the future. Identity, independence, control, and quality in living are all features of the present moment. Isolation, threat, loss of privacy, and bodily disfigurement are all factors that reduce the quality of the current moment. Even adolescents' orientation to the future is a way of looking forward from the present moment to that which is immediately ahead. This refers to the potential inherent in the unfolding present, which does not necessarily contain a long-range vision of the future.

There is much that adults, other adolescents, and even younger children can offer to dying adolescents. We can, for example, use reasonably promising and acceptable interventions to attempt a cure, seek to palliate distressing symptoms, extend compassion (not pity), make a gift of our human presence, and support the hopes that remain open even until the final moments of life. These activities may not always be sufficient, or even welcomed. But they are much better than doing nothing and can, in fact, be precious tokens in times of extreme stress. As Papadatou (1989, p. 31) has written, "we must also believe that we are not helpless or hopeless, but have something valuable to offer: an honest and meaningful relationship that provides the adolescent with the feeling that we are willing to share his journey through the remainder of his life."

Dying adolescents grieve over the losses they have already experienced, those they are currently experiencing, and those they have yet to experience (Rando, 1986). We cannot relieve them of this grief, but we can help them to set aside unjustified guilt, to cope with grief in constructive ways, and to emphasize the life they still have to live. We can determine to be with them throughout that process.

ADOLESCENTS AND BEREAVEMENT

In bereavement, as in dying, there is again a two-sided quality to the experiences of adolescents. Normal adolescent development calls for a set of tasks that Fleming and Adolph (1986) have described as emotional separation from parents; achievement of competency, mastery, or control; and development of intimacy vs. commitment. The conflicts inherent in these tasks are separation vs. reunion or abandonment vs. safety, independence vs. dependence, and closeness vs. distance.

These developmental tasks echo, in significant ways, processes in normal adolescent mourning, which Sugar (1968) has described as protest/searching, disorganization, and reorganization. In other words, both normally developing adolescents and adolescent mourners are faced with a need to achieve some separation or distancing from others, and are likely to protest the harshness of this experience and to search for ways to overcome it. As they move forward in their respective tasks, developing and mourning adolescents face challenges to their competencies to live in new situations that are not wholly of their making. Thus, they may feel disoriented or disorganized in determining what to do next. Finally, developing adolescents are called upon to reorganize their lives in the form of new relationships with the adults who are now their peers, much as mourners must find ways to reorient themselves to a future in which the loved one will no longer be physically present.

This teaches us about the difficulties in distinguishing processes of development in adolescents from those of grief, mourning, and coping with bereavement.

Two other factors complicate our insights into adolescent bereavement. First, much of the literature has focused upon disturbed adolescents or those who were already engaged in psychotherapy when they experienced bereavement. Clearly, this is not a satisfactory basis upon which to generalize interpretations for all adolescents. Grief and mourning are not psychiatric processes, although of course psychiatrically ill people may grieve. What is most needed is detailed studies of grief and mourning in "normal" adolescents. This is just beginning in studies of adolescents surviving the death of a sibling (e.g., Balk, 1983).

Second, in addition to the usual losses that might be faced by many other human beings, such as those involving older persons (grandparents or parents), those of roughly the same age (peers), and those of younger age (younger siblings), adolescents also face the possibility of losses that have not been well studied or understood, such as those involved in elective abortion (Joralemon, 1986) or those arising from parental bereavement over the death of their own children (Barnickol, Fuller & Shinners, 1986; Schodt, 1982). Undoubtedly we have much to learn about how bereaved adolescents deal with the "empty space" in their lives (McClowry et al., 1987).

At the same time, there are things we can do to help bereaved adolescents. Fox (1988) has suggested four tasks for bereaved young children that apply to adolescents as well and can be turned into guidelines for constructive intervention. These tasks are (1) to understand what is happening or has happened; (2) to grieve or express emotional responses to the present or anticipated loss; (3) to commemorate the loss through some formal or informal remembrance; and

(4) to learn how to go on with one's life, i.e., how to come to grips with the loss and integrate it into one's living. In other words, adult helpers can assist bereaved adolescents to obtain accurate information about their losses, to commemorate or memorialize the lost person or object, and to begin the process of interpreting and integrating the loss into ongoing life.

Rather than taking over the mourning process for adolescents (which is never productive), helpers can return to what Calvin and Smith (1986) have called the fundamental goals of the counseling process: providing a safe, caring environment in which adolescents can begin to address their death-related concerns, as well as providing clarification of or assistance with the problem-solving process itself.

ADOLESCENTS AND SUICIDE

Suicidologists have studied their chosen subject for many years, so there is a large body of literature in this field. Literature relevant only to adolescents (e.g., Peck, Farberow & Litman, 1985) is too extensive to include in this chapter. However, the following observations can be made.

First, recent years have seen a tremendous rise in the rate of suicide among adolescents in the United States. That fact, together with the sharp contrast between the vitality of healthy adolescents and elements of desperation in suicide, drives a much-needed search for additional understanding of the dynamics of suicidal behavior in adolescents and for effective intervention processes.

Second, for adolescents in particular, it may be helpful to question the links between suicidal behavior and death. Ambivalence and depression are familiar features in all accounts of suicide. They appear to be highly increased in many suicidal adolescents. Thus, it has been said that much of adolescent suicidal behavior is not about death, but about escape. We need to consider the complexities of adolescent suicidal behavior, the expectation that it may be driven by different motives in different individuals, and the likelihood that it is multiply determined in most cases.

Third, it is worth noting that, while we have rightly placed much emphasis upon protagonists in adolescent suicide, very little attention has been given to those who are the survivors of such suicides (Valente & Sellers, 1986). These are, in the first place, bereaved siblings and peers in cases of completed suicides. We have much to learn about the impact of a suicide upon such adolescents and their development. In the second place, even less attention has been directed to those adolescents who attempt suicide but, for one reason or another, fail to carry it through to completion. Many of these are regarded as troubled youths engaged in desperate forms of communication. Some are perhaps poor problem-solvers, incapable of solving the problem of how to commit suicide. We must worry about failed suicides, cases of adolescents who do not end their lives but damage themselves seriously and irreparably for the remainder of their lives.

Fourth, as suicide education programs are developed—and in some cases, required—in the schools (Berkovitz, 1985; Ross, 1985), it is good to distinguish between education and modeling. Suicidal behavior in families or peer groups has been said to legitimize or give permission in ways that increase the risk of similar behavior in others associated with the family or group. Similarly, reports in the media of suicidal behavior, especially among adolescents, have been accused of providing models for such behavior and encouraging what are called "cluster suicides." To whatever degree these links or charges may be valid, it seems to me that they are quite different from sound education about suicide. Such education is always designed, at least in part, to point out the unfortunate aspects of such behavior and to identify ways in which it can be minimized by constructive processes of intervention. When counselors and friends suspect that young people may be contemplating suicide, they are always urged to raise that possibility directly. The goal is not to incite such behavior, but to address it and thereby to minimize its likelihood. Some people misunderstand this critical point.

CONCLUSION: HELPING ADOLESCENTS
AND HELPING OURSELVES

Helping adolescents to cope effectively with death, dying, and bereavement begins in societies and in families with principles of good communication and with accurate information about these subjects. That directs us to alter the ways in which interactions with the changing face of death have become distorted in contemporary society. We also need to develop social, parental, and familial programs of education. Since peers are so influential in the lives of adolescents, it also suggests the value of constructive educational programs about death, dying, and bereavement for children and adolescents. Adolescents can help themselves and each other if they are provided with accurate information and guided in the development of appropriate behaviors and values.

In coping with grief and the impact of death, adolescents are often well served by assistance from respected adults and from caring peers. These adults need not be their parents, to whom adolescents may not readily turn or who may be grieving themselves. School, sports, religion, and other prominent venues in adolescent life bring young people into contact with responsible adults who can be safe counselors, if they themselves are prepared, sensitive to needs, and willing to help.

Similarly, adolescent peers in self-help or mutual-aid groups, especially where there is a bond of shared experiences, can be a particularly valuable resource (Baxter, Bennett & Stuart, 1989; Ribar & Berman, 1987; Wolfe, 1987). The development of such groups is a relatively new phenomenon, the effectiveness of which may not appear to be well established. However, their value has certainly been demonstrated for many adults; they are congruent with the underlying theme in this chapter of normalizing (rather than professionalizing) interactions with death, and they fit closely with the emphasis upon peers that is so typical a feature of adolescent life.

Jackson (1984, p. 42) has noted that "adolescents are apt to think they are the discoverers of deep and powerful feelings and that no one has ever loved as they do." If that is so, then adolescent grief will be equally unparalleled. In short, to say "I know how you feel" may be even more inappropriate with adolescents than with other grieving persons. Thus, there are many reasons why parents may be unhelpful to grieving adolescents. But when it is the same person who has been lost, even though the grief will be different, a parent can rightly point out that "you lost your grandfather, I lost my father."

The first lesson to learn, here, is that common ground can be found on which adults and adolescents can join hands, if we search for it in careful ways. The second lesson is that if the ground is truly common, then help can run in both directions. A third lesson arises from one of the conclusions drawn by young adolescents in a class on death and dying: "By laughing about death, we learned to laugh more in life" (Sternberg & Sternberg, 1980, p. 81). Adolescents sometimes puncture the pretentious euphemisms and practiced evasions of adults with keen insight and honesty, even as they develop their own baffling idioms.

Francis Bacon (1620/1960) once likened different kinds of philosophers to ants, spiders, and bees. Ants are empiricists who gather lots of raw materials, but often without much selectivity and without modifying what they have gathered for constructive exploitation. Spiders spin theories of marvelous ingenuity and formal perfection out of their own innards, but may not link such theories effectively to the rest of life. Against these, bees both gather materials and transform them in satisfying and productive ways. Adult philosophers of adolescent life must gather data from and about a wide range of adolescent experiences. They must also assess and test what they have gathered in order to interpret it judiciously. And they must reflect with insight upon what they have learned in order to understand the life-related and death-related experiences of adolescents more clearly. Only in these ways can adults help adolescents and themselves to live healthful lives.

REFERENCES

Adams, D. W., & Deveau, E. J. (1986). Helping dying adolescents: Needs and responses. In C. A. Corr & J. N. McNeil (Eds.), *Adolescence and death* (pp. 79–96). New York: Springer.

Adelson, J. (Ed.). (1980). *Handbook of adolescent psychology.* New York: Wiley.

Alexander, I. E., & Adlerstein, A. M. (1958). Affective responses to the concept of death in a population of children and early adolescents. *Journal of Genetic Psychology, 83,* 167–177.

Ariès, P. (1962). *Centuries of childhood.* New York: Knopf.

Attig, T. (1986). Death themes in adolescent music: The classic years. In C. A. Corr & J. N. McNeil (Eds.), *Adolescence and death* (pp. 32–56). New York: Springer.

Bacon, F. (1960). *The new organon and related writings.* Ed. F. H. Anderson. New York: Bobbs-Merrill. (Original work published 1620)

Balk, D. (1983). Adolescents' grief reactions and self-concept perceptions following sibling death: A study of 33 teenagers. *Journal of Youth and Adolescence, 12*(2), 137–161.

Bandura, A. (1980). The stormy decade: Fact or fiction? In R. E. Muuss (Ed.), *Adolescent behavior and society: A book of readings* (pp. 22–31) (3rd ed.). New York: Random House.

Barnickol, C. A., Fuller, H., & Shinners, B. (1986). Helping bereaved adolescent parents. In C. A. Corr & J. N. McNeil (Eds.), *Adolescence and death* (pp. 132–147). New York: Springer.

Baxter, G., Bennett, L., & Stuart, W. (1989). *Adolescents and death: Bereavement support groups for secondary school students* (2nd ed.). Etobicoke, Ontario: Canadian Centre for Death Education and Bereavement at Humber College.

Beardslee, W. R., & Mack, J. E. (1982). The impact on children and adolescents of nuclear developments. In R. Rogers (Ed.), *Psychosocial aspects of nuclear developments* (Task Force Report #20) (pp. 64–93). Washington, DC: American Psychiatric Association.

Berkovitz, I. H. (1985). The role of schools in child, adolescent, and youth suicide prevention. In M. L. Peck, N. L. Farberow, & R. E. Litman (Eds.), *Youth suicide* (pp. 170–190). New York: Springer.

Calvin, S., & Smith, I. M. (1986). Counseling adolescents in death-related situations. In C. A. Corr & J. N. McNeil (Eds.), *Adolescence and death* (pp. 215–230). New York: Springer.

Caplan, M. G., & Douglas, V. I. (1969). Incidence of parental loss in children with depressed moods. *Journal of Child Psychology and Psychiatry, 10,* 225–232.

Conger, J. J., & Petersen, A. (1984). *Adolescence and youth: Psychological development in a changing world* (3rd ed.). New York: Harper & Row.

Corr, C. A. (1979). Reconstructing the changing face of death. In H. Wass (Ed.), *Dying: Facing the facts* (pp. 5–43). Washington, DC: Hemisphere.

Corr, C. A., & McNeil, J. N. (1986). *Adolescence and death.* New York: Springer.

Escalona, S. (1982). Growing up with the threat of nuclear war: Some indirect effects on personality development. *American Journal of Orthopsychiatry, 52,* 600–607.

Field, T. M., Huston, A., Quay, H. D., Troll, L., & Finley, G. E. (1982). *Review of human development.* New York: Wiley.

Fleming, S. J., & Adolph, R. (1986). Helping bereaved adolescents: Needs and responses. In C. A. Corr & J. N. McNeil (Eds.), *Adolescence and death* (pp. 97–118). New York: Springer.

Fox, S. (1988). Psychological tasks for bereaved students: Strategies for schools. Paper presented at the Conference on Helping Young People Cope with Death, London, Ontario, June 1.

Freud, A. (1958). Adolescence. *Psychoanalytic Study of the Child, 13,* 255–268.

Goodman, L. A., Mack, J. E., Beardslee, W. R., & Snow, R. (1983). The threat of nuclear war and the nuclear arms race: Adolescent experience and perceptions. *Political Psychology, 4,* 501–530.

Gordon, A. K. (1986). The tattered cloak of immortality. In C. A. Corr & J. N. McNeil (Eds.), *Adolescence and death* (pp. 16–31). New York: Springer.

Hardt, D. V. (1978). An investigation of the stages of bereavement. *Omega, 9,* 279–285.

Hersey, J. (1959). *Hiroshima.* New York: Bantam.

Jackson, E. N. (1984). The pastoral counselor and the child encountering death. In H. Wass & C. A. Corr (Eds.), *Helping children cope with death: Guidelines and resources* (pp. 33–47). (2nd ed.). Washington, DC: Hemisphere.

Jonah, B. A. (1986). Accident risk and risk-taking behavior among young drivers. *Accident Analysis and Prevention, 18*(4), 255–271.

Joralemon, B. G. (1986). Terminating an adolescent pregnancy: Choice and loss. In C. A. Corr & J. N. McNeil (Eds.), *Adolescence and death* (pp. 119–131). New York: Springer.

Kagan, J., & Coles, R. (Eds.) (1972). *Twelve to sixteen: Early adolescence.* New York: Norton.

Kastenbaum, R. (1972). On the future of death: Some images and options. *Omega, 3,* 306–318.

Kohlberg, L., & Gilligan, C. (1971). The adolescent as a philosopher: The discovery of the self in a postconventional world. *Daedalus, 100,* 1051–1086.

Lifton, R. J. (1967). *Death in life: Survivors of Hiroshima.* New York: Random House.

Lifton, R. J. (1979). *The broken connection: On death and the continuity of life.* New York: Simon & Schuster.

Lonetto, R. (1980). *Children's conceptions of death.* New York: Springer.

Maurer, A. (1964). Adolescent attitudes toward death. *Journal of Genetic Psychology, 105,* 75–90.

McClowry, S. G., Davies, E. B., May, K. A., Kulenkamp, E. J., & Martinson, I. M. (1987). The empty space phenomenon: The process of grief in the bereaved family. *Death Studies, 11,* 361–374.

Mussen, P. H., Conger, J. J., Kagan, J., Geiwitz, J. (1979). *Psychological development: A life span approach.* New York: Harper & Row.

Offer, D., Ostrov, E., & Howard, K. I. (1981). *The adolescent: A psychological self-portrait.* New York: Basic Books.

Papadatou, D. (1989). Caring for dying adolescents. *Nursing Times, 85,* 28–31.

Peck, M. L., Farberow, N. L., & Litman, R. E. (Eds.) (1985). *Youth suicide.* New York: Springer.

Rando, T. A. (1986). *Loss and anticipatory grief.* Lexington, MA: Heath.

Ribar, M. C., & Berman, C. (1987). "Nobody understands": A support group for high school students. In C. A. Corr & R. A. Pacholski (Eds.), *Death: Completion and discovery* (pp. 189–196). Lakewood, OH: Association for Death Education and Counseling.

Ross, C. P. (1985). Teaching children the facts of life and death: Suicide prevention in the schools. In M. L. Peck, N. L. Farberow, & R. E. Litman (Eds.), *Youth suicide* (pp. 147–169). New York: Springer.

Schodt, C. M. (1982). Grief in adolescent mothers after an infant death. *Image, 14,* 20–25.

Snow, R. (1984). Decision making in a nuclear age. *Boston University Journal of Education, 166,* 103–107.

Sternberg, F., & Sternberg, B. (1980). *If I die and when I do: Exploring death with young people.* Englewood Cliffs, NJ: Prentice Hall.

Sugar, M. (1968). Normal adolescent mourning. *American Journal of Psychotherapy, 22,* 258–269.

Thrush, J. C., & Paulus, G. S. (1970). The concept of death in popular music: A social psychological perspective. *Popular Music and Society, 6,* 219–228.

Tolstoy, L. (1960). *The death of Ivan Ilych and other stories.* New York: New American Library. (Original work published 1884)

Valente, S. M., & Sellers, J. R. (1986). Helping adolescent survivors of suicide. In C. A. Corr & J. N. McNeil (Eds.), *Adolescence and death* (pp. 167–182). New York: Springer.

Van Eerdewegh, M., Bieri, M., Parrilla, R., & Clayton, P. (1982). The bereaved child. *British Journal of Psychiatry, 140,* 23–29.

Waechter, E. H. (1984). Dying children: Patterns of coping. In H. Wass & C. A. Corr (Eds.), *Childhood and death* (pp. 51–68). Washington, DC: Hemisphere.

Wass, H. (1984). Concepts of death: A developmental perspective. In H. Wass & C. A. Corr (Eds.), *Childhood and death* (pp. 3–24). Washington, DC: Hemisphere.

Wass, H., Miller, M. D., & Stevenson, R. G. (1989). Factors affecting adolescents' behavior and attitudes toward destructive rock lyrics. *Death Studies, 13,* 287–303.

Wass, H., Raup, J. L., Cerullo, K., Martel, L. G., Mingione, L. A., & Sperring, A. M. (1989). Adolescents' interest in and views of destructive themes in rock music. *Omega, 19,* 177–186.

Wolfe, B. (1987). Children grieve, too: A three-year hospital-based young persons' grief support program. In C. A. Corr & R. A. Pacholski (Eds.), *Death: Completion and discovery* (pp. 177–187). Lakewood, OH: Association for Death Education and Counseling.

Music

"Abraham, Martin and John" (1975). Dion. NY: Laurie.

"And When I Die." In *Blood, Sweat and Tears* (1969). Blood, Sweat and Tears. New York & Los Angeles: Columbia Records.

"Before the Deluge." In *Late for the Sky* (1974). Jackson Browne. Los Angeles, New York & Nashville: Asylum.

"Bridge over Troubled Waters." In *Bridge over Troubled Waters* (1970). Simon and Garfunkel. New York & Los Angeles: Columbia Records.

"But I Might Die Tonight." In *Tea for the Tillerman* (1970). Cat Stevens. Los Angeles: A & M.

"Die Young, Stay Pretty." In *Eat to the Beat* (1979). Blondie. Los Angeles: Chrysalis Records.

"Don't Cry Out Loud." In *Don't Cry Out Loud* (1978). Melissa Manchester. New York & Los Angeles: Arista.

"Don't Fear the Reaper." In *Agents of Fortune* (1976). The Blue Oyster Cult. New York & Los Angeles: Columbia Records.

"Don't Try Suicide." In *The Game* (1980). Queen. Los Angeles, New York & Nashville: Elektra.

"Everything I Own." In *Best of Bread* (1973). David Gates. Los Angeles, New York & Nashville: Elektra/Asylum/Nonesuch Records.

"A Hard Rain's Gonna Fall." In *The Freewheelin' Bob Dylan* (1963). Bob Dylan. New York & Los Angeles: Columbia Records.

"I-Feel-Like-I'm-Fixin'-To-Die-Rag." In *I-Feel-Like-I'm-Fixin'-To-Die* (1967). Country Joe and the Fish. New York: Vanguard.

"I Think I'm Gonna Kill Myself." In *Honky Chateau* (1972). Elton John. Los Angeles & New York: UNI.

"The Living Years." In *Living Years* (1988). Mike and the Mechanics. New York & Los Angeles: Atlantic Records.

"Old Friends." In *Bookends* (1968). Simon and Garfunkel. New York & Los Angeles: Columbia Records.

"Poems, Prayers and Promises." In *Poems, Prayers and Promises* (1971). John Denver. New York, Los Angeles & Nashville: RCA.

"Stairway to Heaven." In *Led Zeppelin IV* (1971). Led Zeppelin. New York & Los Angeles: Atlantic Records.

"Suicide Is Painless." In *M*A*S*H* (1970). New York & Los Angeles: Columbia Records.

The Wall (1979). Pink Floyd. New York & Los Angeles: Columbia Records.

"The Way Old Friends Do." In *Super Trouper* (1981). Abba. New York & Los Angeles: Atlantic Records.

"We'll All Go Together When We Go." In *An Evening Wasted with Tom Lehrer* (1966). Tom Lehrer. Burbank, New York & Nashville: Reprise/Warner Bros.

"When All the Laughter Dies in Sorrow." In *Chicago III* (1971). Chicago. New York & Los Angeles: Columbia Records.

"When I'm Sixty-Four." In *Sgt. Pepper's Lonely Hearts Club Band* (1967). The Beatles. Hollywood, New York & Nashville: Capitol.

"Will the Circle Be Unbroken?" In *David's Album* (1969). Joan Baez. New York: Vanguard.

"You're Only Human (Second Wind)." In Billy Joel's Greatest Hits, Vol. II (1985). Billy Joel. New York & Los Angeles: Columbia Records.

Chapter 4

College Student Death: Postvention Issues for Educators and Counselors

Robert L. Wrenn

In 1976 I opened a course on the psychology of death and loss in the Psychology Department of the University of Arizona. Two hundred students enrolled for my first class. This really terrified me because I had never taught the subject before. As the semester moved on I knew my students were learning—and so was I. This had never happened to me before; usually I taught, and they learned. Then students from my class began coming in, during office hours, to talk about their personal needs related to a death in their lives. In a short time I came to be viewed as the campus expert on the psychology of death, and since I was already a counseling psychologist I became the "target" (I use the word wisely and with due respect for the need) of more referrals than I could handle.

I learned rather quickly that students are worried about death, in addition to grades and interpersonal relations. In recent communication with En-Chang Wu (1989), I have come to realize that this is probably a universal phenomenon although, as far as I know, we have little if any documentation of this presumed fact. In surveys at the National Taiwan University in Taipei, students indicate very strong concern about potential death or illness in the family or among their friends, as well as about failing a course, getting along with others, and finding a career they like.

In fact, offering a course in death education has been a release valve for the anxiety about death many students carry with them inwardly, I am convinced. The course has also raised as many questions as it has answered and was probably the best thing I ever did for myself professionally—as well as for the students at the University of Arizona. Course evaluations over the past 14 years have consistently indicated that students were amazed that they could immediately apply what they had learned. "I never knew when I enrolled that I would be using what I learned the sixth week of class, when my Grandmother died," wrote one student. Another student said, "This should be a required course," and another stated, "It is the only realistic and practical course I've had at the University and I graduate in two months." What they are really saying, I think, is that there is a tremendous need on our campuses to educate ourselves, each other, and our students, faculty, and administrators about how to listen, what to say, and what to do when a death occurs. Nothing nurtures anxiety so well as ambiguity. Students, as well as many of us who are educators and counselors, need some "reality anchors" in our education. If we are to continue teaching and counseling as death and dying facilitators, we need education as much as the students.

This is my main point in what is to follow. In this chapter, I will raise some questions many of us are struggling with, and will suggest some possible answers to the questions. More important, I will encourage the process of gathering facts and procedures that are effective in dealing with student death on our campuses. I will organize this chapter around four key questions that were of concern to me.

1   WHAT HAS BEEN WRITTEN ABOUT THE SUBJECT OF COLLEGE STUDENT DEATH?

In all the texts and articles available on death, dying, and bereavement, very little is specific to the college campus environment. Zinner (1985) has edited an excellent book that offers ideas and help for dealing with student death on campus. There are a few articles in journals, such as those by Halberg (1986) and Donohue (1977), which are individual responses from campus personnel reacting to the issue of student death. There are also articles, such as the one by Morgan (1986), that catch a glimpse of the cross-cultural aspect of death and bereavement attitudes but are not specific to college student death. There appears to be very little information specific to college student death. In addition, very little is known about how we in the United States deal with the death of a university or college student, not to mention how our attitudes and actions relate to those of other cultures.

We know from experience that one of the most difficult events for a college student to deal with is the death of a family member or friend. This is not a matter that is much talked about on campus or even expected to occur. It is certainly not a matter that most college administrators want to discuss or deal with. Nonetheless, it is important for students to become aware of whatever resources are available to them when a death does occur on campus.

2 DO STUDENTS, AS A COHORT, DIFFER IN FREQUENCY AND KIND OF DEATH FROM OTHER GROUPS?

We think they do, largely because of their stage and age in life. But there must be wide differences from campus to campus and from country to country. These differences in rates and in kinds of death should lead to differences in postvention work for those of us on the campus scene. By *postvention* I mean what we do to help the survivors of a student death. Sudden and violent death appears to be much more frequent for the 18–23-year-old group than for other groups at different ages and stages of life. Trying to bring to light information on frequency and cause of college student death, however, is not easy. The American College Health Association indicated it had no data and suggested I consult national reference materials on rates and kinds of death, such as those provided by insurance companies and drawn from national census data. Some generalizations can be drawn from death by age group, but no common source exists, to my knowledge, that offers information specific to the college campus in the United States.

According to statistics taken from *The Chronicle of Higher Education* (1989) approximately 12.5 million college students have enrolled on our nation's campuses during the past few years. This figure varies by a few hundred thousand, depending on the year. Estimates of rates of death per 10,000 students have reportedly ranged from as few as 4 to as many as 15 per 10,000 enrollment. On a national scale this would mean that, annually, we have from 5,000 to 18,750 college student deaths in the United States.

There are good reasons to cite this variation in estimates, since size of the school, location, regulations concerning drinking or driving, competition for grades, and other factors all bear heavily on the given death rate for a particular college or university. Additionally, many schools do not keep records of student death, or if they do, we do not know about it, so some of our estimates are rather loosely constructed at best. The only comparative data come from 53 American colleges and universities responding to my survey, and from a report on these matters given to me by Dr. Junko Nakajima, director of student health at Ibaraki University in Japan, during a personal interview with her on her campus (Table 1). Her data were drawn from 51 universities throughout Japan. The number of universities sampled and the number of students enrolled in

Table 1   Reported Death Rates, Average Student Age, and Causes of Death from U.S.A., Japan, and Other Countries (1989)

	U.S.A.[a]	Japan	Other Countries[b]
Number of institutions reporting	55	51	11
Number of students enrolled at reporting institutions	723,300	311,228	46,525
Average student age	23	20.5	20.4
Death rate reported per 10,000 students enrolled	4.7	4.5	4.7
Percentage of death by cause (rounded)			
Accident	55	31	60
Illness	21	22	14
Suicide	11	37	6
Homicide	2	0	6
Other	11	10	14
Total	100	100	100

[a]States represented include: Alabama (1), Arizona (3), California (3), Colorado (1), Connecticut (2), Delaware (1), Florida (4), Georgia (1), Hawaii (2), Illinois (1), Iowa (1), Kansas (1), Kentucky (1), Maryland (2), Massachusetts (1), Mississippi (1), New York (7), North Carolina (2), North Dakota (1), Ohio (1), Pennsylvania (4), Rhode Island (1), Tennessee (2), Texas (3), Vermont (1), Virginia (1), Washington (4), Wisconsin (1). Also included is the District of Columbia (1).

[b]Other countries include England (4), Canada (3), Indonesia (3), Greece (1). Percentages for cause of death are less reliable due to the small number of schools and students reporting.

these universities are a respectable sample size, totaling 1 million students for all groups combined.

The average undergraduate student age of 23 years reported from the United States is slightly higher than Japan's average of 20.5 due to our community college and adult education emphasis in higher education. Also, the number of reported deaths per 10,000 students varies so little between groups as to be insignificant. Japan reports 4.5 deaths per 10,000 students enrolled and the U.S. figure is 4.7. Of greater interest is the difference in cause of death between the United States and Japan. Homicide in Japan is very rare and even in the United States is reported at only a 2% level. There is a difference between these two countries in reported deaths by accident or by suicide. Japan reports 31% of its student deaths due to accidents, compared to 55% for the United States. However, Japan reports a 37% suicide rate compared to 11% for the United States. It would seem reasonable to believe Japan is more concerned with suicide prevention that we are in the United States, and the nature of Japanese postvention work will probably reflect this fact. In fact, in my travels through Japan, talking with psychologists there, I received the impression that they are now focused on suicide prevention as we were in the 1960s, when Shneidman and others were developing suicide prevention centers and establishing hot lines for emergency referral on campuses.

Another factor that makes these data intriguing is that the kind of response from the campus in one country may differ considerably from that of another due to the way the campus is organized, its mission, its size, and so forth. The United States is unique in its assignment of auxiliary services to students. Most European as well as Asian colleges and universities do not offer the kinds of organized student services, such as housing, health, and counseling, that we do in the United States. It is therefore easy to expect that when a student dies in Japan, or in many other parts of the world, the university representative most likely to respond to the death will be the student's teacher or academic department head. A more important aspect of this difference is that in Japan it is more likely that postvention work does not constitute an assigned role, but rather a natural response from a university member close to the student—most likely a teacher. In addition, an increase in frequency of suicides versus car accidents as a cause of death in our respective countries results in differences in the grief work of all persons concerned.

3 DO OTHER UNIVERSITIES HAVE WRITTEN POLICIES, OFFER TRAINING TO THE UNIVERSITY COMMUNITY, AND HAVE AN AWARENESS OF DEATH NOTIFICATION, AND ARE THEY ABLE TO TALK ABOUT A RECENT DEATH ON THEIR CAMPUS?

These questions came to me as I tried, several years ago, to develop some coordination for efforts on my own campus. I received excellent support from our health center director, Murray DeArmond, recent past president of the American College Health Association, and our dean of students, Rosalind Andreas, who is now vice president of student affairs at the University of Vermont. The three of us looked at our own campus and eventually developed a plan that our vice president, Doug Woodard, put into action.

Investigating whether other schools use student affairs personnel to take care of these matters, I found only two schools from my survey of U.S. campuses (Table 2) that discussed the teacher or academic department as being the most active unit on campus to deal with the aftermath of a student death. These were both schools with small enrollments. In some church-sponsored schools the clergy was expected to take care of coordinating such efforts. As mentioned before, in Japan and in other countries sampled outside the United States, the situation was described more often than not as one in which the student's teacher or department head would represent the university from a nonassigned role basis. I found that most schools in the United States

Table 2   Responses Regarding Management of Student Death from 53 Universities and Colleges in the United States (1989)

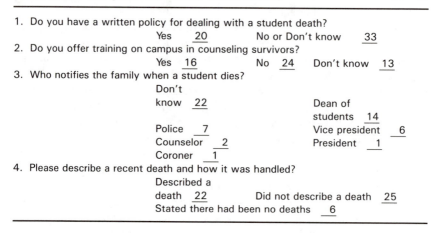

1. Do you have a written policy for dealing with a student death?

    Yes ___20___   No or Don't know   ___33___

2. Do you offer training on campus in counseling survivors?

    Yes ___16___   No ___24___   Don't know ___13___

3. Who notifies the family when a student dies?

    Don't know ___22___   Dean of students ___14___

    Police   ___7___   Vice president   ___6___

    Counselor   ___2___   President   ___1___

    Coroner   ___1___

4. Please describe a recent death and how it was handled?

    Described a death ___22___   Did not describe a death   ___25___

    Stated there had been no deaths   ___6___

do not have a written policy regarding what to do when a student dies, and of the 20 schools that did, many of them referred to a chain of command by which matters were processed. A few schools—and these were for the most part large universities or schools with multiple branches—had detailed policies that discussed contingencies for dealing with the student, as well as a chain of command for handling the situation. In addition, more schools than not have *not* advised, informed, or trained other personnel in the residence halls or in other locations where students tend to congregate concerning how to help survivors of a death. There were a number of schools—these tended to be the smaller colleges—where the sense of community and the close working relationships among faculty and staff would obviously come into play in a very positive way when a student died. The 22 schools out of 53 that did not know how death notification takes place or who does it again were mainly the smaller schools, where the frequency of student death is very low. In one case, it has been 15 years since a student died. The frequency of notifications coming from designated officials, either in the community where the death occurs (police) or from the Student Affairs Office (dean of students, vice president of student affairs, etc.) in fact represents the way things usually work in the United States. Finally, when asked to describe a recent death on their campuses, 22 schools did, 25 did not, and 6 schools said that the frequency of student death was so low that no one would be able to remember one to describe. In two cases, the indication was that "students don't die here." This last statement is reminiscent of what Kübler-Ross found back in the 1960s when she asked fellow doctors in Chicago if she could talk to any of their dying patients, only to be told, "I don't have any dying patients."

4   WHAT MAKES THE POSTVENTION PROCESS EFFECTIVE?

The last question concerns what actions people have found that make a positive difference to all parties concerned when a student dies and what stands in the way of achieving this purpose (Table 3).

An inspection of my survey results in Table 3 leads to at least 10 ideas or steps that prove helpful in dealing with college student death.

1 Students, faculty, staff, and officials from the college or university attend the funeral or memorial service.

2 Letters of recognition of appreciation or achievement are given to the dying student or to the family posthumously.

3 One person is assigned to coordinate or handle information given to the press and to investigators.

4 The presence and support of the president, vice president, dean, department head, and faculty members convey to the family and friends that the student was important and respected.

5 Police have good channels of communication with campus personnel.

6 Professionals are available to work with roommates, friends, and family of the deceased.

7 Some way, place, and time are provided for students and others associated with the deceased to ask questions and express their concern or anger.

8 Follow-up procedures are held with those students or faculty who are most affected.

9 Some public recognition of the death is made, such as the flag flying at half-mast, or letters written to those concerned.

10 Those closest to the deceased are encouraged to be involved in services and other events.

As can be seen from the survey results, all those things we teach and read about as being important at the time of death are taking place on our campuses. More often than not the sensitivity of the people involved and their experience in solid human relations is what makes things work well.

According to the survey, the main factor that stood in the way of helpful postvention work had to do with relaying accurate information about the death in a timely way to those coordinating the events and people involved.

CONCLUSIONS

My conclusions are few in number, simple and straightforward. They have to do with looking not only to our own campus as a place to practice what we preach, but beyond to those regional, national, and international associations, workshops, and forums where we can gain perspective on the matter of college student death. Specifically, we need the following:

Table 3   Specific Deaths and What Helped and Hindered the Process of Postvention Work from 22 U.S. Campuses

School	Cause of Death	Helpful	Hindered
1	Car accident of a well-known student on campus (male)	Many students and staff attended funeral. Tuition refunded. All information went to the press and investigators from one source.	Channels of communication not well defined. We often learn of a death via the evening news on TV or the morning newspaper.
2	Muscular dystrophy death (male)	Hospice called the school two days before the death. Student given certificate of recognition before he died. President spoke at the funeral. Everyone was supportive to the family.	
3	Epileptic seizure injury resulting in death (male)	Police notified vice president's office. Letters sent, records and refunds handled in a timely way. Chaplain, counseling staff activated. Good turnout at funeral.	Hospital policy did not allow release of information to campus officials.
4	Drowning (male)	Church service and burial anyone could attend. Counselors, teachers supportive.	
5	Heart failure (female)	Individual counseling for friends and family of the student. Students, staff, and faculty attended the wake. University held a memorial service.	
6	Drug overdose (female)	Campus coordinator available to family and all others concerned. Arranged later at father's request to ship student's artwork home.	Campus police and city police don't communicate well. Had trouble getting accurate information.
7	Car accident (male)	President spent an hour with the family. Sent representative to the funeral (100 miles away). Sent follow-up letters. On-campus mass offered by the campus chaplain. Flag was lowered to half-mast the next day.	Learned of death from newspaper, like everyone else.

**Table 3   Specific Deaths and What Helped and Hindered the Process of
Postvention Work from 22 U.S. Campuses (Continued)**

School	Cause of Death	Helpful	Hindered
8	Sudden respiratory failure (female)	Counseling director worked with the roommates until they were able to cope. Chaplain met with student groups. An 8-week group was formed for roommates and friends. Staff were trained in these matters.	
9	Car accident (male)	Out-of-town family was notified via family's minister by a call from campus minister. Department faculty and students were notified by personal letter. Memorial service was held. Letter of appreciation of student's achievements was sent to parents. Having dealt with other deaths proved helpful.	
10	Two students killed and 2 severely injured in a car accident (mixed gender)	Everyone from the president on down became involved and were supportive. Counselors, public information office, university lawyers, vice president all agreed on roles. Memorial service was held. Both students who died received posthumous degrees.	80% of students live on campus and rumors (with attendant anxiety) spread like wildfire. Police and E.R. personnel sometimes slow to respond.
11	Car accident (male)	Parents notified the college of the death! Family request for semester grades to be awarded posthumously was granted.	Verification of information when death occurs off-campus is usually a problem.
12	Car accident (male)	Mortuary held the body for choices to be made. Academic dept. held a brief memorial service. Reimbursed tuition and fees.	Verification of information sometimes a problem.
13	Car accident (3 students involved, popular female killed)	Support came from off-campus families and friends and on-campus people close to these students, not from the official sources of support. Sorority and fraternity people became involved and were helpful.	

Table 3   Specific Deaths and What Helped and Hindered the Process of Postvention Work from 22 U.S. Campuses (*Continued*)

School	Cause of Death	Helpful	Hindered
14	Illness (female)	Dean of students worked with family before student died as well as arranging for mortuary, etc. Everyone knew the dean of students' office handled these matters and brought their concerns there for triage.	None, thanks to a known coordinating office.
15	Suicide (male)	Several student affairs people talked to the fraternity president for a plan of action. Vice president talked to the fraternity and answered questions. On-campus memorial service offered. Follow-up made with close friends of the deceased.	
16	Natural causes (male)	Parents notified immediately just before death and were with him at time of death. Good support from all campus offices and campus police.	
17	Airpliane accident (male)	Faculty adviser notified the parents; dean of students, coordinator of religious activities, and others were helpful.	County police sometimes slow in informing us.
18	Drowning (male)	Died on a class outing. Faculty adviser was notified immediately. Memorial service was attended by many people. People were allowed to view the body.	
19	Illness (male)	Family notified by hospital before student died. Mother talked with teachers and collected son's personal belongings. Information and representation at service worked well.	
20	Suicide (female)	Dean of students and campus police went together to notify parents. Counselors worked with residence hall.	Sometimes hard to establish who is next of kin from our records. Communicating with divorced parents sometimes a problem.

Table 3 Specific Deaths and What Helped and Hindered the Process of Postvention Work from 22 U.S. Campuses (*Continued*)

School	Cause of Death	Helpful	Hindered
21	Car accident (female)	University representatives contacted parents and student's husband to offer assistance. On-campus faculty were notified.	In an emergency, written policy is not always followed. Sometimes this is more helpful than hindering, sometimes not. Depends on who is in charge.
22	Homicide (female)	Occurred at home between semesters. Support in the form of individual counseling and information groups was offered at the beginning of the next term in the residence hall.	

- Better sharing of what works and what makes a difference. In the journals, in our associations, at various meeting places, we need to ask questions, to hear what is taking place elsewhere, and to communicate these matters to those who can help make a difference.
- Better data on the frequency of student death and the causes of student death. This record-keeping will open up areas of research for our doctoral students, and the like. We know that better information locally, nationally, and internationally would provide helpful support for prevention as well as postvention efforts. A good example of this need is to ask ourselves the question: what do we know about AIDS death on our campuses, nationally or internationally?
- Knowledge of how student death is handled institutionally so that postvention work can be accomplished. We do *not* need to encourage the development of written policies from some theoretical vantage point for a university or college where things work quite well without one. All over the world there are good things happening within institutions of higher education, and it is important to understand how the culture, the people, and the expectations work together in positive ways. We might even learn and apply something from another culture to our own. For example, at Tsukuba University in Japan there are designated grounds where anyone can go to pay respects to a deceased member of the university. At a university in the United States the flag is flown at half-mast when a student dies. These formal, sanctioned signs of respect are extremely important symbols of the institution's attitude toward students. Family and friends of the deceased student notice and appreciate these symbolic representations of care.

64 DEATH IN WORLD OF CHILDREN AND ADOLESCENTS

REFERENCES

Chronicle of Higher Education, June 28, 1989, p. A24.

Donohue, W. R. (1977). "Student death: What do we do?" *NASPA Journal, 14*(4), 29–32.

Halberg, L. J. (1986). "Death of a college student: Response by student services professionals on one campus." *Journal of Counseling and Development, 64* (February), 411–412.

Morgan, J. D. (1986). "Death, dying and bereavement in China and Japan: A brief glimpse." *Death Studies, 10,* 265–272.

Wu, En-Chang. (1989). "The management of mental health in a university environment." Unpublished report, Department of Psychology, National Taiwan University, Taipei.

Zinner, E. S. (Ed.). (1985). *Coping with death on campus.* San Francisco, Jossey-Bass.

Chapter 5

Preserving Children's Mental Health Under Threat of War

Mooli Lahad and Ofra Ayalon

Childhood is devastated by war. Children who grow up in an environment of continuous, or even intermittent, stress are likely to worry about their existence. They may assume that the world is not a safe place, and that parents—the primary source of children's security—cannot be relied upon for protection at all times, since they leave their children in times of danger (fathers are conscripted), allow separations from them (for example, for evacuation), and let horrific things happen.

The heaviest psychological price paid for war is the trauma of bereavement. Being orphaned, wounded, crippled, or having one's house destroyed cause mental suffering and, in many cases, irreversible mental damage. The concept of "bereft families" includes increasing numbers of children exposed to traumatic experiences of losing loved ones as a result of war or terrorist attacks.

While trauma is a direct injury, the stressful situations of war create indirect injuries. Children are influenced by the moods of their parents and absorb feelings of worry, pain, anger, and frustration. Family functioning is disrupted by prolonged absences of fathers and sons serving in the army. Apart from the family's longing for them and constant worry for their well-being, their absence imposes changes in the distribution of roles in the family and places a heavy burden on the mother and the older children.

When families live near the border, where frequent dangerous incidents occur, they are affected by the constant turmoil and lack of security. The necessity to take refuge in shelters from bombings destroys the daily routine and often disturbs the night's sleep. In emergencies, there is liable to be an evacuation. This means that children are separated from their parents; they are uprooted and taken to a strange place.

The intensity of the experienced stress is determined by additional factors:

- Proximity to the incident, enabling one to see or hear the incident and imposing a strong chance of personal injury.
- Identifying with the injured, because of same age or sex, or similar social status.
- Knowing the injured.
- Repeated incidents within a short period of time.
- Living in a border area or near a hostility zone.

Proximity to the place of the incident increases the stress, but geographical distance from the place of the incident does not always provide protection from stress and anxiety, since immediate reports on television and through other media narrow the psychological distance and increase the general feeling of insecurity. Thus, children living in different regions become directly or indirectly involved. This involvement can explain why psychological investigations have not identified any significant difference between the anxiety level of children in the center of the country and that of those living in border settlements (Ziv, Yisraeli & Verbenhaus, 1972).

"Circles of vulnerability," which become further removed from the point of the incident, can be compared to a pool full of frogs where someone throws a stone: the frogs in the middle will react with great fear whereas the others, feeling the shock waves, will develop reactions of anxiety (Ayalon, 1987).

Large groups of children throughout the country, exposed to the shock waves of enemy attacks, are in danger of developing stress reactions that are liable to affect normal functioning and to cause suffering to some of them as well as to their families.

Once the battles subside, the stress does not completely disappear. Even in times of calm, there are elements of emergency. Living in a situation of "neither peace nor war" imposes a constant emotional burden and exposes both children and adults to messages, rich in internal conflict on behavioral, emotional, and moral levels. The following examples illustrate a number of such conflicts, which result in mixed-up values, confusion, and embarrassment:

- Keeping to the routine of daily life while being ready for war.
- Encouraging trust and openness with other people while being continuously exposed to warnings about suspicious articles or people.
- Education towards peaceful coexistence and respecting the difference in others, while justifying war and dehumanizing the enemy.

These contradictions are liable to bring about conflicts in the morals and values of society and to challenge the norms of wartime, such as violence and depreciation of the value of human life and property, in everyday life. All of these add up to the mental conflict caused by conflicting values (Kubovi, 1980).

SIGNS OF DISTRESS IN CHILDREN

Under these conditions of threat, children tend to exhibit signs of distress, expressed in behavioral changes at home and with friends, in play, in drawings, and in writing. Thus, one can detect signs of insecurity, anxiety, dependence, difficulty in concentration, frustration, anger, and aggression.

Stressful situations create two basic reactions: fight and flight. *Flight reactions* are accompanied by fear and anxiety and are frequently expressed through behavioral regression. *Fight reactions* are accompanied by anger, intensified by children's exposure to adults' violent way of settling international and regional arguments. The functional disturbances arising from these two types of reactions are described below.

Fears

What are children frightened of in times of increased security tension, war, and terror? Are their fears different from those related to the normal process of growth and change? Through careful observation of children's signs of distress during tense security situations, six basic characteristics of fear can be identified:

1. Fear due to Circumstances Fear as a result of threat is called "healthy fear" and is common to both adults and children (Janis, 1975). It has the function of indicating the presence of danger and warns the person to be careful, thus ensuring survival. However, when circumstances interfere with taking the appropriate means of defense or inhibit flight reactions, then physical symptoms of confusion and psychological problems ensue, accompanied by regression in behavioral patterns.

2. Increased Imaginary Fears In young children the fear of war is mixed with many other characteristic fears, and can cause difficulty in distinguishing between real and imaginary dangers. Children take the fear-arousing object into their immediate environment and project it onto external objects. With growth and development, fears of war become more concrete. Even though the confusion caused by alarming incidents disappears once the threat is past, physical and behavioral symptoms can persist for some time.

3. Fear Caused by the Behavior of Those Around the Child Young children experience the world through the significant adults in their life. Overreaction on the part of adults will cause the children in their care to be afraid, whereas an atmosphere of peace and security in times of danger will calm children. It is, however, difficult to request that parents remain calm in a dangerous situation. Some adults try—"for the child's sake"—to pretend all is well, but their denial of fear can make coping all the more difficult. When these adults try to hide or deny their anxiety, they usually require that their children play the part of the hero, thus increasing a feeling of helplessness. Not only do children fail to receive support when they need it, but they are also denied the opportunity of verifying their perception of things—that their parents are worried or annoyed. Instead of being allowed to indulge in their emotions, children are likely to suffer shame or guilt and to feel confused and isolated. Open discussion of feelings and thoughts, combined with expectations of improvement and a better future, may counteract these fears.

4. Fear of Separation from Parents Fear of separation or abandonment is normal during the first years of every child's life. It is heightened by the unavoidable separation from conscripted family members. These fears are intensified in times of war, when children suspect that following the departure of their fathers, they will also lose their maternal support.

5. Fear of Death Concerns about death, which preoccupy the child at various developmental stages, are occasionally examined through the literature. However, the issue still remains mysterious and unknown. In times of war, younger children are exposed to the experience of loss of life, without having the means of dealing with the information and the fear aroused by it. Cases of death around them may increase the feeling of their own vulnerability. The loss of loved ones forces many children to confront bereavement and increases their concern for children their age having a similar fate. Preparing children to cope with the subject of death, expressing feelings of distress and mourning, comforting those bereaved, and understanding the reactions of bereavement have become an urgent social-educational issue (Smilansky, 1978). However, frequent exposure to death can cause flattening of emotions, apathy, and depreciation of the value of life.

6. Traumatic Fears In some extreme cases, exposure to life-threatening incidents or loss of loved ones is likely to cause post-traumatic stress disorder, which includes at least three of the following symptoms: remembering details of the disaster as if they were actually happening; phobic avoidance of places or activities arousing memories of the traumatic event; oversensitivity to sounds; nervousness; flattening of emotions; disruption in one's sense of identity; memory impairment or trouble concentrating; sleep disturbance; hyperalertness for repeated disaster; regrets and guilt about surviving when others have not; and suspicion and alienation with regard to society and its institutions. These symptoms are not likely to diminish or disappear, without special treatment (Ayalon, 1989).

LONG-TERM EFFECTS

Long-term mental damage is hard to gauge, since it is not always possible to distinguish between the effects of war and those of the various life events shaping children's personalities. The time of diagnosis is incidental and does not necessarily reflect the onset of the mental or social disturbance. Conventional instruments, such as questionnaires, observation, projective examinations, and physiological tests, do not provide the full picture with regard to the functioning of the subject, and there is not necessarily correlation among them. For instance, a person may present low scores of anxiety in a questionnaire, whereas physiological or projective tests may indicate high levels of anxiety. Factors such as denial (conscious or subconscious) and social desirability decrease the reliability of self-report instruments. Beyond measurable damage, however, war leaves hidden mental scars, unnamed and unclassified by conventional psychological measurements.

Studies from the time of World War II relate long-term disorders in children to the occurrence of agitation and confusion in parents and other "significant adults" looking after them. Nervousness, bed-wetting, and other anxiety reactions that appeared in children after aerial bombing were related to reactions of overanxiety in their parents (Freud & Berlingham, 1942).

Follow-up studies with mentally affected children, as a result of the civil war in northern Ireland, indicate that in only a few cases do the symptoms of fear and withdrawal persist and become chronic. In most of these cases, children were found to be oversensitive, to have previously exhibited signs of distress, and to have had some kind of developmental difficulties (Fraser, 1973). Most children with normal ability to adapt calmed down with the passing of the storm and gradually returned to normal. Thus, the conclusion drawn is that special attention should be devoted to children defined as "high risk" (such as the physically weak or mentally handicapped; children having suffered desertion, abuse, or the loss of a parent; or those who had been uprooted from their homes). Preventive treatment can decrease the time required for rehabilitation.

War and incidents affecting security turn out to be particularly traumatic for children who have been directly exposed to death, through loss of a parent or sibling, an attack by terrorists, a serious injury, the destruction of their home, or an attack on their settlement. These destructive events are likely to imprint themselves on the child's personality and to affect him or her for many years. Countless testimonies confirm that children suffering from direct injury carry their pain throughout their adult lives like a fire in their souls; the consequences of this pain permeate their lives and are transmitted to the next generation (Nathan, 1981).

The "survivor's syndrome" may appear after years of apparently normal adaptation, as a reaction to stimuli that arouse recollection of the original incident. This syndrome may become apparent in various behavioral, cognitive, and emotional expressions, such as nightmares, unrelenting ideations, fears associated with the place of the incident, expectation of reoccurrence of the incident, suspicion of others, feelings of guilt toward the victims, and various kinds of depression. Even when there are no immediate signs of suffering following a traumatic incident, one should not ignore the need for intervention, support, and rehabilitation among the victims and survivors.

A typical reaction of a society placed in constant conflict due to the security situation is denial of fear. "Playing the hero" receives widespread social applause. This happens at the cost of suppression and ignoring of emotions counter to this image, and of social disapproval of anyone showing signs of fear. The same expectation is also directed at the bereaved family. The long-term effects of such denial are evident in the decrease of emotional investment in relations and the tendency to become hardened in order to prevent showing "signs of weakness."

AGGRESSION: BEHAVIOR AND ATTITUDES

When surrounded by killings and death, young children are liable to have some problem in suppressing their aggressive urges. Through identification with the warring adults and the new norms of violence, the sublimation of verbal and physical aggression is weakened. Children who have already reached a higher stage of control over their impulses are seen to regress to earlier forms of expression, inclining to aggression.

In times of war, the symbolic aspect of war-games declines, and in its place appear activities mimicking models of social violence. The existence of an external, defined enemy alters the subject matter of the game. Instead of imaginary characters, such as cowboys and Indians, the focus of aggression is now on the stereotype of the enemy; imagination and reality become confused. With continued war, terror, and raids the ceasing of this kind of play activity becomes more difficult. It takes on a concrete expression and inhibits the development of a softer, more respectful attitude. The result may be the overflowing of aggressive behavior from play into everyday life.

Adir Cohen's research (1985, 1988) on the attitudes of Jewish pupils towards Arabs, in the context of the Arab-Israeli conflict, revealed a deep-rooted aggression and a strong fear of Arabs. These fears were enhanced in part by the exposure of children to acts of terror and murder, which took place around the time of the research, and were reinforced by stereotype illustrations of the "bad Arab" character appearing in children's literature. Many of those investigated had developed overgeneralizations according to which the entire Arab population was identified as being responsible for acts of terror.

This research reveals the systematic stereotyping of the enemy as a dangerous and preposterous monster, a description engendering contempt, hostility, and a whirlwind of fear and hate. When the enemy is portrayed as the symbol of evil, an alien, a threat, and a danger to the existence of society, all roads to peace, mutual understanding, and the end of hostility are barred.

An important question to consider is, Can these aggressive childhood reactions form the nucleus of aggressive political attitudes in the future? A research study conducted in the United States shows that political views formed in childhood were strengthened during adolescence. Research studies from Ireland indicate that during 150 years of terror-marked civil war, there has been an unceasing escalation in the level of violence and identification with aggressive values, passed on from generation to generation. In the light of these few findings and in the absence of systematic investigation of the long-term effects of war on attitudes and social behavior, it is possible that an ever-increasing escalation of violence and cruelty will occur in society as a result of the socialization of war!

These assumptions, however, are under dispute. Those who doubt the influence of war upon the level of violence in society cite as an example the sanity of the generation that grew up in Europe following World War II, and the antiwar movements that flourished in the United States during the Vietnam War. Nevertheless, the relationship between the influence of war at an early age and the development of adult attitudes and behavior remains unclear; it requires a courageous and thorough research approach.

The upsurge in criminal activity in Israel renews the suspicion that the war situation contributes directly to antisocial behavior. It is worth examining the processes of entrenchment of certain phenomena that in times of war become norms and weaken the structure of society. The cheapening of life manifests itself through the internalization of destructive behavior, as partly evidenced by the increasing number of suicides among soldiers, children, and young people.

Within this reality a number of questions need to be considered: How should we present war to children? How could we describe acts of cruelty and aggression? Do we cushion the description? If we do, is this not a distortion and perversion of reality?

Children's literature gives full expression to war in all its terror, with descriptions of attacks and murders, of guarding of people and property, of protection from infiltrators, of preservation of ground despite the disasters. There are several stories referring to the values of heroism and volunteering, to resourcefulness and participation in the struggle, to the contribution of children in saving the battle, to the feelings of togetherness and of sharing a common fate, to the coping with fear, loss, and mourning, while stressing the righteousness of the cause. Behind the faith in the righteousness of the cause is hidden the inner strength to stand up to the plight of war and its consequences. To help us understand better this contradictory evidence about the long-term effects of war on individuals and society, these effects must be further examined in order to channel them, moderate them, and decrease their potential for causing damage.

CHILDREN'S MENTAL INVULNERABILITY

Despite the child's great sensitivity during the first developmental stages, most children display invulnerability to surrounding pressures, especially if they receive consistent support and calm from parents. There are additional factors enhancing the invulnerability of the child in emergency situations and in war.

Young children tend to take the environment for granted. They have nothing to compare it with, so they adapt to changes imposed upon them by the threatening environment as if these were everyday changes dictated by their parents. To determine adaptability, a distinction must be drawn between children who are objectively aware of the dangers and those who do not perceive the full extent of the situation, due to their age and personality, and whose feelings depend to a large extent on their parents' reactions.

Factors Enhancing Adaptation

Suppression and Denial   The use of these defense mechanisms helps children avoid confronting the stress. Ignoring it, diverting one's attention, or creating the illusion of immunity by saying, "It won't happen to me," are efficient mechanisms for decreasing anxiety whenever there is no opportunity to control the threat.

Compensation   Staying in the shelter, in the permanent presence of adults, is likely to compensate the anxious child for his or her fears. Perceiving the shelter as a safe place enhances the feeling of security. Children enjoy the permanent presence of an adult (parent or teacher) as well as being together with others. The common worry about security is likely to cause some distortion of specific childhood problems, such as learning difficulties and overdependency.

Support Systems The component of support in the stress equation plays a most positive role in coping. In border settlements—where there is a high degree of cohesiveness—inhabitants feel more secure, in spite of the security dangers, than do those in settlements where communal cohesiveness is low (Ayalon, 1983). The small and tightly knit group allows expression of interpersonal distress and gives the individual a kind of "security net," offering a "soft fall" in hard times.

Active Cooperation in the Adult World Children's reactions to war are not always connected with fear and withdrawal. Children who desire change and adventure often greet these novelties in their life with excitement and curiosity. The dramatic events stimulate their imaginations. Heroic deeds and their performers turn into ideals, and thus identification with society's ideals increases. Taking part in the war effort contributes to maturity and raises the self-esteem of the young. As a result of environmental pressures, active coping is expressed though creativity in various fields. Many children mature early, assume responsibilities, carry out family and community tasks, and become aware of and interested in political matters. To increase their own coping skills, therefore, children and young people should be directed to helpful communal activities.

Disadvantages of Adaptation

However, once the security problems pass, some children cannot resume their original role or return to the routine of studies and to games appropriate to their age. These children are usually "stuck" in the war stage and show a lack of confidence in adults. Quite often, they continue to search for dangerous activities in order to preserve the image of the world they created under conditions of stress.

Overuse of denial may cause a distortion of reality and enclosure in a world of illusion, as well as the loss of all ability for active coping.

Dependence on a social support group is not without its disadvantages. Cohesive groups tend to create social pressures and claim behavior according to certain group norms (such as being sociable, spartan, or heroic) that are not always supportive to the needs of each individual. Any individual who cannot stand by the group's demands is punished by isolation and alienation. Some children may develop a complete dependency on adults, making an autonomous and independent existence impossible.

Relying on temporary means of protection, such as shelters and security rooms, may lead to a restriction of freedom of movement—even after the danger has passed—caused by the generalization of the worry of being exposed to danger, out in the open.

STRESS INOCULATION

Increased awareness of the current distress and the possibility of long-term damage has led to a research project on the therapeutic intervention and inoculation against stress, which was initiated by Haifa University and the Community Stress Prevention Centre in Kiryat Shmona, Israel. The aim of this project is to reduce the expected damage due to direct traumatic injury and prolonged exposure to precarious security situations. The intervention is based upon the identification of factors that help the child (or adolescent or adult) to cope under stress; these factors need to be recognized, reinforced, and adjusted to the individual's age, personal needs, and level of understanding and experience.

"Stress inoculation" (Meichenbaum, 1977) enables the channeling of anger, the moderation of fears, the dispelling of anxieties, and the acquisition and development of additional skills to widen the repertoire of coping resources. It is based upon the individual's motivation for change, brought about by exposure to stress and crisis.

Stress inoculation programs, which mainly aim at the development of coping skills, can also be used for intervention during a crisis, in shelters under bombardment, and for rehabilitation following an incident, such as treatment given to those surviving a terrorist attack or to children recently bereaved. In order to take into account the wide range of reactions to stresses—influenced by age, life history, personality, and intensity of exposure—inoculation programs must encompass all areas of personality.

Our program is based on the understanding of risk factors that determine the child's well-being. If we suspect that the moral code of ethics and respect for human rights are at risk, we then work towards enhancing the children's belief system, making them more aware of their values and beliefs and convincing them that it is part of their choice to be aware of their moral code.

War affects the emotions of all human beings; therefore, an important part of the program is to enable children to express feelings and to work through and process feelings that are socially undesirable and at times rejected. Only by being able to express their feelings and to understand what causes them can children sublimate their behavior.

Society undergoes turmoil, and children see the abolishment of social norms and their replacement with new ones. Sometimes children are deprived of parental attention and at others, they are separated from their parents. They need social skills, a support group, and a role to perform, in order to feel part of the events and able to make a significant contribution to their community.

In times of war, individuals develop horrific fantasies. At the same time, the world is often incomprehensible, and the threats are too great to understand. Under those circumstances the children's imaginations need attention and permitted channels of expression. Children want to know the facts of life, of death, and of war. They want to be informed and to make sense of their experiences.

However, their ability to solve problems and to process the information is at times underdeveloped. It is therefore in their best interest that we help them develop their cognitive skills.

The most unacceptable, albeit the most normal, aspect of human reaction to stress is the somatic one. It is classified as "psychosomatic reaction," signifying that one has failed to cope. Such interpretation stems from the adult world of ignorance and fear. The body needs its outlets, which are as valuable as any other mode of coping. It is true that some physical reactions need alternative channeling, but to discard them altogether is a mistake. Children need to be allowed to get rid of their physiological tension as well as to learn to relax. It is, therefore, the adults' responsibility to provide children with such guidance and support. According to a model of stress inoculation we developed, named the *BASIC Ph Model*, we believe we can enhance children's coping ability (Lahad, in press).

The initials of the *BASIC Ph Model* stand for:

Belifes, attitudes, meaning
Affect, verbal and nonverbal
Social skills, roles, and support
Imagination in creative problem solving and in the use of attention direction
Cognition, information, and problem solving
Physiology, action, and relaxation

Our research has shown that it is possible to enhance coping skills. And since it is adults who make war, it is they who should support the children of war.

REFERENCES

Ayalon, O. (1983). Face to face with terrorists. In A. Cohen (Ed.), *Education as a meeting place* (81–102). Haifa University. (Hebrew)

Ayalon, O. (1987). Living in dangerous environments. In B. Germain, H. Brassard & S. Hart (Eds.), *Psychological maltreatment of children and youth* (pp. 171–182). New York: Pergamon Press.

Ayalon, O. (1989). Mental and community treatment of terror victims. In C. Desberg, Y. Itsikson & G. Speller (Eds.), *Short-term psychology* (206–229). Jerusalem: Agnes.

Cohen, A. (1985). *An ugly face in the mirror.* Haifa: Reshafim. (Hebrew)

Cohen, A. (1988). *Pictures in children's stories.* Haifa: Ach. (Hebrew)

Fraser, M. (1973). *Children in conflict.* Harmondsworth: Penguin.

Freud, A., & Berlingham, D. (1942). *War and children.* New York: Willard.

Janis, I. (1975). Healthy fear. In I. Markowitz & R. Rabinowitz (Eds.), *The individual and the community in emergencies.* Jerusalem: Ministry of Interior Affairs.

Kubovi, D. (1980). Therapeutic teaching, applications in emergencies. In A. Raviv,

A. Klingman, & M. Horowitz (Eds.), *Children under stress and crisis.* Tel Aviv: Otsar Hamoreh. (Hebrew)

Lahad, S. *BASIC Ph.* (In press). In J. Jennings (Ed.), *Drama-therapy and practice, Vol. 2. London: Routledge.*

Meichenbaum, D. *(1977). Cognitive behavior modification.* New York: Plenum.

Nathan, T. (1981). *Second generation Holocaust survivors in psychosocial research.* The Holocaust Research Institute. (Hebrew)

Smilansky, S. (1978). The concept of death in Israeli schoolchildren, *Opinions, 9.* (Hebrew journal)

Ziv, A., Yisraeli, R., & Verbenhaus, A. (1972). Anxiety level of children under stress. *Joint Education.* (Hebrew journal)

Chapter 6

Suicidal Attempts and Suicides in Greek Adolescents

Stavroula Beratis

Adolescence is a period of human development that is considered as particularly vulnerable to psychopathology (Freud, 1958) due to the fluidity and reorganization of the personality structure. All components of a personality are modified through a complicated interplay between internal forces and external experiences.

One of the main factors involved in the changes of adolescence is the increase in energy of the instinctual drives, both sexual and aggressive, and the setting up of new sexual aims, different for males and females—that is, the transition from childhood sexuality into adult sexuality.

Another important function that undergoes changes is the relationships of youngsters to the people around them. During this period an important emotional breakaway from the family takes place; adolescents withdraw from their parents, separate from them, and become more independent and autonomous. They move from the world of childhood into that of adulthood.

The primary task of adolescence, however, is the development of an identity. Erikson (1968), who associates each developmental stage with a task that takes the form of a crisis, refers to the task of this period as the *identity crisis*.

At the end of it, the individual will have, an integrated identity as opposed to an identity confusion. A successful outcome does not mean that the individual will not have any insecurities or any confusions, it just means that there is a balance between the two, thus allowing the individual to maintain a sense of identity most of the time. The concept of identity is a very broad one and involves several aspects. The most important of these are: (1) sexual identity, which refers to the individual's sexual behavior and gender identity, meaning the inner sense of being male or female; (2) body image and self-image, which refer to external and internal characteristics, including the concept of self-esteem; (3) role experimentation, which involves various identifications and a balance between dependency and independency; (4) work identity, which relates to the ability to pursue a career; and (5) interest in various ideologies and values.

The formation of identity makes adolescence a period of great fluidity and turmoil. There are controversies in behavior, in relationships, in affective discharge. It is an interruption of the smooth peaceful growth of the latency period. It is possible to observe extreme unpredictable mood swings, loosened defenses, and regressive trends. Under the circumstances, discharge of aggressive impulses may occur, in the form of either violent delinquent behavior or self-destructive suicidal behavior. In this chapter, we will examine the latter of these alternatives.

SUICIDAL BEHAVIOR OF YOUNG INDIVIDUALS

Suicidal behavior includes suicidal attempts and completed suicides. Suicidal attempts are nonfatal acts of self-aggression; completed suicides are fatal ones. It has been shown that the epidemiological characteristics of the two categories differ. However, the two populations do not include mutually exclusive types of personality, and an individual can belong to both (Stengel, 1970).

Several factors related to individuals and their families have been implicated in the etiology of adolescent suicidal behavior. Psychiatric conditions—especially affective disorders (Garfinkel et al., 1982; Robbins & Alessi, 1985), borderline personality (Crumley, 1981), and substance abuse (Robbins & Alessi, 1985)—are factors of the individual psychopathology contributing to the etiology of adolescent suicidal behavior.

The psychopathology of the family, which may lead to adolescent suicidal behavior, includes early child abuse or neglect (Deykin et al., 1985); suicidal behavior by a family member (Bergstrand & Otto, 1962); parental psychiatric disorders, particularly depressive disorders (Carlson & Cantwell, 1982; Garfinkel et al., 1982); and family disruption and disorganization, with absence of one or both parents (Haider, 1968; Schrut, 1968; Kosky, 1983). It has been suggested that parental loss through separation or divorce may predispose to attempted suicide, whereas parental loss through death may predispose to completed suicide (Dorpat et al., 1965).

Certain countries report a significant increase of completed suicide among the young in recent years (Brooke, 1974; Sainsbury et al., 1980; McClure, 1984). Suicide is the third leading cause of death among adolescents in the United States (Holinger, 1978). It has been suggested (McAnarney, 1979) that the increase of the suicide rate among youth in the United States and certain other countries may be due to: (1) the changing status of the family, which distances children from their parents; (2) the transition from a religious system to none, rendering the youngster vulnerable to isolation; (3) the high mobility and transition of certain adolescent groups; (4) the extreme pressure put on the young for achievement; (5) inwardly directed aggression due to cultural characteristics.

In general, boys outnumber girls in completed suicides, with a ratio of males to females of at least 2:1 (Holinger, 1978; Shaffer & Fisher, 1981; McClure, 1984). It has been reported, however, that 14 of 73 countries showed suicide rates for girls to be equal to or greater than those for boys. Nine of those countries were Latin American, four were Asian, and one—Portugal—was European (Barraclough, 1987).

SUICIDAL BEHAVIOR OF GREEK ADOLESCENTS

Suicidal Attempts

In a study of suicidal behavior of Greek adolescents, we evaluated youngsters up to 16 years of age who, because of a suicidal attempt, were brought to the emergency room of the Department of Pediatrics of the University of Patras Medical School. A suicide attempt was defined as a nonfatal ingestion of a toxic substance or of a medical remedy, well in excess of the recommended therapeutic dose, or a self-inflicted injury accompanied by a statement of suicidal intent. The suicidal youngsters were compared to a control group matched for age, sex, and parental socioeconomic status. The psychiatric diagnosis of the subjects was based on the diagnostic criteria of the *Diagnostic and Statistical Manual III (DSM III)* of the American Psychiatric Association (American Psychiatric Association, 1980). Of the 29 youngsters who attempted suicide, 27 were female and 2 male.

The findings demonstrated that half of the adolescents who attempted suicide were subjected to severe restriction of their personal freedom, which they claimed as the reason for the attempt. The youngsters' parents kept them under close supervision and limited their independent activities outside the house to almost none, fearing that the adolescent individuation and growing autonomy would lead them to sexual delinquency and drug abuse. These fears were not justified by the youngsters' behavior or by the incidence of sexual delinquency and drug abuse among adolescents in the area. However, as Greek society seems to be going through a change in moral values and customs, some parents face their female children's growing quest for autonomy with increasing anxiety, and therefore impose extreme restrictions on their social freedom.

The restriction of freedom was significantly greater in the attempters than in the control subjects and emerged as the major environmental factor leading the Greek adolescents to suicidal attempts. This oppressive parental behavior acts as a strong stressful factor, which increases the adolescent turmoil and intensifies the youngster's susceptibility to suicidal ideation and action. The fact that boys are generally less restricted than girls may account, at least in part, for the much higher female proportion of suicide attempts observed in this study than mentioned in other reports (Garfinkel et al., 1982; Hawton et al., 1982; Kahn, 1987).

Although social isolation has been identified as a major characteristic of adolescents involved in suicide attempts (Rohn et al., 1977; Hawton, 1982), in the population we investigated, 57% of the attempters were socially isolated, but in 46% of them the isolation was imposed upon them by their parents.

Quarrels and poor communication between the attempters and their parents were observed in 2/3 of the cases, but in 3/4 of them, the quarrels were the direct result of the restriction of personal freedom imposed on the adolescents by their parents. It should be noted that the extreme restriction of the teenage girls' freedom and the strained relationship between them and their parents coincided with the beginning of adolescence and the blooming of sexuality.

At least one psychiatric disorder was identified in 1/2 of the attempters studied, dysthymic disorder being the most frequent. The other 1/2 of the attempters demonstrated other conditions—not attributed to a mental disorder—that required attention or treatment. It is possible that the presence of psychiatric disorders contributed to the suicidal behavior of the youngsters.

Several other factors associated with adolescent suicide attempters were noted to occur with a much lower frequency in the population of this study than in those reported by others (Hawton, 1982). Only 1/4 of the attempters had experienced broken homes through divorce, death, or separation of the parents. Parental drinking, child abuse, or previous suicide attempt by another family member, and physical ill health, marriage, or use of drugs by the attempters were noticed infrequently.

Completed Suicides

We investigated all completed suicides in Greece of individuals between 10 and 19 years of age, from 1980 through 1987. During the eight-year period of the study, 3,044 cases of completed suicides were recorded. Of those who committed suicide, 118 were 10–19 years old.

Of the 118 individuals, 10–19 years old who committed suicide in the whole country, 66 were boys and 52 were girls. The difference between boys and girls is not significant ($p > 0.3$). The average suicide rate per 100,000 adolescent population per year in the whole country was 0.98 (boys: 1.07, girls: 0.89). The suicide rates of the adolescent population in the metropolitan area of Athens and in the rest of the country except Athens were 0.48 and 1.19, respectively.

The rate of suicide in the total adolescent population of Greece is among the lowest reported in the world (Brooke, 1974; Holinger, 1979; McClure, 1984). This parallels the low suicide rate observed in the adult population of the country (Bazas et al., 1979; Beratis, 1986). We can speculate that the low adolescent suicide rate is due to certain Greek cultural characteristics, such as strong family ties, warm family environment for the growing child, and ability to discharge anger easily. Similar factors have been implicated for the low suicide rate of all ages in other European countries (Farber, 1975; Retterstol, 1975; Retterstol & Juel-Nielsen, 1983).

Boys showed a greater suicide rate than girls in both the metropolitan area of Athens and the urban areas, but this difference in the rate of suicide was not significant ($p > 0.2$ and $p > 0.3$, respectively). On the contrary, in the rural areas girls committed suicide more frequently than boys, but the difference again was not significant ($p > 0.5$).

It should be noted that the rate of suicide in the mixed population of boys and girls was significantly greater in the rural areas than in the area of Athens ($p < 0.001$) and the other urban areas ($p < 0.05$). In addition, girls committed suicide significantly more frequently in the rural areas than in the area of Athens ($p < 0.001$) and the other urban areas ($p < 0.02$). Similarly, boys committed suicide significantly more frequently in the rural areas than in the area of Athens ($p < 0.05$). However, the difference in the suicide rate between boys living in the rural areas and other urban areas but Athens was not significant ($p > 0.5$).

It is of interest that the adolescent suicide rate was lowest in the area of Athens and highest in the rural areas, as well as that there were differences in the relative rates of suicide between boys and girls among the populations of these areas. These observations may reflect existing differences among the population in the urban and the rural areas. These include differences in moral, social, and family values, in the attachment to traditional customs, in the degree of parental interference in the youngsters' life, and in the ability of adolescents to find emotional outlets (frustrations may result from limited opportunities in the rural areas).

Psychiatric disorders were the most frequent reason for suicide recorded in the total population of the country, being significantly more frequent in boys than in girls ($p < 0.001$). This was particularly true for boys and girls living in the metropolitan areas of Athens and other urban areas.

However, significant differences in the reasons for suicide were observed between the rural areas and the rest of the country (area of Athens and other urban areas). The most frequent reasons for suicide in the rural areas were family problems in the form of strained relationships between the young victims and their parents, and romantic problems, psychiatric disorders ranking third. The impact of family problems on the frequency of suicide in the rural areas was significantly greater in girls than in boys ($p < 0.05$).

Although a failed love affair was a major reason for suicide in female adolescents throughout the country, its frequency was greatest in the rural areas. This factor was three times less frequent in male suicides, being again more frequent in boys from the rural areas than in those from the rest of the country. This observation seems to reflect the difference in ethical values regarding adolescent sexual freedom between the rural and urban areas, as well as the greater oppression of female youngsters, for whom premarital sexual relations are less accepted than for males.

The finding that psychiatric disorders were the most frequent cause of suicide in male adolescents underlines the different etiologies that lead to suicide in adolescents of the two sexes. It indicates that factors related to individual psychopathology may be more prevalent in boys, whereas environmental factors may be more prevalent in girls.

CONCLUSIONS

The findings on suicidal behavior of Greek adolescents allow us to draw several conclusions.

1   Cultural factors and customs are determining the relevant importance of the causes that may lead adolescents to suicidal behavior.

2   A suicide attempt, in some cases, may be an alternative for the female youngster to indicate that she feels emotionally suffocated and is trying to find escape from parental oppression, which impedes her progress to autonomy and individuation.

3   Greece has a very low adolescent suicide rate, indicating that Greek youngsters are relatively protected from suicide, particularly in the urban areas.

4   The variability of the factors exercised within the country on adolescents residing in cities, towns, and villages is illustrated by the different suicide rates, the different male to female suicide ratios, and the different relative importance of the reasons leading to suicide observed in the urban and rural areas of the country.

REFERENCES

American Psychiatric Association. (1980). *Diagnostic and statistical manual of mental disorders* (3rd ed.). Washington, DC: APA.

Barraclough, B. (1987). Brief communication, sex ratio of juvenile suicide. *Journal of the American Academy of Child and Adolescent Psychiatry, 26,* 434–435.

Bazas, T., Jemos, J., Stefanis, K., & Trichopoulos, D. (1979). Incidence and seasonal variation of suicide mortality in Greece. *Comprehensive Psychiatry, 20,* 15–20.

Beratis, S. (1986). Suicide in southwestern Greece 1979–1984. *Acta Psychiatrica Scandinavica, 74,* 433–439.

Bergstrand, C. G., & Otto, U. (1962). Suicidal attempts in adolescence and child-hood. *Acta Psychiatrica Scandinavica, 51,* 17–26.

Brooke, E. M. (1974). *Suicide and attempted suicide.* Public Health Paper No. 58. Geneva: World Health Organization.

Carlson, G. A., & Cantwell, D. P. (1982). Suicidal behavior and depression in chil-dren and adolescents. *Journal of the American Academy of Child Psychiatry, 21,* 361–368.

Crumley, F. E. (1981). Adolescent suicide attempts and borderline personality disor-der: Clinical features. *Southern Medical Journal, 74,* 546–549.

Deykin, E. Y., Alpert, J. J., & McNamara, J. J. (1985). A pilot study of the effect of exposure to child abuse or neglect on adolescent suicidal behavior. *American Journal of Psychiatry, 142,* 1299–1303.

Dorpat, T. L., Jackson, J. K., & Ripley, H. S. (1965). Broken homes and attempted and completed suicide. *Archives of General Psychiatry, 12,* 213–216.

Erikson, E. H. (1968). *Identity: Youth and crisis.* New York: W. W. Norton.

Farber, M. L. (1975). Psychocultural variables in Italian suicide. In N. L. Farberow (Ed.), *Suicide in different cultures* (pp. 179–184). Baltimore: University Park Press.

Freud, A. (1958). Adolescence. *Psychoanalytic Study of the Child, 13,* 255–278.

Garfinkel, B. D., Froese, A., & Hood, J. (1982). Suicide attempts in children and adolescents. *American Journal of Psychiatry, 139,* 1257–1261.

Haider, I. (1968). Suicidal attempts in children and adolescents. *British Journal of Psychiatry, 114,* 1133–1134.

Hawton, K. (1982). Attempted suicide in children and adolescents. *Journal of Child Psychology and Psychiatry, 23,* 497–503.

Hawton, K., O'Grady, J., Osborn, M., et al. (1982). Adolescents who take over-doses: Their characteristics, problems and contacts with helping agencies. *British Journal of Psychiatry, 140,* 118–123.

Holinger, P. C. (1978). Adolescent suicide: An epidemiological study of recent trends. *American Journal of Psychiatry, 135,* 754–756.

Holinger, P. C. (1979). Violent deaths among the young: Recent trends in suicide, homicide and accidents. *American Journal of Psychiatry, 136,* 1144–1147.

Kahn, A. U. (1987). Heterogeneity of suicidal adolescents. *Journal of the American Academy of Child and Adolescent Psychiatry, 26,* 92–96.

Kosky, R. (1983). Childhood suicidal behavior. *Journal of Child Psychology and Psy-chiatry, 24,* 457–468.

McAnarney, E. R. (1979). Adolescent and young adult suicide in the United States: A reflection of societal unrest. *Adolescence, 14,* 765–774.

McClure, G. M. G. (1984). Recent trends in suicide amongst the young. *British Journal of Psychiatry, 14,* 134–138.

Retterstol, N. (1975). Suicide in Norway. In N. L. Farberow (Ed.), *Suicide in differ-ent cultures* (pp. 77–94). Baltimore: University Park Press.

Retterstol, N., & Juel-Nielsen, N. (1983). The differences in the Scandinavian suicide rates. In J. P. Soubrier & J. Vedrinne (Eds.), *Depression and suicide* (pp. 111–114). Paris: Pergamon Press.

Robbins, D. R., & Alessi, N. E. (1985). Depressive symptoms and suicidal behavior in adolescents. *American Journal of Psychiatry, 142,* 588–592.

Rohn, R. D., Sarles, R. M., Kenny, T. J., et al. (1977). Adolescents who attempt suicide. *Journal of Pediatrics, 90,* 636–638.

Sainsbury, P., Jenkins, J., & Levey, A. (1980). The social correlates of suicide in Europe. In R. D. Farmer and J. Hirsch (Eds.), *The suicide syndrome* (pp. 38–53). London: Croom Helm.

Schrut, A. (1968). Some typical patterns in the behavior and background of adolescent girls who attempt suicide. *American Journal of Psychiatry, 125,* 107–112.

Shaffer, D., & Fisher, P. (1981). The epidemiology of suicide in children and young adolescents. *Journal of the American Academy of Child Psychiatry, 20,* 545–565.

Stengel, E. (1970). *Suicide and attempted suicide.* Harmondsworth: Penguin.

Part Two

Grieving Children and Families

Chapter 7

A Child's Perception of Death

Janna A. Excell

After a child has been told that a loved one has died, it is very important to prepare him or her for the experience of mourning. The process that I propose here has evolved over the years, from my work with children as a bereavement counselor and teacher. This process encompasses grief experiences resulting from sudden deaths as well as deaths occurring after a short or long illness. It is a process that can be used with preschool children from ages 3 and older, and it can be implemented in a classroom setting or in a one-to-one consultation. Most likely, this will be a new experience for the child, and the unknown always holds an element of fear. Therefore, the discussion between the professional and the child needs to focus on the following objectives:

1 To allow for an open, honest, and nonjudgmental environment where questions may be asked by the child and feelings may be discussed without fear.

2 To understand the experiences that the child has already had with death and how he or she interprets these experiences.

This study is dedicated to my mother, Blandine Schoppa Rummel (1910–1988).

3 To provide correct and factual information for any misperceptions the child may have concerning death.

4 To identify a model or overview for the many feelings involved in the process of mourning.

5 To provide alternatives for the child in saying good-bye to his or her loved one.

OBJECTIVE ONE

This objective calls for an open, honest, and nonjudgmental environment where questions may be asked by the child and feelings may be discussed without fear. In achieving this, body language and opening statements are very important. You may sit on the carpet with the child and make a comment about how he or she must feel. For example:

"This must be a time when you are confused or mixed up."
"This must be a scary time for you."
"Sometimes, it must be scary not to know what's happening."
"Death is sad for all of us. Let's talk and see if we can help one another."

These comments build rapport as the child realizes that someone knows how he or she feels. As the environment becomes more familiar, the child will begin to feel more at ease and comfortable in asking questions or telling part of his or her story. In this way, you provide for an open flow of feelings.

CASE STUDY

One case study I will use throughout this chapter is that of a 5-year-old boy, Cory, whose mother held him hostage for 3 hours in their home. During this time a Special Weapons and Tactics (SWAT) team had been summoned to the house as officers were trying to negotiate Cory's release. However, before this could be accomplished, Cory escaped through a side door. His mother followed and aimed her rifle at him. At this point, Cory was pulled to the ground by an officer as another officer fired one shot over their heads, killing the mother instantly and thereby saving Cory's life.

Cory's stepfather and two aunts scheduled a conference with me the following day. Cory had not cried or spoken about the incident, and the family was concerned. Moreover, they had decided to protect Cory and not talk about the situation in any way. They were, however, willing for me to see him, and the conference was scheduled for that afternoon.

Cory came to my office looking down and rarely making eye contact with anyone. As we sat on the carpet, Cory took off his shoes and I followed by removing mine. It was then that he made eye contact with me, and the following conversation ensued.

Janna: Cory, you must be so confused.

Cory: What does *confused* mean?

J: Mixed up.

C: Yeah, I'm mixed up.

J: And scared?

C: (Nodding) Mixed up and scared.

J: Tell me what scared you the most.

C: (Angrily) My mamma wanted to kill me.

J: Did you think she would?

C: Yeah. She had the rifle at me and said she would kill me and then herself.

J: What did you do then?

C: Stayed quiet. Didn't move.

Cory had finally begun to tell his story. He felt safe. More important, he realized that I was willing to listen to his reality without judgment. In a few minutes I would begin to ask Cory about his perceptions of death and, surprisingly, I would learn how he thought death looked.

OBJECTIVE TWO

The second objective demands that we understand the experiences that the child already has had with death and how he or she interprets them. Each child comes to this situation with some ideas of what he or she thinks death is. Therefore, we cannot clarify any misperceptions without knowing what ideas the child brings to this encounter. The following questions can help with this task.

"What do you think you will see [when viewing the body]?"

"What happened when your———died?"

"Have you ever attended a funeral? What was it like?"

"What questions do you have at this time?"

From this information, you can begin to clarify misperceptions and reinforce or supply correct information. It is important to listen carefully to what the child is trying to say. If you do not know for sure, you can ask again or simply say, "Tell me more." If you do not have an answer to a question, you can simply say, "I don't know."

CASE STUDY CONTINUED

The last memory Cory had of his mother was her effort to shoot him as he escaped out a side door. She had died instantly. It was extremely important that he be allowed some time with her if he wished to see her body. Our conversation continued:

C: Is my mamma here? I heard she was. *(Referring to the mortuary).*

J: Yes she is. Do you want to see her?

C: Yeah! But no one will let me.

J: (Having talked with the stepfather earlier and advised him how important viewing could be for Cory) I will let you.

C: Okay, let's go.

J: Before we do, tell me what you think you will see.

C: (Without hesitation) A pile of bones.

J: Why do you think you will see a pile of bones?

C: Because we have a dead person in our room at school.

J: Oh, you have a skeleton in your room.

C: Yeah, a dead person.

From this conversation, it becomes apparent how important it is to know what experience the child brings to this encounter. Misinformation cannot be corrected until misperceptions are known. We must, therefore, understand how the child perceives death before any information can be given and accurately processed by the child.

Other than asking questions about how the child perceives death, you may also ask the child to draw what he or she thinks death is. This process is different from open-ended drawings, as you are asking for specific feedback to a direct question, How do you see death? In my work with children, I have designated three categories of drawings: (1) *the way death may occur* (through shooting, knifing, heart attacks, illnesses, or accidents); (2) *personification of death* (as a bogey-man, a monster, a death angel, a devil, or any religious figure); (3) *what happens after a death*, (scenes from the funeral, viewing, cremation, burial, and drawings depicting mourning).

When analyzing any of these drawings, it is important to look for the child in his or her own drawing. If he or she is totally absent, the child has most likely been an observer of grief rather than a participant. However, if the child has experienced grief, the role as a participant in the mourning process will be a part of the drawing, as well as depicting other mourners. Any significant death may include the death of a beloved pet or person. Following are examples from each category.

How Death May Occur

If the person or pet who died was extremely significant to the child, then the child may draw the cause of death, but also include himself or herself depicting fear or great sadness. The drawing of the child may be very large because of the immense grief, or extremely small as the child feels overwhelmed by the incident. On the contrary, a child who draws from an observer's viewpoint will usually be absent from the drawing, focusing more on how the death occurred. This may be from an event in real life that the child heard about or saw on television, or it may be purely fictional. The key is to look for the anticipated grief reactions that would result from having been a participant in the loss. If you are unsure, simply use open-ended comments or questions such as, "What is this about?" or "Tell me about your drawing." (See Figures 1 and 2.)

Personification of Death

In this category the child will draw a figure of death coming to take away the one who has died, such as an angel of death meeting the deceased. Is this a child who has been a participant in mourning, or an observer who is drawing a religious depiction of what he or she thinks death may be? Again, look for the child and any grief reactions, such as tears or standing alone or off to one side of the drawing. If these or any other grief reactions are present, then most

Figure 1 How death may occur (observer).

Figure 2 How death may occur (participant).

likely the child has experienced the mourning process. Otherwise, the child would not have included this as a part of the drawing. (See Figure 3.)

What Happens After a Death

This category may be subdivided into *factual* and *symbolic* depictions. Factual drawings may include depictions of any cultural or religious ritual involving viewings, funerals, cremations, or burials. These may represent a view from a passing car, such as viewing a cemetery from a distance. This is the drawing of an observer of grief, rather than a participant. However, a more detailed drawing of a funeral or burial may show mourners and include a name on the memorial or tombstone. The child who portrays such details may have attended a funeral with his or her parents of someone insignificant to him or her, and therefore, was more an observer of grief than a participant. However, if the deceased was someone significant, then the child will include himself or herself as a person who has felt the pain of mourning the death of a loved one. (See Figures 4 and 5.)

Symbolic depictions representing what happens after a death are almost always those of a bereaved child who has experienced deep pain. The child may leave the paper blank or draw a line around the border to portray a large vacant area that is expressive of great loss and increased feelings of isolation. Children who have a higher level of cognitive development may sketch a philosophical approach and may include in their drawings words such as, "God is somewhere." This response reflects life experiences with death and loss in which the child has searched for meaning to make sense of this experience. Otherwise, the child's drawing would not have portrayed this searching process. (See Figure 6).

An impressive drawing by an 8-year-old boy (Figure 7) depicted a circle with ³/₄ of the circle shaded in with a black marker. He defined bereavement with a clarity that comes only from the immense pain of experiencing a significant, personal loss. Above the circle he printed, "I feel like three-fourths of me has left."

OBJECTIVE THREE

This objective says we should provide correct and factual information for any misperceptions the child may have concerning death. Since a young child takes our words literally, death needs to be defined or explained in simple yet factual terms. For example, telling a sibling that his sister is now a star in the sky may be simple, but it is certainly not factual. The following explanation is simple,

Figure 3 Personification of death (observer).

Figure 4   What happens after a death (factual drawing; participant mourner).

honest, and factual and has never presented a problem for any culture or religion that I have dealt with:

> When someone dies, that means their body is no longer working. The heart stops beating, they no longer need to eat or sleep, and they no longer feel any pain. They don't need their body any longer. That means we will never see them again as we could before.

At a young age, a child first perceives death as reversible. Therefore, be prepared to repeat this definition to a child of 6 or younger, as he or she will rarely understand that death is final. This will occur when the child asks a similar question, such as, "Now, when is Mommy coming home?" A reply would be, "Remember, Mommy died. When someone dies, that means their body is no longer working. . . . " As the child develops in cognition, the child will eventually perceive death as final and inevitable.

When a child is going to view the deceased, it is important to describe what he or she will see. If possible, let the child see a casket similar to the one that will be used. If no casket is used, then explain what will be seen. Also, describe any facial cuts that may have occurred, so that the child will be prepared for these changes.

A young child is naturally curious and will touch to gain understanding and to make sense of this new experience. Therefore, prepare a child for touching the body. Otherwise, the child will be frightened! Simply say, "You may touch your mother if you want. However, now that the body is no longer working, it will feel different. Instead of being warm and soft, your mother's body will feel cold and hard."

CASE STUDY CONTINUED

Knowing that Cory thought he would see a pile of bones when viewing his mother now gave me the opportunity to clarify his misperceptions. The conversation continued:

J: No, Cory, you won't see a pile of bones. You do have a dead person in your room at school, but that person has been dead for a very long time. Your mother just died yesterday, so she will be in her same body. She will have her

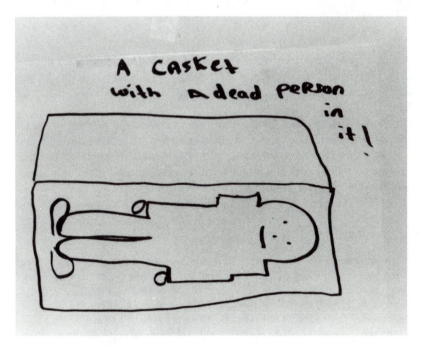

Figure 5   What happens after a death (factual drawing; observer).

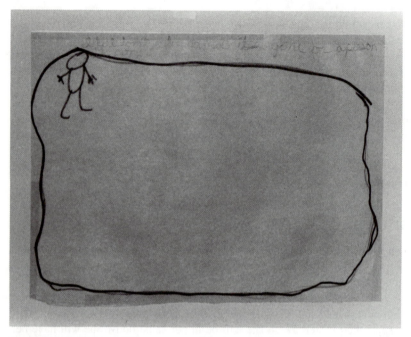

Figure 6 What happens after a death (symbolic depiction; participant). The handwriting says, "I feel lonely because its gone or a person is gone."

hair and skin just like before when she was alive. You may touch her if you want, but remember she will feel different now that her body is no longer working. Instead of feeling warm and soft, your mother's body will feel cold and hard.

If this explanation seems harsh, remember that the child is trusting you to provide correct information. Children's acceptance of a situation can only develop if what they have been told corresponds with what their perceptions tell them is true. A child can deal with the truth. Hopefully, the adult in this situation will be able to do the same.

Depending on the child's age, prior experience, and what information the child needs to understand what has happened to the body, you can explain all or part of the following:

> When someone dies, we must decide what to do with the body. Some people choose to put the body in a box called a casket and bury it below ground in a cemetery. Some place the body in a box and put it above ground in a building called a mausoleum. Sometimes, people choose to burn the body and place what is left, or the cremains, in a container called an urn. This urn can be placed in a building, in a space called a niche, or buried below ground in a cemetery. Some choose to scatter the cremains or keep them.

In my experiences with young children, cremation is difficult to understand. Burning the body is usually not the major concern, when the child realizes that pain is not an issue. For the child, the puzzle of cremation is one of proportion. I have been asked many times, "But how did my mother's body get in that small box/jar?"

The process Cory had been through regarding his mother's traumatic death left two major issues that needed to be addressed immediately: his mother's behavior, especially on that day, and the way she died. We continued our conversation:

J: Cory, your mother loved you very much and what she did had nothing to do with her love for you. She acted this way because she was very sick. We could not see her sickness, like we can when someone has chicken pox, measles, or even a broken bone. But we could see her sickness by the way she acted when she was angry or mixed up. You did not do anything to make her sick. What happened was not your fault. It happened because she was so sick.

C: Then, maybe she wasn't just mad at me. Maybe she was sick?

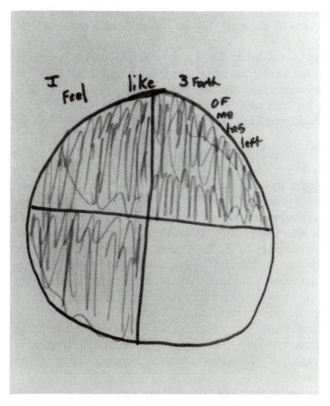

Figure 7   What happens after a death (symbolic depiction; participant).

J: Yes, Cory, her illness made her act that way. I'm sorry that she was that sick. It must have been scary for you.

C: Uh hm.

J: Cory, there is something else I want you to always remember. The police wanted to help you and your mother. However, because of the way things happened, they had to make a very hard decision. If they had not made this decision, you might have been hurt too. It is a very sad thing, but that is what happened.

These are honest and factual explanations of what occurred between Cory, his mother, and the SWAT team/police. These explanations make no attempt to assess moral blame or guilt on anyone's part. Neither is there an attempt to deny the truth or to make the situation better with partial truths. We cannot make the pain better. However, we can increase the pain by not talking about it and by making the child feel isolated or, even worse, leaving the child alone with self-inflicted guilt. In any situation involving loss or death, the bereaved child needs two actions on the part of adults. The first one is recognition of the child's pain. Following that is the need for correct and factual information so the child can try to make sense out of what has occurred. As awful as the truth may be, it is the only way to place the child on a path of healing through the process of mourning.

Before taking Cory to view his mother, I asked him if he had any questions. He wanted to know if his mother would be sitting up. Although he wanted to see her, his fear of her was still within him. This opportunity to see her gave him a chance to face his fears and then let go of them. Otherwise, his inner child would have carried these fears with him into adulthood.

OBJECTIVE FOUR

The fourth objective calls for identifying a model or overview of the many feelings involved with the process of mourning. It is possible to accomplish this objective to some extent before a death occurs by discussing the array of feelings people experience after small losses. This will help a group of children to realize that they experience many of the same feelings. Likewise, after a death has occurred, it is important for the child to know that his or her feelings are normal. It will help the child to feel less isolated. This is not an attempt to alleviate pain, for the pain will still be present. However, it sheds some light on an unfamiliar and often frightening path.

One way to accomplish this is by drawing a graph of feelings resulting from a loss. Even with most 4- and 5-year-olds, this can be effective. Instead of using lines with the graph, you could draw something more expressive such as happy, sad, or angry faces.

Another method is having the child draw self-portraits of his or her feelings. These can be made into a small book, which I call a "small people's journal.'' Portraits could be added as the child experiences different feelings. The following example shows how the process of mourning can be incorporated with self-portraits in understanding where misinformation has occurred.

Tommy was almost 4 years old when his mother was diagnosed with cancer and died 16 months later. His grandmother set up an appointment with me 3 months after her daughter's death. Tommy had become very destructive with other children, adults, and personal property belonging to anyone. His acting out had disrupted not only his life, but everyone around him.

When death from a terminal illness is involved, the process of loss starts long before the death. We should always look for the process that the child has experienced with the death of a significant person. By analyzing the process from the child's perception of what he or she thinks happened, we will find the answer or clue to the behavior we are trying to understand.

In Tommy's case, he had the memory of a beautiful, healthy mother; later, of a frail, sick mother; and, finally, of no mother at all. Therefore, bearing this in mind, I asked Tommy to draw a series of self-portraits. These included pictures of himself in four different situations, which outlined the process that he had experienced. These self-portraits were (1) Tommy when his mother was well; (2) Tommy when his mother was sick; (3) Tommy when his mother died; and (4) Tommy now.

During the next three meetings, I repeated this exercise with him, altering the sequence of the drawings. Changing the sequence never affected the outcome. His self-portraits were always the same. As expected, he would draw himself happy when his mother was well, sad when his mother was sick, and then draw himself angry in the present. However, he always drew himself happy when his mother died. Each time I repeated this exercise with him, I would ask him why he drew himself so happy when his mother died, and his reply was always the same, "I don't know."

Having worked with many families whose loved ones had died from terminal illnesses, I tried to recall all the explanations I had overheard when a well-intentioned adult gave incorrect information to a child to try to ease the child's pain. The following conversation with Tommy gave me the information I needed to correct misinformation that was making him very angry.

J: Tommy, did someone tell you after your mother died that she is happier now because she is free of her pain?

T: Yeah! *(Very angry and agitated)* And tell me this: how can she be happier without me?

J: Tommy, sometimes adults make mistakes in how they say things, even though they may not know it at the time. That's what happened here. What they meant is that your mom's body no longer hurts from her illness. But remember this always. If your mother had had a choice, she would have stayed with you, because she loved you very much. But she had no choice. She was so sick for so long, and finally her body quit working. Most of the time, people get well again when they are sick, but sometimes they become so sick they die. That's what happened to your mother. It is very sad, but that is what happened.

T: Then, my mom didn't want to leave me?

J: No, she didn't. She loved you very much.

One can see how a well-intentioned statement not only turned into misinformation for Tommy, but also resulted in his being angry. Another method is to have puppets talk about how they feel after someone has died. This is an extremely effective way to give permission to the child to express and own feelings of anger, guilt, or sadness. You can also present the feelings of different family members, using the puppets and also role-model healthy coping behaviors.

The feeling a child experiences most frequently in connection with death is guilt. This is often fostered unknowingly by adults who refuse to give a child information, or who decide to change the truth altogether in order to "protect the child." This is often the case when a suicide has occurred. The child will eventually learn the truth from someone. When this happens, the only conclusion a child can come to is that he or she cannot trust the adult who gave the misinformation. Even worse, the child receives the tacit message that the death and subsequent grief cannot be discussed openly and honestly. This isolates the child during the mourning process and causes more confusion. One point to remember is that the more horrendous the facts of the death, the more it needs to be discussed. Adults who cannot do this are not protecting a child, but are merely disguising the truth for themselves.

CASE STUDY CONTINUED

I asked Cory directly if he felt responsible for what happened.

J: Do you think you caused this?

C: Yeah.

J: Why?

C: Because I wanted some candy [icing] off my birthday cake. Mama said no, but I climbed up on the table anyway to get some. Then, she got the gun out.

J: Cory, you did absolutely nothing to cause this. If your mother had not been so mixed up and sick inside, she would have given you some. It is normal to want some of your birthday cake. However, it was not normal for your mother to get so angry that she got the gun out. Remember, she was very sick, and that was one way we knew she was sick, because she was so angry she wanted to hurt you. It is very sad, but you must always remember that you did not cause this to happen.

In the context of objective five, Cory will be able to release his feelings more openly, as he begins to have some understanding of what has happened to him.

OBJECTIVE FIVE

This objective says we must provide alternatives for the child in saying good-bye to his or her loved one. The child needs an opportunity to say good-bye, either before or after the funeral. Following are some examples for beginning this process before the funeral or burial.

Viewing the deceased This is very effective in helping children accept the reality of the death. For Cory, viewing was a very helpful element in letting go and saying good-bye to his mother. My conversation with Cory continued before he saw his mother:

J: When you see your mother, she will not be able to talk to you. However, you can say everything you wished you could have said to her before she died. I know it was a confusing time for you, but now that we have talked about what happened, you may have something to say to her. If you want time alone, just ask me.

Cory not only viewed his mother, but provided an open door for his family to view also. Cory did ask for time alone and spent about 5–7 minutes talking with his mother. After this, he lay on the carpet in the viewing room crying and kicking his feet. As I had learned to do from Elisabeth Kübler-Ross so many years before, even though I was present, I left him alone so as not to interrupt his natural flow of grief. He had now begun his journey of mourning.

Cory was later adopted by one of his aunts and moved to another state. He has done very well in school and in his personal life. His family continues to be very open about what happened, and Cory is free to ask questions as they arise. One of his later drawings summed up his readjustment. Below a self-portrait he printed: "What happened to me was sad, but I [will] always know, my mama loved me. She was sick."

Drawing a picture for a loved one This is a simple but excellent way of assisting a child in the "letting go" process. The drawing can be placed in the casket and/or cremation container. Either let the child place the drawing in the casket or let the child watch someone else place it there. Make a copy for the child to keep. It will help the child later in remembering how he or she said good-bye. Being able to review this is healing and a source of comfort.

Placing an article in the casket This could be any article that is meaningful to the child, such as a photo, letter, card, cassette tape, books made by the child or a favorite book, or toys. This is frequently very helpful. The act, not the article itself, is what is of primary benefit to the child. The act provides an avenue for saying good-bye.

Children's participation in the funeral service A child may take part by reading a poem or letter, as long as the child expresses the wish for attending this event. Again, the act of participating in the service is what is of value.

Sometimes, there may be joint participation, as in a children's choir or a reading.

If the funeral or memorial service is over, there are still many ways a child can say good-bye to the loved one. The child could draw pictures of a loved one's life and make them into a book. A child may wish to visit the grave and leave a toy or other small memento for the loved one. Another may wish to make a holiday decoration to place on the grave. Bereaved children will benefit from reviewing photographs and making an album of the person's life. You can always use role-playing with puppets or an "empty chair" in which the child tells the loved one good-bye.

There are unlimited ways to say good-bye. The factor that will make it work for one child may not work for another. The key to "letting go" is finding a way that is meaningful to the child. Most often, the child has the answer to this within himself or herself.

For example, I once encountered a 4-year-old boy who would not leave his grandfather's grave after burial. After 20 minutes or so, his parents became frustrated with his insistence not to leave Grandpa. Not knowing what would help him, I simply asked him what would make him feel better about leaving his grandfather. He had an immediate reply. "I want to get Grandpa a large eegees [soda drink]." Buying "eegees" was a meaningful experience that he and his grandfather had shared many times. His parents agreed to this solution and returned a few minutes later. The 4-year-old placed the giant "eegees" on his grandfather's grave, and then he and his parents sat on the grass drinking their own "eegees." They talked about Grandpa and the many memories they would always have of him. This process enabled the young boy to say good-bye for that day, as he now felt that he had not abandoned his grandfather. The family continued this ritual for several months, and it helped everyone to let go and to readjust to a different life without Grandpa.

In summary, there are three major points to keep in mind when implementing this process of mourning. The first one is understanding that a child needs to be included. As Earl Grollman has so aptly stated, "A child understands inclusion rather than exclusion and what is mentionable is manageable." If the child is excluded, he or she must rely on imagination. Imagination can make things a thousand times worse and never has a chance to end. It is often more frightening than understanding the actual event. In order to say good-bye, let go, and get on with reinvesting in life, the child needs a clear understanding of what has occurred in a simple but factual way.

The second point is to be a healthy role model for the child. Tell the child, "When someone we loved dies, we grieve. You may see grown-ups cry because they also loved your mother. It is okay for them to be sad too." When a child sees a healthy response to loss, it is not only of value to him or her in the present, but also in the future as the child experiences other losses.

The third and final point is extremely important to remember: A child's personal boundaries must be respected. The child may choose to react in one way or another. Forcing the child into any of these alternatives is as unhealthy to emotional and mental health as excluding the child from any participation. However, discussing these alternatives with the child is a caregiver's responsibility. The final decision belongs to the child. Our job as counselors and teachers is to make the child and family aware that these alternatives are available. You may be the only link in this human chain that will provide the child with an opportunity to understand and respond to the mourning process in a positive way. The child you help now is the future adult who will be able to view the cycle of life and death in a natural way. It makes for a happier ending for all.

BIBLIOGRAPHY

Bowlby, John. (1980). *Attachment and loss, vol. 3.* New York: Basic Books.

Dass, Ram, & Gorman, Paul. (1986). *How can I help?* New York: Knopf.

Grollman, E. A. (Ed.) (1967). *Explaining death to children.* Boston: Beacon.

Grollman, E. A. (1976). *Talking about death: A dialogue between parent and child.* Boston: Beacon.

Kavanaugh, R. E. (1972). *Facing death.* New York: Nash.

Kübler-Ross, E. (1983). *On children and death.* New York: Macmillan.

Mellonie, Bryan, & Ingpen, Robert. (1983). *Lifetimes.* New York: Beacon.

Rosenthal, Nina Ribak. (1978). "Teaching educators to deal with death." *Death Education, 2*(3), 293–306.

Siegel, Benjamin S. (1986). "Helping children cope with death." *Research Record, 3*(2), 53–62.

Wrenn, Robert, & Mencke, Reed. (1975). *Being: A psychology of self.* Chicago: Science Research Associates, Inc.

Chapter 8

Group Intervention
with Bereaved Children

Stephen Fleming and Leslie Balmer

The Bereaved Families of Ontario (BFO) located in Toronto, Ontario, Canada, is a mutual-help organization established in 1978 to assist families when a child has died. In addition to offering support to bereaved parents, BFO also mounts programs for grieving children, adolescents, and young adults as they struggle with the loss of a parent or sibling. In this chapter we describe one of BFO's programs, namely, the groups offered for bereaved children. Following a brief discussion of the groups' structure and format, we will focus on facilitation strategies that have been effective in encouraging exploration and aiding expression of children's reactions to the death of a parent or sibling.

The material presented in this chapter is drawn principally from the second author's group experience. We are indebted to Tricia McGovern, Karen Kerekas, and Lynda Cumberland-Macri, the bereaved-sibling coleaders who participated in the groups described here. Their wisdom and sensitivity, born of their personal loss, provided much of the insight embodied in their paper.

Further, the authors gratefully acknowledge the support of the Hospital for Sick Children Foundation (Grant XG 88–55) and the cooperation of the Bereaved Families of Ontario in the preparation of this manuscript.

GROUP PARTICIPANTS
AND GROUP STRUCTURE

At BFO, groups are available for children between the age of 6 and 12 who have experienced the death of a parent or sibling. The groups are designed to provide a safe environment in which children can explore the emotional vicissitudes of their grief and have their grief experience validated and normalized. In addition, the groups educate with respect to the nature and dynamics of the child's reaction to loss.

The majority of bereaved-sibling participants are referred to the program by their parents, who are often themselves involved in the BFO adult groups. When a parent has died, the surviving parent usually refers the child to BFO on the basis of information obtained from the family physician, community health nurse, or school guidance personnel.

Communication with the parent(s) is a priority before, during, and at the conclusion of the groups. More specifically, the group coleaders provide information regarding the purpose of the groups, how they are conducted, the topics to be discussed, and the emotional responses likely to occur. With respect to the last-mentioned, it is not uncommon for the children to report "having fun" in these sessions. This is a particularly difficult concept for the parent(s) to identify with, given the depth of their pain. The parent(s) are invited to call the professional coleader if they have questions or concerns during the course of the groups. Finally, at the conclusion of the groups, feedback is provided jointly to the parent(s) and child. Where indicated, a referral is made for additional individual or family counseling.

Participants are placed in one of two groups as a function of age, either a 6–9- or a 10–12-year-old group. Whenever possible, siblings are placed in separate groups. It has been our experience that when siblings attend the same group there is often resistance to disclosing feelings (particularly negative ones) or to discussing intimate details of family life. In addition, in some families, one sibling (often the eldest) plays the role of the strong child and caretaker of the other. As a result, both children feel inhibited and unable to express openly some of their more worrisome and frightening feelings.

The groups are composed of a minimum of 5 children and a maximum of 10. While some groups have been conducted with fewer than 5 participants, there is a tendency to lose some of the richness of the group experience when numbers dwindle. When groups have more than 10 members, there is less time for each child to be involved and contribute to the discussion; moreover, there is not the same opportunity for the leaders to interact individually with each child during the session.

The groups are led jointly by a professional with expertise in child development and children's grief, and a bereaved sibling. The use of a bereaved sibling coleader is a unique feature of BFO's approach; this individual has not only completed an eight-week training program, but also has participated in a BFO adolescent or young adult group.

Groups meet once a week, for one hour, over a seven-week period. The way each group evolves depends on several factors including: (1) the individual leadership and counseling styles of the coleaders; (2) the age and developmental level of group participants; (3) factors unique to the composition of the group (i.e., sibling versus parental death, cause of death, the recency of the loss); and (4) the mode(s) of expression found most useful by the individual group members (i.e., expressing feelings verbally, in written form, in drawings, or in clay).

TOPICS/THEMES AND FACILITATION STRATEGIES

Although there is considerable flexibility in the way the seven weekly meetings are conducted, each session has a general topic or theme for discussion. The weekly discussion topics/themes are:

Theme 1   Getting Acquainted
Theme 2   The Relationship with the Deceased
Theme 3   The Funeral
Theme 4   Feelings
Theme 5   Changes
Themes 6-7 Looking to the Future and Saying Good-bye

Usually themes 1, 2, and 6-7 ("getting acquainted," "the relationship with the deceased," and "looking to the future and saying good-bye") are maintained in the order presented here. The remaining themes are not necessarily discussed in a fixed order; for example, more pressing issues like anniversaries/birthdays or how the child/family copes with upcoming major religious holidays may affect the order of discussion and result in the displacement of some themes.

The remainder of this chapter will be devoted to a discussion of the above-mentioned themes. We will discuss each theme in conjunction with a specific facilitation strategy that has been found useful in group work with bereaved children. Some of the facilitation methods have been adapted from widely used children's therapy techniques; others originated with colleagues working with bereaved children. In addition to their usefulness in a group format, these strategies are also effective tools in individual therapy and, with slight modification, for intervention in adjustment situations that are not death-related.

THEME 1: GETTING ACQUAINTED

The first session is very important in setting the atmosphere for the remaining group meetings. It is not uncommon for children to arrive at the initial session feeling anxious and somewhat intimidated by the prospect of meeting with such a group. The purpose of the first session, then, is (1) to outline the rules and format of the group, (2) to help the children become acquainted with each other, and (3) to introduce the death of a family member as a common theme for all participants.

Facilitation: Telling Your Story

An important aspect of the first session is the provision of an opportunity to "tell your story." For most children, the group experience marks the first time they have been invited to discuss their sibling's or parent's dying and death. They may have overheard family members' discussions or they may have attempted to broach the subject with friends, but more often than not, people discourage children from approaching their pain.

One of the many advantages of having a bereaved sibling coleader is that this individual can be the first group member to tell his or her story. Then the children are invited to ask questions. Each child, in turn, is offered the opportunity to relate the details of his or her loss.

Throughout this time, the coleaders indicate significant similarities and differences in the children's experiences. Discussing similarities not only serves to establish elements of trust and cohesion, but also validates the child's experience and reinforces the notion that "I am not the only one." Helping group members recognize the differences between thoughts, feelings, and behaviors initiates the process of recognizing and realizing that their grief may not be "the worst one" after all. We speculate that it is the children's recognition of both the similarities and the differences that facilitates their ability to step outside their own pain and begin to empathize with other group members. This process is viewed as an integral first step in the healing process (Parkes & Weiss, 1983).

The invitation to tell one's story has additional therapeutic impact. Invariably, as the circumstances of the dying and death unfold, some children are seen to possess more information than others. It is not uncommon for those who lack details or have unanswered questions to seek out additional information. Puncturing the "conspiracy of silence" that frequently exists around the dying and death of a family member may appreciably alter the child's conception of who or what caused the death, issues that result in problematic guilt for the young survivor (Fleming, 1985). An 8-year-old participant, whose younger sister had died, illustrates this:

> Over a number of months, the boy's 6-year-old sister had been complaining of pain in her right leg; their parents, however, did not think it serious enough to warrant medical attention. One day, while the children were playfully wrestling on the family sofa, his sister accidentally toppled off, clutched her right knee, and began screaming in pain. Medical examination revealed cancer of the bone, and despite treatment, the girl died soon after. This young survivor struggled with the nagging

notion that the accidental fall from the sofa actually caused the cancer that eventually took his sister's life. It was only after witnessing the extensive information possessed by other group participants that he approached his parents, discussed his perception of the cause of his sister's death, and consequently felt his guilt alleviated.

THEME 2: THE RELATIONSHIP WITH THE DECEASED

In the second session, the focus is on the child and his or her relationship with the family member who died. The technique described here, "pictures and significant objects," involves bringing to the group tangible reminders of the deceased. This technique has several therapeutic values. Like the "telling of your story," it gives the child an opportunity to talk about life events shared with their sibling or parent. As previously noted, bereaved children are often reluctant to talk about the deceased as, all too frequently, family and friends alike avoid the topic. The children are left feeling that a big part of their life (everything they shared with their sibling or parent) is a subject considered taboo. The group setting—which provides an environment where peers are not embarrassed but rather interested, curious, and supportive—assists the child in feeling more comfortable talking about the life shared with the deceased.

Facilitation: Pictures and Significant Objects

At the end of the first meeting, each child is asked to bring something special to the next session in the form of significant pictures of the deceased or an object associated with a special memory. The actual choice of what the child brings to the meeting often reveals potentially problematic thoughts or feelings that may impede grief resolution. The following examples highlight this point.

A 10-year-old boy experienced the death of his two brothers within an 18-month period. The brothers died at 24 and 13 months of age, from a genetically linked disease. This boy brought the shoes his brothers were wearing at the time they became ill and died. The diminutive size of the shoes served to highlight their short life. As revealed during the session, a very significant part of this boy's sadness was related to the fact that he had never had the chance to know his brothers. Being now an only child, he was grieving for the fantasized brothers he would never have; the brothers he would never play baseball with or take to hockey games.

In another group, a boy of 12 brought a bookmark that his 21-year-old sister had given him six months before she committed suicide. The handwritten inscription on the bookmark said, "To the best brother in the whole world." What was highlighted, in this case, was the closeness of the relationship and the pain and confusion this boy felt that his sister had chosen to kill herself. Secondly, this boy was now an only child. His "brother" status had been taken away, and he could no longer be "the best brother in the whole world." He also had to deal with the loss of all the fantasies attached to growing up with an older sister.

THEME 3: THE FUNERAL

For most participants, the funeral of a sibling or parent represents the first experience with rituals surrounding death. It comes at a time when children are grief-stricken, confused, and in most cases, lacking the emotional support of their parent(s). As a result, they often entertain numerous unanswered questions and misconceptions about the funeral, the associated ritual, and burial. Thus, it is important during this session to include a strong educational component to correct misconceptions and misunderstandings that may exacerbate the already problematic and painful emotions and thoughts associated with the death of a loved one.

Toward this end, the coleaders must be knowledgeable about developmental issues and particularly the cognitive ability of the child (Fleming, 1985). For example, in the case of a younger child who believes that the dead can feel, placing the sibling's body in a casket and then into the ground may conjure up thoughts and images that are sorely in need of exploration and clarification. Similarly, if a child believes death to be reversible, this will certainly influence the depth of his or her despair at the death of a loved one (Wass, 1984).

In assessing the child's affective and cognitive appreciation of death and the rituals surrounding it, the following strategies have proven to be helpful.

Facilitation: The Question Box

"The question box" is based on the assumption that children are sometimes reluctant to ask problematic personal questions or to introduce worrisome issues, either because they are uncertain of the appropriateness of the question or because they believe they should already know the answer. This technique is quite simple. On arrival, group members are given several small pieces of paper and asked to write any questions they might have about funerals (children who cannot print can be assisted by older group members or by one of the coleaders). All the questions are placed in a container or "question box," which is circulated. Each member is then offered the opportunity to select a slip of paper from the box, read a question, and then lead the ensuing discussion.

The following are some examples from one group's question box:

Figure 1 was written by a 10-year-old boy who witnessed the murder of his father, shot in the head during a robbery. At the funeral, he was quite shocked to see that his father's face bore little resemblance to the face he remembered. At the same time, he said he felt some relief in seeing his father "at peace" because his last image of him was a very violent one. This revelation led to more general questions and discussion about the body and the physiological changes that occur at the time of death.

A 12-year-old boy wrote the note in Figure 2. His sister committed suicide, and her body was found the day before his birthday. At the funeral, he became, in his own words, "hysterical," screaming his sister's name and smashing his fist into

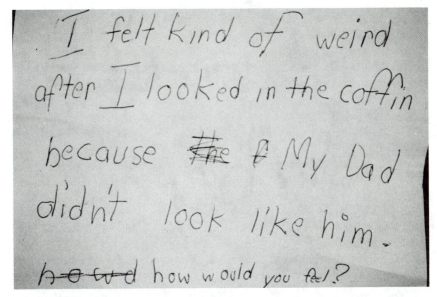

Figure 1 Question written by a 10-year-old boy who witnessed the murder of his father, who was shot in the head during a robbery.

the wall. Since that time, which was three months earlier, he had felt a great burden of unexpressed guilt for being disruptive and causing problems for his grief-stricken parents. This is illustrated in his question. Initially, he wrote "Did you shout why?" Then he crossed out the word *shout* and replaced it with the word *think*. During the discussion, children focused initially on the specific question, "Why did this happen?" which was paramount in all of their minds. Further, they were effective in normalizing the survivor's funeral-home behavior, some reframing it as "gutsy" and "brave." They, too, had wanted to express their pain and anger by screaming and pounding walls but felt inhibited by the crowd of mourners, many of whom were strangers.

The 10-year-old girl who wrote the question depicted in Figure 3 suffered the death of her mother. This woman was diagnosed with cancer two years before her death. The child's family was Catholic, and members were very devoted to their religion. Throughout much of her illness, the mother remained optimistic and encouraged her family to have faith in God's plan. When the mother became aware that her condition was terminal, she talked at length about her faith in an afterlife. For this child, part of remaining true to her mother was to maintain an unwavering belief in an afterlife. Even uncontrollable, intrusive thoughts and dreams, in which she questioned the notion of an afterlife, represented a breach of her faith. Once again the group discussion prompted by this question managed to normalize her feelings. Most group members also wondered about an afterlife. Further, the bereaved coleader added that this was a common question in the original group that she attended after her brother died five years previously.

Figure 2 Question written by a 12-year-old boy after the suicide of his sister.

Facilitation: The Weather Inside*

It is not uncommon for children to give very concrete and action-oriented descriptions when talking about the funeral. As a result, the discussion can, at times, become a cognitive exercise void of affective content. Moreover, when children are asked how they felt on the day of the funeral, they often reply, "I don't know," or "I can't remember." The following technique assists children in assessing feelings connected with this often overwhelming, frightening, and confusing time.

First, the group members are given the opportunity to "tell the story" of the funeral. After some discussion, each child is asked to briefly describe what

*This technique was developed by Janneke Koole, an art therapist from Toronto, Canada, who was instrumental in establishing the children's program at Bereaved Families of Ontario.

the weather was like on the day of the funeral. A large piece of paper is then placed on the floor, large enough for all group members to have a space, and the group is asked to paint a picture of what the "weather" was like inside of them on the day of the funeral. The children typically draw very expressive, vivid interpretations, which contrast sharply with their verbal descriptions of the funeral.

The following are several examples of children's interpretations of the "weather inside":

> Figure 4 was drawn by a 10-year-old boy whose sister had died only six weeks previously. He drew a bright red heart split in two by a lightening bolt and surrounded by black rain clouds. Beside the heart he wrote "scared." This boy had not been able to articulate any feelings with regard to his sister's funeral.
>
> Figure 5 was drawn by a 12-year-old boy whose older sister committed suicide. He drew a tornado beneath rain clouds. To the left of the tornado are two lightning bolts. To the right is a black sun with a question mark in the middle. At the bottom is the world "confused." In describing this picture, the artist commented that his sister had left a suicide note, indicating that for the first time in her life, she felt at peace. This boy wanted to believe it (thus the sun) but really questioned whether she could find peace in death.

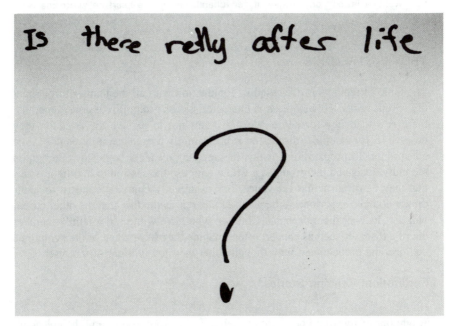

Figure 3 Question written by a 10-year-old girl whose mother, a devout Catholic, died of cancer.

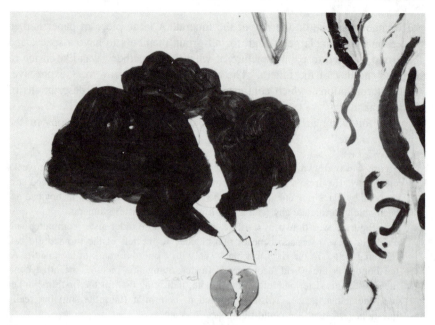

Figure 4 Drawing by a 10-year-old boy six weeks after the death of his sister, showing his "weather inside" on the day of her funeral. Beside the heart he wrote the word "scared."

THEME 4: FEELINGS

The topic of feelings is discussed in conjunction with all the themes throughout the seven weeks. However, as is characteristic of group discussions generally, there is a tendency for some relevant issues not to receive the attention they deserve if, for example, discussion is prematurely terminated as a result of time constraints. In preparation for this theme, the coleaders begin to reflect upon the individuals and the group as a whole, and use the session to highlight issues that may be of particular relevance. For example, a common concern for children who have experienced the death of a parent is the fear that the other parent will die, leaving them orphans. Children who have witnessed a family member die of a disease, such as cancer, often imagine they have some of the symptoms and become preoccupied with thoughts that they too will die of the disease.

Facilitation: Reading Stories

A number of relevant books are available in the group room, and the coleaders encourage participants to borrow them. With specific reference to feeling states, the reading of stories can assist in the stimulation of discussion. Books of particular value are those containing contributions by bereaved children and adolescents themselves (Krementz, 1988; Richter, 1987).

A story is selected reflecting the age and circumstances of the majority of group participants. After the coleaders have read the story to the group members, children compile a list of feelings they think the child in the story might experience. This technique, commonly known to child therapists as a displacement activity (Kalter, Schaefer, Lesowitz, Alpern & Pickar, 1988), permits the child to disclose feelings in an indirect, nonthreatening way. This leads to a discussion of the appropriateness of the various feelings.

It is often difficult for children to acknowledge what they judge to be inappropriate or unacceptable feelings. These include affective responses such as anger (at God or the deceased), fear (that they, too, may die), suicidal ideation (not necessarily wanting to die but wanting to be with the deceased), guilt (that somehow they were responsible for the death), and relief (in the case

Figure 5 Drawing by a 12-year-old boy whose older sister committed suicide, illustrating his "weather inside" on the day of her funeral.

of a chronic, painful illness). By first discussing these feelings in an indirect and nonthreatening manner, what were once believed to be inappropriate or unacceptable feelings can be reframed for the children as appropriate, common, and healthy responses to the death of a loved one.

Once again, the bereaved sibling coleader can be a valuable role model in relating his or her grief experiences. In addition, the professional coleader can assist through the use of what Kalter and colleagues (1988) refer to as "universalizing" statements, such as "Most children tell me . . . " or "Children in other groups felt . . . ."

As participants reveal feelings of guilt or fear, or thoughts of suicide, they frequently come to the realization that (1) they are not alone with their feelings, and (2) maybe their responses are normal after all. Once various feelings are acknowledged, the discussion can turn to coping with responses associated with grief.

Facilitation: The Mandala

A powerful technique, based on a structured version of the Jungian mandala, can be effectively used in conjunction with story reading and discussion (Sourkes, 1980, 1988). The child is asked to think back to, and focus on, a specific time or event (i.e., when they were informed that their sibling or parent was dead). Then, the coleaders introduce a series of index cards; on each card is a word describing an emotional response (e.g., *sad*, *angry*, *scared*, *shocked*, *relieved*, *guilty*, or *lonely*). One card is left blank so that other responses can be added if the participant desires.

Each group member is given a piece of paper with a blank circle and a number of colored pens or crayons. The coleaders ask the children to choose the words that describe how they feel, to choose a color representing the feeling, and then to color the proportion of the circle representing this emotional response. For example, a child who is feeling very lonely might choose the color purple to represent this feeling, and color much of the circle purple. Upon completion, there is a visual representation of the child's feelings, which can be applied in a number of ways:

> Figure 6 was drawn by an 11-year-old girl whose mother died of cancer 18 months previously. This child is the eldest, having two younger brothers. She verbalized anxiety about being involved in the group and felt pressure from her family to set a good example for her younger siblings. For her, setting an example meant not only being strong and not crying, but also accepting her father's remarriage. From the mandala it can be seen that she has not only chosen various colors but also has drawn symbols to represent her feelings. At the bottom is "sad," which is represented by tears (blue). In the center is "angry," represented by lightning bolts (red). At the top is a word that she chose, "crammed" (black), depicted by circles compressed into a small area.

Figure 6 Mandala drawn by an 11-year-old girl 18 months after the death of her mother from cancer. She chose colors and drew symbols to represent her feelings. From top down: "sad" (drawn in blue); "angry" (colored red); "crammed" (drawn in black).

Figures 7a–b illustrates how this technique can be used to explore actual or perceived changes in affect over time. These two mandalas were drawn by a 9-year-old boy whose father died of a heart attack six months previously. Figure 7a represents the boy's perception of how he felt "when I found out" (that his father had died). At the top of the picture he wrote "mad" in bold red letters. The circle was colored completely green, which he said was "sad." The face was purple, symbolizing "falling apart." Figure 7b was drawn to represent "how I feel now." Much of the anger was gone, nevertheless, he was still very much engulfed in the intense pain of grief. He wrote "brocken" (broken) at the top of the page. The sad face is drawn in purple, which as in the first illustration, symbolizes the feeling "falling apart."

THEME 5: CHANGES

A myriad changes, internal and external, occur after the death of a parent or sibling, including residence relocation, school relocation, disruption of family finances, strain on family cohesion, wavering support of friends, concentration problems in school, and alterations in role and position in the family. The purpose of this session is to allow the children to compare notes as they describe the changes they are struggling with and the coping strategies they employ to survive.

Facilitation; Before/After Pictures

It is not only difficult but also frequently threatening for children to verbalize the numerous changes that have occurred in their family since their sibling or parent died. Rather than subject the participants to the trials of articulation, this technique requires an artistic representation of how their lives and family have changed. Each child is presented with a piece of paper and asked to draw a line down the center. On one side, they draw a picture of their family before the death and, on the other side, a picture depicting the family at the present time.

Each child is then invited to present his or her drawing to the group. Generally, children are much more comfortable and adept at describing the changes in their pictures than directly addressing changes in the family. Therapists trained in the interpretation of children's drawings can also use this material as a way of gaining valuable information about the child and how the child views himself or herself in the family.

Figure 8 was drawn by an 8-year-old girl. Her father, to whom she was extremely close, was killed in a car accident 13 months before the drawing of this picture. Since the death, her relationship with her mother had become increasingly conflicted. As is shown in the "before" picture (on the left), this was originally a family of four. The artist of the picture is between her parents saying, "I'm so

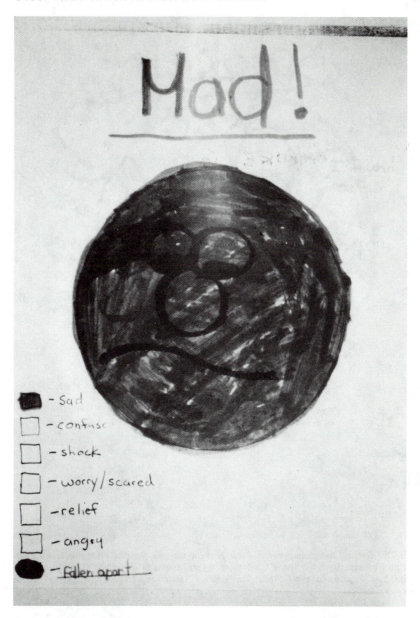

Figure 7a First mandala drawn by a 9-year-old boy six months after his father died of a heart attack to represent how he felt when he found out his father had died. At the top of the picture he wrote "mad" (originally in bold red letters). The circle was colored green, for "sad." The face was originally colored purple, symbolizing "falling apart."

Figure 7b Second mandala drawn by a 9-year-old boy six months after this father died of a heart attack to show "how I feel now." The face was originally drawn in purple, which as in Figure 7a symbolizes the feeling "fallen apart." At the top he wrote "brocken" (broken).

happy." The mother (far left) is laughing; the father is saying, "Let's go for a walk"; and the youngest sister (age 6) is also laughing. When describing her drawing, this girl reflected that the only change since her father's death was that she now had a dog. However, a closer look at this picture suggests that before the death, the family was close and happy (as they are pictured going on a walk together, talking and laughing). After the death, the family is not portrayed as a unit. The two sisters are alone, comforted by the dog. This suggests that the current lack of closeness in this family represents a major change for this child. Furthermore, she does not perceive support or nurturance coming from her mother, who is not portrayed in the "after" picture. Even the deceased (seen at the top of the picture in heaven) is more present in this child's life than is her mother.

Figure 9 serves to illustrate the fact that something remaining unchanged can also be significant. This 10-year-old boy, who has an expressive speech and language disability, experienced the death by drowning of an older sister five years before being in the group. When asked to draw before/after pictures, he persisted in asking the coleader if he could draw a bicycle. The leader continued to explain the instructions, thinking that the boy was having some difficulty understanding what she said. Eventually, the boy drew the bicycle, the first drawing he had been willing to complete in the group. He spent 20 minutes drawing the picture with a great amount of detail. When showing his picture to the group, he explained that this was the bike his sister had received just months before her death. Five years later, the brand-new BMX bike remained untouched in the attic.

Figure 8 Drawing by an 8-year-old girl 13 months after her father was killed in a car accident: left, her family as it was before the death (her father is saying, "Let's go for a walk"); right, the girl, her sister, and their dog "now" (the father is shown in heaven). Note that the girl's mother is not portrayed in the "now" picture.

Figure 9 Drawing by a 10-year-old boy five years after the death by drowning of an older sister. The sister had received a bike just months before her death, and it remained stored in the family's attic.

THEMES 6–7: LOOKING TO THE FUTURE
AND SAYING GOOD-BYE

The last two sessions are characteristically devoted to "saying good-bye." A prominent topic for discussion during this period of leave-taking is fear of the future. At this point in the group process, the leaders are somewhat familiar with each child's personality, relevant family history, coping style, support system, and relationship with the deceased. Highlighting similarities and differences between the experiences of group members, the coleaders facilitate discussions in which the collective group "expertise" and wisdom assist the children in preparing for the days, months, and years ahead. For example, children who have been bereaved over a longer period of time can offer their experiences to the children who have suffered more recent losses:

> A 10-year-old boy, whose brother had died three months previously and had been cremated, worried about the family's plans to spread the deceased's ashes the following summer at the family cottage. He had been very frightened and uncomfortable at the funeral, had watched his parents' pain, and anticipated a similar trauma during the spreading of the ashes. In the same group, a 12-year-old girl had been involved in a similar ceremony the previous summer. Her mother had died in the winter, having requested that she be cremated and her ashes spread at the family cottage, which was her favorite place. The girl remarked that she had also detested the funeral. However, she felt grateful to have participated in the ritual surrounding the spreading of the ashes, for on this occasion, she was no longer in shock and in fact used this ceremony, rather than the funeral, to say good-bye to her mother. She added that it was difficult, "but nowhere near as bad as the funeral."

A second prominent theme during these final sessions involves saving the precious memories of the deceased (many of which are portrayed in the children's artwork, which they are allowed to keep). Because children are at different points in the bereavement process, some are able to comment that they "enjoy" reflecting upon their life with the deceased. It is important that these children be given the opportunity to share their experiences, as this serves to offer hope to others who are still engulfed in the intense pain associated with the earlier phases of the grief process. Sometimes, just knowing that memories of the deceased will eventually be less painful is of great assistance in easing fears about the future.

A final important issue, addressed in the last two sessions, is the preparation for the termination of the group. The group is encouraged to reflect upon specific memories from the group meetings, such as (1) how they felt during the first meeting as compared to now, (2) discussing their favorite activity and least favorite one, (3) remembering significant group occurrences, and (4) how sad it is to say good-bye.

Participants are also invited to contribute their expertise to other bereaved children by suggesting specific ways of improving the group and by volunteering to have specific pieces of their artwork used to educate professionals with regard to children's grief. One group consented to participate in the production of a videotape describing their reactions to the death of a parent or sibling and how the group was beneficial to them. The result will be used by BFO to educate teachers, therapists, and interested members of the community about children's grief and more specifically about the children's group program.

The final week usually is a pizza party. A group picture is taken so that the children can have a visual keepsake of their time together. Friendships that develop over the seven weeks are encouraged. Children and parents often exchange phone numbers and keep in touch long after the official completion of the group. After a few final words of parting, the children (often quite reluctantly) gather up their art folders and leave the group for the last time.

CONCLUSIONS

When a child or parent dies, children are often left to mourn alone. Not only have they lost a sibling or parent to death, but the remaining adult family members are lost in a functional sense, for they, too, are immobilized by grief. In addition, the support of friends is often wavering, short-lived, or lacking completely. Groups, then, fill an important void in the provision of support for bereaved children during a highly traumatic period of their lives.

A particularly noteworthy feature of the children's program of Bereaved Families of Ontario is the involvement of a bereaved sibling coleader. These individuals enrich the group experience by offering a unique perspective. They possess a familiarity and expertise in adjustment to loss, unmatched by any professional. The parent(s), as well as the children, view the bereaved sibling as living proof that one can not only survive the death of a loved one, but also use one's experience to benefit others. For many of the bereaved children, the ability of the bereaved coleader to describe their grief experiences over time, in combination with the clear message that "you will be able to laugh and enjoy life again," does much to alleviate destructive fears and apprehension, and offers hope for a brighter future.

REFERENCES

Fleming, S. J. (1985). Children's grief: Individual and family dynamics. In C. A. Corr & D. M. Corr (Eds.), *Hospice approaches to pediatric care* (pp. 197–218). New York: Springer.

Kalter, N., Schaefer, M., Lesowitz, M., Alpern, D., & Pickar, J. (1988). School-based support groups for children of divorce: A model of brief intervention. In B. H. Gottlieb. (Ed.), *Marshaling social support* (pp. 165–186). Newbury Park: Sage.

Krementz, J. (1988). *How it feels when a parent dies.* New York: Knopf.

Parkes, C. M., & Weiss, R. (1983). *Recovery from bereavement.* New York: Basic Books.

Richter, E. (1987). *Losing someone you love: When a brother or sister dies.* New York: G. P. Putnam's Sons.

Sourkes, B. M. (1980). Siblings of the pediatric cancer patient. In J. Kellerman (Ed.), *Psychological aspects of childhood cancer* (pp. 47–69). Springfield: Charles C. Thomas.

Sourkes, B. M. (1988). What the butterfly sees: Resilience in the face of loss. *Canadian Pharmaceutical Journal, 121*(3), 177–181.

Wass, H. (1984). Concepts of death: A developmental perspective. In H. Wass & C. Corr (Eds.), *Childhood and death* (pp. 3–24). New York: Hemisphere.

Chapter 9

Responses of Children
to the Death of a Sibling

Betty Davies

My interest in the field of death and dying had its origins in my experiences as a student in nursing school. My lifelong goal was to be pediatric nurse, and I relished the days spent in the children's wards. Like many others who worked in hospitals during the late 1960s, I became aware of the plight of patients who were dying in the lonely and barren atmosphere of the hospital setting. In particular, my heart went out to those children who had no hope of being cured, and I concentrated my efforts on caring for them and for their parents. Somewhere along the line, however, I realized that those sick children were often not the only children in their families. They had brothers and sisters who, though not hospitalized themselves, were experiencing the effects of their sibling's illness and subsequent death. I wondered what effect this experience had on these children. In particular, I wondered what the long-term effect of sibling loss would be on the surviving children. I knew from my experience in my own family that the effect of sibling death can be very long lasting; and as a nurse, I wondered what nurses and other health care professionals might do to help lessen the impact of the loss on the surviving children.

Siblings are known to fulfill several functions for each other (Bank &

Kahn, 1975). Siblings protect one another, and older ones often help to care for younger ones. They teach one another, and share times of learning. They come to each other's defense on the playground, and often against parents, in the form of sibling alliances. They confide in one another and share secrets from the rest of the world. I believe that understanding the siblings' experience provides clues as to how we—as adults, as health care workers, as child care professionals—might better help these children in ways that would promote their optimal development. This was the reason for my research.

Relatively little has been written about the impact of a child's death on siblings, even though the child's response to major loss has been a source of much interest and considerable study in recent years. There have been clinical theoretical considerations of the younger child's capacity to mourn (Bowlby, 1960; Wolfenstein, 1966); epidemiological studies attempting to link adult depression to childhood loss (Blinder, 1972; Birtchnell, 1970; Brown, Harris & Copeland, 1977; Hilgard, 1969); and descriptive studies of children's bereavement responses to the death of a parent (Furman, 1974) and siblings (Biner, Ablin, Feuerstein et al., 1969; Cain, Fast & Erickson, 1964; Lewis, 1967; Stehbens & Lascari, 1974).

Studies of children's bereavement reactions indicate a range of possible responses. Several researchers (Biner et al., 1969; Cain et al., 1964; Lewis, 1967) reported a wide variety of behavior problems in children following the death of a sibling. Other researchers (Spinetta, 1977; Stehbens & Lascari, 1974) have found few behavior problems. Discrepancies between these sets of findings may be due to differences in the definition of what constitutes behavior problems or in the nature of the samples. Most studies relied on anecdotal and descriptive observation of the children. What has been written focuses primarily on a description of these responses without consideration of how these behavioral responses compare with the behavior of "normal" nonbereaved children and without consideration of moderating factors that may influence the children's responses. Consequently, I have attempted to build on this previous work by using reliable and valid tools to measure the behavior of bereaved children and then comparing the responses of these children to norms for children's behavior. I have also attempted to collect systematically and to organize interview data from siblings themselves in order to describe accurately the responses of children to the death of a sibling.

SOURCES OF DATA

Four studies concerned with the long-term outcome of sibling loss are presented in this chapter.

The first study (Davies, 1983) looked at the responses of one child in each of 34 families who had had a child die from cancer within the past three years from the time of data collection, and who had a surviving child between 6 and 16 years of age. Families lived in the western United States and Canada.

The second study (Davies, 1985) included all the children aged 6–16 in these same families. The overall purpose of the three-year postdeath studies was to investigate bereaved children's behavioral responses to the death of a sibling and to examine these responses in relation to a number of selected individual, situational, and environmental characteristics. *Individual variables* included age and sex of both the surviving and the deceased children. *Situational variables* were duration of illness, type of cancer, and time since death. *Environmental variables* were sibling closeness, sibling involvement, and family environment; my clinical experience suggested that these variables were of importance to bereavement outcome in children.

The third study included 58 families, followed seven to nine years after the death of their child from cancer. This study—under the direction of Ida Martinson at the University of California, San Francisco—was a follow-up study of the families that participated in a Home Care Program for their dying children in Minnesota in the early 1970s. I had the privilege of working with Martinson on this project as a postdoctoral fellow in 1986. The study had several components, of which a few selected aspects are presented in this chapter.

The fourth study is one that I am presently conducting. It focuses on experiences of individuals, now adults, who in their childhood lost a sibling. Interviews have been conducted with 16 individuals, ranging in age from 25 to 75 years. The death of their sibling occurred between 12 and 65 years before the time the interviews were conducted.

I have chosen to organize the data into categories, according to four conclusions that result from my work so far:

1   Children are affected by the death of a sibling, and the effect is demonstrated in behavior changes. During the first three years following the death, siblings were reported to demonstrate certain behaviors, which their parents, and they themselves, attributed to the death.

2   The death of a sibling in childhood has long-term implications for surviving siblings. At seven to nine years after a child's death, siblings continue to report various behaviors that they attribute to the death of their sibling.

3   The death of a sibling is not an isolated occurrence, which children forget. Rather, it is a major life event that leaves its mark on the subsequent development of the surviving children. Adults who, in their childhood, lost a sibling report that the effect of that loss continues throughout adult life.

4   The responses of children to the death of a sibling are affected by characteristics of the sibling relationship and of the family environment. The behavioral responses of the children in the three-year study were affected by certain variables, specifically the closeness of the relationship between the siblings, and the cohesiveness of the family environment. The responses of the siblings in the seven-to-nine-year study were also affected by similar characteristics. Adults recall similar variables affecting their responses. Therefore, the closer the relationship between the children, the greater the effect of the death of one of the children on the surviving ones. Furthermore, selected aspects of the family environment contribute to the effect of the death on surviving children.

RESULTS: BEHAVIORAL RESPONSES OF BEREAVED SIBLINGS

Up to Three Years Postdeath

In the three-year study, I assessed the children's behavior using the Child Behavior Checklist (CBCL), designed and tested by Achenbach and Edelbrock (1981). The CBCL includes assessment not only of behavior problems, but of behavior competencies as well, and was therefore selected as the instrument of choice for measuring child behaviors. The CBCL was designed to obtain parents' reports of the behavioral problems and competencies of their children in a standardized format. It comprises 118 problem behavior items, including statements such as:

- acts too young for his/her age
- can't concentrate, can't pay attention for long
- disobedient at home
- overtired

It also includes items for reporting a child's school performance and the amount and quality of the child's participation in sports, games, hobbies, chores, organizations, and social relationships. The CBCL provides standardized norms for age and sex. It has demonstrated test-retest reliability (Achenbach, 1979) and discriminative validity (Achenbach & Edelbrock, 1981). The CBCL gives four summary scores: (1) Internalizing Behavior Problem Score; (2) Externalizing Behavior Problem Score; (3) Total Behavior Problem Score; and (4) Total Social Competency Score.

The bereaved children demonstrated a wide range of behaviors following the death of a sibling. Three behaviors that occurred with the greatest frequency were to be noted in at least 50% of the children, and were observed by the parents, and by many of the siblings, to be linked directly to the death of the child. These behaviors were: (a) nervous; (b) likes to be alone; and (c) unhappy, sad, or depressed.

Including these 3 problems, a total of 21 problems was reported for $1/3$ of the bereaved children. Some of the other behaviors included psychophysiological responses in the form of headaches, generalized aches and pains, and stomach cramps, reported for approximately $1/4$ of the children. Close to $1/3$ of the children were reported to have sleeping disorders, including trouble in sleeping, nightmares, or walking and talking in their sleep. Nearly $1/4$ of the children were not eating well. Anxiety, loneliness, and poor school work also occurred in ¹/₃ of the children.

Looking at the average total scores for the bereaved children, their behavior problem scores were all higher than the standardized mean scores, their internalizing scores being significantly higher. Internalizing scores reflect a turning inward on the part of the children. Furthermore, their social competency scores decreased with time.

These findings imply that siblings respond to the death of a brother or sister with a range of behaviors; most notably they turn inward and become sad and lonely, and with time, they may become socially withdrawn.

Assuming that we expect modifications in children's behavior following any significant change in their lives, it is perhaps not unusual that these behaviors were reported for the bereaved children. The occurrence of these behaviors up to three years after the death may be considered unusual in light of previous studies on childhood bereavement. However, few studies of childhood bereavement have assessed children beyond the few weeks or months immediately following the death. Therefore, it has been assumed that, with time, children's behavior returns to "normal." Consequently, the long-term impact on children of a sibling's death has been negated.

Seven to Nine Years Postdeath

Seven to nine years after the death, siblings reported that they continued to experience several of the same behaviors that the siblings in the other study reported at three years postdeath (Davies, 1987). Several continued to dream of their deceased brother or sister; such dreams were not disturbing, but rather comforting in that they provided a feeling of closeness to the sibling. Nearly all siblings indicated that at the time of death, loneliness was a great problem. Feelings of loneliness and sorrow persisted, not always in the forefront of the siblings' mind, but still identifiable. Such feelings accounted, in the siblings' view, for aspects of their present personality. Matthew, for example, said: "If my sister were still here, somehow my personality would be different. I'd be more outgoing . . . because the sadness got in the way."

These siblings continued to think about their brother or sister. The majority of them reported that they thought about the deceased sibling at least once a day. Such thoughts were more prevalent at certain times, for example, when they themselves reached the age at which the sibling had died, or when they had children of their own.

Experiencing a sibling's death does not only result in problem behaviors, since many surviving siblings report that they experience growth as a result of the loss. Analysis of siblings' and parents' interview data indicated that the siblings had gained maturity, and had grown psychologically as a result of their experience (Martinson, Davies & McClowry, 1987). For example, one 16-year-old boy commented: "I have a better outlook on life now; I mean, I realize how important life is as a result of my sister's death.'' Furthermore, the siblings, as a group, had significantly higher self-concept scores than would be expected from the norms for the self-concept measure that was used (the Piers-Harris Self-Concept Scale; Piers & Harris, 1969).

Adults Who Lost a Sibling in Childhood

Years after the death of a sibling, surviving siblings recounted persistent effects of their experience (Davies, 1988a). Looking back over a long period of time, many perceived positive outcomes resulting from their experience. These siblings felt comfortable with death and were able to help others with death-related events instead of avoiding such experiences. Encountering death also contributed to the siblings' viewing life in a constructive way. Feeling comfortable with death, being able to help others, and developing a sensitive outlook on life contributed to these siblings feeling generally good about themselves. There was, however, another effect of the earlier death of their brother or sister. For many, the newly found maturity was accompanied by a seriousness about life that left no room for the normal developmental antics of childhood and adolescence. As a result, these individuals withdrew from socializing; they were often lonely, never having learned, during critical periods of development, to develop and foster social relationships.

Behavioral Responses and Influencing Variables

The data provide some clues as to factors that influence siblings' responses to the death of a brother or sister. First, the degree of closeness between two siblings made a difference in the surviving siblings' response. The closer the stated emotional closeness between siblings, the greater the trend for the surviving sibling to demonstrate more behavior problems after the death of the other child. Closeness did not necessarily have to do with closeness in age, but rather with perceived emotional closeness (Davies, 1988b).

Second, characteristics of the family environment were related to siblings' responses. In the first study, for example, both internalizing and externalizing behaviors were negatively related to cohesion within the families (as measured by the Moos Family Environment Scale; Moos, 1981). That is, the greater the feelings of closeness among family members, the fewer behavior problems reported for the children (Davies, 1988c).

Third, in looking more closely at the self-concept scores of the bereaved siblings, we examined differences between those children who had the highest scores and those with the lowest ones (Martinson, Davies & McClowry, 1987). The children in the lower group shared one common characteristic: they felt as though they were "not enough." Feelings of being "not enough" came about through several means: they were compared unfavorably to the deceased child, and most often such comparisons had occurred even before the death ("Johnny was always smarter that I was; I can never be enough to take his place").

Feeling somehow responsible for the death added to feelings of not being good enough, as did feeling displaced by the addition of new children into the family ("If I were enough, why do mom and dad need another baby?").

The psychosocial environment, therefore, played a potentially significant role in how children responded to the death of a sibling. Particularly important was the message the child received about his or her own worth and place in the family.

IMPLICATIONS FOR CLINICIANS

These findings provide several suggestions for those who work with the families of children who die. Such caregivers should be knowledgeable about the behaviors that were reported to occur most frequently in bereaved children. Generally, they need to know that behavior problems of an internalizing or withdrawing nature tend to increase, and social competencies tend to decrease after the death of a sibling. In particular, professionals should know that children become sad, withdrawn, and lonely; that their performance in school may diminish; and that their interests in other social activities may lessen. Many professionals realize that these are expected behaviors of grieving children; in addition, however, caregivers must realize that such behaviors may continue for long periods of time.

Professionals should look for such behaviors in bereaved siblings; they can also use their knowledge of these behaviors to help bereaved parents cope with their surviving children. Professionals can forewarn parents of the behaviors they might expect to see in their grieving children. Further, they can advise parents to be alert to continuing patterns of sorrow and withdrawal in their children, as indications that the sibling needs additional support in coping with the death.

Furthermore, professionals should be aware of those children who may be especially affected by a sibling's death. Those children who shared a close relationship with their sibling may be in need of greater support. Those children who already have a diminished self-concept, or whose families are not cohesive, are also at risk of persistent sorrow and withdrawal.

Finally, professionals must also remember that many siblings, in retrospect, perceive their experience in a positive light. Therefore, professionals must not make the morbid mistake of thinking that a sibling's death bodes *only* negative consequences for the surviving children. Professionals must, however, overcome the previous assumption that a sibling's death has *no* effect on the surviving children. The responses of children to a sibling's death can be profound and long lasting. Only be appreciating the nature of the impact of a sibling's death can caregivers be sensitive to and supportive of the bereaved siblings.

REFERENCES

Achenbach, T. M. (1979). The child behavior profile: An empirically based system for assessing children's behavioral problems and competencies. *International Journal of Mental Health, 4,* 24–42.

Achenbach, T. M., & Edelbrock, C. S. (1981). Behavioral problems and competencies reported by parents of normal and disturbed children aged four through sixteen. *Monographs of the Society for Research in Child Development, 46* (1, Serial No. 188).

Bank, S. & Kahn, M. D. (1975). Sisterhood–brotherhood is powerful: sibling subsystems and family therapy. *Family Process, 14,* 311–337.

Binger, C., Ablin, A., Feurerstein, R., Kushner, J., Zoger, S., & Mikkelsen, C. (1969). Childhood leukemia: Emotional impact on patient and family. *New England Journal of Medicine, 2804,* 414–418.

Birtchnell, J. (1970). Depression in relation to early and recent parent death. *British Journal of Psychiatry, 116,* 299–306.

Blinder, B. (1972). Sibling death in childhood. *Child Psychiatry and Human Development, 2,* 169–175.

Bowlby, J. (1960). Grief and mourning in infancy and early childhood. *The Psychoanalytic Study of the Child, 15,* 9–52.

Brown, G., Harris, T., & Copeland, J. (1977). Depression and loss. *British Journal of Psychiatry, 130,* 11.

Cain, A., Fast, I., & Erickson, M. (1964). Children's disturbed reactions to the death of a sibling. *American Journal of Orthopsychiatry, 34,* 741–745.

Davies, E. B. (1983). Behavioral responses to the death of a sibling. (Unpublished doctoral dissertation, University of Washington.)

Davies, E. B. (1985) Behavioral responses of children to the death of a sibling (Final report). Alberta Foundation of Nursing Research.

Davies, E. B. (1987). After a sibling dies. In M. A. Morgan (Ed.), *Bereavement: Helping the survivors. Proceedings of the 1987 King's College Conference* (pp. 55–65). London, Ontario: King's College (Ont.).

Davies, E. B. (1988a). Long term follow-up of brothers and sisters who have died. Paper presented at the 1988 King's College Conference, London, Ontario.

Davies, E. B. (1988b). Shared life space and sibling bereavement responses. *Cancer Nursing, 11*(6), 339–347.

Davies, E. B. (1988c). The family environment in bereaved families and its relationship to surviving sibling behavior. *Children's Health Care, 17*(1), 22–32.

Furman, E. (1974). *A child's parent dies: Studies in childhood bereavement.* New Haven: Yale University Press.

Hilgard, J. R. (1969). Depressive and psychotic states as anniversaries to sibling death in childhood. *International Psychiatry Clinics, 6,* 197–207.

Kaplan, D. M., Smith, A., Grobstein, R., & Fishman, S. (1973). Family mediation of stress. *Social Work, 18*(4), 60–69.

Lewis, I. C. (1967). Leukemia in childhood: Its effects on the family. *Australian Paediatric Journal, 3,* 244–247.

Martinson, I. M., Davies, E., & McClowry, S. G. (1987). The long-term effect of sibling death on self-concept. *Journal of Pediatric Nursing, 2*(4), 227–235.

McClowry, S. G., Davies, E. B., May, K. A., Kulenkamp, E. J., & Martinson, I. M.

(1987). The empty space phenomenon: The process of grief in the bereaved family. *Death Studies, 11,* 361–374.

Moldow, D., & Martinson, I. M. (1980). From research to reality: Home care for the dying child. *The American Journal of Maternal–Child Nursing, 51,* 41–45.

Moos, R. M. (1981). *Family environment scale manual.* Palo Alto, CA: Consulting Psychologists Press.

Payne, J. S., Goff, J. R., & Paulson, M. A. (1980). Psychological adjustment of families following the death of a child. In J. L. Schulman and M. J. Kupst (Eds.), *The child with cancer: Clinical approaches to psychological cancer—research in psychosocial aspects.* Springfield, IL: Charles C. Thomas.

Piers, E., & Harris, D. (1969). *The manual of the Piers-Harris Children's Self-concept Scale.* Nashville, TN: Counselor Recordings and Tests.

Spinetta, J. J. (1977). Adjustment in children with cancer. *Journal of Pediatric Psychology, 2,* 49–51.

Stehbens, J. A., & Lascari, A. D. (1974). Psychological follow-up of families with childhood leukemia. *Journal of Clinical Psychology, 30,* 394–397.

Wolfenstein, M. (1966). How is mourning possible? *Psychoanalytic Study of the Child, 21,* 93.

Chapter 10

Family Intervention with Families Bereaved or About to be Bereaved

Dora Black

This chapter will focus on how we can best help children and their families to cope with death, dying, and bereavement. I have had long-standing clinical and research interest in bereaved children (Black, 1978) and particularly in using family intervention to reduce morbidity in children who lose a parent by death (Black & Urbanowicz, 1985, 1987; Black, 1981; Lieberman & Black, 1982). There is now enough evidence to show that various counseling interventions can reduce the high morbidity found in bereaved children and adults (Black & Urbanowicz, 1985, 1987; Black, 1981; Lieberman & Black, 1982; Parkes, 1980). This led me to consider whether an intervention before bereavement might also be preventive (Black, 1989). In this chapter, I will briefly describe the results of family intervention with bereaved children and our clinical work with families in which a parent or a child has a life-threatening illness. Issues that need to be addressed when working with these families will be presented.

FAMILY INTERVENTION WITH BEREAVED CHILDREN

An unselected group of children aged 16 or under, at the time of the death of the parent, was identified with the aid of the records clerks of hospitals and 12 general practices. The sample consisted of all consecutive families where a parent had recently died in hospital or practice, over a three-year period. The families were randomly allocated to treatment and control groups. About two months after their bereavement, the treatment families received a letter from "Cruse," the national charity for bereavement care in Great Britain. The letter was sent by a Cruse social worker/therapist, who offered to visit the family, in order to help with any problems that might have arisen since the death. The therapists were all experienced psychiatric social workers who worked in child guidance or child psychiatric settings, and who had received training in bereavement counseling. They offered six family therapy sessions to the treatment families, spaced at two- to three-week intervals. These therapy sessions took place at the families' home starting two to three months after their bereavement.

The aims of the therapists were to promote mourning in both the children and the surviving parent and to improve communication between them, especially in regard to the death. The families were invited to review for the therapist the events leading up to the death, and to show photographs and mementos. The therapists used play materials, appropriate to the ages and developmental stages of the children, to encourage them to talk about the dead parent and their feelings of loss and grief. They used techniques to encourage the expression of grief in the family, which included modeling of appropriate verbal behaviors and responses. Very often, this was the first time that parent and children sat together to talk about the loss and share their feelings.

One year and two years after the death, follow-up interviews were undertaken, for both the treatment and control group, by a research psychologist. For the control group, this was the first time they were contacted. The interview was structured and covered issues related to (a) the parental health and psychiatric state, (b) the children's health and behavior, and (c) the death and events surrounding it. Eighty families were contacted. About 2/3 of the families allocated to the treatment group accepted the first interview, and almost 1/2 completed the treatment. This acceptance rate is about the norm for bereavement counseling in adults. Of those families completing the treatment, all but one agreed to follow-up interviews. About 3/4 of the controls consented to the first follow-up interview and about 1/2 to the second one.

Results

There were no significant differences between treatment and control groups in regard to the number and age of children, social class, and sex of the surviving parent. There were no significant differences in regard to the cause of death (mostly due to heart disease or neoplasm), length of illness, or place of death. In addition, no significant differences were found in regard to financial or work worries, housing problems, moves, school, or work changes. Table 1 summarizes the major differences that were found between the treatment and the control group at the first-year follow-up. The treatment group had slightly higher scores in terms of behavior, mood, and health.

Table 2 summarizes the variables examined. On the whole the "life event" variables did not differ between the two groups, while the outcome variables (i.e., those relating to mental and physical health) showed a trend in favor of the treatment group that was not always statistically significant.

A favorable outcome was associated with children—especially those over 5 years of age—having cried and talked about the dead parent in the month following bereavement. These older children who cried more had fewer and less serious behavior and emotional problems. The treatment was associated with increased crying scores and a decrease in behavioral problems. Another association with a good outcome in the total group of children was the well-being of the surviving parent.

Table 3 summarizes the major differences between the treatment and con-

Table 1 Summary of Major Differences between Treatment (T) and Control (C) Groups at First-Year Follow-Up

Variable	N	%	Significance
Children	T(38)	21	
Behavior problems	C(44)	41	n.s.
Sleep problems beginning after bereavement	T(33)	15	
(age >5 years)	C(33)	33	n.s.
Had parents who were depressed	T(33)	18	
(age >5 years)	C(34)	50	$P = 0.01$
Talked about dead parent	T(33)	91	
(age >5 years)	C(34)	71	n.s.
Restless (Rutter A Scale,	T(27)	7	
age >5 years)	C(33)	36	$P = 0.02$
Nailbiting (Rutter A Scale	T(27)	18	
age >5 years)	C(33)	45	$P = 0.05$
School problems	T(34)	12	
	C(41)	27	n.s.
Parents			
Health problems	T(21)	14	
	C(24)	42	n.s.
Depressed mood	T(21)	14	
	C(24)	38	n.s.
Sought help from professional	T(21)	0	
agencies	C(24)	25	$P = 0.05$

Source: From Black & Urbanowicz, 1987.

Table 2   Variables Examined at First-Year Follow-Up (Treatment Versus Controls)

Factors significantly less common in the treatment group, $P < 0.05$	Factors possibly less common in the treatment group, $P < 0.1$	Factors more common in treated group	Factors not discriminating between the two groups
Parents depressed	Behavior problems	Crying about dead parent	Health of extended family
Restlessness (Rutter A Scale)	Behavior changes	Talking about dead parent	Death in extended family
Nailbiting (Rutter A Scale)	Sleep problems	Lower score on Rutter A Scale	Closeness to family
Sought help from professional agencies	Health problems in parents	Lower score on Parkes	Money worries
	Health problems in child	Health questionnaire	Work worries or changes
	Learning problems		Housing worries
			Moves
			Time for children
			Discipline problems
			Social contacts as a family
			Outings
			Acquisition of parent substitute
			Supports
			Adequacy of help
			Rutter B Questionnaire
			General communication
			Child smoking, drinking, drugs
			Child's appetite

Source: From Black & Urbanowicz, 1987.

trol groups at second-year follow-up. Although most of the significant findings had disappeared, the trends still pointed in the same direction. The treated children were still talking more about the dead parent and had fewer adverse behavior changes, and their parents were in better physical health. By the second-year follow-up, about 50% of the children had some kind of substitute for the dead parent, although only seven parents actually remarried. There seemed to be an association between the avoidance of talking and the provision of a substitute parent: significantly fewer children talked about their dead parent if a substitute existed. The attentuation of differences that were observed between the first- and second-year follow-up appears to be due to the attrition of the control sample, which did not occur with the treated sample. The control children who did not participate in the second-year follow-up interview were those who, at the first-year follow-up, were the most disturbed and had inhibited their grief. Although statistical evidence shows only a very modest difference in favor of the treatment group, there are indications that the intervention was helpful. Concern had been expressed by some colleagues that arousing children's grief and eliciting their feelings of sorrow might be harmful, but this does not appear to have been the case. On the contrary, those who cried more seemed to do better at follow-up. Looking at all the variables, almost all the outcome measures were more favorable in the treatment group, although they failed to reach statistical significance.

In this study we were able to conclude that our intervention had done no harm and had made a modest contribution to shortening the period of distress following bereavement. The findings of Harris and her colleagues (Harris, Brown & Bifulco, 1986) supported the suggestion that whether a woman who had been bereaved in childhood developed an adult psychiatric disorder was dependent on whether her care subsequent to the loss was adequate. Bearing

Table 3   Major Differences between Treatment (T) and Control (C) Groups at Second-Year Follow-Up

Variable	N	%	Significance
Children			
Behavior changes[a]	T(38)	39	
(for the worse)	C(34)	62	n.s.
Talking about dead parent	T(38)	82	
	C(35)	60	n.s.
School problems	T(31)	0	
	C(29)	14	n.s.
Behaviour problems[b] (as measured	T(22)	33	
by aggregate score)	C(15)	56	n.s.
Health (children under 8 years)	T(12)	50	
	C(15)	13	n.s.
Parents			
Health problems	T(20)	5	
	C(18)	39	$P = 0.03$
Depressed	T(21)	14	
	C(18)	33	n.s.

[a]Behavior changes = no change, regressive, conduct, emotional, other.
[b]Behavior problems = sleep, appetite disorders, mood, crying, ease of communication, smoking, drugs, alcohol.
Source: From Black & Urbanowicz, 1987.

this in mind, it may be that by our intervention we enhanced the coping skills of the surviving parents, thus enabling them to feel less helpless, more in control of family life, and more able to give better care to their children.

CHILDREN FACED WITH MURDER OF MOTHER

Because of my interest in bereaved children, I recently discovered that I had seen a large number of children bereaved by the death of their mother who had been killed by their father. We published our findings on a group of 28 children (Black & Kaplan, 1988) and have now seen a further 22 children. These children have suffered many losses. Not only have they lost their mother, but also they have been parted from father, home, school, friends, and often siblings. The issues for these children include not only bereavement (due to a sudden, violent, unexpected death) but also often the trauma of witnessing their mother's violent death at their father's hand, followed by posttraumatic stress disorder characterized by repetitive nightmares (Pynoos & Eth, 1985). In addition, problems arise if children live with relatives, since the mother's relatives will often alienate the children from the father and his relatives, and the fathers' relatives may denigrate the dead mother as one who "deserved to die."

What should these children be told about their mother's death? Should the children visit their father in prison? Should the father retain custody rights? Should therapy be available routinely for these children? What happens when the father is released from prison? In my opinion these children—who are fortunately rare, in Great Britain at least—deserve the best available expertise if we are to prevent or minimize later mental health problems. Our experience is that all the children are aware of the nature of their mother's death and desperately need an opportunity to understand what happened. We are presently offering sibling group psychotherapy and family therapy with these children and their foster parents.

CHILDREN WITH A LIFE-THREATENING ILLNESS

Chronic or life-threatening illness in a child or parent has effects on all individuals in the family, and on their relationships to each other and to people outside the family (Black & Wood, 1989). Children with fatal illnesses are more concerned about death and perceive themselves to be more isolated (Clunies-Ross & Lansdown, 1988). The incidence of behavior problems in leukemic children is high, and this may be related to the lack of openness within the family. Child cancer survivors have significant psychological sequelae (reviewed in Black & Wood, 1989). Studies of morbidity in the siblings of sick children show high rates (up to 75%) of psychological disturbance. The parents, too, present high levels of psychological problems. Marriages are put under stress by the demands of the sick child and by the treatment needs, which often separate parents and increase work and financial strains. The siblings of dead children also show high rates of disturbance.

Given this high morbidity, there seems to be a role for therapeutic intervention with at-risk families. The best way of helping children in these situations has not been systematically studied (see review of the literature in Black, 1989). In our department at the Royal Free Hospital, London, a team of child psychiatrists, psychologists, social workers, family therapists, psychotherapists, and psychiatric nurses offers services to families facing the life-threatening illness of one of their members. We become involved with all the children who are having a bone-marrow transplant for leukemia and all children in end-stage renal failure in our hospital. We are currently evaluating the relative efficacy of individual and family therapy with children in end-stage renal failure, who are undergoing dialysis and transplantation. In a pilot study we have found high levels of morbidity in these children (McFadyen, Black & Trompeter, 1991), affecting compliance with medical treatment (Altschuler, Black, Trompeter & Fitzpatrick, 1991). Other issues that need to be addressed are connected with changes in the child as a result of treatment (e.g., intellectual deterioration) and child care issues, particularly those of siblings.

Illness changes families. If a mother accompanies a child to hospital, the family life is disrupted and the family unit is reorganized. An aunt or grandmother may become a substitute parent. Frequently, the elder sister is recruited or offers herself as a substitute mother, an act that may have long-term effects. A sick child can be overprotected by both parents and siblings. There are particular problems when a family member acts as a donor for a sick child—for example, a bone-marrow transplant from a sibling or a kidney transplant from a parent. The donor is likely to have emotional problems, particularly if a graft is unsuccessful.

Finally, it is important to address issues of death and dying in an open way within the family. Parents try to protect children from the realization that an illness is potentially fatal, but various studies have shown that, at some stage, children learn about their prognosis, although they may protect parents from becoming aware of their knowledge. Bluebond-Langner (1978) has written about "mutual pretense," which is maladaptive and certainly results in loneliness and isolation for the child.

Taking into account the development of the child's concept of death (Lansdown & Benjamin, 1985), the therapist's task is to model appropriate open communication and help families find a language that children can use to talk about death. It is important to work within the family's belief system while helping parents to reframe religious beliefs in a mentally healthy and developmentally comprehensible way. In a recent article (Black, 1989) that reviewed the results of various family therapy studies with children facing life-threatening illness, only one study evaluated family therapy and it was found to be effective (Bellomo, 1986).

PARENTS WITH A LIFE-THREATENING ILLNESS

When a parent has a life-threatening illness, both parents may need help with understanding and facing the implications of the diagnosis for their family and themselves. The task of the family therapist is to ascertain what is known, what is understood, and who knows and understands it. It is essential to address child care issues. Parents often feel helpless to plan for the care of their children. Attachment bonds are disrupted and child care compromised in the acute emergency surrounding the diagnosis and hospital admission. The therapist should be able to help parents explore the available options, such as negotiating time off work on compassionate grounds for the healthy parent or grandparent. The therapist should also help them find the least detrimental solution for the care of their children. It is important to bear in mind the principles of continuity of care and gradual transfer of care of young children, as well as the maintenance of some constancy in the lives of these children.

A further task is that of helping to cope with the psychological effects that the diagnosis has on the patient and family. These can often lead to feelings of hopelessness, and the task of the therapist is to find some way of helping to infuse a feeling of mastery to counteract the psychological dangers of giving up and feeling helpless. Dying parents may need help with such tasks as making a will, assigning guardians for the children, preparing children to face their death, and giving permission for life to go on without them. In making plans, the dying parent exercises some control over the future, and this aids mastery. One way of doing this is for the parent to imagine the children, birthday by birthday, and write letters to each child, to be opened at the appropriate time. This act requires some guidance and supervision, or it may leave the child with the imperative to carry out the dead parent's expressed wish, which may be too costly. A study by Rosenheim & Reicher (1985) compares the levels of anxiety in children who were told, and those who were not told, of the terminal nature of their parent's illness. Those who were told showed significantly less anxiety, even within the same family. The authors note that most uninformed children have some knowledge of the ominous nature of the parent's disease. It is important too, to address issues of intimacy between the couple, and in particular the maintenance of physical closeness in the absence of the ability to have sexual intercourse. Needless to say, any work carried out with families facing terminal illness must be continued after the death of the sick member.

In summary, help for the bereaved child should start before bereavement. It is essential to maintain a family viewpoint even though treatment may be at an individual level.

REFERENCES

Altschuler, J., Black, D., Trompeter, R., & Fitzpatrick, M. (1991). Systemic factors in adherence to a medical regime in adolescents with renal failure. Manuscript submitted for publication.

Bellomo, P. A. (1986). An initial investigation of the effects of family therapy on adaptability and cohesion in cancer patient families. *Dissertation Abstracts International, 47*(2A), 419–420.

Black, D. (1978). Annotation: The bereaved child. *Journal of Child Psychology & Psychiatry, 19,* 287–292.

Black, D. (1981). Mourning and the family. In S. Walrond-Skinner (Ed.), *Developmental family therapy.* London: Routledge & Kegan Paul.

Black, D. (1989). Life-threatening illness, children and family therapy. *Journal of Family Therapy, 11,* 81–101.

Black, D., & Kaplan, T. (1988). Father kills mother. *British Journal of Psychiatry, 153,* 624–630.

Black, D., & Urbanowicz, M. A. (1985). Bereaved children—Family intervention. In J. E. Stevenson. (Ed.), *Recent research in developmental psychopathology.* Oxford: Pergamon.

Black, D., & Urbanowicz, M. A. (1987). Family intervention with bereaved children. *Journal of Psychology & Psychiatry, 28,* 467–476.

Black, D., & Wood, D. (1989). Family therapy and life-threatening illness in children or parents. *Palliative Medicine, 3,* 113–118.

Bluebond-Langner, J. (1978). *The private worlds of dying children.* Princeton: Princeton University Press.

Clunies-Ross, C., & Lansdown, R. (1988). Concepts of death, illness, and isolation found in children with leukaemia. *Child: Care, Health and Development, 14,* 373–386.

Harris, T., Brown, G. W., & Bifulco, A. (1986). Loss of parent in childhood and adult psychiatric disorder. *Psychological Medicine, 16,* 641–659.

Lansdown, R., & Benjamin, G. (1985). The development of the concept of death in children aged 5–9 years. *Child: Care, Health and Development, 11,* 13–20.

Lieberman, S., & Black, D. (1982). Loss, mourning and grief. In A. Bentovim et al. (Eds.), *Family therapy: Complementary frameworks or theory & practice.* London: Academic Press.

McFadyen, A., Black, D., & Trompeter, R. S. (1991). Psychosocial aspects of end-stage renal failure in children. Manuscript submitted for publication.

Parkes, C. M. (1980). Bereavement counselling—Does it work? *British Medical Journal, 181,* 3–6.

Pynoos, R. S., & Eth, S. (1985). Children traumatized by witnessing acts of personal violence. In S. Eth & R. S. Pynoos (Eds.), *Post-traumatic stress disorder in children.* New York: American Psychiatric Press.

Rosenheim, E., & Reicher, R. (1985). Informing children about a parent's terminal illness. *Journal of Child Psychology & Psychiatry, 26,* 995–998.

Part Three

Dying Children, Families, and Professionals

Chapter 11

The Dying Child

Elisabeth Kübler-Ross

As human beings, each of us consists of four quadrants (see Figure 1). We are not simply made of a body, a brain, and a heart. In the new era, modern medicine begins to work with all aspects of human beings—the physical, emotional, intellectual, and spiritual quadrants. The latter develops automatically when the other three are in balance and when individuals have the courage to be honest with themselves.

THE PHYSICAL QUADRANT

Taking care of the *physical quadrant* is a priority during the first year of life. This is true for both healthy, "normal" children, as well as for disabled and retarded ones. When you take care of babies, you nurse them by touching them, hugging them, smooching and kissing them, and thus providing them with a lot of necessary physical contact. In some cultures of American Indians—the

Copyright 1991 by Elisabeth Kübler-Ross. All rights reserved.

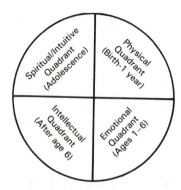

Figure 1 The four quadrants of each human being.

aboriginals—natives carry their babies during the first year of their life, in a pouch at either the front or the back of their body, so as to maintain this much-needed physical contact.

Unfortunately, in modern society, children who are very sick and placed in an intensive care unit, where they are hooked to machines, are deprived of physical contact, since nobody touches them. These children have a very bad prognosis, even if they physically survive. The same is true of 3,000 AIDS babies in the United States. They are not hugged, loved, kissed, or touched. In the old days in 1981, when I started working with AIDS patients, caregivers were terribly afraid to get close to them. They used to go to these children with goggles, masks, gowns, and boots! They looked like robots and were very scary to the children.

Physical contact, which is so important during the first year of life, is also mandatory during the last years of life. Unfortunately, old people—who end up in nursing homes—are not hugged and touched any more. They become senile and just sit and stare into space; they live in a world of fantasy. My big dream—before I die—is to change all nursing homes and develop "E.T. Centers" instead.

E.T. is the movie of unconditional love. In E.T. Centers, *E* stands for elderly people and *T* stands for toddlers. Old people who have contributed to society for 70 or 80 years deserve a place of peace, love, compassion, and understanding. They could have their own place in these centers, but they would have to make their payment for it, not in money but by taking care of a toddler. Working parents could send their toddlers to these E.T. Centers without worrying about sexual or physical child abuse or baby-sitting payments. They could just drop them at the E.T. Centers, and the elderly would each pick the child they would love the most. Old people could be biased and prejudiced in choosing redheads or black curly-heads, boys or girls. Everyone has his or her preference, and when I am very old, I know, I will choose a little boy with black, curly hair. The rule would then be for each one to spoil one child rotten, not by buying them things, but rather by taking them on their laps, by telling them stories of their homeland, by rocking, and stroking them, by touching them, and by loving them totally. Little children love old-looking faces with wrinkles. The more wrinkles, the better they like it. Every wrinkle is a story of one's life. We spend 6 billion dollars in America to erase wrinkles, when children love them; if you have pimples on top of that, it is a gift from heaven, as children will play piano on the pimples!

These E.T. Centers would provide old people with a reason to live, since they would feel wanted, needed, and of service. They could share their total, unconditional love. They would never say stupid things like those parents tend to say: "Oh, I will love you if you bring good grades from school," or "I will love you if I can say my son is a doctor." There are no "ifs" for older people. Therefore, if children grow up with unconditional love and old people are loved, touched, hugged, and kissed again, I can guarantee there will be less senility in those E.T. Centers. What I am suggesting also holds true for dying adults and dying children.

THE EMOTIONAL QUADRANT

The *emotional quadrant* is developed between the ages of 1 and 6, when a child receives enough love and physical contact. However, it is during this period that most people develop hang-ups and unnatural fears, because frequently they are not allowed to express their natural emotions (see Table 1). Think of how many million fears we adults have: fear of failure, of rejection, of death, of war, of hunger, of being unloved, of being rich, of being poor. Children are not

Table 1   Natural and Unnatural Emotions

Natural Emotions	Distorted, Unnatural Emotions
Fear: Of falling from high places, of loud, unexpected noises	Fears of failure, rejection, not being loved, success, suffering, violence, boss, neighbors' opinions
Grief: How we deal with loss, expressed by tears and sharing	Self-pity, extended bad moods, depression, guilt, shame, self-reproach, blame
Anger (takes 15 seconds): Brings about change, assertiveness, self-protection	Prolonged anger, rage, hate, revenge, bitterness, resentment
Jealousy: Stimulus and motivator for growth	Envy, competition, possessiveness, self-condemnation
Love (unconditional): Care, concern, nurturance, ability to say no, set limits to help others become independent, self-worth, self-trust, self-love	I love you, if . . . (conditional): leads to pleasing others, to "buy" their love and/or approval (we call this prostitution)

born with these fears. They experience only two natural fears: the fear of falling from high places, and the fear of sudden loud noises. Both fears are important for survival. Later on children are naturally afraid of separation, since abandonment and the absence of a loving caretaker affect their development in a negative way. All other fears we develop are totally unnatural.

Hurt and *grief*, expressed by tears, are natural emotions. How many of us between the ages of 1 and 6 were allowed to sob and cry, without being inhibited by anybody. Most adults tend to say to children who cry: "Stop crying," or "Here she goes again," or "Are you a sissy?" or "If you don't stop crying, I'll give you something to cry about." When you are not allowed to cry, you develop into an adult marinated in self-pity and depression. The "poor-me syndrome" originates from the time you were stopped from crying naturally. Healthy children cry. For instance, when children fall off their bicycle, they cry, but if nobody makes a big fuss over it, two minutes later they are back on the bicycle again.

Anger is also a natural emotion. Think what happened when you were angry as a child. What punishment did you get? Were you spanked, belted, beaten with all sorts of instruments? What you probably learned was that you are not allowed to be angry. When you repress and sit on your anger for years and years, you become a head-lock. There is a head-lock in all of us, and we need to have courage to get rid of our piled-up anger, resentment, and negativity.

Jealousy is another natural emotion, which children experience as they copy and emulate other children. However, they learn to repress it, since adults consider it an inappropriate response. Thus, they develop into very envious, competitive adults.

Finally, *love* is a natural emotion, but also the biggest problem, in our western societies. All we have learned is "I will love you *if* . . . " and we raise our children with statements such as "I will love you *if* you become this or that." We therefore raise a whole generation of prostitutes. Prostitutes are people who do things to please others, not because they really want to, but because they think that other people will like them if, for example, they dress right, shave their beard, or go out with a guy from the same congregation.

By repressing all these natural emotions, we become individuals full of unnaturalness, full of unfinished business, individuals who deprive ourselves of the chance to develop our spiritual quadrant.

Repressing natural emotions also has physical consequences. Repressed grief will affect your gastrointestinal and pulmonary system; repressed anger along with repressed fear will wear down your coronary system. Unfinished business can have repercussions on your physical health. I am not saying that repressed grief is the sole cause of asthma, but it can be an important contributing factor to it.

One day I went to visit a 6-year-old boy who was dying of cancer and who was able to talk about it, since he knew that his time was very limited. His parents were also quite open about it, and I was surprised at how easy it was to talk with the three of them. Usually when I make home visits, I take with me some sheets of paper and a box of crayons and ask family members to draw a picture. Grown-ups take forever to draw a picture, so I always tell them I have to catch a plane in 15 minutes and then they draw it in 10. Children on the other hand, draw it in 2 or 3 minutes. The less they use their heads, the more genuine the drawing.

The father, mother, and boy each drew a picture, which was very easy to understand. After I had explained the drawings to them, and I was ready to leave, I saw at the other end of the living room another little boy, sitting on the floor, doodling on a piece of paper. I thought he was a visiting neighbor and walked toward him, asking, "Who is this?" The boy with cancer said, "Well, this is my brother." I was surprised. The brother of the boy who had cancer? I wanted to ask why he wasn't included. Why was he an outsider? Why wasn't he allowed to draw a picture and be a part of the family? But I did not say anything. I just walked over to him and said, "I want you to walk me to my car." In a split second he grabbed my hand and held it tightly. Through the open door he said very loudly, "I presume you know I have asthma," to which I replied, "This doesn't surprise me." His mother looked shocked and wanted to walk me to my car, but I gave her a sign and said, "You stay right here. I am going to my car with this little boy, just he and I." When we reached the car, you could already see she had pulled the curtain. Some parents are very snoopy. They want to peek and to hear what is said, but children need confidentiality and privacy, just like adults. So I half-closed the door, so she could not see us, and we both sat in the front seat of the car.

I then said, "So you have asthma," and looked at him questioningly. "Yes, but it is not good enough," he replied. "Ah, it's not good enough. Why are you saying that?" I asked him. "Look at my brother who has cancer," he said, "he gets everything. They take him to Disneyland, he gets an electric train set, he gets anything he wants or asks for. The other day I really needed a football so I went to my father and said 'I need a football' and he answered, 'You can't have it'." This boy had enough natural anger to say to his father "Why not?" and the father, who was very angry with him, said "Would you rather have cancer?" What he was really saying was "your brother is dying and we have to try and catch up because he is going to miss so much. So he has to get everything he can now. You have your whole life ahead of you." This is the wrong message to give to siblings of dying children. In fact, this is why this boy developed asthma and believed it was probably "not good enough." Such messages need to be addressed and discussed with the parents. Preventive interventions could have contributed to preventing this boy from developing asthma and becoming a psychosomatic cripple, just because he felt left out. To include siblings is a very important part of work in preventive psychiatry. This also holds true for grandparents, who are often left out. It is especially difficult for grandmothers and grandfathers who suffer the sorrow of their own child's experience as well as that of their grandchild.

I will share another example of repressed anger and rage from my own personal experience. After 15 years of running workshops and trying to teach what unconditional love is all about, I got in touch with my own unfinished business. One day I received a phone call from Hawaii and was asked to give a workshop to help people with their unfinished business. I accepted, providing they would find a nice convent, plenty of land around, a nice kitchen, a small chapel, and hopefully some decent food for about 100 people. Unfortunately, Hawaii does not have such places, since all it has are Hiltons, Sheratons, and locations that are not conducive to this kind of sharing.

A year later, as I was about to give up the trip to Hawaii, a woman whom I did not know called and said she had just the right place for me. The only drawback was that the workshop would be held sometime in April of the following year. I sent a deposit, to be certain I would get the place, and then forgot all about it. Shortly before the beginning of the workshop, I received a letter with the details. I was outraged and had a temper tantrum such as I have not had since I was 3 years old. When your emotional quadrant overreacts, the intellectual quadrant comes to your rescue with rationalizations: "You are entitled to be mad for the following reasons . . . "

One reason I was furious, I thought, was because the workshop had been scheduled for Easter week. Easter week is a terrible week for workshops, since you cannot celebrate Easter. I thought I was a terrible mother, being away from home and from my own children, and felt "poor me." But I knew well that this was all nonsense, since it was not the reason I was having a temper tantrum. So I assumed I was in rage because Catholics and Jews would not be able to attend my workshop, due to holidays. I was aware that all these excuses were phony. I finally went to Hawaii. I had to teach about unconditional love, and I was miserable. I tried to control myself, but I was still angry. I had to put a lid on something, yet I did not even know what it was.

The workshop was being held in a residential school for girls. The owner of the school, a very sweet minister (I hate people who are sugarcoated and sweet), invited himself to the workshop. He showed me the room I was supposed to stay in for the entire week. The moment I opened the door, I said to him, "I can't stay in this room." The teenagers had not been told that their rooms had been rented out to other people and had, therefore, left their belongings on their desks or tables, which made me feel like an intruder. The reason I felt so neurotic was because I grew up as a triplet and never had any privacy. We had to share everything—shoes, dresses, even grade cards—because the teacher could not tell us apart. Therefore, intruding on somebody's space was for me inconceivable. At that moment, I really hated the minister.

By the end of the first day, he came up to me, and in front of 90 people said, "Your group eats too much." I could not tell him that teenagers eat more than my old people, but I took my revenge at the end of the meal when I suggested to the participants, "How about finishing the spaghetti? Would you like to finish the meatballs? There is another piece of bread left, let's clear up." The first night he requested 25 cents for a cup of coffee; later, he asked 10 cents for a sheet of paper for the drawings, and finally 60 cents for a box of crayons. It went from bad to worse. I did not have the courage to tell him that he was a cheap, stingy man, so I was revengeful the whole week.

When I left the workshop I was drained. I had done my work as long as I did not have to look at this man in the corner, but I knew he had pushed a button in me that nobody had ever pushed before. Yet I had gone through seven years of medical school, three years of psychiatry, three years of child psychiatry and classical psychoanalysis, and nobody had ever pushed that button. As I was flying home, I was thinking intently, what buttons had this man pushed? By the time the plane landed, I had discovered I was allergic to stingy men, without knowing where this feeling had come from and what it meant.

My friends who met me at the airport asked repeatedly how the workshop had gone, and I reluctantly answered, "Nice work, fine." But they did not let me off the hook. They became very sweet, stroked my hair (a thing I hate), and said, "Tell us all about bunnies." I instantly had a temper tantrum: "I am 50 years old, I do not believe in Easter bunnies any more, so don't you talk to me like this." Suddenly, everything poured out, the anguish, the agony, the sense of unfairness and insensitivity.

As my emotions poured out, my memory returned, and I remembered the time when my sisters and I were tiny, identical triplets. My mother always had one triplet on one side of her lap, a second on the other, and there was no third side left. My salvation became my bunnies. I raised them, and when I needed love, a hug, a touch of fur, or warmth, I would go to them. They were the only living creatures that knew me from my sisters, and I loved them beyond anything I can ever describe. The tragedy was that my father was an authoritarian, stingy Swiss, who wanted to eat a roast rabbit every so often. So once every six months he insisted I take one of my bunnies to the butcher.

I therefore had to pick my love object, take it in my arms, try to explain to it that I had no choice, and take it to the butcher. Later the butcher would come out with a paper bag in his hand, with the warm meat inside. I had to carry it home—half an hour in the mountains—and sit at table, watching my family eat my beloved pet. I never cried because I thought they did not love me and therefore did not deserve to know I was hurt. Every six months, after I had recuperated from the death of one of my bunnies, the next one's turn would come, and then the next. My last bunny was named Blacky (that is why I love black-haired children). I was 6½ years old when my father said I had to take Blacky to the butcher. I knelt down and begged Blacky to run away, since that would be the only way it could live. But Blacky loved me so much that it did not move. So I had to pick it up and take it to the butcher (who was a redhead, and that is why I don't like redheads). When he came out with the warm meat in a paper bag, he said: "Damn shame you had to bring this rabbit . . . in a day or two she would have had babies." I did not even know that it was a female! I was devastated. I remember walking up the mountain like a zombie, with no feelings, absolutely no emotions whatsoever. I delivered the meat to the kitchen and needless to say, I never ever had a rabbit pet again.

Reflecting upon this experience, from the point of view of a psychiatrist, I can now understand that each time I meet a stingy or thrifty man, the memory recurs, so I have to put a lid on it, tighter and tighter. If you keep a lid on a pressure cooker, or on a volcano, you can only do it for 10, 20, perhaps 50 years. But then a moment will come when someone pushes the pressure cooker and it explodes. This is how people become mass murderers. Two years after I resolved my problem with the black bunny, I went to a prison and asked the authorities to allow me to work with the criminals and to help them discover the "black bunny" in them. There are no bad people in this world. There are people who have been damaged or abused as children, and all we need to do is help them grow and develop more naturally.

THE SPIRITUAL QUADRANT

The *spiritual quadrant* is the greatest gift you ever give yourself. You do not have to work for it, you just have to be natural, the way you were created. When children are raised naturally, they develop their spiritual quadrant during adolescence. This means that as teenagers they know what they want to be, whether they wish to leave the country or to follow a different profession from what their parents had in mind, and they actually have the courage to go ahead and accomplish their goals.

These people do not die sad, bitter, and resentful. They do not end up saying, "You know, Dr. Ross, I made a good living, but I've never really lived." To which I respond, "What does it mean for you to have 'really lived'?" They answer, "I was a successful doctor and I am sure I helped a lot of people, but I really wanted to become a dancer." It is very sad that some people look back on their lives as if they had never lived.

We have to find out what we want early in life, so as to have the chance to change our profession, even at the risk of being broke for a couple of years, and even if all must be provided for. When our spiritual quadrant is opened up, then we know that if we follow our heart and not some other person's expectations, we will be provided with all we need.

The spiritual is the most important quadrant. It is developed through unconditional love we receive from grandparents, sometimes from a cleaning woman, at times from a stranger. If we have received five minutes of unconditional love in our early life, those five minutes will sustain us through time and help us through the windstorms of life.

These windstorms are all the tragedies in our life. If you shield the Grand Canyon from windstorms, you will never see its beauty. This symbolism refers to the wrinkles you develop in your life and spend so much money trying to erase.

WORKING WITH DYING CHILDREN

The spiritual quadrant is most important, especially when working with dying children who use a symbolic language almost exclusively. All children know, even 2- and 3-year-olds, when they have terminal illness, and they all know when they are dying. They can teach us things we do not know, but which they know from their spiritual quadrant. There is not a single child, not even a child who has been murdered—and I have worked with thousands of parents of murdered children—who has not left a message behind, in which one could see in retrospect that they "knew" their life was going to end. Even when it is a totally unexpected, accidental death, they all "know." They do not know it cognitively—and therefore cannot talk about it—but they know it intuitively.

If you become a helper to a dying patient—an adult or a child—and your spiritual quadrant is open, then you will understand the communication of these children. They do not look *at* you, but rather *through* you. They know if you are phony and afraid; if so, they will not share their knowledge with you. If, however, you are totally unafraid, then they will tell you things they would never tell anybody else. This does not take weekly or monthly sessions, but simply the open heart of someone who sits with the child and holds his or her hand. Some children share everything with a parent who is open and receptive; however, most of the time they tend to protect parents and use a third person who is not so close. If you work with dying patients, I would suggest you work during night shifts and sit at their bedside, when no visitors are around. Within a few minutes they will tell you more than they would during the daytime.

When you work with dying children, you realize that they are not born with the fear of death, but are mostly afraid of being buried. They have watched funeral scenes on television, or have seen their grandparents buried—placed in a box that is nailed down, put in a big hole, and then covered with mud—and they are mostly afraid that their grandfather or grandmother will not be able to breathe anymore.

We have developed a model to help us explain death to children. According to it, the physical body—which is either cremated or buried—is represented as a cocoon. This cocoon is what each of us looks like. At the moment of death—whether it is a sudden death or a slow, lingering one, whether it is homicide, suicide, or other forms of death—the cocoon opens up and releases the individual's butterfly, which is even more beautiful than the cocoon. What is buried is the cocoon, not the butterfly.

Research work on death and life after death reveals that when the physical body is no longer able to maintain life—when there are no vital signs, no blood pressure, no pulse—then the "butterfly" is released and the individual enters a state of total awareness. It is important to distinguish *awareness* from *consciousness*. With awareness one knows everybody's thoughts. This state is referred to as a "near death" or "out of body" experience. The person is not dead yet, because he or she is still connected to the cocoon, but is in a place or state of transition. In this place or state of transition, the person can go anywhere with the speed of thought—close to family members or to whomever else he or she needs to be with. In addition, all those the person has loved, and who preceded the person in death, are waiting to accompany him or her in the afterlife. No human being can die alone.

Dying children know that when they think of their mother or father they are already with them. Many children, after long periods of having their parents sitting at their bedside, suddenly send them home: 'Mommy, why don't you go home, take a rest, and have a shower. I am really all right." And usually the mother goes home and takes a shower and a nap and then receives a phone call: "Sorry, Mrs. Johnson, your little girl just died." Then all these mothers wonder why they left the hospital at this crucial moment, after having been there for months and months. In fact, what really happens is that children want to be able to let go and usually mothers, who are at their bedside, say to them, "Honey, don't die. I cannot live without you," and thus make children feel guilty for dying.

There comes a time, after you have tried everything that science and medicine have to offer, when you hear a child say, "It's enough now." If you love someone unconditionally, you will be able to hear that, no matter how much it hurts, and you will have the courage to let go.

Jeffrey had had six years of leukemia in nine years of life. What happens when $2/3$ of your life has been spent in pain, in chemotherapy, with hair loss, throwing up, diarrhea, or other side-effects? God's gift to you is the ability to use a compensatory mechanism whenever you lose something. Children who suffer a lot develop their spiritual quadrant at an earlier age, thus compensating for their declining physical health. This is why dying children are so wise. When you talk to them, you think you are talking to a wise elder. Jeffrey was a boy like that. He had said loud and clear that this was the last treatment he wanted. I expected that his parents would really be able to hear that and respect his wish. One day, as I went back to the hospital, I saw the door of his room open. Jeffrey was lying on the bed, looking devastated and pathetic. As I walked into the room, I saw a young doctor talking to the parents about Jeffrey, but not to Jeffrey. "Don't worry," the young physician said, "we will just try another experimental chemotherapy." I looked at Jeffrey's face, which had dropped, and asked, "Did anyone ask Jeffrey if that is what he wants?" To which the doctor replied, "You don't ask a 9-year-old child what kind of therapy he wants." I then said, "I know, but he should be included because if he doesn't want the therapy, if he doesn't fight, if he doesn't participate, there is no chance of it being effective . . . no chance! Do you mind if I ask him?" They didn't dare say no, so I asked Jeffrey, "How about it?" He gave me the most beautiful answer any child has ever given me: "I don't understand these grown-ups who have to make me so sick to get me well." Finally, the parents got the message: why should they make him more and more sick if he was not going to get well anyway? Jeffrey insisted he be discharged from the hospital right then and there.

Initially I thought that I had just happened to be there. But on second thought I do not believe it was a coincidence. What other people refer to as coincidence, I call *demand manipulation*. I knew I was there for a purpose, to make sure that somebody was there with Jeffrey.

This boy insisted, "You will come home with me." As I looked at my watch, he said, "Don't worry, it will only take 10 minutes." I can give 10 minutes to a dying child, no matter what my next appointment is. So we drove home, and as the car pulled into the garage, Jeffrey looked at his watch, because he had promised it would take only 10 minutes. He crawled out of the car, very weak, very pale, barely able to move his arms, and said to his father, "I want you to take the bicycle down." The bicycle had been hanging on the wall for two years. Jeffrey's biggest dream had been to ride—under his own power—around the block once more, but he had never been able to do it. The father took the bicycle down, and I stood there. Nobody knew what was going to happen next. Then, with tears in his eyes, Jeffrey said to his father, "Pop, put the training wheels on my bicycle." Can you imagine how much courage it takes for a 9-year-old boy to ask for training wheels? The father put the training wheels on the bicycle to make it more stable, and the boy looked at me with a big smile on his face and said, "You, Elisabeth, are only here to hold my Mom back. My father could not do it, so you will have to do it."

The mother wanted to allow this frail, weak boy to get on the bicycle, but she would have run around the block holding him the whole way. She would thereby have cheated him out of his triumph: to ride around the block once in his lifetime, on his own. I held Mom back, the father held me back—because I am a mother too and I felt very tempted—and we all restrained our impulse to help and rescue. Jeffrey drove off like a drunken man, and when he returned it was as if he had won a gold medal at the Olympics. He was all smiles and full of happiness. He then turned and said to me, "You can go now." I was dismissed! No sentimentality, nothing! That was the last time I saw Jeffrey. It was the biggest gift he could ever have given me. His parents could also keep the memory of Jeffrey's triumphant tour around the block on his bicycle, rather than a memory of him hooked to machines undergoing another experimental chemotherapy.

THE LANGUAGE OF DYING CHILDREN

If you open up your own spiritual quadrant you will hear the young patients' symbolic language. This symbolic language can be verbal and nonverbal. They look at you and know if they can trust you. To make sure that you are what they think you are, they use symbolic language, and if you shake your head and pretend to be a psychiatrist, without having the slightest idea of what they are talking about, they will dismiss you and will not talk to you any more. If, on the other hand, you are very honest and say, "I think you are trying to tell me . . ." they will respond and will correct you if you are wrong, by giving you several examples until you finally get their message.

If you are not able to hear the verbal symbolic language, give them a sheet of paper and a box of crayons and ask them to draw any picture. Through this nonverbal language, children can express the awareness of their illness, the localization of their tumor, and even the years or months they have left to live. Then, they observe how you react to their drawing. If you say, "Very nice," and just put it away, they are not likely to give you another picture, feeling they have overestimated you.

Your task is to understand and to explain to the parents what the child is trying to tell them, so that they can stop lying. Lying to children, whether you are a physician, a nurse, a clergyman, or a social worker, is detrimental, because they will then never trust you again.

I would like to share an experience I had in Switzerland, a year ago. After a lecture I gave to a large audience, several people came up wanting to tell me their stories. Some of them had lost someone, while others were seriously ill. Usually the ones who come do not really need help, while those who stay back in the audience are the ones most in need.

That day, I noticed a man in the audience who was the picture of pain and anguish. I left everyone and walked over to him and said, "You need to talk." He replied, "Here?" "No," I said, "it doesn't need to be here, we can go into the bushes." This sounded awful, but he had a smile on his face. Anyone who is the picture of pain and anguish and can smile about some stupid verbal expression still has some hope. I then said to him, "Let's go." We went out and literally stood behind some bushes, and I asked him to be brief. He said he had a 15-year-old son who had just been diagnosed as having a sarcoma of the leg and who was dying. The physician had told the father that his son would have to undergo a leg amputation, but even so, the prognosis was very, very poor. All this was bad enough, but the tragedy was that he had left his wife and only son a few years ago, to marry another woman with four children. Since divorce is not recognized by the Catholic Church, he believed he was living in sin and was convinced that God had sent him this punishment for leaving his wife and son. I then said to him, "I am sorry, I cannot help you. I do not know of a revengeful God who punishes parents by taking the life of a child or making a child suffer. I do not know of a revengeful, punishing, mean God. I know only of a God who is all, total, personified, unconditional love. Since this is the only God I know, I cannot help you with your God, but I can help you with your boy." He then said, "Well, you cannot help me because we promised the physician not to reveal the truth to my son." In the parents' presence, the physician had told this young, athletic boy that he only had a virus. They had all covered reality with a lie.

I suggested to the father that he meet me with his son at ten o'clock at my hotel, bringing along a box of crayons and some sheets of paper. At ten o'clock sharp, they came. I asked the boy to draw a picture. He said, "I can't draw." "I will have to leave without helping you," I replied. He drew very fast. He drew a dead tree, with dirty brown and black branches and no leaves. There was only one leaf hanging in the lower right quadrant. On the left side of the trunk of this tree was a cockroach, eating up the tree from the inside, thus making a huge hole in it. You had the feeling that if this ugly bug would eat for another day or two, the tree would collapse and die. When the father saw the picture he wept. I then suggested that I should take him into another hotel room so as to read in privacy the picture drawn by his son.

Since the boy was going to wait, I asked him, "Do me a favor, draw one more picture after the treatment." He had a smile on his face. Note, I did not say "after chemotherapy" or "after amputation." I do not break the rules and laws the treating physician sets, even if I do not agree with them. While the father was listening to the reading of the drawing, this boy made the most fantastic picture I have ever seen. It was exactly the same tree, with lots of branches and baby green leaves, and on the right quadrant, where the lonely leaf was hanging in the previous drawing, there was a fat bird singing its lungs out. I looked at the picture and asked, "What is this bird doing here?" The boy answered, "Stupid, it just ate the bug." The last I heard of this boy was that he did not have a leg amputation and he was doing well.

This is the symbolic language dying children use. We use the same technique with adults when we want to find out what treatment is most effective in certain forms of terminal illness.

An example is an adult who was asked to portray his cancer. He drew a body filled with red concentric circles. These circles reflected his cancer, which had spread all over. His oncologist, a good man who really cared for him, wanted to treat him with a specific chemotherapy protocol, which statistically had a good prognosis. When I asked the man to portray the chemotherapy his physician had in mind, he drew black arrows, each of them pointing to these cells. His drawing was revealing that the chemotherapy treatment would not be effective, as the arrows only touched—without penetrating—the cells. I looked at this man and asked him, "What did the doctor tell you about the chemotherapy?" He answered, "He told me that in a split second the chemotherapy kills the cancer cells." He added, "Thou shall not kill." "Not even your cancer cells?" I asked. "No," he replied, "I was raised as a Quaker and was told I should not kill. I have lived according to these universal laws all my life and I cannot kill, not even my cancer cells." Then I said to him, "I really admire you for your courage in standing up for your convictions, but being a physician, wanting my patients to get well, I will ask you to do me a favor: go home and work out how you can get rid of your cancer."

A week later, the same man with the same cancer, the same oncologist, and the same chemotherapy returned. I handed to him a sheet of paper and a box of crayons. In his drawing, the body was now filled with little gnomes, tiny little dwarves. Each of the gnomes—and there were many of them—lovingly carried a cancer cell away. All I had to do then was to call the oncologist and tell him that he could now begin the treatment.

When you practice holistic medicine, you are able to hear where your patients are, without judging, criticizing, or mocking them. You just listen to them and respect what they have to say, while you take care of the physical, emotional, intellectual, and spiritual quadrants. This is how we are working currently with AIDS patients. I am very happy to inform you that of the 3,000 AIDS babies, 3 of them have become HIV-negative. They were born with AIDS, were repeatedly evaluated as HIV-positive. But as they were given love, nothing but love, they became HIV-negative.

Let me tell you the story of an Australian woman, who could not have children of her own. Being deeply religious, she prayed to the Virgin Mary, "You have to send me a child, I want to be a mother and take care of a child. Whatever child you pick will be fine for me." Two days later she received a telephone call from the hospital, saying they had a child for adoption. As she was ready to go and pick up this child, the social worker told her that the child had AIDS. "Fine, don't worry," the woman said to the social worker, who thought that she was dumb and did not realize what it meant to adopt a child with AIDS. This woman could not explain to the social worker that she had talked to the Virgin Mary and that she trusted that Mary would send her the child she needed.

This baby was HIV-positive during the first year of his life. A year later, this woman, her husband, and their adopted child went back to the hospital for the AIDS test and returned to their home in the mountains. A few days later they received a phone call telling them to come back to the hospital since something was wrong: the baby had been found HIV-negative! "I knew that," the woman said. Today the child is still HIV-negative and will stay that way.

Most people perceive AIDS as a terminal illness, a death penalty, since there is nothing that can be done about it. We know of 154 persons who have had all the positive symptoms of AIDS, and who, today, are well and healthy.

What we really need to learn when caring for dying patients is to love, not to judge. Be honest with ourselves and with our fellow human beings. I believe it is the only way we can really help.

Chapter 12

Utilizing Art and Imagery in Death and Dying Counseling

Sheryle R. Baker

For the past 16 years, my professional work in hospitals and private practice has focused upon terminally ill children and children grieving the death of a loved one. As we explored together the physical, emotional, psychological, and spiritual components of facing stressful illness or death, these children became my teachers. They often communicated their internal awareness of life losses, illness, death, and heaven through pictorial language and imagery.

The purpose of this chapter is to explore the therapeutic strategies of nonverbal communication in understanding and working with children's dying and/or grieving process. Using examples of spontaneous drawings, this work sheds light on the intuitive awareness of dying or grieving children. Combining examples of creative imagery exercises with these spontaneous and guided drawings, I will demonstrate the power of nonverbal communication. I will also describe experiential techniques, which are used to help reduce the internal stress in children who are dying and/or grieving the death of a loved one. In addition, I will offer guidelines to help facilitate caregivers' basic appreciation and interpretation of children's drawings and other nonverbal responses, and suggest that these techniques can help explore the reconciliation tasks of mourning and foster a sense of healing and reconnection to life. My objective is to enrich professionals' intuitive and intervention skills in death and dying counseling, and to offer tools to support nonverbal expression of loss in children.

SPONTANEOUS DRAWINGS AND THE DYING CHILD

The use of spontaneous drawings as a form of symbolic communication helps objectify the child's perspective of inner and outer reality. To understand the language of drawings, we need to accept three premises (Furth 1988, p. 16):

1 That there is an unconscious, and that pictures come from the same unconscious level as dreams.
2 That the picture is a valid and dependable method of communication with the unconscious.
3 That mind (psyche) and body (soma) are inherently linked.

These premises serve as internal guidelines to help therapists be aware of the interconnection between the unconscious and conscious expression as it is conveyed through pictures where there are no words.

Because terminally ill children are often unable to verbalize their feelings, their many concerns, fears, and conflicts may go unnoticed. Art therapist Susan Michal (1979) describes how seriously ill children are able to release tension through lines, colors, and forms in their drawings. In cases where there is amputation due to tumor growth and there is traumatic fear of lost limbs, these children illustrate pictures with body parts missing, even though they cannot talk about their own lost limbs. Their artwork conveys their genuine fears. Furth (1988) elaborates on the relevance of omission, or missing parts, as an interpretive focus in children's drawings. Susan Bach (1966) notes that significant omission of a particular body part or area shows evidence of new disease.

When seriously or terminally ill children lose a sense of control over themselves and their personal environment, they may mask it in withdrawn behavior and yet experience increased dependency upon others. Sometimes, in resisting the painful feelings accompanying this loss of control, dying children are caught in the emotional struggle between the need for contact and intimacy and the need to let go and wean themselves from those closest to them. As Judith Rubin (1978) points out, to experience letting go yet simultaneously remaining aware and ultimately in control is a profound lesson.

I have seen many children regress to infantile behavior to avoid the pain inherent in this paradoxical situation. For example, a young dying adolescent drew a self-portrait of a little girl in a crib with bars all around to express her isolation and fear of being trapped with no way out. In a guided imagery exercise, she explored what it would be like to float above and beyond the bars, freeing herself from her body that she described as "too cramped to live in anymore.'' She completed this experience by creating a drawing representing her floating body as a big golden balloon with a smiling face, flying freely upward away from the hospital bed. Thus, she was able to externalize her pain and gain control by finding a medium for her own resolution to the physical entrapment she originally experienced.

This example demonstrates how symbolic language provides the opportunity to objectify self-knowledge and hidden feelings or conflicts by translating symbolic clues from the unconscious into creative form. The drawing itself becomes part of the inner healing process, whereby chaotic unacceptable or repressed feelings are brought to light and given a form to which another person can relate (See also Edwards, 1979).

Through nonverbal symbolic art, children allow us a glimpse into their inner secret world. This art form provides a bridge to access their intuitive awareness and may ease some of their sense of isolation and fears of abandonment. Pictures often express children's internal knowledge of their disease, treatment, and prognosis, sometimes long before medical staff and protective families are able to share factual information with the child (see Figure 1).

A 9 1/2-year-old girl drew the picture in Figure 1 six months before she was diagnosed with terminal brain cancer. She expressed her inner knowledge that she would not live to celebrate her 10th birthday through her "life cake"—a strawberry cake with four strawberries inside it, symbolizing the connection to her four significant family members. The amazing predictive part of this drawing is her awareness of dying, drawn in the form of nine "life" candles and one "death" candle in black, falling over, broken, yet simultaneously releasing a butterfly, which flies freely towards the upper left corner. Bach (1966), Perkins (1976), and Furth (1988) interpret this direction as "setting sun," or death awareness. (See also Greenberg and Blank [1970], who refer to the unconscious recognition of death through images, themes, and symbols often appearing before the diagnosis of an illness, or despite conscious knowledge of the disease process.)

Elizabeth Kübler-Ross (1981) used the technique developed by Susan Bach, a Jungian analyst, to interpret drawings of dying children. Through this method, allowing free choice of form, color, and design, children often reveal knowledge of their impending death to those sensitive to such symbolic language. This was also confirmed in a study based on the collected artwork of 35 children, 20 of whom had life-threatening to terminal conditions, and 15 of whom were healthy (Perkins, 1976). The seriously ill children showed distinct death awareness through two key aspects of their artwork: *consistent color frequency* (e.g., the use of black to represent negative dark symbols, such as monsters, snakes, or skeletons, or the use of red in association with blood, especially with leukemic children); and *the situation of the sun* (drawn in the upper left-hand corner in all but one picture of the 20 children facing life-threatening illness and showing a correlation between symbols drawn on the

Figure 1 "Life cake" drawn by a 9½-year-old girl 6 months before she was diagnosed with terminal brain cancer, revealing her inner knowledge that she would not live to celebrate her 10th birthday.

left, which represented the past (setting sun), versus those drawn on the right, which represented the future).

Of the 16 children with life-threatening illnesses who drew houses, 10 showed possible indications of their diseased state within the body of the house, the most common symbol of self. Perkins illustrates this in a case of a 12-year-old girl with osteomyelitis of the right leg, meningitis, and congenital heart disease, who outlined, in heavy black marker, the lower right corner of the house she drew.

Both Perkins (1976) and Bach (1966) noted a seemingly universal phenomenon of a "soul window" (a small round window drawn under the high eaves of a house occurring in the drawings of houses by seriously ill children). An ancient Swiss folktale tells how the soul of a recently deceased person will leave the house through this window. Despite the fact that there is no evidence of this belief in America, seven of the terminally ill children in the Perkins study drew these windows on their houses (Tate, 1989).

Spontaneous drawing often evoked stories told in the third person, revealing how children related to their illness. They depicted what was happening inside their bodies and what parts hurt or had tumors or "bumps" that couldn't be fixed. Dying of an inoperable heart disease, a good-natured 5-year-old boy with whom I worked, drew his body shape with one big heart with broken lines through it. Then he shouted, "Color me gone!" as he angrily crossed himself out in black crayon. The drawing was a vehicle through which his inner feelings were mirrored, indicating his internal knowledge that he would not survive the surgery (see Figure 2).

This case history illustrates the ideas of Lowenfeld and Brittain (1975): "A child's art is an extension of his or her world. The images produced may reflect the child, his/her perception of position within environment, and areas of question, concern, conflict or need."

Kübler-Ross (1981) cautions, however, that if a child uses an object or drawing to relate what he or she cannot verbally express, one should not push the child to talk about it. That may be a projection of the caregiver's need and not of the child's. It is important to avoid personal projections that may lead to false assumptions. For example, a child who draws only with a red crayon may not necessarily be terminally ill; it may be his or her favorite color, or the only crayon available.

Figure 2 Self-portrait drawn by a 5-year-old boy dying of an inoperable heart disease, who crossed himself out in black crayon, shouting, "Color me gone!"

Furth (1988) differentiates between drawings that are *impromptu* (guided or suggested) and drawings that are *spontaneous* (free style). The following are some focal points (guidelines) to help decipher unconscious content as revealed in pictures:

1 What feelings does the picture convey to the child? Capture the initial spontaneous impression: how the child felt while drawing (happy, sad, afraid).

2 Have the child carry himself or herself into the picture. (Question for the therapist: What is the image or symbol saying or doing? Attempt to become particular objects in order to feel, hear and see their relationship to the whole.) An example is a child's drawing of a boat tossing in stormy waters. The therapist asks the child to tell a story about what it's like to be that boat rocking inside the storm.

3 What is odd or seems out of place (e.g., a car flying in the sky or a person with three hands)? This conveys a specific problem area.

4 What barriers are used (e.g., a person, a tree, a wall, or any object that blocks or constricts)?

5 What is missing or absent (e.g., missing feet to stand on)?

6 What objects stand out, or are underlined or filled in for emphasis?

7 What is the size or proportion of objects and people? Are there any shape distortions? Excessive or reduced perspective (e.g., a big head and/or tiny body may show a problem or affected area).

8 Count repeated or recurring objects, such as sun rays or birds in the sky. Numbers may suggest important units of time, age, sequence, or number in family present or missing.

Other therapeutic media include any process that enable a child to control or release feelings. Dying children who are physically restricted in movement can use the medium of clay to discharge or redirect aggressive behavior. The movement of throwing, pounding, or manipulating clay helps release anger, helplessness, and frustration. Other suggested forms of interactions with dying and bereaved children include:

- Scribbling or doodling (Note the shades of intensity and pressure.)
- Dramatic play with puppets or clay sculptures
- Finger painting
- Art collage (Collect and cut out pictures from magazines describing different people and varied scenes. The grieving child may choose to talk about a picture that reminds him or her of the lost loved one. This may be less threatening to the child than talking about the actual death.)
- The child's drawing of a favorite animal followed by pretending to be an angry, happy, or sad animal through sounds and movement (If a dying child is too debilitated, the therapist can draw for the child, following the directions of the child as to objects, placement, and colors.)

Each of these methods provides the opportunity for energy release and integration of mind and body in a pleasurable, nonthreatening activity.

The therapeutic process is multidimensional. It involves knowledge of techniques and of interpretive skills in order to assess children's awareness. Yet psychological information about children is not enough. Also required is an intuitive approach that is not intrusive and enables children to communicate their inner needs and find some peaceful resolution on their journey towards death.

SPONTANEOUS DRAWINGS
AND THE GRIEVING CHILD

Expressive therapy works just as well for grieving children who have lost a parent, sibling, or peer. According to Robert M. Segal (1984), bereaved children may exhibit one or more of these behaviors: (1) denial of trauma; (2) guilt and blame for tragic event; (3) internalization or acting out of anger; (4) repressed feelings; (5) obsession with fear of loss of remaining family members; (6) search for immediate ways of regaining control over their life.

Contrary to the parents' belief that children are unaware, children's drawings of the family often depict their knowledge of a serious life crisis, such as in the case of a terminally ill parent. One of my clients, a 6-year-old boy whose father was dying, knew nothing about the impending death, according to his mother. When I asked her if she had noticed any behavioral changes, she replied that her son's grades had dropped and that he now picked fights at school with children with whom he used to play. He also visited his dad less often in the upstairs bedroom. Subsequently, it was revealed that he had secretly told his teacher that he was afraid that he could "get sick like his dad." In my first session, the boy was shy and reluctant to talk. Instead, he picked up a sad-looking puppet and forcefully threw it, several times, against a big pillow. He stated that "the puppet was so mad and wanted to hurt them." I asked the puppet if he could draw a picture of "them" and tell "them" how mad he was. Holding the crayon in the puppet's hand, this child drew his family in black. No one was touching. All had sad faces and limp, lifeless forms. His father was separated out to the left edge of the paper, opposite the rest of the family on the right side. The child placed himself alone in the far upper right corner as a tiny, barely visible and faint-colored figure with no arms (see Figure 3).

This picture portrayed the child's hidden anger and hurt, as well as his inner knowledge of the situation. The exaggeration of distance and isolation from others and the helplessness of this child with no arms may indicate his unexpressed need for love and inclusion in the family. His previous attempts to control a part of this environment at school through rebellious behavior decreased when his parents began to share the truth of his dad's condition and to communicate as a family unit.

Figure 3 Family portrait drawn by a 6-year-old boy whose father was dying, but who supposedly did not know this. Placement of figures reveals his inner knowledge of the situation.

Based on personal case histories, I observed an unspoken conspiracy of protection that often involved the child whose parent was dying. C. M. Binzer and colleagues (1969) noted a breakdown in communication with parents of leukemic children as well. When children saw their parents' discomfort in sharing feelings, they then suppressed their own. Because of the need to repress painful thoughts and memories, as well as negative emotions (e.g., anger, guilt, helplessness), a child may maintain a mask of noncaring attitude and display little visible affect. The child may perceive any attempt to help him or her verbalize as interrogation, and may resist. Such a situation, as described above and portrayed in Figure 3, may offer the opportunity for nonverbal communication, since this provides an unconditional environment for self-expression. It may evoke a natural unplanned response that potentially reduces the child's underlying anxiety and establishes a bond to share the helplessness.

IMAGERY AND THE DYING CHILD

"The imagination is sun in the soul of man," said Paracelsus. The truth of this is seen in the value of relaxation techniques and guided imagery, followed by spontaneous or impromptu drawings, for children facing life-threatening illness and intrusive treatment procedures. They serve to help reduce the stress and anxiety that provoke helplessness, and they increase a sense of self-regulation and control over the often uncontrollable external forces.

Bernie Siegel (1989) describes how a hemophiliac successfully created imagery to stop his bleeding by visualizing himself flying a plane through his blood vessels and dropping off loads of Factor 8 to control bleeding. In an account by Porter and Norris (1985), a 9-year-old boy with an inoperable brain tumor visualized a *Star Wars* scenario to fight his tumor. Guided imagery and active use of imagination can provide meaningful validation of a child's inner feelings. The intensity of physical and psychological suffering caused by illness can be diffused through new perceptual and sensory information, which enters through the central nervous system, altering and affecting the states of physiological and emotional response.

Images conveying feelings, attitudes, and internal messages must be translated by the right hemisphere of the brain (where emotions and kinesthetic experiences evolve) into nonverbal terminology before they can be understood by the involuntary or autonomic nervous system (Achterberg, 1985). Such images are preverbal and are only transmitted by physiological connection with the left hemisphere (the logical and analytic thought patterning). Arising from memories and/or visual fantasies, these images engage several or all of the primary senses (visual, auditory, and kinesthetic) and can affect brain waves, blood flow, heart rate, skin temperature, gastric secretions, and the immune response (Achterberg, 1985).

The translation of nonverbal symbolic language from internal to external communication is demonstrated in the following guided imagery exercise, which I have found to be useful with the seriously ill child. I ask the child to draw a picture of his or her body and the place(s) where it hurts. The child is then encouraged to talk to the hurt part (external dialogue) and imagine the sound or words that "hurt" would say (e.g., "no, no" or "get out"). The following questions and suggestions often result from this experience.

1   What would you like to do with pain? Where would you like it to go? How could the pain change in size from bigger to smaller? From hot to cool? What color is it?

2   Who or what could help to make the pain less and less? (Bettelheim [1981] describes how superhero characters, such as the Incredible Hulk, Superman, or the Bionic Woman, "help to stimulate the child's fantasies about being aggressively strong and invulnerable, thus offering some relief from being overwhelmed by the powerful adults who control his existence.")

3   See the pain become smaller and smaller, gradually dissolving (e.g., melting into a puddle on the ground).

4   See the pain gone. Where does it go (e.g., down into the ground or up into the sky)?

5   Think of your favorite color and breathe it in deeply to the place where the pain was. Allow your whole body to become like a sponge, soft and gentle, absorbing the beautiful color inside.

After this imagery, I encourage the child to illustrate and complete the drawing to find some resolution in the process. This combination of imagery and art affords a conscious integration of the way the child represents his or her world visually and kinesthetically. In helping objectify the pain or fear, it reinforces a sense of bodily control. Samuels and Bennett (1974) describe the difference between *receptive imagery*, which involves tuning in and allowing spontaneous images to occur, and *programmed visualization*, specifically designed to achieve certain physiological control and change. Suggestions may be used (with medical or biological information) to erase infections and viruses, replace damaged cells, build new ones, make hot areas cool, reduce pain, and relax tension. Dossey (1988) outlines more specific practices on pain control used by nurses on their patients. Heidt (1978) asked her patients to take mental journeys through the body, and then draw pictures imagining their disease or discomfort. Imagery provided information that was not necessarily obtainable from medical histories.

IMAGERY AND THE GRIEVING CHILD

For the grieving child (approximately 8 years and over), I have obtained excellent results from the exercise I call "Inner Resource Circle." Deep breathing and progressive relaxation techniques are used first (relaxing muscle sets), reinforced by the use of soft music to create a nonthreatening environment. I then ask the child to imagine himself or herself in the center of a special circle, a safe magical place. The exercise proceeds as follows:

   1 Within your circle, picture someone who cares about you very much. See that person looking at you, and feel the experience of being loved just as you are. Breathe in this love through your abdomen and then into your chest. Let it swirl and dance through you. (If the child does not have such a loved one, suggest he or she make one up.)
   2 Who else would you want to be in this special circle? Think of a special friend or playmate who makes you feel happy.
   3 Picture someone you admire greatly: a teacher, a movie or television star, or a magical hero.
   4 Picture someone whom you cared about or loved very much who has died and left you.
   5 With each of your loved ones surrounding you in the circle, speak to the person in your life who has died. Is there something you would like to say to this person? What would you want him or her to know about you now? Catch up. Breathe in deeply, feeling a light filling your whole body that helps you let go, exhaling any sad or mad feelings that you may have held inside from the

time you experienced your loved one's death. Feel his or her support and permission to do this now. If you have any questions or unfinished concerns or problems, share them with this person. Open up to receive an answer, a gift, a message, or a symbol as a helpful reminder or way of remembrance. When you are ready, let yourself really experience your "good-bye," however different at this moment. Then see him or her leave the circle, with the understanding that you can return to this safe inner place anytime you choose to be with or talk to your loved one. (Option: Invite the child to do a spontaneous drawing to deepen the above exercise and amplify the experience.)

The exercise can also be adapted for use with a dying child as he or she feels surrounded by loved ones and says good-bye to each one, completing any unfinished business.

The archetypal image of the circle, used in "Inner Resource Circle" exercise, is a mandala, in which the individual becomes the center. Mandalas can be traced back to ancient times and are found in all religions. They symbolize wholeness and unity, and reflect the inner awareness of and relationship to the source of all things (Samuels and Samuels, 1975). According to Wadeson (1980), images came before words. Prehistorically, pictures drawn on cave walls, depicting human cultural needs and feelings as well as power images (e.g., animals and religious symbols) indicated the connection of the healing force to the human spirit.

Behaviorist Donald Meichenbaum (1977) described the use of imagery techniques as a clinical tool for cognitive restructuring as applied in grief therapy. To illustrate further the effect of guided imagery when combined with art drawings, I turn to the case history of a grieving 6-year-old girl whose father had died suddenly the previous year. The mother brought the girl to see me because she was repeatedly acting out self-destructive behavior, the latest being an attempt to hurt herself with a kitchen knife. On her first visit, the child appeared depressed and withdrawn. Initially she was reluctant to verbalize her feelings. However, she agreed to draw a picture of herself: a drooping figure with a sad face. When I asked her to tell me a story about why the little girl looked so sad, she replied, "Because I want to be with my daddy." Next, I asked her to imagine what it would look like if she could draw the sad part that wanted to be with her daddy. Her response came in the form of a big black blob, drawn with numerous intense colors of red and black lines throughout (see Figure 4).

When I questioned where this blob was located inside the little girl, she pointed to her chest and said, "It hurts here." I then asked her to take a deep breath, filling her tummy, and tell me what the hurt would say if it could talk. She expressed the words *ouch* and *stop* using hand motions for emphasis. With her permission, I wrote these words inside the blob. I wondered out loud what her daddy might say to the hurt (blob) if he were here. She closed her eyes for a second, and in a stronger, more authoritative tone, exclaimed, "Stop hurting

Figure 4   Self-portrait drawn by a 6-year-old girl whose father had died suddenly, show-ing "blob" of hurt and sadness inside her chest.

my little girl," and, "I'm gonna take you away." I invited her to make a second picture based on her daddy's words. She drew him carrying the hurt (blob) away in a big bubble (towards the upper right corner of the picture).

After a few moments, we explored how her mother might respond to all this. Upon careful reflection, the child replied that she would say to her, "I love you and don't leave me to join your daddy." At that time she was projecting her mother's fears in response to her previous self-destructive attempts. She then pointed to her doll and spoke in a tiny doll voice, "Stay and play with me. I'm lonely."

After this dialogue was finished, I used a deep-breathing exercise and sug-gested that she fill her chest area with her favorite color. When I asked her how it felt there, she told me, "Only a little pain is left and it is melting away—and that's okay." To complete the session, I invited the child to remember a special fun time with her daddy that she could think about whenever she felt sad or lonely. She imaged it and then drew a picture of her daddy holding her hand, the two of them walking happily in the park. Ten weeks later, she shared that she had often used the image of going to her secret heart place in the park, "holding daddy's hand and talking to him." This confirmed the continuous existence of her father's love in her life, helping her change her perception of the loss and find a means of lasting comfort.

This example combines the use of stress reduction techniques to evoke an altered physiological and emotional state of being with nonverbal impromptu art drawings to externalize the feelings. Guided verbal images and cues from the drawing helped further to avoid identification with the pain, while giving to the image form, movement, and a means of expression. The second drawing helped to concretize her new solution, "daddy carrying the hurt blob away in a big bubble," while simultaneously diminishing the helplessness. Other resources were presented to reinforce her connection to life in the here and now (e.g., mother and doll), and to validate her mourning process. The use of the deep-breathing exercise and color imagery helped to diffuse the intensity and focus, and to provide feedback about the changed physiological response. As Singer (1974) points out, the efficacy of imagery as a way of personal mastery lies in:

- The ability of the client to discriminate fantasy processes
- Clues from the therapist on how to approach uncomfortable situations
- The rehearsal of alternatives (or changed internal dialogue and adaptive response)
- Consequent decrease in fear approaching situations that were previously avoided or hidden.

CONCLUSION

Since more than half of all communication is nonverbal, such tools as art drawings and creative imagery provide access to a child's intuitive awareness, especially in dealing with the illness or loss of a loved one. Pictures reveal the relationship between mind and body, translating symbolic clues from the unconscious into creative life forms. Often, the experience of drawing itself becomes part of the healing process that occurs when we appreciate the language of our hearts as well as our minds. Counseling dying or bereaved children requires sensitivity to their nonverbal expressions of internalized emotions, which are frequently masked. Therapeutic intervention at the time of loss can help minimize some of the potential problems resulting from repressed grief.

The greatest of human potential is to acknowledge and to empower one another. We all do this, but rarely do we appreciate the quality of empowerment that we give to others. To be acknowledged, especially in times of confusion, loss, or despair, is to be given a rare moment for transformation. This is the opportunity therapists or caregivers provide when they successfully use nonverbal communication with children undergoing the greatest stresses of their lives. By giving form through creative imagination and focusing on the hurt (illness, loss, or death), it is possible to release the energy absorbed by the suffering, thus allowing possible new growth, knowledge, and transformation (Houston, 1987). Such a process can be attributed to death and dying counseling with children when we effectively listen to the language of the intuitive heart, and speak from a inner place of wisdom, where true healing can occur, even in death.

REFERENCES

Achterberg, J. (1985). *Imagery in healing.* Boston: Shambhala Press.

Bach, S. (1966). Spontaneous paintings of severely ill patients. *Acta Psychosomatica, 8,* 1–66.

Bach, S. (1975). Spontaneous drawings of leukemic children as an expression of the total personality, mind and body. *Acta Paedopsychiatrica, 41*(3), 86–104.

Bettelheim, B. (1981, October). The art of moving pictures. *Harper's Magazine,* pp. 80–83.

Binzer, C. M., Ablin, A. R., Fuerstein, R. C., Kushner, J. H., Zoger, S., & Mikkelson, C. (1969). Childhood leukemia: Emotional impact on patient and family. *New England Journal of Medicine, 280*(8), 414–418.

Dossey, B. M. (1988). Imagery: Awakening the inner healer. In B. M. Dossey (Ed.), *Holistic nursing* (pp. 239–240). Rockville, MD: Aspen.

Edwards, B. (1979). *Drawing on the right side of the brain.* New York: St. Martin's.

Furth, G. (1988). *The secret world of drawings; Healing through art.* Boston: Sego.

Greenberg, H., & Blank, H. (1970). Dreams of a dying patient. *British Journal of Medical Psychology, 43*(4), 355–362.

Heidt, P. (1978). Patients tell their stories. Paper presented at Second Annual Conference on Imaging & Fantasy Process. New York.

Houston, J. (1987). *The Search for the Beloved: Journeys in Mythology and Sacred Psychology.* Los Angeles, CA: J. P. Tarcher.

Kübler-Ross, E. (1981). *Living with death and dying.* New York: Macmillan.

Lowenfeld, V., & Brittain, W. L. (1975). *Creative and mental growth.* New York: Macmillan.

Meichenbaum, D. (1977). *Cognitive Behavioral Modification: An Integrative Approach.* New York: Plenum.

Michal, S. C. (1979). Art therapy on a children's cancer unit. In American Art Therapy Association, *Art therapy: Expanding horizons. Proceedings of the 9th Annual Conference* (p. 120–121). Baltimore: American Art Therapy Association.

Perkins, C. (1976). The art of life threatened children: A preliminary study. In American Art Therapy Association, *Creativity and the art therapist's identity. Proceedings of the 7th Annual Conference* (pp. 9–12). Baltimore: American Art Therapy Association.

Porter, G., & Norris, P. (1985). *Why me?* Walpole, NH: Stillpoint.

Rubin, J. A. (1978). *Child art therapy: Understanding and helping children grow through art.* New York: Van Nostrand Reinhold.

Samuels, M. & Bennett, H. (1974). *Be Well* (p. 144). New York: Random House.

Samuels, M., & Samuels, N. (1975). *Seeing with the mind's eye.* New York: Random House.

Segal, R. M. (1984). Helping children express grief through symbolic communication. *Social Casework: The Journal of Contemporary Social Work, 65*(10), 590–599.

Siegel, B. (1989). *Peace, love and healing.* New York: Harper & Row.

Singer, J. (1974). *Imagery and daydream methods in psychotherapy and behavior modification.* New York: Academic Press.

Tate, F. B. (1989). Symbols in the graphic art of the dying. *The Arts in Psychotherapy,* *16*(2), 115–120.

Wadeson, H. (1980). *Art psychotherapy.* New York: John Wiley & Sons.

Chapter 13

The Seriously Ill Child: Management of Family and Medical Surroundings

Ginette Raimbault

Every chronic disease, beyond the somatic aspects, presents important psychological problems, which accompany all processes that inevitably evolve towards either permanent invalidity or foreseeable death within a variable period of time. Chronicity entails an irreversible transition from a normal state, "just like the others," to a state out of the norm, "unlike the others."

When a chronic disease affects a child, the whole family group is affected as well. The application of a therapeutic program is thus carried out by the triad of child–parents–doctor, and the chronic illness becomes the focus of these interpersonal relationships.

The effects of the disease and treatment upon the body, its development, and its functioning overlap with the conscious and unconscious reactions to the disease and to the treatment. These effects constitute the boundaries of a process of adaptation to whatever emanates from a permanent aggression. Although the aggression is permanent, the aggressors may alternate: at one time it is the disease, at another it is the sick child, sometimes it is the doctor and the nursing team, while at other times it is the family. It is, in fact, a question of unconscious circulation, expressed in behavior and/or affects intimately connected with everyone's defense mechanism against the "bad object"—the ill, the aggressor, the aggression. During this movement to and fro, the fluctuation between hope and despair revives the love-hate conflict. This conflict becomes the source of certain patterns of behavior that are paradoxical because they are ambivalent.

The need for global care, embracing the psychological and the somatic problems of the sick person, is being debated among specialists. Whatever apparent relationships develop among family, child, and staff, the therapeutic relation in its strictest sense is heavily loaded with a charge of conscious, but mainly unconscious, affects—forcing those who share the caring load to be particularly painstaking in regard to their actions and to their own reactions. Suggesting that these problems do not affect the therapeutic process (as well as the therapeutic conduct) is a euphemism, stemming from the therapist's unconscious denial of the reality, and undoubtedly from a denial of the reality of the unconscious itself.

This mechanism of denial arises from an ideal, or rather an idealized image, of the physician as the perfect worker or the perfect researcher, serving medical science and capable of abstracting himself or herself from this work. As a matter of fact, wittingly or unwittingly, everyone is concerned about the sick child's survival, quality of life, and life-style, and everyone reacts from a personal problematic point of view. Moreover, everyone is engaged in this struggle and uses all possible means of repression in order to cancel the psychological dimension—one's own, as much as the others'. The psychological dimension is frequently conceived in terms of imagination, illusion, and eventually delusion. Ignoring the psyche leads to attitudes of rationalization, justification, and judgment of others' behavior. At the same time, it invites responses of the same kind. For example, a young child's passivity or an adolescent's aggression is labeled "normal" or "abnormal," without prior analysis of this behavior—which is, basically, the expression of what the child is trying to say, both to others and to himself or herself.

This is a matter of less importance in the case of a benign and shorter illness. But the effects can hardly be disregarded when the disease necessitates long-term treatment for children whose personality is in the process of development, and for the family group whose structure and material, psychological, and affective life-style are undergoing a total transformation, whether brutal or progressive.

We can pose the following questions:

• Upon whom should fall the task of assuming the therapeutic function concerning the physical illness or the difficulties in the psychic adaptation?

• Does the responsibility lie with the physician, the specialist in organic pathology?

• What models of intervention exist?

• Should these models be standardized?

CASE HISTORY OF MICHEL B.

The following example illustrates a method of psychological intervention on a pediatric oncology ward.

Michel B., age 15, is diagnosed with acute myeloblastic leukemia. He is admitted to a French provincial hospital. Both parents are panic-stricken when the diagnosis and prognosis are clearly revealed to them by the physicians. Michel systematically resists treatment, as well as therapists. Denying the severity of the illness and rebelling against the new constraints, he states his wish to regain his independence and return home. In fact, he experiences panic when confronted with the physical aggression caused by the treatment.

Staff members are overwhelmed by this conflictual situation, which develops into a keen contest for power. Doctors "threaten" Michel with a mortal prognosis in order to compel him to accept the treatment. It is suggested that Michel be admitted to the Institut Gustave Roussy (a Parisian oncology center) both for medical reasons (continuation and adaptation of treatment) and psychological ones (due to the conflict between Michel and the staff).

At the Institut Gustave Roussy, the parents seem to accept and desire the separation from their son; they are at the end of their tether. Both are taking antidepressive medication and have medical certificates to justify their absence from work. Michel agrees to stay at the Institut Gustave Roussy. He is impressed by the hospital and by team members, whom he prefers to the ones at the provincial hospital. A catheter helps him sustain the treatments. Initially Michel accepts his solitude, but is then bored with the television and some electronic toys, and suffers from lack of affection. Identifying himself with his father, who has built their house, he starts planning to rearrange his room and study at home.

In an attempt to overcome Michel's affective isolation, the physician decides to have the parents be present daily in the ward. The social service from the father's company assumes all the expenses and obtains an extension of the medical certificate that excuses both parents from work. The parents manage to move, with their little daughter, to a cousin's home in the suburbs of Paris.

The mother stays at Michel's bedside at night and often during the day, while occasionally the father takes over. Since the family's reorganization, Michel feels better, but still maintains a resistance in his relation with the medical team, and with the nurses in particular. He experiences the medical treatment as a painful offense against his narcissistic envelope, and grants no one the right to take possession of either his individuality or his body.

The mother often mentions that she should take care of Michel's little sister, thus expressing her ambivalence over the necessity to devote herself exclusively to her son. According to her, Michel is as difficult as his father, and he becomes intolerant and panic-stricken when confronted with the illness and the treatment.

Gradually, however, the parents feel better and accept the new situation. Then Michel starts pressuring them to return home with him. He wants to see his grandparents, who have raised him and think highly of him, and he expresses the wish to rearrange his room. In spite of the treatment's failure, the team complies with his request, and the family returns home. They agree to come back after 10 days in order to evaluate his condition and to decide about further therapy.

At home, everything goes well for some days. Then Michel's health deteriorates, a fact that he attributes to a "liver attack" due to his overeating and overdrinking in an attempt to regain strength. His parents agree to return to the hospital before the scheduled appointment.

Back in the hospital, Michel and his parents are rather well disposed towards the staff; however, the boy is opposed to the proposal of a new chemotherapy treatment. Finally, he accepts the physician's decision, but only because he wishes to please his parents who are pressuring him.

The nurses' opinions regarding the new therapeutic cycle are divided, since they believe it provides little hope of being effective, and offers Michel and his parents a mediocre quality of life.

After a relatively calm period, the treatment again proves to be ineffective, and Michel's condition begins to deteriorate. He breaks through his habitual reserved attitude towards his parents, and particularly towards his mother. She cannot stand Michel's declarations about his approaching death: "You'll take me back in a coffin," "When I'm in heaven, I'll do everything I can for you." The mother finds the situation—both physically and psychologically—more and more burdensome. Michel cannot bear to stay alone, especially at night, and always seeks company. In the meantime, his father feels better and plans to start working again.

When Michel's condition becomes even worse, the doctors decide to inform the parents of the irreversible progress of his disease and ask them to take the boy home that same day. Michel is then admitted to a provincial hospital, in which the staff has been informed of his condition. In fact, the parents cannot bear the idea of Michel dying at home. Considering that they have done their best for their son, they feel no guilt. A few days later, the parents call the ward physician, announce Michel's death at the hospital, and thank him for his care.

Some Comments About Michel's Case

Isolation   Michel cannot bear being excluded from his family and from his sports activities. Neither can he bear being plunged into a universe over which he has no control and which aggresses him incessantly.

Communication   During a rather long period, Michel speaks to no one of his anxiety about his illness, although he is aware of its severity. He rebels against it and openly denies it. He oscillates between making future plans, and frankly admitting his realistic pessimism concerning the prognosis. During the preterminal phase, his relationship with his parents becomes intimate. They seem more prepared to face the reality and listen to him speaking of his fears and convictions now that death is imminent.

EVALUATION OF THE PSYCHOLOGICAL AND SOCIAL INTERVENTION

The Initial Phase

Michel opposes the treatment and the team members. He also denies his illness. There is a discordance between the social facade he wishes to maintain, on one hand, and his infantile affective desires, on the other, which stems from his narcissistic, fragile, and defensive personality.

Michel's parents initially collapse and resign (although the geographical distance should not be ignored). After the initial dramatic experience at the provincial hospital, they present a passionate general mobilization.

The hospital staff presents several solutions:

• A temporary separation between Michel and his parents gives the parents the opportunity to breathe and Michel the chance to be less affected by their panic.

• Negotiations are carried out with Michel on a footing of equality. He seems to have rather good contacts with male physicians, while his relationship with female nurses is more difficult and at times conflictual.

• To cope with Michel's affective isolation, the physician insists on the importance of the parents' daily presence and manages to get social aid (which helps extend their permit for being absent from work and arranges for the family to move to the suburbs of Paris).

• The parents, together and separately, have frequent discussions with the doctors and with a psychologist. They are thus able to air their anxieties and difficulties and receive encouragement and counseling.

The Preterminal Phase

Michel's mother speaks to the nurses and physicians about her son's pessimistic-realistic discourse, which she considers as a heavy affective burden. Team members, taking advantage of the relatively stable period following the failure to the first cycle of chemotherapy, and considering the actual split in the family's life, allow Michel and his parents to return home for a week. Michel feels better psychologically and agrees to return to the hospital in Paris when his symptoms reappear. The parents agree, since they prefer Paris to going back to the provincial hospital.

The Terminal Phase

Michel wishes to return home. His parents do not want him to die at home, out of fear of being unable to face the medical and psychological situation. A compromise is reached: Michel is sent home for "Christmas" and is told that the situation will be reexamined after the holidays, and a decision will then be made about his readmission to the hospital. The parents are informed that the treating physician has made arrangements with the provincial hospital to hospitalize Michel during the terminal phase. This way, the parents are able to decide to stop the treatment, without collapsing. As far as Michel is concerned, he declares his satisfaction with the idea of going home, but he has no illusions.

QUESTIONS RAISED BY THERAPEUTIC INTERVENTION

During the course of the formation of the psychological team—whose objectives are both therapeutic and research oriented—certain questions are raised. The following kinds of therapeutic intervention raise some of these questions:

Conflict Between the Mother of a Child Under Treatment and the Hospital Team

The hospital team is deeply shocked and intolerant of a mother who speaks frankly, in the presence of her 7-year-old child, of the severity of his disease, of the risks involved, of being affected by her child's treatment, and of being obliged to do certain things, such as leaving her family back in the province and spending her days in the hospital.

A discussion with the mother enabled the therapeutic team to understand her attitude. She had already lost two very young children. The boy under treatment, suffering from iatrogenic leukemia, had been treated for a kidney cancer since he was 1 year old. Moreover, she was bound to support the family and earn a living as a small shopkeeper, since her husband, a carpenter, had lost his clientele and had taken to drink.

In this case it was the psychotherapist who helped the mother express her despair and hatred for her husband, her child, and the doctors. She felt that all of them had kept her from realizing her own desires and compelled her to sacrifice her desires to medical and family needs, while simultaneously they did not acknowledge her suffering. This cry of despair and hatred had to be heard by someone who would neither deaden its sound by wrapping it up in fine words, nor condemn or reject her. With the help of the psychotherapist, this woman was able to feel that, in spite of her hatred and envy, she was being accepted and acknowledged as a subject whose desires had been mutilated. Thus, she and her child were no longer toxic, bad objects for each other.

Effort to Establish a Therapeutic Relationship
Between a Nurse and a Patient

In some cases, where there is a spontaneous transference by a patient to a member of the therapeutic team, we try to entrust that team member with the major part of the psychotherapeutic work. That was the case of a 20-year-old girl, who had undergone a bone marrow transplant and was isolated for two months in a laminar airflow. Her passive and negative attitude made treatment difficult, and the team members found her intolerable. The team, however, noticed that she responded favorably to the care given by a male nurse, whereas the contact with a female psychotherapist was very mediocre.

We suggested that this male nurse should assume the psychological support of this young girl, and we volunteered to help him by meeting with him regularly and providing him with supervision.

It is noteworthy that the girl had lost her father some years earlier and showed no apparent signs of suffering or sorrow. Her pathological mourning was expressed in terms of a very passive and infantile attitude, reinforced by the protection of her elder sister. The mother had devoted her energies to the task of replacing the father in handling the family business.

The girl was unable to face her medical problem, which was hardly explained to her. She did not ask any questions. It seemed as if she was only interested in flirting with boys of her age. In the laminar airflow she was incapable of taking care of herself. The nurse thus represented for her a male figure to be seduced, as well as a guiding and caring pedagogue, so to speak, an affectionate protector. This involvement allowed her, once more, to assume an active part in the therapeutic enterprise, in which she had been passive.

Unfortunately, she died a few weeks later, in another hospital. It goes without saying that the male nurse was severely affected, both physically and psychologically.

Therapeutic Intervention in Conflicts
Among Staff Members

In a conflict between physicians and nurses concerning the terminal phase of an 8-year-old boy suffering from acute myeloblastic leukemia, we were asked to act as mediators.

The possibility of a bone marrow transplant was considered, and the boy's parents set their hopes on it. Unfortunately, and in spite of chemotherapy, the boy's further relapse put an end to the project and to the parents' hopes. The physicians told the parents that there was no treatment left and that they could take their son home. Upon reflection, the parents declared that they preferred for their boy to die in the hospital. They felt more secure and expressed the fear of not having the courage to face their son's death at home, particularly in the presence of the other children.

A week later the situation became critical. On the one hand, the nurse thought the child was suffering a great deal, they noticed that the mother kept silent, and they felt they had lost touch with both parents, who until then had trusted them. On the other hand, physicians reported having a good relationship with the father; the treatment they had prescribed for the child's pain was effective. They would not put an end to a situation that was not as disastrous as the nurses had described it.

By the end of the discussion with staff members, it was decided that a psychotherapist would have a discussion with the parents in the presence of a physician. At this meeting, the parents reported that their son was actually suffering less. Since his improvement, he had again actively started to control the treatments and tests he underwent, and to fight for his recovery, which he seemed to desire in order to return home.

After the parents had expressed their views, the doctor decided not to change the treatment, for the time being. Then, the nurses were invited to talk with the parents and to hear their point of view, so the interrupted dialogue could continue. At the very moment when everyone was getting up, ready to leave the meeting, the parents asked how long their son was still expected to live and what was the reason for the current palliative treatment. Then, little by little, they expressed the view that there was no point in prolonging their son's life any further. After this declaration, which confirmed the nurses' intuition, it was decided to organize a staff meeting in the presence of the ward chief. During that meeting it was decided that the child would no longer be kept in isolation and would play with other children, while the palliative treatment would be reduced to a minimum.

Two days later, the child died of a hemorrhagic syndrome. He was not conscious of his agony, due to a rapidly administered injection. While he was dying, there was an atmosphere of peace and calm in the ward, with both team members and parents present.

Our role in this case was fourfold:

1 To allow and assist nurses and physicians to express their feelings so as to perceive their personal involvement and identifications: nurses had a tendency to identify with the mother, who was already mourning over the child's death, whereas physicians identified with the father and the boy.

2 To help the young doctors face the parents' anxious discourse and thus the implicit risk of being charged with failure; also, to enable them to probe the parents' psychological and ethical attitudes towards their child's death, and to help them become aware that the fear of cutting the child-parent tie, and of somehow being responsible for the child's death, was hidden behind their therapeutic prudence.

3 To help the nurses understand that the parents' attitude of apparent rejection to the team was an expression of their withdrawal into deep and painful mourning.

4 To allow the parents to realize that they had attained a state of painful detachment from their son, and then to say that henceforward they expected the hospital to put an end to an intolerable situation: that of giving care and affection to a child who was still alive, but to their minds was already almost dead.

Hence, in certain cases it is possible to alter the therapeutic decisions in accordance with psychological estimations, elaborated and discussed during either "synthesis meetings" or informal conversations. It is also possible to organize meetings that include the patient, the psychotherapist, and a nurse or physician, with the purpose of providing psychosocial care for the patient and his or her entourage. In some cases, the team becomes aware that, before making any decisions, more work is needed (e.g., assessment of the family's need for information and support, preparation of the patient and entourage for the details of the therapeutic protocol). This process of awareness leads some members of the therapeutic team to ask for regular psychological training.

THERAPEUTIC GOALS

Opposition to the introduction of psychological and social dimensions into daily practice is fairly frequent. This is often due to various factors, such as: a priori objections (from all parties involved), an overinvestment in techniques and performances of material activities, and a feeling of unease among staff members who are involved in intersubjective relationships with patients and families in anguish (these relationships may prevent some of them from trying to cope with their feeling of unease in an articulate manner).

Every human being is faced, at one time another, with the reality of death—essentially the death of someone else. This happens even with infants. Denying this fact and the knowledge that comes with it creates the fiction of an innocence ("The Lost Paradise"), which causes severe damage and impairs the psychoaffective development of any human being. Seriously ill children who are confronted with the possibility or certainty of their own death, and in spite of the best care they may apparently or actually receive, will find themselves in a state of moral, affective, and psychological abandonment, mostly due to a total lack of exchanges with others in their environment. Even when "others" who care for these children watch over them, love them, and try to do their best for them and their life, comfort, and well being, even then, conscious as well as unconscious distortions of these exchanges are inevitable.

The child's quest for knowledge, for truth—his or her own truth, not necessarily the "objective" medical truth—is mobilized by anxiety and suffering, by the trauma imposed through the illness and the therapeutic requirements. The child's quest for truth will confront with the different barriers raised by adults whose conscious aim is to protect the child, but whose unconscious aims and desires are manifold.

Clinical experience bears the evidence that the child—just like any adult—left alone with his or her illness and personal drama is prey to an imaginative process, whereby the child is altogether a vehicle for aggressive, hostile feelings and a victim of this aggression and hostility. This conflict can only reinforce the child's sense of loneliness. Therapeutic goals should therefore include taking these feelings and tendencies into account and helping the child symbolize them. Symbolization is, we must realize, the human being's privilege, assisting people in their efforts to overcome traumas, wounds, anguish, or threats. This, however, can seldom be achieved by any human subject alone: it requires the help of others, and as far as children are concerned, this requirement is total. Important figures surrounding children—namely families and caring staff—can best help them achieve this necessary therapeutic goal.

As a psychoanalyst in a pediatric ward, where seriously ill children are treated, I have listened to them speaking of their daily life at home and in the hospital, of their illness and of death. Death is not children's only topic of interest, and it does not necessarily keep them from enjoying life, as long as those in their environment are willing and able to listen to them, without trying to induce false hopes or telling lies. As soon as a child is able to freely express himself or herself, no further age-dependent progress can be observed about the concept of death. Faced with sickness and death, children are led to the same images and conclusions, to the same order, disorder, and sequence of ideas, as adults. Their clear-sightedness may be expressed more openly, and is thus more impressive—without, however, preventing the occurrence of defense mechanisms. If children are then faced with silence or lies, even well-intentioned ones, they are caught up in loneliness and will shut themselves off from this empty world, which prematurely isolates them from other human beings.

This is not what children want. Their desire is not to be lonely. As they approach death, their desire is to be *recognized*, which is synonymous with being recognized as near death *and* alive. According to Jacques Lacan, "the anthropogenous and human desire for recognition . . . is man's desire to see all other men attribute an absolute value to his *free* and *historical individuality*" (Lacan, 1977).

To let children talk about death, about their fears and feelings, their hopes and despairs, their certainties and uncertainties, their love and hate, means we are allowing them to talk about life, *their* life, and we are providing them with the only possible help: the presence of another human being until the end. By fostering children's epistemophilic drive, their quest for what could be considered as their own specific, personal, subjective truth, and maintaining those exchanges with them, we will keep them "alive" even though they are close to death (Raimbault, 1973).

However the question still remains: How can we—adults, parents, nurses, physicians—achieve this part of our role and function when we are so deeply grieved by the thought of this particular child's near future? Is it possible to help parents at this time? Parents can help their child if they are able to listen, accept what he or she is saying without trying to underestimate or annul by any possible means what the child is stating and trying to convey to them.

As far as the medical team is concerned, I would like to make a distinction between physicians and nurses. Most often, under the pressure of a demagogical bias, they are referred to as a group: in French, "equipe soignante," or "caring team," even though they do not share functions, roles, or objective and a fortiori subjective positions

As far as nurses are concerned, they are still, at least in France, mainly female. There is no need to analyze the nurse-child relationship, which is so often a duplicate or forerunner of the mother-child relationship. Nurses perform both acts that are part of the child's daily care, and act dependent on the doctor's instructions. Their daily contacts lead to a physical intimacy, which may in turn lead to a psychological one, as long as they are not unconsciously frightened of such closeness and deterred from it.

We may give advice, provide actual knowledge about the disease, or teach cognitive or psychodynamic concepts and developmental psychology, but these procedures remain useless, from the patient's point of view, if all concerned professionals are not encouraged, helped, and trained to work on and elaborate their feelings. Teaching has, all too often, the function of molding according to an ideal. This moral ideal hampers the expression of feelings and fantasies and censors whatever is considered unsuitable and inappropriate. Although we know that these values differ according to cultural norms, we still cling to them as though they were the universal incarnation of wisdom. Thus guilt can be aggravated, since it is always present when a child dies, present within both the child and those who have reared or cared for him or her.

There is no knowledge to be taught about death. There are beliefs, faiths, and feelings that have to be expressed and heard. Can we listen and can we hear? How? This is my final question.

REFERENCES

Lacan, Jacques. (1977). *Ecrits*. London: Tavistock.
Raimbault, Ginette. (1973). *L'enfant et la mort [Child and Death]*. Toulouse: Privat.

Chapter 14

On the Choice to Live or Die

Mina Bouras

In this chapter I will describe a case. Even though it is just one case study, I am convinced that similar ones occur every day in all parts of the world.

Some years ago, when I was working as a psychoanalyst at a children's hospital in France, the pediatric nephrologists asked me to help a particular child. His name was Samuel, and he was 7 years old. He suffered from a number of congenital deformities, the most severe of which was a deformation of the ureters, which had serious effects on his kidneys. When physicians asked me to see him, Samuel was in danger of dying from a kidney complication if his ureters were not operated on.

In addition, Samuel suffered from cryptorchidism, and had a minor deformation of the legs that made it necessary for him to use crutches. He had spent long periods in hospital, particularly during his infancy, to avoid coming in contact with his mother who at the time displayed symptoms of tuberculosis. His hospitalization as an infant went some way towards explaining why Samuel had been so late in walking and talking. Despite these delays, Samuel seemed to present no psychological problems and was highly intelligent. He belonged to a family of immigrants, coming from a poor country, but he spoke perfect

French, and was in this respect indistinguishable from the rest of his peer group at school. His father worked as a manual laborer.

The pediatricians asked me to help Samuel because, in their opinion, he was suffering from depression. As I found out, his nephrological condition was deteriorating, and if the operation on his ureters was not carried out, he would soon die. I also discovered that the physicians had decided not to operate, arguing that "the parents would never understand the purpose of such an operation." I often came across similar situations in pediatrics: ordinary people were regarded as being of limited intelligence, unable to understand a particular treatment or unable to carry it out.

Samuel's parents—his mother in particular—had accepted the physicians' decision, and repeated monotonously, "The doctors have decided. . . . In any case, operations are always dangerous."

As for Samuel, he expressed something quite different. From the day I met him and until his death, eight months later, Samuel always talked about a boy—obviously himself—whom the others were killing, whom they attacked, who was big but kept falling down. Everyone fought each other and finally there were all killed. This was expressed in his own words:

> Bombs, lots of bombs, to blow up the little man. . . . Why are they attacking him? Why are they killing him, beating him up? He goes away, he's big . . . why is he killing him? Look, he has fallen down . . . he has sticks [clearly a reference to his crutches]. Why does he have sticks? Why doesn't he want to let him come into the house? Why is he killing him? My mother doesn't want me to talk too much. They'll plant a bomb to blow up the sticks. They are all dying . . . A big bomb, are you deaf? A stick . . . he's big . . . lots of bombs. . . . Why do mummy-kidney and daddy-kidney hit each other? The kidneys, why are they hitting each other? Tell my parents that I spoke about it, and ask why they are hitting each other?

The above is a condensed selection of the words Samuel constantly repeated in our sessions. Given I was aware of the whole context in which these words were said, it was clear to me that Samuel was talking about himself, that it was *he* who was being killed, attacked, and beaten. It was he who despite all the difficulties in walking with crutches, had grown up and was "big," a reality that the others were unwilling to tolerate. His parents could not bear it and did not want him home. He was a reject. He was the one who had to die.

Note the order in which the free associations take place. Each time Samuel mentions being big, this is followed by death—the bombs. The word *why* dominates everywhere, a *why* that remains unanswered: why is he not wanted at home? why are they killing him? It is clear that there is no room for Samuel at home, that he is not allowed to grow up, that he must die. But the sad consequence is that the others die too. As Samuel said, "They're all dying." When a psychopathological act is completed, the problem often does not end there, but is spread to the whole family. When the rejected member of a family dies, problems ensue.

Lastly, Samuel is clearly and expressly asking me to talk to his parents, his parents who "hit each other."

It was in fact true that Samuel's parents did not agree about the fate of their child. The father wanted Samuel to live, while the mother's wish was exactly the opposite, since she had always wanted him to die. This, for a clinical psychologist, explains Samuel's difficulties in walking and talking in his early childhood. His difficulties were not only the result of his frequent admissions to the hospital, but also were due to a negative desire towards him on the part of his mother. Since the mother had experienced an attack of tuberculosis when pregnant with Samuel, she probably held him responsible for the possibility of her own death. In fact, she said one day, as I was attempting to talk to her and to her husband: "I am ill too, but who thinks of me?" It is not fortuitous that Samuel said: "My mother doesn't want me to talk too much." Despite the particularly mild and friendly tone in which I spoke to her, the mother said to me, "Oh, you are a psychologist. No questions. It is best to leave things as they are." Despite my almost superhuman efforts to talk to her, to lighten her burden and to convey Samuel's message, the mother reacted to me with silence and deafness. Her fear and refusal to talk were so strong that when she was present Samuel, who talked nonstop when we were alone, fell silent.

I gradually discovered that the decision that Samuel was to die had been made by his mother and one female pediatrician. Samuel's father was completely passive and took no part in the conspiracy. He had been unable to oppose his wife and give Samuel a chance to live. He was totally overshadowed and dominated by his wife, and was unable to work through—when talking with me—the position that Samuel occupied in his wife's desires.

One day when I asked him why they had given the boy the name Samuel, he replied, "Because it is Jewish." Then I asked him, "Are you of Jewish descent?" He replied, "No." "Don't you know what happened to the Jews in World War II?" I asked, and he answered, "No, I know nothing." Even in terms of his name Samuel had the position of the one who had to die.

When a child occupies a place of this kind in the desires of his mother, can the psychoanalyst make the child's wish be heard? Can he or she help the parents realize that the child's wishes differ from their own, that the child disagrees? This, which is part of the psychoanalyst's work, is sometimes possible, at other times not.

In the case of Samuel, as I have already described, the parents were unable to hear their son's message and were also unable to work with me to verbalize their fears and ambivalence, thus helping to free their child from his pathological position.

There is another aspect to the problem. The physicians had decided the child's fate in advance based on the assumption that the family was incapable of having an opinion because of its socioeconomic status. This decision on the part of the physicians coincided with the mother's psychopathology and validated it.

I attempted to convey Samuel's message to the pediatrician who had undertaken his case as a representative of the medical team. I asked her, "Do you know that the child wants to live, and he is clearly expressing it when he talks to me?" The physician replied, "No child of 7 knows what life or death is. How could he want to live?" It was quite impossible to discuss Samuel's' case with the physician. Furthermore, the medical team, influenced by the immigrant origins of the family and their supposedly low level of intelligence, remained apathetic. The female pediatrician had the first and last word.

Samuel died shortly afterward and I was left with a message and no one to deliver it to. I am delivering it now.

The case of Samuel undoubtedly has certain unique features. Not all children who are dying hold the position of "a reject" in their families, or the position of the one who has to die. But his case does quite clearly raise the following questions: Who decides whether a child will live or die? Does the child himself or herself have a say, and if so as from what age?

I believe that the child has a say from the moment of birth. We all know this is true, and that will to live or resignation to illness and death may be observed even in the behavior of any infant, no matter how small. However, it is difficult for an adult to approach an infant who does not have the power of speech, and ask what his or her desires are. As soon as the child begins to speak, as soon as he or she enters the world of language as a subject and actively uses the parents' linguistic code for the purpose of communication, then—according to linguistics—the child knows why he or she is talking and understands the nomenclature of words. As soon as children use the word *death* in their discourse, they know what that word applies to. According to psychoanalytic theory and clinical experience they know as much about death as adults do. This has also been clearly my personal experience during the 15 years I have worked with children suffering from serious and fatal illnesses, involving encounters with death, and also with survival—thanks to the advanced techniques of modern medical science.

In the past, and even today, there have been psychoanalytical theories that located the child's capacity to know what death is at a much later date, usually around 10 years of age.

However, since the work of the great French psychoanalyst Jacques Lacan and his theory of the structure of the unconscious as discourse, it has ceased to be possible to place the child's knowledge of death at such an advanced age. If the structuring of the unconscious begins with primary repression between 6 and 18 months, the child has also access to the "symbolic," the symbolic function of language and the ability to have desires as a subject.

With primary repression, the child is born as a desiring subject and his or her desire is related to the desire parents have for him or her, though it is not identical to theirs. Thus, children are capable, at this early age, of having a desire of their own, which may be distinct from that of their parents. They are therefore capable of having an opinion about the decisions that the medical team takes in relation to their treatment, their life, or their death. Other theorists besides Lacan (1966), such as Barnes (1964), Kolansky (1960), Rosenblatt (1969), Scharl (1961), and Wolfenstein (1969), have also situated the child's ability to know the meaning of death in early childhood.

We all know that as opposed to the past, recent clinical and psychological research has further and further lowered the age at which the child is aware of his or her environment and communicates with it. Therefore, the medical team has a duty to see every child as a subject desirous of having an opinion concerning his or her fate. I consider it essential that when the medical team has to make a decision concerning the life or death of a child, the child's opinion should be the first to be taken into consideration. This is a fundamental right for children, and in my view it ought to have legal protection.

One last point I would like to make is the position of the psychoanalyst in the pediatric team. Of course, every psychoanalyst knows that he or she has chosen an "impossible profession," as Freud put it. The psychoanalyst knows that people do not want to know, that they find it convenient not to know the truth, and prefer to lead a pseudolife. However, a pediatric team that requests the help of a psychoanalyst ought perhaps to trust him or her a little more than the pediatrician did in the case of Samuel. Of course, the ideal orientation would be to expand the psychoanalytical training of pediatricians so as to allow them to do the obvious: to ask children their own opinions about their futures. In addition, a pediatric team that requests the help of a psychoanalyst ought to know that there is a price to be paid: the loss of convenience and the experience of anxiety. In the case of Samuel, the pediatric team was surprised when a child they had condemned to death became depressed. Perhaps it was inconvenient for the pediatrician who made the decision to realize that the child, too, had an opinion, and it was certainly not convenient for her to understand the position that Samuel occupied in the desires of his mother and his family.

The pediatric team asked me to treat the child for depression. I listened to the child until the very last moments and tried to convey his message. Psychoanalysts can never totally obey the wishes of the pediatric team; at best they can hope to rouse the team from its inertia.

REFERENCES

Barnes, M. J. (1964). Reactions to the death of a mother. *Psychoanalytic Study of the Child, XIX,* 334–357.

Kolansky, H. (1960). Treatment of three year old girl's infantile neurosis: Stammering and insect phobia. *Psychoanalytic Study of the Child, XV,* 261–285.

Lacan, J. (1966). *Ecrits.* Paris: Editions Seuil.

Rosenblatt, P. (1969). Young boy's reactions to the death of his sister. *Journal of American Child Psychiatry, VIII,* 321–335.

Scharl, A. (1961). Regression and restitution in object loss. *Psychoanalytic Study of the Child, XVI,* 471–480.

Wolfenstein, M. (1969). Loss, rage and repetition. *Psychoanalytic Study of the Child, XXIV,* 432–460.

Part Four

Programs for the Care of Dying Children and Their Families

Chapter 15

Care of the Child Dying from Cancer: Home vs. Hospital

John J. Hutter, Jr., Fran Zappia Farrell, and Paul S. Meltzer

Over the past 20 years there has been an increasing interest in providing terminal care for the child dying of cancer in the home rather than in the hospital (Martinson et al., 1978; Chambers, Oakhill, Cornish & Curnicle, 1989; Lauer, Mulhern, Hoffmann & Camitta, 1986; Lauer & Camitta, 1980; Martinson et al., 1986). The rationale for this approach is the simple fact that most children are more comfortable in the home environment as compared to the less familiar and more invasive hospital setting. Surveys of parents whose child with cancer died at home have reported general satisfaction with the home care experience (Martinson et al., 1986) and more favorable parental adaptation patterns (Lauer, Mulhern, Wallskoad, Camitta, 1983). The family adjustment of both parents and siblings has also been observed to be more adequate following participation in a structured home care program (Mulhern, Lauer & Hoffmann, 1983).

A retrospective analysis of the management of death in the child with cancer in our pediatric oncology program at the University of Arizona has resulted in the identification of factors that are involved in the decision to provide care in the home as opposed to the hospital. We use a model of family network intervention from the time of diagnosis, which has been helpful in providing psychosocial support to the children and families who unfortunately enter a terminal phase of their illness.

PATIENT POPULATION

Over a 12-year period at the University of Arizona, we provided care to 143 children aged 4 months to 21 years who died of cancer. Our review included all pediatric cancer deaths in our program and was not limited to the children who had been defined as terminal by medical staff and family.

Approximately 50% of the patients were U.S. Caucasian, 40% Hispanic, and 10% Native American. In about 20% of our patients, Spanish rather than English was the primary language. The diversity of this patient population has enhanced our appreciation of the importance of assessing individual, family, and cultural factors in developing a program for the management of terminally ill children.

The frequency of newly diagnosed cancer in children treated in our program was similar to that reported in other parts of the United States. Approximately $1/2$ of the children have leukemia or lymphoma, while the remainder have solid tumors, such a neuroblastoma, Wilms' tumor, CNS tumors, rhabdomyosarcoma, or bone tumors.

FAMILY NETWORK INTERVENTION
SUPPORT SYSTEM

One of our approaches to assessing family resources and developing a treatment program in our cross-cultural setting has been to assemble the family members and extended family shortly after the diagnosis of the child with cancer. Some of the issues addressed at the family meeting include: diagnosis, prognosis, present condition of the child, optimal means of treatment of the child's condition, as well as issues relating to child care, transportation, and financial and other needs of the family. The meeting also allows us to assess the background, belief system, and available resources of each family.

Family networking is an intervention model that we have used and found effective in our work with families of children with cancer. The term *family network* refers to the people who have a major relationship to a particular nuclear family at a particular time. The observation that human beings are held together by bonds of association is as old as the literature about human behavior. In essence, we are referring to the "clan" or "tribe." Assembling the tribe at a time of crisis and setting an expectation that something is about to happen probably had its origin in prehistoric times. Tribal meetings for healing purposes are certainly well known in many cultures. The bond of shared love and caring is what tribal meetings exemplify.

Previous authors have discussed the use of family network and its implications (Litwick, 1959–1960; Salloway & Dillon, 1973; Speck & Attneave, 1973; Farrell & Hutter, 1984). The work of Speck and Attneave (1973) has had a major influence on our model.

At the time of establishing the diagnosis, the physician and other members of the team, such as the social worker, nurse, and pediatric resident, will meet with the parents to inform them of the diagnosis, its treatment, and potential side effects. The parents are subsequently encouraged to immediately share the information regarding diagnosis and the proposed treatment plan with the patient and his or her siblings. The patient, siblings, and parents are reassured that none of them have done anything to bring about the illness, neither by their wishes nor by their actions. Although questions are encouraged and answered, an effort is made to avoid overwhelming the family with too much information during the initial meeting.

Within the next few days the social worker will meet with the family and seek to identify questions and concerns that may have arisen since the meeting. Discussion focuses one (1) individual fears and needs; (2) past experiences with any type of catastrophic illness; and (3) social support and resources. A list of immediate concerns related to such issues as child care, household assistance, job, transportation, and other problems related to activities of daily life is then developed. The parents are invited to make a list of extended family members, such as friends, neighbors, schoolteachers, church associates, and other significant individuals in their lives. The concept of family networking is introduced to the parents and patient as a means whereby everybody will have the opportunity of airing their questions and concerns associated with the illness. The meeting is scheduled within the next few weeks. It is scheduled (at a time convenient for the family) in a large conference room within the hospital setting where interruptions will be unlikely. One and a half to two hours are allowed. Present at the meeting are the physician and other team members, such as the social worker and oncology nurse, who open the meeting by introducing themselves and inviting the individuals present to introduce themselves and state their relationship to the patient. The major purpose of the meeting is to discuss openly the diagnosis, the proposed treatment, and the potential side effects of the illness. Attention is given to the emotional response of the individuals and the acknowledgement of feelings. The concrete needs the family has previously identified are then presented, and suggestions are invited from the group toward problem resolution. Information regarding hospital and community resources is also provided. At the conclusion of the meeting, literature about the illness and its treatment is distributed. Members of the group are invited to accompany the patient to the hospital when he or she receives subsequent treatment.

The meeting allows the health care team to assess the background, belief system, and available resources of each family. It is important to remember in the assessment of a family that each is unique in its constellation; style of communication; values, life-style, and philosophy regarding life and death; external support systems; and strength of marital and family relationships. The number of individuals attending the family network meetings has varied from as few as 4 or 5 to as many as 45. These individuals, when involved *early* in the course of the illness, become potential valuable resources for support of the family throughout the course of the illness. The family meeting conveys the message that the family is part of the treatment team and creates a sense of relatedness among everyone caring for the child. The challenge for each health care team member is to learn *nonjudgmental acceptance* of each family and their differing belief systems.

FAMILY NETWORK SUPPORT FOR THE DYING CHILD

When the child does not achieve a cure and when the team has exhausted all treatment possibilities, the patient enters the terminal phase of illness. In providing comprehensive care during the terminal phase, the foundation of relatedness established by the family network process becomes vitally important (Figure 1). This relatedness helps the team facilitate the family's choice of where to care for the child until death. The mutual trust and communication that have evolved enable the team to assess the needs and desires of the patient and the family network and to balance them with the ongoing medical requirements of the patient. The health care team must provide for holistic care and enable participation of members of the family network in total care.

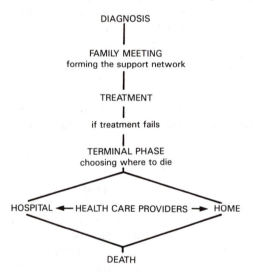

Figure 1 A family support network is established shortly after diagnosis. This support network forms a framework in the management of patients who enter a terminal phase.

For the child and family choosing home care, the health care team's role is one of reaching out beyond the walls of the hospital, to let the home become the hospital. This requires that the health care team be committed to home visits and facilitate the medical care needed by the child at home. The following comments were made by the mother of a 13-year-old boy who elected to die at home. Although she was living alone at the time of the child's diagnosis, her parents and exhusband were included in the family network and became part of the support network during the terminal phase of the child's illness. These comments were made six years after the child's death.

> Later on, it became obvious that things just had to change, that any preconceived notions of how the house was supposed to be, just had to go out the window. The living room became his bedroom and the bedroom became another room for the time we needed to get away. I have a very tiny house and for the physical planning of it, I needed help with [it]. We borrowed a hospital bed, a hospital tray, a portable commode, and eventually our little living room was just like a hospital. Most everything we needed, we could do at home. There were times that were difficult, but the nurse and the team helped out a lot because they made a list of emergency phone numbers that I could call and brought hospital supplies and a lot of other little things that we needed.
>
> I didn't know that the dying process took as long as it did or that there were lots of sounds and motions in the body that I wasn't familiar with. . . . I had never seen the death of a human being before. Actually, what it reminded me of was childbirth, in lots of ways, because there is a whole kind of process that the body goes through and I didn't quite know whether it would go on a for a long time. It helped that someone from the health care team came because one of the first things they said was, "It won't be long now," and I was relieved. I didn't know if it would go on for months or nights or whatever it would be. He was making sounds I hadn't heard before. And then it helped when they said it wouldn't hurt. He had been in such pain for so long that I could hardly touch him. I hadn't really hugged him for months, and I certainly hadn't held him for a long time. And so they helped me to get into the bed and to hold him and I really wanted to do that. . . . I held him for a long time. I feel very glad with having him at home because I didn't need to have him rushed off right away. In fact, I kind of shocked the funeral people who came. I told them to go away, I wasn't ready, and so I got to have him there quietly, just at home with the rest of the family for a few more hours. That was beautiful.

The sense of communication and compassion among everyone who cared for the patient extends beyond death and supports the family through the grieving process. In this model the health care team and the family network system are the crucial elements that link the home and the hospital. They enable the home to become the hospital, and vice versa. For the patient and family choosing the hospital as the place for the patient to die, the team's role becomes one of helping the family to bring the home within the hospital walls and to help the patient and family maintain ties to what is going on outside the hospital.

Follow-up interviews were conducted with four parents who were involved in family networking; two elected home care for their child, and two decided to have their child die in the hospital. The time of the follow-up interviews from the death of the child spanned five to nine years. In all four cases, there was no evidence of ambivalence in the decision they had made regarding where their child would die: home or hospital.

As they reorganized their lives after the death of their child, there was a strong sense in each parent of "not taking life for granted" and a deeper appreciation of life. The follow-up interviews identified three themes related to the loss of the child that are reflected in the current lives of each of the parents: attitudes towards death, personal growth, and family involvement (Table 1).

Each of the parents interviewed acknowledged the pain and suffering they had experienced in the illness and death of their child, but they indicated they also felt stronger and more committed to living a full life. They all expressed greater value for humor and whimsy, and mentioned that they had experienced a shift in their perception, enabling them to view life as a dynamic process rather than a static condition. For these parents, the suffering and pain have not dimmed their delight in the wonder and mystery of life. Their grief has not negated the joy of living, and they report a better quality of life.

CARE OF THE DYING CHILD: HOME VS. HOSPITAL

Of the 143 children who died of cancer in our program, 84 were hospitalized and 59 died at home. In recent years, we have developed a system enabling us to provide care at home to as many terminally ill children as possible. During the last five years of our review (1984–1988), 53% of the children dying of cancer in our program died at home. This contrasts with the earlier years when children more often died in the hospital. Also, of the 84 children who died in the hospital, 10 of these were primarily managed at home until a complication developed requiring a terminal hospitalization. Examples of these complications included intestinal obstructions, spinal cord compressions, and severe hemorrhages.

We retrospectively reviewed our management of the 143 children who died and attempted to identify the factors that caused us to provide care for a dying child in the hospital setting rather than in the home setting. Three general categories of important factors could be identified: medical, sociocultural, and psychological.

Medical Factors

The perceived possibility of a cure of the illness by physician and family was the single most important medical factor resulting in hospital care for the child who eventually died of cancer. These cases included children who were treated during the initial phases of their illness, as well as those whose disease had recurred and who were receiving newer treatment regimens, such as bone marrow transplantation. In both situations, there was hope that the treatment would control the illness, so maximum medical support was provided to the child in the hospital.

Another important medical factor helps determine the feasibility of home care for the dying child; this is the availability of professionals to provide care within the home setting. Our team has included pediatric oncologists, nurses, and social workers. The University of Arizona Health Sciences Center also has a major educational function. With appropriate supervision, trainees, such as nursing students, medical students, and pediatric residents, have been allowed to be active participants and have been accepted by the families. Other special services (home hospice, skilled pediatric home health nurses) have been successfully incorporated and are an integral part of the home health team for the dying child. However, due to close relationships of the oncology team with the family, the pediatric oncology care providers must remain actively involved in terminal care management. Otherwise, families may feel they have been abandoned by the oncology team. Professionals must be on

Table 1 Themes Identified by Parents Related to the Loss of Their Child

Attitudes toward death
    Death cannot be controlled
    Death is no longer feared
    Permission for open expression of feelings regarding death
    Respect for other family members' individual feelings and attitudes
    Gratitude for time spent with child (although abbreviated)
    Respect for the value of life ("life is a gift")
Personal growth
    Able to love more deeply
    Able to be with others in pain and suffering, more compassion
    Desire to be of service to others
    More aware of feelings—all feelings involved in living life
    Respect and acceptance of own process
    Life is painful and sorrowful, also joyful
Family involvement
    Families more unified (deeper marital bond and strong bond with family network)
    Stronger bond with siblings
    Families do more activities together
    Families take nothing for granted

call to provide help when needed and to attend to the child at home if indicated. For the dying children who resided far from the oncology center, home care was still feasible if a primary care physician with a relationship to the family was willing to assume a major role in the delivery of home care. The center's oncologists and other members of the team remained available by telephone in order to answer specific questions asked by this physician in the local community.

Other medical factors that contributed to the hospitalization of the terminally ill child with cancer included severe infections, such as pneumonia, and major neurological complications, such as seizures that could not be managed by the family at home. Some of the specific medical interventions required for optimal home management of the child with cancer have recently been described (Chambers et al., 1989).

During the earlier years of our review, children were occasionally admitted to the hospital for intravenous administration of medication for pain that could not be managed with oral medications. Oral administration of analgesics constitutes the preferred initial approach to pain management in the child with cancer. However, with the increased use of permanent indwelling venous access, such as the Hickman catheter, and development of portable infusion pumps, it has become more feasible to deliver intravenous pain control in the home. This access to the vascular system also allows for the administration of chemotherapy, other intravenous medication, blood products, intravenous fluids, and nutritional support.

Sociocultural Factors

An important sociocultural factor is the presence of a supportive extended family. Also essential is the availability of a comfortable home environment for the sick child. This does not necessarily mean that a large house with ample space is an absolute prerequisite. In fact, we have successfully managed children whose families were of less affluent socioeconomic background and lived in small quarters. More important than the area of living space is the willingness and ability of the family to adjust and to meet the needs of the sick child.

The cultural religious belief system is an additional factor in the decision to manage a child at home rather than in the hospital. A family's belief system may, on occasion, require permission from a religious authority to accept the death of a child. For example, a Hispanic Roman Catholic family will often require the assistance of a priest in resolving issues relating to death. If the child is being managed at home, it is important that visits to the home be made by the priest as well as medical professionals. Another example is the role of the medicine man in Native American cultures. The medicine man, or folk healer, is often a powerful figure to whom families turn for advice and guidance. In addition to providing advice for the child at home, the medicine man occasionally needs to visit the dying child in the hospital in order to satisfy the belief system of a particular family.

Psychological Factors

The final set of determinants involved in the decision to provide care at home rather than in the hospital involves individual psychological factors. Some of these can be modified by working with a family during the course of a terminal illness, but occasionally an individual belief is so strong that it becomes a major factor in the child's management. One individual factor is fear, usually on the part of a parent or significant member of the extended family (e.g., a grandparent), that the child's death will be uncomfortable and too painful to be managed at home. Some of these fears can be alleviated in part by the professional team, which recognizes that this is an issue and presents a realistic but reassuring picture of death and its management.

Other factors include individual beliefs about the meaning and acceptance of death. An extreme example of the latter occurred with the family of one of our patients whose cancer was unquestionably out of control and progressive. However, despite realistic presentations by professional staff, the parents sincerely believed that the illness would be cured with more prayer. In this particular situation, acceptance of death in the home environment was obviously not possible.

Another factor is the patients' desire to protect their family. Two teenage patients who were aware of the impact of their terminal illness on their very supportive families deliberately chose to die in the hospital because they believed it would make their death process easier for their families.

DISCUSSION

The preparation for the death of a child with cancer or other life-threatening chronic disease must begin at the time of diagnosis of the child's illness. Over the past 25 years, there have been markedly improved results in the treatment of certain childhood malignant diseases. As a result, pediatric oncologists have become increasingly optimistic in the presentation of information to the patients and their families at the time of diagnosis of cancer. This is appropriate because of the improved success rate and probable cure rate of certain childhood cancers, such as acute lymphoblastic leukemia (ALL), the most frequently occurring cancer in U.S. children. The care provided is appropriately focused on the survival of the child with cancer. However, 20% to 30% of children with ALL do eventually die. Thus, the professional team providing care assumes an important role in recognizing the possibility of death and in making an assessment from the time of diagnosis as to the resources and capabilities of that particular child and family in managing the overall illness, which includes the possible death of the child.

Decisions regarding the management of the child's death should be individualized with full participation of both child and family. A home care program for the terminal child is often feasible, efficacious, and less expensive than a similar level of care provided in a hospital (Lauer & Camitta, 1980; Moldow, Armstrong, Henry & Martinson, 1982). The selection of a child and family for home care is influenced by a large number of factors, including the child's medical condition, the availability of adequate resources to support the family, the cultural beliefs of the family, the acceptance of death by the family, and the willingness of physicians to accept a new model of health care delivery. An analysis of the physician's participation (Edwardson, 1985) and the model developed by Martinson and colleagues (1978) indicated that oncologists referred patients to the program not because they found it desirable, but rather because these were patients whom they judged technically and emotionally able to receive care in the home. Our experience in providing terminal care to children with cancer supports the observations of Lauer and Camitta (1980) that children of all ages, diagnoses, family structures, and socioeconomic status can be successfully managed at home, should other individual factors, outlined above, be conducive to this setting.

Maintaining open lines of communication between the child, family, and health care team is an important aspect of total care for the dying child. Nitschke and colleagues (1982) evaluated the effects of a conference that included the child, family, and physician to discuss the therapeutic options for children with end-stage cancer. This open approach enabled patients and family members to communicate with each other, and severe behavioral problems were rarely observed.

Evaluations of home care programs for children dying of cancer have revealed overall parental satisfaction with the program (Martinson et al., 1986), and better family adjustment when compared to similar families whose children died in the hospital (Lauer et al., 1983; Mulhern et al., 1983). Mulhern and colleagues (1983) compared 24 families who participated in a home care program with 13 families of similar children who died in the hospital, 3–29 months following the death of the child. Parents of patients who received terminal care in the hospital were found to be more anxious, depressed, and defensive while siblings of hospitalized patients were more emotionally inhibited, withdrawn, and fearful than their respective counterparts in the home care program. Preliminary observations on follow-up several years after the death of our patients would suggest that although the death of a child is a devastating loss, the adjustment to illness provides for some individuals an opportunity for personal growth and for the strengthening of family relationships. If the decision of where a child should die is made in an open, forthright manner, with support mechanisms provided for the family, it would appear that families have long-term satisfaction from their choice of whether death should occur at home or in the hospital.

An additional issue to be considered is the question of autopsy consent for children who die at home. Autopsy findings are useful for educational and research purposes. Also, autopsy information is often helpful to some families. It is possible to obtain autopsy consent and perform autopsies on children who have died at home. However, it must also be clearly recognized that the consent of the family for autopsy is an essential factor. Certain cultural beliefs and/or burial practices often preclude autopsy consent. In this regard, it is sometimes difficult for Native Americans and perhaps those of some other cultures, such as those with strong Islamic beliefs, to consent to an autopsy. We would, however, strongly recommend that a home care program for children dying of cancer include a mechanism allowing for obtaining autopsies when appropriate consent is given.

In summary, the following are essential elements in a comprehensive program for the management of a child dying of cancer either at home or in the hospital:

1 Availability of a team of professional caretakers to meet the needs of the child.

2 Identification and delivery of medical supplies necessary for care.

3 Well-defined mechanisms to maintain communication with the family.

4 Flexibility in allowing the child to enter and leave the hospital as necessary.

5 Attention to the impact of the situation for the extended family (particularly siblings) and provision of postdeath counseling.

6 Incorporation of educational and research objectives within the program.

REFERENCES

Chambers, E. J., Oakhill, A., Cornish, J. M., & Curnick, S. (1989). Terminal care at home for children with cancer. *British American Journal.*

Edwardson, S. R. (1985). Physician acceptance of home care for terminally ill children. *Health Services Research, 20,* 83–101.

Farrell, F. Z., & Hutter, J. J., Jr. (1984). The family of the adolescent: A time of challenge. In M. Eisenberg (Ed.), *The impact of chronic disabling conditions on self and family: A life span approach.* New York: Springer.

Lauer, M. E., & Camitta, B. M. (1980). Home care for the dying child: A nursing model. *Journal of Pediatrics, 97* 1032–1035.

Lauer, M. E., Mulhern, R. K., Hoffmann, R. G., & Camitta, B. M. (1986). Utilization of hospice/home care in pediatric oncology: A national survey, *Cancer Nurse, 9,* 102–107.

Lauer, M. E., Mulhern, R. K., Wallskog, J. R., & Camitta B. M. (1983). A comparison study of parental adaptation following a child's death at home or in the hospital. *Pediatrics, 71,* 107–112.

Litwick, E. (1959–1960). The use of extended family groups in the achievement of social goals: Some policy implications. *Social Problems, 7,* 177–187.

Martinson, I. M., Armstrong, G. D., Geis, D. P., et al. (1978). Home care for children dying of cancer. *Pediatrics, 62,* 106–113.

Martinson, I. M., Moldow, D. G., Armstrong, G. D., Henry W. F., Nesbit, M. E., Kersey, J. H. (1986). Home care for children dying of cancer. *Research in Nursing and Health, 9,* 11–16.

Moldow, D. G., Armstrong, G. D., Henry, W. F., & Martinson, I. M. (1982). The cost of home care for dying children. *Medical Care, 20,* 1154–1160.

Mulhern, R. K., Lauer, M. E., & Hoffman, R. G. (1983). Death of a child at home or in the hospital: Subsequent psychological adjustment of the family. *Pediatrics, 71,* 743–747.

Nitschke, R., Humphrey, G. B., Sexauer, C. L., Catron, B., Wunder, S., & Jay, S. (1982). Therapeutic choices made by patients with end-stage cancer. *Journal of Pediatrics, 101,* 471–476.

Salloway, J. C., & Dillon, P. B. (1973). A comparison of family network and friend network in health care utilization. *Journal of Comparative Family Studies, 4,* 131–142.

Speck, R., & Attneave, C. (1973). *Family networks.* New York: Vintage Books.

Chapter 16

Home-Based Palliative Care for Children: A Feasibility Study

Ciarán M. Duffy, Pamela Pollock, Maurice Levy,
Elisabeth Budd, Lisa Caufield, Stephen P. Spielberg,
and Gideon Koren

In a malignant fatal illness a time is usually reached when aggressive treatment should be withheld and palliative care commenced. This is the stage of management aimed at controlling the most troublesome symptoms rather than combating the disease itself. It is also the time to consider the benefits of caring for the patient at home. This is, perhaps, of special significance when applied to children because of their greater dependence on the family and on the home environment.

Approximately 70% of Canadians ultimately die in institutions, and available evidence suggests that health care professionals have been remiss in identifying their overall needs (Mount, 1976; Shepard, 1977). Some 10% of adult patients admitted to hospital are terminally ill and would most likely benefit from the introduction of a properly coordinated palliative care program (Lunt & Hillier, 1981; Reid, 1985). However, few such programs exist in Canada. In Europe and the United States, a number of programs have been developed both for adults and children. The diversity of pediatric palliative care programs illustrates that care can be administered in a variety of ways and settings (Siegel, Rudd, Cleveland, Powers & Harmon, 1985; Wheeler, Foerster & Bertolone, 1985; Wilson, 1985; Dominica, 1982). Previous studies have outlined the practical and emotional benefits for the pediatric patients, parents, and siblings when the child is cared for and dies at home (Mulhern, Lauer & Hoffmond, 1983; Lauer, Mulhern, Bohn, & Camitta, 1985). The feasibility and desirability of home care for the dying child have been alluded to previously (Martinson, 1976; Martinson et al., 1978; Martinson, Moldow & Henry, 1980). When parents have received professional assistance and support, they have been shown to be emotionally and technically more competent to provide care in the home environment for their terminally ill children (Martinson et al., 1978).

For these reasons, we conducted an analysis of all terminally ill children admitted to the neurosurgical unit at our hospital, the Hospital for Sick Children (HSC), Toronto, Canada, over a defined time period, in an attempt to identify their needs and to assess the feasibility of introducing a home-based palliative care program. This chapter describes this feasibility study and the program that was instituted as a result of the study.

PATIENTS AND METHODS

We studied all terminally ill children admitted to the neurosurgical unit at HSC over an 18-month period, from March 1984 to September 1985. These patients had been diagnosed as being terminally ill by the admitting neurosurgeon, and medical intervention aimed at curing their underlying disease had been deemed to be no longer appropriate.

We conducted a retrospective chart review on these patients. We collected data on diagnosis, sex, age at diagnosis as terminally ill, total number of days from diagnosis as terminally ill until death, total number of hospitalized days from diagnosis as terminally ill until death, proportion of days hospitalized from diagnosis as terminally ill until death, and place of death, for all patients for whom adequate data had been recorded.

During the last six months of this time period, patients admitted to the neurosurgical unit and diagnosed as being terminally ill were studied prospectively to determine the extent of their symptoms and to ascertain whether these children could have been managed at home. In addressing this particular issue, we were interested in identifying the most troublesome symptoms occurring in this group of patients and the interventions that were required to alleviate these problems. The main reason for obtaining these data was to determine the skills required of the caregiver, in order to ascertain whether these therapeutic interventions could be conducted by the parents at home, under the supervision of a palliative care team. The assessment tools used to conduct this evaluation were adopted from Martinson and colleagues (1980). Additional data as indicated above were also collected for these patients.

RESULTS

A total of 30 patients (18 males, 12 females), with a mean age ± Standard error of the mean (SEM) of 6.75 ± 1.20 years (range from birth to 18 years) at the time of diagnosis as terminally ill, were studied. Of these, 22 (73.4%) had central nervous system tumors, 6 (20%) had myelomeningocoele/hydrocephalus and 2 (6.6%) had arteriovenous malformations. A wide variety of central nervous system tumors was noted among this group of patients and represented the usual pathological types seen in childhood.

The mean ± SEM for the total number of hospitalized days, from diagnosis as terminally ill until death, for the 23 patients who died and for whom adequate data were available, was 28.8 ± 4.77. The mean ± SEM for the total number of days from diagnosis as terminally ill until death was 88.11 ± 27.49, and the proportion of this time spent hospitalized was 0.327. In all, 16 (70.6%) of these 23 patients died in hospital, while only 7 (30.4%) died at home. The remaining 7 patients were excluded from the above analysis, since 3 are alive and there was inadequate documentation for the other 4 patients.

The most troublesome symptoms identified in the 9 patients studied prospectively and the therapy required to alleviate these symptoms are shown in Table 1.

The most commonly identified symptoms were related to the gastrointestinal tract. Seven patients (77.8%) had feeding difficulties and required

Table 1 Most Commonly Occurring Symptoms in Patients and Therapy Required to Alleviate Them

Symptom	Percentage of patients affected	Treatment
Feeding Problems	77.8%	Nasogastric tube (57.1%) Nasojejunal tube (42.9%)
Vomiting	66.7	Dimenhydrinate (100%)
Breathing difficulty	66.7	Repositioning (100%) Oropharyngeal suctioning (100%)
Pain	55.6	Nonnarcotic analgesics (100%) Narcotic analgesics (20.0%)
Seizures	44.4	Anticonvulsants (100%)
Temperature fluctuations	33.3	Acetaminophen (100%) Tepid sponging (100%)
Urinary retention	22.2%	Catheterization (100%)

intubation for feeding assistance—4 by way of nasogastric (NG) tube and 3 by way of nasojejunal (NJ) tube. None required gastronomy feeding. Vomiting was a significant problem in 6 patients (66.7%) and was relieved quite readily by the administration of antiemetics, usually dimenhydrinate (gravol).

Breathing difficulty was the next most commonly noted symptom. This was noted in 6 patients (66.7%) and was managed for the most part by repositioning and oropharyngeal suctioning. The occasional administration of oxygen was required in all 6 patients. Pain was noted in only 5 patients (55.6%) and was treated in all by the administration of nonnarcotic analgesics, usually acetaminophen. Only 1 patient was treated with a narcotic analgesic, namely codeine. Seizures were noted in 4 patients (44.4%). They were usually generalized, tonic-clonic seizures and were managed by the administration of anticonvulsants which were given per os, per NG/NJ tube, or per rectum. Administration of medications parenterally was very rarely required. Temperature fluctuations were noted in 3 patients (33.3%). These were managed by the administration of antipyretics and tepid sponging. Two patients (22.2%) developed urinary retention and required intermittent urinary catheterization.

Based on these observations, we felt that patients admitted to our neurosurgical unit represented a significant problem and that their overall care could perhaps be improved. Two points of particular concern were (1) the fact that so few of these children were felt to require narcotic analgesics, despite their diagnoses, and (2) the fact that the predominant problems encountered by these patients were such that they could be managed by administration of medications per os, per NG/NJ tube, or per rectum or by simple procedures carried out by a nurse. Therefore, we felt that we had demonstrated not only that there was a need to develop a palliative care program for these children, but also that it was feasible for this to be developed as a home-based program. The following section describes our program and how it functions.

THE PALLIATIVE CARE PROGRAM AT HSC

The palliative care program for children admitted to the neurosurgical unit at HSC, and diagnosed as terminally ill, was instituted in March 1986. This program consists of a nurse coordinator, three palliative care nurses, and a pediatric clinical pharmacology fellow who is supervised by the chief of the Division of Clinical Pharmacology. The program works closely in association with the primary care physician, other services available at HSC (including the neurosurgical service), and community services (including home care nursing services).

The nurse coordinator is primarily responsible for ensuring that all aspects of the program run smoothly. She is employed solely for this purpose. She is the point of first contact for all new referrals. Following her review of a referred case, she will automatically discuss all aspects of the case with the pediatric clinical pharmacology fellow. The fellow will then see the patient and the parents. Thereafter, a decision will be made regarding the suitability of the case for admission to the program. All aspects of the required care for the patient are discussed, with the ultimate objective being to discharge the patient home, as soon as this is feasible. The parents are trained to perform any procedures indicated for their child that they would feel comfortable in carrying out at home. Available resources in the community, including the primary care physician and home care nursing services, are notified of the child's impending discharge from the hospital. When all these facilities are set up and the parents indicate that they feel comfortable about caring for their child at home, then the patient is discharged from the hospital.

The nurse coordinator maintains once- to twice-weekly contact with the parents of all currently active patients, in an effort to identify problems early on, so that they may be dealt with in an appropriate manner. The nurse coordinator and the pediatric child pharmacology fellow meet on a regular basis to familiarize one another with ongoing patient problems. Both are available to be contacted at all times should problems arise. If needed, a staff pediatric clinical pharmacologist is also always available. Most problems can be handled over the phone. Occasionally the nurse coordinator may be required to make a home visit, and very occasionally the pediatric clinical pharmacology fellow is required to see the patient in the emergency room.

Three palliative care nurses who are part of the nursing staff of the neurosurgical unit also play a role in ensuring the success of this program. They are involved with the intimate care of patients while they are hospitalized and are also available on a call shift basis as the point of first contact for the program patients on nights and on weekends. They are available to conduct home visits, if this is required, or may consult with the nurse coordinator or the pediatric pharmacology fellow should the need arise. The nurse coordinator herself shares this duty with the other palliative care nurses. This format ensures an adequate amount of time free from the service for these nurses, while ensuring that an excellent standard of support is available for these families.

After the child dies a referral is automatically made to the Bereaved Families of Ontario. Contact with the family is maintained by the coordinator, who calls the parents approximately four weeks after the death. The offer of continued support is made, and the decision to accept this support is left entirely to the family.

Since this program is primarily funded as a nursing palliative care program, the available funds are small. Sufficient funds are available to finance the nurse coordinator's salary, together with some administrative costs. For this reason this program has maintained its links to the neurosurgical unit and has not expanded beyond it. When further funds become available, it is hoped that the program can expand. Given this restriction, the following are the current criteria for admission of patients to the program:

1　Diagnosis of the child as "terminally ill" by the admitting neurosurgeon; withdrawal of treatment aimed at affecting the natural history of the underlying disease or disorder.

2　An estimated life expectancy of less than one year.

3　The family's understanding and acceptance of the aims of the program.

DISCUSSION

Although not the first individual to develop the concept of specialized care for the terminally ill, Cicely Saunders is often quoted as being one of the pioneers (Saunders, 1981). She was responsible for the development of St. Christopher's Hospice in London in 1964, and this is still the best-known hospice of its type worldwide. It functions entirely independently of any general hospital. It was after having spent several months at St. Christopher's that Balfour Mount set up the palliative care unit at the Royal Victoria Hospital in Montreal (Mount, 1976). This unit differs from St. Christopher's in that it is actually located within the general hospital. However, the philosophy of management differs dramatically from that of a typical general hospital ward. In this regard it is similar to St. Christopher's, where the main emphasis is on pain management and the overall well-being of the patient.

This move towards hospice care for the terminally ill cancer patient continued through the latter part of the 1970s and into the 1980s (Krant, 1978; Holman, Noce & Montgomery, 1985). In recent years, greater attention has been paid to the plight of children who have been diagnosed as terminally ill, resulting in the development of several hospices especially for children (Siegel et al., 1985; Wheeler et al., 1985; Wilson, 1985; Dominica, 1982). However, the emphasis of the majority of these hospices has been institutionalized care, rather than home care. Martinson (1976) has been responsible for bringing this fact to light. The wisdom of continued hospitalization is questionable if the required care could be provided at home. The advantages for the child, the parents, and the whole family are innumerable when the terminally ill child is cared for and dies at home, provided that there are adequate supports to guarantee the overall well-being of the child and family (Mulhern et al., 1983; Lauer et al., 1985).

Our study demonstrates that a large number of children diagnosed as terminally ill were admitted to our neurosurgical unit over the study period. It also demonstrates that the care provided for these children could be improved, particularly in the area of pain management. Only 55% of the children admitted over the study period were felt to require analgesics, and only one patient received narcotic analgesics. This is out of keeping with the current state of knowledge, which suggests that all children dying as a result of malignancy require narcotic analgesics to control pain. One of the great problems in assessing the level of pain in young children is the lack of adequate indications of pain. This may result in undertreatment. We have recently attempted to devise ways of gaining a better indication of the level of pain in these patients. Our experience suggests that the introduction of appropriate analgesics, in adequate dosage, early on is associated with an overall improvement in the patient's condition.

In excess of 70% of our study patients ultimately died in the hospital. The second component of our study illustrates that the most commonly occurring symptoms in these patients were such that the patients could have been managed at home. All patients exhibited feeding difficulties and required some assistance. Vomiting and seizures, although they occurred in most patients, were not difficult to control, requiring only standard medications. For those patients in whom vomiting was most troublesome, relief was achieved by placement of a nasojejunal tube. This procedure can be carried out without requiring the patient to be admitted to the hospital.

Based on these findings, we instituted our palliative care program in March 1986. It differs from St. Christopher's Hospice and the palliative care unit at the Royal Victoria Hospital in that it is a home-based program, where the parents take on the role of primary caregiver. The emphasis is placed on ensuring that children are cared for in the comfort of their own home in a familiar setting, rather than on a busy hospital ward. The success of this type of program is totally dependent on ensuring that an adequate level of expertise is always available to meet the family's needs. We have achieved this by instituting a program with a nurse coordinator working closely with a physician skilled in the therapeutic management of children who are terminally ill, both of whom are readily available to handle problems as soon as they occur. In addition, there is an adequate number of palliative care nurses available to ensure that home visits can be made as the need arises. The continued success of this type of program is also dependent upon adequate links to ensure the continued involvement of other health care personnel in the community, especially the home care nursing services and primary care physicians.

This study demonstrates that it is possible to care for children, who have been admitted to a neurosurgical unit and diagnosed as being terminally ill by the introduction of a home-based palliative care program. Recently we have been able to demonstrate that this program is truly beneficial (Duffy et al., 1990). Although it has had a narrow focus so far, we hope that with the acquisition of additional funds, we may expand this service beyond care for terminally ill children admitted to our neurosurgical unit.

REFERENCES

Dominica, F. B. (1982). Helen House—A hospice for children. *Maternal and Child Health, 7,* 355–359.

Duffy, C. H., Pollock, P., Levy, M., Budd, E., Caufield, L., Spielberg, S. P., & Koren,

G. (1990). Home-based palliative care for children: An established program. Submitted for publication.

Holman, K. G., Noce, J. J., & Montgomery, P. J. (1985). Hospice care: Not available to everyone. *Journal of Family Practice, 20,* 539–546.

Krant, M. J. (1978). The hospice movement. *New England Journal of Medicine, 299,* 546–549.

Lauer, M. E., Mulhern, R. K., Bohn, J. B., & Camitta, B. M. (1985). Children's perception of their sibling's death at home or in hospital: The precursors of differential adjustment. *Cancer Nursing, 8,* 21–27.

Lunt, B., & Hillier, R. (1981). Terminal care: Present services and future priorities. *British Medical Journal, 283,* 595–598.

Martinson, I. M. (1976). Why don't we let them die at home? *RN,* 58–66.

Martinson, I. M., Armstrong, G. D., Geis, D. P. et al. (1978). Home care for children dying of cancer. *Pediatrics, 62,* 106–113.

Martinson, I. M., Moldow, D. G., & Henry, W. F. (1980, June). *Home care for the dying child with cancer.* CA 19490. Minneapolis: University of Minnesota, School of Nursing.

Mount, B. M. (1976). The problem of caring for the dying in a general hospital: The palliative care unit as a possible solution. *Canadian Medical Association Journal, 115,* 119–121.

Mulhern, R. K., Lauer, M. E., & Hoffmond, C. B. (1983). Death of a child at home or in the hospital: Subsequent psychological adjustment of the family. *Pediatrics, 71,* 743–747.

Reid, D. B. (1985). Hospice palliative care. *Medical Journal of Australia, 142,* 619.

Saunders, C. (1981). The hospice: Its meaning to patients and their physicians. *Hospital Practice, 16,* 93–98.

Shepard, D. A. (1977). Principles and practice of palliative care. *Canadian Medical Association Journal, 116,* 522–526.

Siegel, R., Rudd, S. H., Cleveland, C., Powers, L. K., Harmon, R. J. (1985). A hospice approach to neonatal care. In C. A. Corr & D. M. Corr (Eds.), *Hospice approaches to pediatric care* (pp. 127–152). New York: Springer.

Wheeler, P. R., Foerster, L., & Bertolone, S. J. (1985). Improving care for hospitalized terminally ill children: A practicable model. In C. A. Corr & D. M. Corr (Eds.), *Hospice approaches to pediatric care* (pp. 43–60). New York: Springer.

Wilson, D. C. (1985). Developing a hospice program for children. In C. A. Corr & D. M. Corr (Eds.), *Hospice approaches to pediatric care* (pp. 5–29). New York: Springer.

Chapter 17

Coping with Terminal Care in Pediatric Cancer

**G. B. Humphrey, W. A. Kamps,
J. E. H. M. Hoekstra-Weebers, J. L. Littlewood,
and C. M. J. Boon**

It is amazing how little we know about the circumstances surrounding the death of a child, while we know so much about the demographic aspects of death, such as age, sex, duration of therapy, and the biological functions of the most important organ systems of the body.

While we can determine the duration of the illness (the time from diagnosis to death), it is almost impossible to know how long a child was *terminally ill*. This is not surprising, as the cure rates for pediatric cancers are approximately 60% at present. The initial intent of the therapy is to cure the child, but as this cannot be guaranteed, the child and the family enter into a period of uncertainty. The point in time when the child is no longer thought to be curable and thus, enter the terminal phase can be very difficult to determine.

In the recent medical literature about terminal care of seriously ill children,

The research reported in this paper was supported by: Pediatric Oncology Foundation of Groningen (SKOG), Dutch Cancer Society (NKB), Universities of Groningen and Loughborough, University Hospital Groningen, and the Domino Foundation.

articles can be grouped into four categories based on their definition of the *onset of the terminal phase* of life:

1   There is no definition or mention of the onset of the terminal phase.
2   The terminal phase is said to begin when therapy is discontinued.
3   The terminal phase is said to begin when the child is transferred to a hospice or a terminal care team.
4   The terminal phase is said to begin when the child is no longer responding to curative therapy, no further curative therapy is available, and the patient is eligible for an experimental drug trial or a drug efficacy trial.

We have used the fourth definition in three different studies and the first definition in retrospective studies, in which we gathered information from parents and siblings concerning events surrounding the death of a child. While we have not used the other two definitions, we have nonetheless, obtained useful information regarding the stress of dying at home versus dying in the hospital.

There are difficulties in initiating a study on terminal care other than the lack of a standard definition of this difficult condition. One of these may be the attitude of the physicians. An orientation towards terminal care as such, is in general not part of physicians' training. Most hospitals do not require that physicians record patients as being "terminally ill," although they are required to record patients as "critically ill." Even if a physician believes that a certain patient is terminally ill, his or her therapeutic strategy may not allow the disclosure of such information to the patient. Finally, every health professional who has practiced medicine for a number of years has seen a "miracle"—a patient assumed to be terminal who somehow recovered. Thus, stating that a patient has entered the terminal phase suggests a high probability of death or a certainty of death, which makes many physicians uncomfortable.

Other difficulties in conducting research in the field of terminal care may relate to the coping style of the family, who may not wish to discuss the issue with any member of the health care team and may feel very strongly about not discussing the topic with the patient. Differences of opinion concerning disclosure among members of the health care team, other than the physician, may also cause conflicts. Finally, there are issues of informed consent and ethics.

We have been involved in a series of studies with the objective of improving the management of the terminally ill child with cancer (Nitschke, Wunder, Sexauer & Humphrey, 1977; Nitschke et al., 1982; Kamps, Akkerboom, Kingma & Humphrey, 1987; Kamps, Kingma, Akkerboom & Humphrey, 1986; Humphrey, Kamps, de Bruin, Bosma & Kingma, 1988; Hoekstra-Weebers, Littlewood, Boon, Postma & Humphrey, 1990). The following are some of the questions that were of concern to us:

- What role should the child play in the decisions to be made regarding the care that can be given during this period?
  - When should the child decide his or her own fate?
  - What type of information should be included in the disclosure?
  - What role do parental coping styles play in parents' perceptions of the terminal care received?

The purpose of this chapter is to discuss the results of our studies, which were guided by the above-mentioned concerns, especially those relating to the disclosure of the onset of terminal care. Although these studies have provided us with additional information on issues related to ethics and informed consent (Kamps, Nitschke, Kingma, Holmes & Humphrey, 1985; Humphrey, Kamps, Kingma, & Nitschke, 1989), these issues will not be discussed.

BACKGROUND, METHODS, AND RESULTS OF FOUR STUDIES

First Study: 1975–1982 (University of Oklahoma)

One of the goals of this study (Nitschke et al., 1977; Nitschke et al., 1982) was to gain experience with explicit disclosure of the *onset of terminal phase,* defined as the time when the child was no longer responding to curative therapy, no further curative therapy was available, and the patient was eligible for an experimental drug trial or a drug efficacy trial (fourth definition). A special conference was scheduled for parents whose child had had a relapse or had a progressive disease. Both parents were informed in advance why the conference was scheduled and what was to be discussed. They were encouraged to include the child in this meeting.

At this conference one of the pediatric oncologists and one of the pediatric nurse oncologists were present. The following topics were discussed: (1) review of the disease, (2) recent progression of the disease, (3) unavailability of curative therapy, (4) availability of new experimental drugs, and (5) the imminence of death. When the child was present, he or she was told, "Most likely you will die from the disease very soon," or other words to that effect.

A checklist was used by the team member who conducted the conference in order to avoid overlooking any topic and to maintain homogeneity across conferences. The family was asked to choose between supportive care plus experimental therapy or supportive care only. Only self-interest issues were discussed; altruism or prosocial behavior was not approached as a topic. For example, we discussed how experimental therapy might prolong life but would necessitate visits to the hospital for drug infusions, vein punctures, or bone marrow aspirations. The possibility that the child's participation in an experimental trial might help future patients was not mentioned.

Sixty-eight parents were asked whether their child could be included in the conference; 25 excluded the child, and 43 included the child. In the first group, where the child was excluded, the choice for experimental therapy versus supportive care alone was relatively equal (14 to 11). In the second group, where the child was included, the choice for experimental therapy was approximately $1/2$ that of supportive care (14 to 29). Despite the small number of subjects in this study, we believe that the truly informed child and parents are more likely to consent to supportive care than experimental therapy.

We also concluded that the child and family coped relatively well with the disclosure of the onset of terminal care. When the child was included in the conference, our general impressions were the following: the child understood his or her declining health; he or she decided alone or together with the family; severe depression and severe behavioral problems rarely occurred during terminal care; communication between parents and child increased.

Second Study, 1985, and Third Study, 1986
(University of Groningen)

One of the major goals of these two sequential studies (Kamps et al., 1987; Kamps et al, 1986; Humphrey et al., 1985) was to gain some insight into Dutch attitudes towards a terminal care conference in which the imminence of death would be disclosed and in which the family would be given a choice between supportive care plus experimental therapy versus supportive care alone. The fourth definition of terminal care was used. We raised the following questions: (1) Should the child be included, and if so at what age? (2) Should the child be involved in the decision-making process, and if so at what age? (3) At what age should the child be allowed to decide alone on his or her fate? (4) Should disclosure about the child's possible participation in experimental therapy include altruism as well as self-interest issues? These two studies were limited to cured children and parents of cured children. Parents of deceased children were excluded for ethical reasons, as very few experimental drugs were available in Groningen before 1986.

The second study focused on parental attitudes, which we evaluated by means of a questionnaire sent to 164 homes, 137 of which responded.

The third study evaluated patient attitudes. The same questionnaire was used to conduct a two-hour interview in the child's home. Most of the parents who participated in the second study agreed that their child be interviewed. Time and personnel however, allowed for only 25 children to participate. The children were assured that their answers would be confidential and that we would not compare their answers to those of their parents.

A comparison of these studies is given in Tables 1 and 2.

Not surprisingly, children thought that the child should be included in the conference and should be involved in the decision-making process at a slightly higher frequency and at a slightly lower median age; a wide range of opinions was expressed by both parents and children (Table 1). More than the majority of

Table 1   A Terminal Care Conference: Parental Attitudes Towards Disclosure
and Associated Decisions

Possibilities	Parent's response (study 2)	Children's response (study 3)
The child attends	85% + [M = 12 (4–20)][a]	96% + [M = 10 (3–15)]
The child is involved[b]	89% + [M = 12 (4–20)]	100% + [M = 12 (6–16)]
The child gives consent alone[b]	67% + [M = 16 (7–20)][a]	92% + [M = 16 (8–19)]

Note: + = Positive or affirmative answer.
[a]M = 12 (4–20): median age in years with range.
[b]For those answering in the affirmative to the first question, should the child attend.

both parents and children felt that disclosure of a possible experimental drug trial should include altruism as well as self-interest; this affirmative answer was given by a higher percentage of children than adults (Table 2). It is difficult to discuss this finding in any detail due to the small number of children participating in the study and to the study's retrospective method. Children who were cured may have been biased to some extent; some of them probably assumed that the drugs used to cure them were at one time experimental agents.

Fourth Study (Active): 1989 (University of Groningen/University of Loughborough)

The principal goals on this current study (Hoekstra-Weebers et al., 1990) are: (1) to determine if there are differences in the ways parents of younger children and parents of adolescent children cope with the death of their child, and whether this has an effect on psychological well-being in the bereavement period; and (2) to gather information from parents about the circumstances surrounding the death of their child. This study was designed and is being analyzed

Table 2   A Terminal Care Conference: Attitudes towards Inclusion of Self-Interest vs. Altruism as Reasons for Choosing an Experimental Drug Trial

Possibilities	Parent's response (study 2)	Children's response (study 3)
Self-interest and altruism	68%	96%
Self-interest only	27%	0%
Altruism only	1%	4%
"Don't know"	4%	0%

in collaboration with Jane Littlewood of the Department of Sociology, Technology University of Loughborough, U. K.

For the first part of the study, data were collected from 33 parents using the Utrecht Coping List and the Goldberg General Health Questionnaire. Findings revealed no differences in coping styles used by parents of younger children versus parents of adolescents during the bereavement period, apart from the active, problem-focused coping style (Hoekstra-Weebers et al., 1990), which is used more by parents of younger children. For the second part of this study, a semistructured interview, conducted in the homes of these parents, was used to gather information, which is currently being analyzed.

FUTURE DIRECTIONS

What are the events surrounding the death of a child? If discussion is limited to the child with cancer, then these events can be better understood by referring to the time of diagnosis. Even though early deaths (within the first few days) still do occur, most children who eventually die undergo a period of uncertainty and die after going through a terminal phase. The process may last a few months or a few years. The child is accompanied through this process not only by the members of the immediate family but also by members of a health care team and individuals from the child's social environment.

The events surrounding the death of a child suggest that a certain process develops before the death (*terminal care*) and another after death (*bereavement*). If terminal care is to be studied, it seems that we need to know what stressful events occurred before the onset of terminal care. This is our reason for suggesting that research on terminal care needs to begin at diagnosis. The child who may die, as well as the people the child comes in contact with, are all potential subjects of investigation. Investigators should search for factors that cause stress throughout all stages or phases the child undergoes (including the time after cessation of therapy for those who are cured). "State of the art" interventions should be evaluated during these periods, and the results should be used to develop the next generation of intervention strategies. Obviously, interventions should also apply to those who are bereaved by the child's death.

More research into the events surrounding the death of a child is necessary. Inherent in this advice is the need for members of the health care team to recognize terminal care as a research priority and to recruit their patients and families actively into psychosocial protocols with the same enthusiasm they recruit their patients into therapeutic protocols.

REFERENCES

Hoekstra-Weebers, J.E.H.M., Littlewood, J. L., Boon, C.M.J., Postma, A., & Humphrey, G. B. (1990). A comparison of the bereavement process following a death from childhood malignancy: Parents who have lost adolescents versus parents who have lost younger children. Manuscript submitted for publication.

Humphrey, G. B., Kamps, W. A., de Bruin, E., Bosma, H., & Kingma, A. (1988). Terminal care of the child with cancer: An analysis of parent/child attitudes. In A. Gilmore & S. Gilmore (Eds.), *A Safer Death* (p. 161). New York: Plenum.

Humphrey, G. B., Kamps, W. A., Kingma, A., & Nitschke, R. (1989). Serial studies of the ethics of informed consent in children. In D. V. Razis, G. Mathe & M. Jodeay-Grymberg (Eds.), *Medical ethics and/or ethical medicine* (p. 201). Paris: Elsevier.

Kamps, W. A., Akkerboom, J. C., Kingma, A., & Humphrey, G. B. (1987). Experimental chemotherapy in children with cancer—A parent's view. *Pediatric Hematology and Oncology, 4,* 117.

Kamps, W. A., Kingma, A., Akkerboom, J. C., & Humphrey, G. B. (1986). Attitudes of children with cancer towards their personal involvement in informed consent [Abstract]. *Proceedings of the UICC Congress,* 475.

Kamps, W. A., Nitschke, R., Kingma, A., Holmes, H. B., & Humphrey, G. B. (1985). Altruism and informed consent in chemotherapy trials of childhood cancer. *Archives of the Foundation of Thanatology, 11,* 4.

Nitschke, R., Humphrey, G. B., Sexauer, C. L., Catron, B., Wunder, S., & Jay, S. (1982). Therapeutic choices made by patients with end-stage cancer. *Journal of Pediatrics, 101,* 471.

Nitschke, R., Wunder, S., Sexauer, C. L., & Humphrey, G. B. (1977). The final stage conference: The patient's decision on research drugs in pediatric oncology. *Journal of Pediatric Psychology, 2,* 58.

Chapter 18

Hospice Care for Children: Their Families and Health Care Providers

Ann Armstrong-Dailey

Children are not supposed to die. The death of a child violates society's norms and flies in the face of everything parents and health professionals expect and desire for that child. But children do die.

According to former U.S. Surgeon General C. Everett Koop (1986), "approximately 100,000 children in the United States die annually. Many more will be diagnosed with life-threatening illness. Most parents of dying children want involvement and some control over their children's care."

According to the U.S. General Accounting Office (1989), "Ten to fifteen percent of all U.S. children have a chronic health condition . . . about one million of these have a severe form of the condition. . . . Advances in medical technology have moved much of the treatment to the home."

In addition to all of the hospice-type support services needed by these children with life-threatening conditions and their families, bereavement support services are also needed by thousands of families each year who lose a child through accident, drug use, war, or other forms of sudden death.

Without hospice-oriented support and practical assistance to pediatricians, nurses, other health care professionals, and family members, too many of these children face death with unnecessary physical pain, loneliness, and isolation. Children with life-threatening conditions, their families, and caregivers must deal with the pain, grief, fear, frustration, and profound sense of failure that inevitably accompany the prospect of a child's death.

Timmy, a 5-year-old child with nephortic syndrome, spent his last few weeks of life in a leading children's hospital. He received much support and attention from his physicians and nurses while there was still hope for his recovery. However, along with the terminal prognosis, he was moved to a room at the end of the corridor.

His health care providers, trained to cure, were experiencing understandable denial. So were Timmy's parents who, although they did come to visit, were not able to bring themselves to stay long to provide him with the love and support he needed.

Children tend to know they are dying, and want to know what it is going to be like: "Will someone be with them to hold their hand? Will a grandmother who died last year be there to greet them? Families need to cry together, to tell how much they are going to miss each other." (Gamarekian, 1987).

Everyone evaded Timmy's anxious questions. Isolated from the world he knew, and, seemingly abandoned by those he loved, Timmy, in typical 5-year-old fashion, blamed himself and tried to figure out what he had done to drive everyone away. Timmy died without physical pain but very much alone, without the reassurance of his parents' love. To paraphrase Mother Theresa, the greatest pain on earth is not the pain of hunger or poverty, but rather, the pain of isolation, abandonment, and feeling unloved.

Not coincidentally, both staff members and Timmy's parents suffered prolonged guilt after his death. If only Timmy's health care providers had been equipped with appropriate education and training to encourage the provision of care, even when they could no longer cure, and if they had had an appropriate support system for themselves, they could have helped Timmy's parents to focus on the time they had left with him and to deal in an appropriate manner with their guilt.

Through such hospice-type support, Timmy, his parents, and his health care providers could have known what they were feeling was normal. They could have cried together and expressed how they would miss one another. They could have shared the picture of the butterfly, bearing the words, "I Love You," which Timmy drew just before he died—alone.

And rather than the devastating guilt that Timmy's family members felt following his death, they could have felt the satisfaction of knowing that they had helped him live every moment of his life to its fullest and that they had done everything possible for their child.

Children's hospice care provides much-needed services by encouraging the ongoing involvement of family members and health care professionals with the dying child, and implementing practical knowledge of effective and appropriate palliative measures in children with life-threatening conditions. The hospice concept of care involves an interdisciplinary team working together to provide appropriate medical, psychosocial, and spiritual support. Application of the hospice concept can significantly enhance the lives of dying children, their families, and health care providers.

The landmark volume, *Bereavement: Reactions, Consequences, and Care* (Osterweis, Solomon, & Green, 1984) provides a critical analysis of the available research on the physical and psychological effects of loss. The editors conclude that preliminary data demonstrate the potential long-term impact of traumatic loss on a person's immune system. They cite some evidence to suggest that bereavement intervention can help people to move through the grieving process, but stress the need for controlled studies to measure short- and long-term outcomes of different types of interventions.

Bernard Nigro, chief of psychiatry at Alexandria Hospital in Virginia, U. S. A., regards hospice care as "preventive psychiatry." He estimates that as many as 80% of his patients have problems linked to unresolved grief. According to Nigro (1983), "hospice care provides the opportunity to help families deal with emotional issues as they occur and to work through those issues in the process. Thus, it helps minimize or prevent subsequent depression, anxiety, guilt and possible dysfunction within the family and in the lives of individual bereaved family members."

Children's hospice is a concept of care addressing the physical, psychological, social, and spiritual aspects of the lives of people who have lost a child, as well as of children with life-threatening conditions and their families. Children's Hospice international advocates the implementation of hospice-type care immediately upon the occurrence of a sudden death or from the time of diagnosis and throughout bereavement follow-up, as long as the family and/or significant others desire.

Hospice denotes a philosophically "old-fashioned" approach to medical care and services, which focuses on helping people with expected relatively short life-spans to live their remaining lives to the fullest without pain, with choices and dignity, and with family support.

According to Otis R. Bowen, former secretary of the U.S. Department of Health and Human Services (1986), "children's hospice care facilitates the participation of parents in assuming the role of primary caregiver. It supports the inclusion of the patient and the family in the decision-making process to the best of the family's capability and commensurate with their desires. . . . Hospice is a concept of care which can take place in a hospital, at home or in a residential care setting."

When provided to surviving family members or to the child with a life-threatening condition and his or her family, children's hospice care is a comprehensive, interdisciplinary continuum of care. It can and should be thoroughly integrated into all aspects of pediatric health care. It is provided by a "hospice team," which includes—depending on individual needs—physicians, nurses, social workers, clergy, therapists, teachers, trained volunteers, and others. The child and family are integral members and leaders of the team.

According to Milton Glatt, a child psychiatrist (personal communication, April 21, 1989), "Whenever incurability is confused with untreatability, an attitude (either expressed or tacit) of 'there is nothing more I can do' often results. However, much can be done to aid the child with the life-threatening condition, his family and health care providers in coping with the stress and fears involved in dealing with the likely death. Children's hospice care can turn this potentially devastating experience into one of growth for the child and his support system."

As stated in the National Hospice Organization's *Standards of Care* (NHO, 1981), "admission to a hospice program of care is on the basis of patient and family need." This philosophy of admission based on need (rather than on need plus ability to pay) reflects the idealistic and largely noninstitutional origins of the hospice movement.

Hospice care focuses on patient and family needs to the extent possible. This requires considerable flexibility on the part of hospice workers and other caregivers involved with the hospice programs, since every patient and every family present different needs, hopes, values, religious beliefs, and prior experiences with death.

Hospice provides support and care for persons who are seriously ill so that their lives can be as full as possible. Hospice care neither hastens nor postpones death. The hospice movement affirms that through personalized services in a caring community, the dying and the soon-to-be-bereaved family can be guided in the necessary preparation for a death with understanding and dignity. Children's hospice does not turn away from the reality of death, but rather affirms life and living.

In this direction, Children's Hospice International creates a world of hospice support for children by providing medical and technical assistance, as well as research and education, for them, their families, and health care professionals. Children's Hospice International promotes the "circle of care" that multidisciplinary resources should create in service to the families and those close to a child who has died, to children with life-threatening conditions, and to their families. The resources involved in creating effective hospice services for children include not only hospitals, physicians, and nurses but also therapists, volunteers, spiritual counselors, home care specialists, social service representatives, and support groups.

Since its inception in 1983, Children's Hospice International has focused on improving the availability and quality of hospice care for children with life-threatening conditions and their families. As a nonprofit organization advocating hospice care for children and adolescents, it grew out of the recognition that most hospice programs in the early 1980s were not able to accept children as patients.

To gain broader acceptance of the patient- and family-centered approach to care, this international organization serves as a resource and advocacy center. Undertaking educational efforts with parents, professionals, policy makers, and payers (government health care reimbursement, private insurance companies, and others) enables Children's Hospice International to move towards four interrelated goals:

1 The implementation of the hospice philosophy throughout pediatric care facilities.
2 The inclusion of children in existing and developing hospice and home-care programs.
3 The inclusion of the hospice perspective in all areas of pediatric care and education.
4 An enhanced public awareness of the needs of children with life-threatening conditions and their families.

Toward these ends, Children's Hospice International has conducted training seminars, held national and international interdisciplinary conferences, published various training manuals, and supported numerous local, regional, national, and international efforts to expand awareness of the benefits of children's hospice care. The organization supports a clearinghouse for information and technical assistance, which fields requests from around the world.

Children's Hospice International continues to strive to meet the needs of communities worldwide. Communities' needs, like families' needs, vary from one to another. The central goal in every case, however, is the same: to celebrate and enjoy every moment of each child's life and the life of the family.

REFERENCES

Bowen, Otis R. (1986). Remarks (presented at the opening of new headquarters for Children's Hospice International, Alexandria, Virginia, September 11, 1986).

Gamarekian, Barbara. (1987, June 25). A support network of hospice groups for dying children. *The New York Times.*

Koop, C. Everett. (1986). Introduction (presented to Children's Hospice International Pediatric Hospice Conference: Enriching the Circle of Care, May 8, 1986).

The National Hospice Organization. (1981). *NHO Standards of Care.* McLean, VA: NHO.

Nigro, Bernard. (1983, August 7). Interview. Washington, DC: WDC Radio.

Osterweis, M., Solomon, F., & Green, M. (Eds.). (1984). *Bereavement reactions, consequences and care.* Washington, DC: National Academy Press.

U.S. General Accounting Office. (1989). *Health care, home care experiences of families with chronically ill children.* Washington, DC: U.S. Government Printing Office.

Part Five

Parental Bereavement and Adjustment to the Loss of a Child

Chapter 19

Parental Adjustment to the Loss of a Child

Therese A. Rando

When you lose your spouse, it is like losing a limb; when you lose your child, it is like losing a lung.

Words of a woman who was both a widow and a bereaved parent

The relationship between parent and child is such that its severing typically affects the parent's innermost core. Although the loss of any close, significant relationship can leave a person feeling maimed, the loss of a child seems to strike even more deeply into the very being and integrity of the mourner. This is one of the main reasons why parental bereavement, when compared to other bereavements, appears more complicated, intense, and long lasting (Rando, 1986b), leaving bereaved parents looking "atypical," "abnormal," or "pathological" in their mourning when, in fact, they are not.

The parent-child relationship addressed in this chapter is the "ideal" one. To the extent that any particular relationship departs from this ideal, one can expect to see corresponding variations in the parental bereavement from that discussed here.

One of the major differences in the centrality of the injury from this type of loss seems to stem from the nature of the attachment. In other relationships, a person has "an attachment to" someone else, for example, a spouse. One is "separate from, but connected to" that beloved other. When that other dies, among other things, the mourner must emotionally disengage himself or herself from one with whom he or she has been intertwined on many levels and in countless ways, and must ultimately transform the relationship to one based on memory. The parent-child relationship, however, is by definition, the closest and most intense that life can generate, not only physically but psychologically and socially as well. In this situation, the other—that is, the child—"has sprung from" the mourner. Therefore, the child is "part of, and the same as" the parent. Such a different relationship mandates a different disengagement after a death, since what the parents have lost is also very much a part of them, and it is therefore extremely difficult for them to disengage.

There are additional reasons why the death of a child has such an intimate impact on the surviving parent. One of these derives from the parental process of projecting feelings, concerns, thoughts, beliefs, hopes, needs, and meanings onto the child-to-be from the moment of parents' knowledge of conception, continuing on through birth and to the existing child. Consequently, each child has a particular accumulation of meanings to the parent. In fact, no relationship has the potential for being as multiply determined (that is, influenced by a number of conscious and unconscious factors and conflicts) as the parent-child relationship.

Because the child stems from and is a product of the parents, their feelings about the child are an admixture of feelings about the self and the partner, as well as about the individual child. These feelings about the self and the other can range from "delight" to "the worst part of the self." Meanings of the child, and corresponding feelings, attitudes, thoughts, and expectations are many and varied for each individual parent. They originate from the past (the child may symbolize a link with the parent's ancestors or serve to resurrect or resolve past sibling or parent-child conflicts), from the present (the child as a source and object of love, providing proof of worth or competence, or acting as a replacement to compensate for the parent's own deprived childhood), and from the future (the child may afford the opportunity to start over or to rectify past mistakes, or may help assure the parent's immortality).

There are *no* unselfish reasons for having a child; many needs, hopes, feelings, attitudes, thoughts, and beliefs are represented in every child. This is the case despite the fact that whatever the child represents to the parent, he or she is also a unique person—a product of and connected to the parent, yet a separate individual as well. Even if the parent has a child for socially acceptable reasons—such as to have someone on whom to shower love, to create new life with a beloved partner, or to raise an individual who will make a positive contribution to society—these reasons all are "selfish." They are selfish not in a pejorative or negative sense, but in the sense that they derive from the self of the parent and are therefore fundamentally egotistic. This is not necessarily negative, for there should be a healthy amount of egotism in any person. It merely clarifies that reasons for having a child represent something of the parent, which in turn affects what is projected onto that child by the parent. It is important to understand what is projected onto the child and to know what the child symbolizes and embodies for the parent, since these projections and symbolizations represent a significant amount of that which is lost along with the child who dies.

Another factor contributing to the unique trauma of parental loss of a child comes from the normal process of parents incorporating a number of roles into their parental identity. Parents are accustomed to being self-sufficient and in control of what happens to and with the child. They can "fix" what happens to the child, be it soothing feelings of rejection from a peer or repairing a broken toy. Parents are protectors, providers, problem solvers, and advisers. All of these roles are taken in and combine to define parents' sense of self, role, and identity.

Finally, as parents people are exposed to the most inappropriate and unrealistic set of social expectations that exist. Parents are expected to be superhuman and to be all loving, all good, all concerned, totally selfless, and solely motivated by the child and his or her welfare. These expectations leave no room for normal human ambivalence or healthy assertiveness. Unfortunately, these expectations are not only socially assigned by culture and society, they are internalized by the parents as well.

Even in day-to-day situations less dramatic than the death of a child, parents have many difficulties reconciling these unrealistic parental expectations with normal human interaction. The expectations establish standards that are simply impossible for parents—or anyone else—to meet. The consequences of this are severe, since parents tend to evaluate themselves based on how effectively and how closely they meet these standards, unrealistic and irrational though they are. Since it is impossible to meet these standards consistently, parents often experience guilt and uncomfortable feelings arising from the recognition of failing to meet them. This is despite the fact that no other role is subject to such unreasonable expectations, which do not allow for normal ambivalence, frustration, anger, and setting of limits.

By definition, the failure to meet any expectation or standard, albeit an impractical one, causes guilt. When, therefore, parents have failed to meet the expectation of "protecting" the child (i.e., the child dies) or when they look back and recall times during the child's life when their feelings towards that child were less than positive (which is expectable and normal, but still a violation of the unrealistic parental standard), guilt and negative feelings ensue. This is one of the primary reasons why bereaved parents tend to have the greatest guilt feelings of all mourners, and why they feel such failures in their parental roles.

For these reasons, the three issues that are difficult enough for parents under the best of circumstances—understanding what responsibilities and expectations are appropriate to have of themselves as parents, appreciating the limits of parental control over any child, and knowing how to take care of themselves as individuals—end up becoming serious impediments to uncomplicated mourning after a child dies.

MOURNING FOR ONE'S CHILD

When a child dies, the aspects of the relationship between parent and child that defined its intimacy and uniqueness are precisely those that intensify bereavement. While the death of a child certainly contains a number of elements found in a variety of other types of losses (e.g., the loss of a spouse, parent, sibling, other relative, or friend), no other death has such a constellation of complicating factors as when parents lose their child. In this chapter, I will present arguments to support the following contentions:

1 Parental bereavement is an exception to the general conceptualizations of mourning.

2 Bereaved parents are predisposed to be exceptionally vulnerable to complicated mourning.

3 Bereaved parents are susceptible to erroneous diagnoses of pathology.

4 There is a mandate for both a new model of parental mourning and new criteria for identification of pathology in bereaved parents (Rando, 1986b).

It must also be noted that in most regards the age of the deceased child is irrelevant, so that the issues of parental bereavement pertain equally to the parent who has sustained a perinatal loss and the parent whose adult child has died. Curiously, there has been a social phenomenon of denying the importance of parental loss of a child at both ends of the age span—that is, in miscarriage, perinatal, and infant deaths, and in the deaths of adult children. In the media, whenever parental bereavement is addressed, it is most commonly portrayed through stories of parents whose school-age or adolescent children die. While this exemplifies a particular type of parental loss, it does not circumscribe it. There are bereaved parents of all ages who lose children of all ages.

The age of the child does have *some* relevance in influencing some of the specific issues to be addressed in parental mourning. For example, if an infant dies, the family will typically experience a deep wound as the little person to whom they were oriented to providing care is ripped from them. In many cases, others outside the family may not have had the opportunity to develop a bond with the child or to experience him or her as an individual. They may mistakenly believe that the loss is minimal because the life was so brief. They fail to appreciate that the family has had a bond with this child since pregnancy, and that although the actual life to be mourned may have been short, the hopes, dreams, feelings, thoughts, and meanings of the child and his or her existence—the numerous secondary losses (Rando, 1984) that accrue—are enormous and quite painful.

In the situation of the death of an adult child with his or her own family, parents again tend to be overlooked, as the primary attention, control, and decision-making responsibilities are given to that child's spouse and children. There are numerous issues compromising the parent's bereavement in this case; notably, the effects of a relationship with an adult child, the psychosocial circumstances of the parent at the time of the death, the incredulity since the child has been successfully reared through more dangerous times, and the difficulty of witnessing the child's responsibilities left unattended (Rando, 1986c). These can contribute to special bereavement problems, such as the compromising of successful accommodation to the loss, the exclusion of the parents from the concern of others, a preponderance of factors that contribute to complicated grief, the parent's significant lack of control, and a host of special secondary losses (Rando, 1986c). It should be noted that this population of bereaved mourners can be expected to increase dramatically as compared to others, since with today's longer life-span, greater numbers of parents will be alive to witness the deaths of their adult children. In earlier eras, these parents would themselves have been dead by the time their middle-aged child was fatally stricken.

SPECIFIC DILEMMAS

At least 10 specific dilemmas are encountered by bereaved parents as a consequence of the loss of the child, who has such a unique role with regard to the parent.

First, there is a failure to sustain the basic function of parenthood, which is to preserve some dimension of the self, the family, and the social group (Jackson, 1977). The parents are supposed to protect and provide for the child so that one day that same child will bury the parents. This is failure of the highest magnitude, since it violates the basic tenet of the aspect of adult life that is taken most seriously. We need only look at how other relationships are more frequently made the butt of adults' jokes (e.g., jokes about spouses or in-laws as opposed to children) to observe how this parental responsibility is perceived with greater solemnity than others.

Second, as compared to other deaths, there are more losses of parts of the self when a child dies. This is a result of the numerous specific investments placed in the child, and the fact that they are extremely significant ones. This also occurs because parental attachment to a child consists of love both for the child and for the self, given that the child is a part of the parents. As a consequence, the death of a child intensifies the losses to self that are usually felt after the death of any close one.

Third, multiple "secondary losses" (Rando, 1984)—physical and symbolic, psychosocial losses—occur as a consequence of the death. With the death of a child, parents lose not only all the dreams and hopes they invested in that child, but also a very special love source, someone who needs, depends upon, admires, and appreciates the parents in a unique and most gratifying way.

Fourth, there is a monumental assault on the parental identity. The parents often report feeling "mutilated," not only from the loss of the child as an extension of the self, or from the loss of self in relation to the child, but from the ripping asunder of the adult identity, which is centered on providing and caring for the child. Because of the death, parents are robbed of the ability to carry out the functional role of parent. This causes an oppressive sense of failure, the loss of power and ability, a deep sense of violation, a monumental decrease in self-esteem, and an overwhelmingly confused identity. In turn, these assaults lead to additional secondary losses, which derive from the diminished sense of self and include disillusionment, emptiness, and insecurity. Ultimately, these culminate in the necessity for a profound identity shift, in which the old identity must be mourned and relinquished, along with former beliefs and assumptions about the self and the person's capabilities as a parent, and a new identity must be formed to reflect the reality of the death and its specific effects upon the parent.

Fifth, there is a loss of a sense of immortality. Children are the parent's future. Although death may claim the parents physically, it cannot do so in terms of the parts of the parents perpetuated by the child. Through the child and that child's offspring, the parents live on genetically, and are kept "alive" through the continuation of the thoughts, values, attitudes, and beliefs they have instilled in the child, and via the numerous ways the child chooses to commemorate the parents, such as memory, ritual, identification, and so forth (Rando, 1988). In this manner, as long as parents have a surviving child, death will not put an end to their influence in the world.

Sixth, the unnaturalness of the child dying before the parent is a major stumbling block often underestimated by professionals and laypersons alike. The loss of the child is incomprehensible because it violates the laws of nature, in which the young grow up to replace the old. This is death out of turn, and it causes the apparent order of the universe to be undermined (Gorer, 1965). There is an unmet expectation that the parents will die before the child, and the intensity of the emotion generated by the discrepancy between what should be and what is becomes overwhelming. The guilt of parents surviving their child in such unnatural circumstances becomes a tremendous burden. It just shouldn't be this way.

Seventh, with the death of the child, there is the loss of the family as it has been known. This comes in part from the irretrievable loss of the presence and role-fulfilling behaviors and functions of the child, but also from the loss of parts of each parent's self in relationship with the child; that is, the special interactive part of the parent who was in a unique relationship to that child (e.g., the special part of the woman who was mother to the particular child who died). When the child dies, that special part of the parent dies too, notwithstanding the fact that there may be other surviving children whom he or she is still called upon to care for.

Eighth, there are problems when the death is sudden and traumatic, like the deaths of many children and adolescents that occur from accidents, suicide, or homicide. This automatically involves the sequelae of unanticipated loss, which has been well documented to lead to complicated bereavement responses (Parkes & Weiss, 1983). In many cases it also involves violence, mutilation, and destruction, which are known to leave all survivors with a greater sense of helplessness and threat, prompting enormous efforts to find meaning in the death, determine who is to blame, and regain a sense of control. In situations where these dynamics overlay the loss of a child, reactions are intensified and bereavement is significantly more complicated.

Ninth, where the death of a child results from genetic or unexplained medical illness, the biological role of the parents predisposes them to assume an even greater guilt and responsibility than usual. This happens even when the parents "know" better; for example, in the case of a psychologist who "knew" his child's cancer was not hereditary, but who said, "My daughter died from cancer. Her genes allowed her to develop cancer. I gave her her genes. Therefore, I killed my daughter." Logic, rationality, and scientific understanding often fare poorly against parents' belief in their responsibility for the death of a child.

Lastly, although frequently not admitted, the loss of a child can portend the loss of a future caretaker. Children are "supposed" to care for their parents when parents can no longer care sufficiently for themselves. In situations where the parents currently depend on the child for emotional, physical, financial, social, or spiritual support, as is often the case with older parents and adult children, the death of that child may leave the parents not only with the enormous difficulties of parental bereavement, but also at high risk in the areas formerly supported by the now-deceased child.

Perhaps one of the most important aspects of parental bereavement is that it typically involves grief and mourning that are more intense, more complicated, and more protracted than those encountered following the loss of other individuals in other role relationships (Rando, 1986b). This means that not only must bereaved parents struggle with additional issues that complicate mourning and compromise adjustment, but also they must do so while contending with an intensity and duration of grief and mourning which further debilitates the parents; makes them vulnerable to more grief-related conflict and fear than ordinarily seen in mourners; increases the possibility for misunderstanding, intolerance, and misdiagnosis by others unaware of the unique difficulties of the loss of a child; and can interfere with successful accommodation to the loss.

While a bereaved parent typically experiences intensified responses in all manifestations of "normal" or "uncomplicated" mourning, several reactions are particularly fueled in intensity because of the dynamics involved in child loss. These include:

• Guilt, especially intense due to inappropriate and unrealistic parental expectations, and the falling short of the self-image caused by the assault on the identity

• Anger, intensified because of what the loss of a child means given the role of parent and because it is so unnatural for a child to predecease a parent

• Pain of separation, heightened because of the incomparable closeness of the relationship with one's child

• Search for meaning, accelerated due to the unnaturalness of the death, the parents' sense of guilt and failure, and their experience of a loss that does not make any sense

• Problems with social support and unrealistic expectations, maintained for the mourner by others, aggravated by society's increased problems with child death (it represents the worst fears of others) and consequent avoidance of the bereaved parents, who suffer from the loss of this support and are harmed by the inappropriate expectation that this loss is like any other bereavement

• "Growing up with the loss," a variation of anniversary phenomena (referring to brief upsurges of acute grief at the time of events that never occurred, such as the time when the child would have been graduating from high school or getting married), both magnified and increased in number by the parental tendency to demarcate life in terms of the events of their children.

MARITAL AND FAMILY COMPLICATIONS

In addition to the personal, intrapsychic problems the individual parent sustains after the loss of a child, difficulties also arise in the marriage and the family. Although space precludes a full discussion of these issues here, they are noted below. Readers should refer to Rando (1986b) for a more complete discussion of these pivotal concerns.

The Marital Dyad

One of the particularly difficult aspects of bereavement following the death of a child is that when one spouse is mourning, the other, to whom the first would normally turn in his or her grief, is mourning as well. Consequently, in this instance, the parents' most therapeutic resource is taken away. Added to this difficulty is the fact that each is actually mourning a different loss, despite the fact that the same child has died. This is because relationships are unique; since what the parents mourn is the loss of the relationship, so each spouse mourns something different. This difference in relationship also influences other critical issues, such as what each spouse misses and when it is missed. This is why, for example, one spouse may especially miss conversation with the child after school, while for the other, the child's absence during football games on Sundays may be exceptionally difficult.

Despite the fact that people say they understand that idiosyncratic variables influence the way in which a mourner experiences grief and mourning, this tends to be forgotten when a couple has lost a child. There is no one correct way to grieve. Spouses must not only remember this and give each other the necessary space and permission to mourn in their own fashion, but also they must refrain from inappropriately drawing conclusions about a lack of love for the child or themselves when witnessing differences in the bereavement of their mate.

There are 29 documented sets of variables that influence any mourner's response (Rando, 1984). In this scenario it appears that a major factor impinging on bereaved parents is sex-role conditioning; in many Western societies what is required in mourning is incompatible with traditional male upbringing. This can bring husbands into conflict with wives when both are mourning their deceased child. For example, what males are taught as proper in situations of stress (and what is typically seen in their mourning), such as identifying and taking specific courses of action, not being "passive," and minimizing emotions while employing rational intellectualization, is often misinterpreted by their mourning female partners who may tend to need more sharing, listening, and reminiscing from their mates than may be condoned by male socialization. Their differences in approach and needs can cause disruption in the couple's life together. This does not mean that there are no mourning-related problems for females. Traditionally they have difficulty with anger, some aspects of problem-solving, and the ability to take action. Nevertheless, the types of skills and behaviors required in successful mourning are more consistent with the traditional female role than with the male role.

Other reasons for asynchronicity in the grief and mourning of a bereaved couple stem from their having personal differences in "grief work" (such as how to handle emotions, what to do for support, whether to put up the child's photos, how to approach work and daily activities in the midst of grief, deciding if holiday rituals should be altered, responding to surviving children, or conducting a search for meaning). Additional dissimilarities are due to their unique individual identities, and to their seldom being at the same "place" at the same time because of normal fluctuations in grief and mourning. Spouses must come to the recognition that differences do not mean a lack of love, and grant one another a wide latitude in their mourning.

Communication problems are not uncommon, as day-to-day stresses may not be confronted due to the spouses' preoccupation with the death, their lack of strength, and their desire to protect one another or to avoid a mutual downward spiral. Unfortunately, this can frequently lead to an accumulation of unexpressed emotion, which can explode inappropriately. Asking the unanswerable "Why?" and making unrealistic demands on each other can exacerbate these problems.

Sexual difficulties are also not unusual for several years following the death of a child. They can stem from the fear of having and losing other children, guilt over pleasure, or the depletion caused by grief and depression. While the intimacy of sexual contact may be precisely what one spouse needs, it may be something the other cannot endure at that time, for if one lets down the barriers to be close, one may get in touch with the pain one is attempting to avoid. It is important for spouses to explore gently each other's underlying feelings and needs, and to avoid interpreting each other's actions without proper information. This requires open communication to minimize this potentially huge area of misunderstanding. The loss of sexual intimacy can be a major secondary loss to bereaved parents who have already lost so much.

The changes in themselves occasioned by the death of the child will necessarily lead to a changed marital relationship. Each spouse will have to recognize that any major loss changes people, for the better and worse. Consequently, their relationship will be altered, since the people composing it are altered. It is important for each spouse to recognize these changes, and to work to accommodate them and integrate them positively into the relationship. It is critical to avoid coping mechanisms that systematically direct attention away from the mourning process or from the marriage, such as overuse of alcohol and drugs, overwork, overinvestment in other areas of life, and extramarital affairs.

Notwithstanding the stresses and burdens the loss of a child can place upon even the healthiest and strongest marriage, it is absolutely untrue that the death of a child inevitably leads to divorce. Some studies have estimated that the divorce rate can be as high as 75%–90%. This is an unsupported, although prevalent, myth! Certainly, parents do suffer significant distress after the death of a child, but many marriages remain intact or even improve. Recent evidence suggests that when there is a divorce after a child's death, it often stems from the reordered priorities and newly recognized strength of one of the bereaved parents who decides that he or she no longer wants or has to stay in an unsatisfactory marriage tolerated before the child's death (Klass, 1986–1987). Far too many parents have been traumatized by incorrect data on divorce based on inappropriate conclusions from poorly designed studies. They need to be informed that marriages *can* and *do* survive. In fact, some actually become healthier as they determine that they will make some good come out of the tragedy and, for example, develop reordered priorities, deeper family commitments, and greater personal growth.

The Family System

As with the loss of any other family member, the family system must reorganize itself after the death of a child (Rando, 1988). After any death in the family, but especially after the death of a child where there are surviving siblings and/or children born subsequent to the death of that child, it is imperative to ensure that role reorganization, role reassignments, and identity ascriptions are appropriate. Many deleterious situations and much pathology have been reported in the thanatological literature attesting to the negative consequences when this fails to occur (Rando, 1986b).

It is not unusual for bereaved parents to report some difficulties with remaining or subsequent children. These children can evoke many feelings in their parents. They may serve as reminders of the one who died. They may be the recipients of the parents' displaced negative feelings stemming from the loss. They may suffer their parents' resentment that they continue to live and appear (to the parents) not to have mourned enough or to have adjusted too quickly. Some bereaved parents fear that their relationships with surviving or subsequent children are less intense than with the one who died, or that they have lost their ability to love.

In most cases, these feelings arise from the parents' normal preoccupation with the one who has died. Indeed, the typical attribution of "most special" qualities to the deceased child reflects this quite clearly. For instance, the child who died is described as the "most intelligent," the "most sensitive," or the "most like me." This sanctification process, not dissimilar to what has been described as occurring with widows, reflects the parents' focus on and desire to reunite with the lost child. Other real, live children with everyday problems compare poorly with the sanctified deceased child. However, in most cases, unless there was a clear preference before the death, the parent would mourn similarly any other lost child and would focus on the special things about that child.

In their desire to protect their other children, and also to ensure that they never again have to undergo the trauma of losing a child, many parents overprotect their surviving and subsequent children. This can have an untoward result, as often the inappropriate "tightening of the reins" serves only to push children further away, and can impair all areas of their development. Often bereaved parents realize their deficiencies in parenting that result from their grief and mourning. It is important that the parents hold and maintain the proper perspective. They should be told by professionals:

- Do the very best you can under the circumstances, recognizing your importance to and effects on the child(ren).
- However, be realistic about what you can expect of yourself since you are mourning too.
- Tap into other resources to assist you in parenting by identifying the deficits and limitations in your ability to parent your child(ren), and find appropriate and concerned others who can temporarily help fill the gaps (Rando, 1988).

Many difficulties and misinterpretations could be eliminated if the parents developed an understanding of children's grief and mourning. Without this, too often parents incorrectly assume what a child feels or thinks. This creates serious problems originating from the misinterpretation, but when it combines with the parents' lack of appreciation of the necessity for children to be included in the family mourning and of the importance of their being given explicit permission to address the loss, it can culminate in the parents "protecting" the child by not providing the requisite information and/or support to cope with the death. Such "protection" contributes to further problems and the possible development of pathology (Rando, 1988).

"Protection" does not only occur on behalf of children; adults may try to protect other adults as well. Not uncommonly, one parent may attempt to protect the other in addition to the children. Actually, anyone in the family can try to "rescue" another by ignoring his or her own needs and concentrating on the needs of others or by creating distractions from the grief (for example, a teenager may begin to "act out" at school to get his parents' minds off the death of his sister). Either course is unhelpful. It is unrealistic for parents (or anyone) to think they can rescue others from pain. The attempt only interferes with the healthy mourning process for all parties. (At times such rescuing may be an attempt to escape one's own pain, and not necessarily stimulated solely by the desire to focus on another.)

If there are surviving siblings, bereaved parents must be aware of the issues involved in losing a sibling. By definition, the sibling relationship, no matter how close, is ripe for ambivalence (Rando, 1988). Ambivalence always makes it difficult to mourn, regardless of who has been lost. Therefore, this is something that the surviving children will have to contend with, and the parents should be aware of this and the other dilemmas posed by the loss of a brother or sister. These include:

Siblings will be called upon to live longer with this loss than anyone else.

The death not only illustrates to siblings that they can die too, but also, because of genetic similarities, may hold implications concerning their own deaths.

Depending on their age, siblings often feel anger toward the parents for their inability to protect the child who died.

Siblings must contend with the emotional turmoil and family changes secondary to their parents' mourning.

Siblings may try to set and/or meet unrealistic expectations in order to "replace" the child for whom the parents long or to be "perfect" (or some other superlative) in order either to take away the parents' pain or not to contribute to it.

Siblings' changed role in the family may not be appropriate to them or, even if it is, may present them with numerous stresses to contend with or surmount.

Reaching the age at which their sibling died may be quite anxiety provoking and can elicit new grief.

If they have been given their deceased sibling's effects (such as clothes, toys, sports items, or bedroom) this can bring up a number of issues requiring sensitive handling.

The "family" often comprises other relatives and close friends, in addition to family members. These individuals are frequently overlooked as mourners. Some are doubly bereaved; for example, grandparents not only lose a grandchild through death, but also lose their child to bereaved-parent status. There may be total incomprehension as to why the grandparents, with their advanced age, did not die instead. There is much clinical evidence to suggest that grandparents and other extended relatives, as well as very close friends, can be either a blessing or a curse. Precisely because many of them are so close, there are expectations that they will be very supportive to the bereaved parents. To the extent that this happens, the bereaved parents are helped enormously. However, when these individuals fail to acknowledge the parents' pain sufficiently, do not help enough, are too egocentric, resent the parents' receiving attention when perhaps they themselves did not receive such attention when they needed it, or when they place inappropriate expectations on the bereaved parents, this can become the origin of enormous stress for the parents and can be a major source of secondary losses as parents are let down by those expected to help.

There are two final complications to the loss of a child with which bereaved parents must contend. The first is not unique to child loss, but the intensity of the response to that type of death certainly magnifies it. The "multiplier effect" is the phenomenon in families in which one member can potentiate and exacerbate another's grief response. With so many intensely mourning individuals all living together in the narrow confines of one house, it is amazing that the roof doesn't blow off with the volatility of the acute emotion being experienced. Related to this is the dilemma of trying to modify and balance the particular idiosyncratic needs of one member versus another in the family. It can become quite a thorny issue when what one needs in order to minimize the pain or assist in the mourning, is diametrically opposed to what another requires; for example, one needs to display the photographs of the deceased child while another needs to put them out of sight. Such discrepancies are bound to occur in the mourning of different individuals, yet in practical day-to-day existence finding a health compromise to meet family members' needs is an enormously difficult task. Bereaved parents and families have the best chance of reaching this goal in cases where:

- Familial communication is honest, open, and fluid
- Boundaries are appropriate
- There is a recognition that each person's needs are just as important as everyone else's

- Compromise at one time means assurance that at another time one's needs will take precedence
- There is a commitment to the survival of the family and its individual members
- There is an understanding and allowance for personal differences in mourning, and family members do not expect each other to have the same needs or to mourn in similar fashion along an identical course, and do not assume that each has lost the same relationship
- Family members recognize the dual aspect of families in grief and work to maximize its positive side and minimize its negative one, that is, to assist one another most effectively rather than to complicate the mourning process for one another due to their physical and psychological proximity, their common experience with the deceased and each other, and their knowledge of one another

The final difficulty for bereaved parents that pertains specifically to the family is the situation they find themselves in if they have surviving or subsequent children. In these cases they still must function in the same role (parent) that they are trying to relinquish. It is an extraordinarily difficult psychological task to attempt to surrender (around the deceased child) and maintain (around living children) the same role simultaneously. This is one of the reasons why parental mourning is so complicated and fails in many ways to be explained or understood by the general conceptualizations that society, as well as the field of thanatology, have for mourning.

PARENTAL BEREAVEMENT: AN EXCEPTION
TO GENERAL CONCEPTUALIZATIONS OF MOURNING

It has become increasingly apparent that: (1) parental bereavement fails to be adequately explained and understood in terms of the general conceptualizations that are held for grief and mourning; (2) bereaved parents are predisposed to be exceptionally vulnerable to complicated mourning and to erroneous diagnoses of pathology; and (3) evidence now provides a mandate for both a new model of parental mourning and new criteria for identification of pathology in bereaved parents. Space considerations prevent a full consideration of these issues here, but readers are urged to see Rando (1986d) for a full discussion and an analysis of supporting arguments. A brief discussion of each of these issues follows.

Parental Bereavement Fails to Be Adequately
Explained and Understood in Terms of the General
Conceptualizations Held for Grief and Mourning

Until fairly recently, most of the general conceptualizations about mourning, and indeed much of our knowledge about grief and bereavement, came from the study of white, middle-class women whose husbands had died. Very simply, they were the easiest mourners to investigate. However, it is now quite apparent that different role relationships give rise to different bereavement experiences, which in turn mandate different treatment interventions. Thus, for example, what is experienced and needed in the loss of a spouse is necessarily distinct from what is found in the loss of an aged parent, or in the loss of a child.

When this understanding about unique dilemmas posed by specific losses is integrated with comprehension of the fact that no two bereavements are exactly alike (because of the idiosyncratic constellation of 29 separate sets of factors known to influence any mourner's bereavement [Rando, 1984]), it becomes evident why it is not only unrealistic but inappropriate to hold similar expectations and treatment strategies for bereavements arising from different losses. It becomes incumbent upon the caregivers to command knowledge both of the commonly experienced reactions in similar losses and of the idiosyncrasies of the particular mourning experience of the person they seek to assist.

In the death of a child, the mourning of the bereaved parents is compromised because what is required in successful mourning is exacerbated or even made impossible by the consequences of the severing of the parent-child bond. For example, if analyzed according to Worden's (1982) delineation of the tasks required in mourning, it is clear that bereaved parents have built-in obstacles.

Accepting the reality of the loss   Bereaved parents have difficulty accepting the reality of their loss because: (1) it violates their basic function and defies the laws of nature; (2) it multiply victimizes the parents and savagely assaults their sense of self and their abilities; (3) it is complicated if they have more than one child, as continuing in the same role with the same expectations and demands makes it easier to deny that the child has died since there is no dramatically changed function to confirm the loss; and (4) often there is a social negation of the loss.

Experiencing the pain of grief   Bereaved parents have difficulty in experiencing the pain of grief because: (1) this type of loss results in intensified pain; (2) there are more losses to self in this bereavement; (3) the pain persists for a longer period of time; and (4) experience of it is subverted by the lack of social support, the loss of the spouse as the most therapeutic resource because he or she is grieving too, and the inappropriate expectations held for bereaved parents.

Adjusting to an environment in which the deceased is missing   Bereaved parents have difficulty adjusting to their new environment because: (1) if there are surviving children, the parents continue to operate in the same environment with the same people (except for the deceased child) and the same roles and expectations, thus lacking the reassignment of roles and assumptions of skills and responsibilities needed to indicate loss and confirm the change; and

(2) in the loss of an infant or adult child, whose not being present has been the norm, there is no dramatic absence to signal that the death has occurred.

Withdrawing and reinvesting emotional energy   Bereaved parents have difficulty investing their emotional energy in other relationships because: (1) there is a mutually incompatible task as parents are expected simultaneously to relinquish the role of parent (with the deceased child) and maintain it (with surviving children); (2) any decathexis that must occur is obscured by the fact that the child is an extension of the self, making it problematic to withdraw investment from the self/child, to define what belonged to the child and to the parent, and to relinquish some aspects of the self (in the child and in the hopes and dreams for the child) while retaining others (in surviving children); (3) in this death there are more losses to self than are usually sustained after the loss of a significant other; (4) identification (an intrapsychic process that assists in withdrawing and subsequently transforming emotional energy, and in the formation of a new identity) is more problematic because of the role of parent to child, and because of inherent problems with identifying with a young child when the mourner is an adult; (5) it is harder to assume the required new identity when much of the world remains the same, whenever there are other children; (6) it is relatively more difficult internally to develop a new relationship with a deceased child than with someone in a different role; and (7) reinvestment in other relationships similar to the lost one is more possible after the death of a spouse, sibling, or parent—since there is often more social support for such reinvestments—than after the loss of a child.

Bereaved Parents Are Predisposed to Be Exceptionally Vulnerable to Complicated Mourning and to Erroneous Diagnoses of Pathology

Three compelling sets of data delineate why bereaved parents are so predisposed to be exceptionally vulnerable to complicated mourning and to erroneous diagnoses of pathology. These pertain to the number of factors inherent in losing a child that are known to promote failure to mourn; to influence grief and mourning negatively; and to lead to complicated mourning.

Lazare (1979) proposed six psychological reasons and five social reasons why any person may fail to mourn. As documented in the preceding discussion, bereaved parents must typically contend with five out of the six psychological issues that are known to interfere with appropriate grief and mourning: guilt, loss of an extension of the self, reawakening of an old loss, multiple loss, and idiosyncratic resistances to mourning.

Additionally, bereaved parents must (especially, although not exclusively, if the child is an infant or an adult) typically contend with four out of the five social factors that have been identified to interfere with any mourner's grief and mourning (Lazare, 1979): social negation of the loss, socially unspeakable loss, social isolation and/or geographic distance from social support, and assumption of the role of the strong one. Thus, the experience of child loss inherently contains a number of factors known to interfere with any person's grief and mourning.

Coinciding with this, the death of a child is the situation that contains the greatest negative constellation of the 29 sets of factors (Rando, 1984) known to have an impact on any person's bereavement. Below is a listing of factors that for bereaved parents represent the most salient negative influences on their grief and mourning. (Personal factors of the mourners have been omitted here, in order to focus on those inherent in this particular type of loss.)

The unique nature and meaning of the loss sustained and the relationship severed

The individual qualities of the relationship lost

The roles the deceased occupied in the family or social system of the mourner

The characteristics of the deceased

The amount of unfinished business between the mourner and the deceased

The mourner's perception of the deceased's fulfillment in life

The suddenness of the death (if it was unexpected) and the death surroundings

The timeliness of the death

The mourner's perception of the preventability of the death

The number, type, and quality of secondary losses

The presence of concurrent stresses or crises

The mourner's social support system and the acceptance and assistance of its members

The funerary rituals

For a bereaved parent, the role of the child and the typical personal, familial, and social reactions subsequent to the child's death combine to yield a situation in which this type of loss, more than any other, appears to confront the mourner with the highest number of adverse influences on mourning.

Research (Raphael, 1983) has delineated the characteristics most often associated with the main three categories of complicated mourning. The loss of a child inherently contains a number of those characteristics that would tend to lead any individual to complicated mourning.

Inhibited, suppressed, or absent mourning   These types of mourning with problems in expression often occur when one simply cannot accept the loss.

Distorted mourning   There are two patterns of distorted mourning. The first is manifested in extreme guilt, and the second in extreme anger. This is usually seen after the loss of dependent relationships, when there has been a sudden or unexpected death for which someone is blamed, or where the loss is special and irreplaceable.

Chronic mourning This results after the loss of dependent and irreplaceable relationships, when there has been an unexpected death, and when there has been an extraordinary investment in the person who died.

In each case, it is clear that what is associated with the complicated (previously termed "abnormal" or "pathological") mourning is characteristics that are part and parcel of the parental bereavement experience following the death of a child. The inherent aspects of the loss of a child are the *same* aspects that in any other situation of loss predispose a mourner to complications. Therefore, it is no wonder that bereaved parents have traditionally been diagnosed with pathological mourning.

A Mandate for Both a New Model of Parental Mourning and New Criteria for Identification of Pathology in Bereaved Parents

If most bereaved parents evidence responses that make them look abnormal when we use the traditional criteria for determination of pathological mourning, then by definition their mourning cannot be "abnormal." The simple fact is that what is considered abnormal or pathological in other losses is typical after the death of a child. This explains the consistent research findings that, when compared to other losses, parental bereavement is much more intense, complicated, and longlasting (Rando, 1986b).

For this reason, it is imperative to delineate a model of mourning that will be appropriate for bereaved parents and to establish new criteria for what constitutes pathology within this special group of mourners. Failure to do so will result in the maintenance of inappropriate and unrealistic expectations for these individuals, who cannot be expected to mourn like or to have the same bereavement experiences as other types of bereaved persons. Also, it is critical that bereaved parents recognize the unique aspects of their mourning, as well as those they share with other mourners, and develop appropriate expectations of themselves in order to avoid the negative evaluations of self, feelings of failure, and guilt that arise when individuals do not meet their own standards or expectations. For professionals not to assist them in doing this by failing to develop an appropriate model and by lacking valid criteria for detection of pathology will only add to the burdens of these already overwhelmed individuals.

TREATMENT IMPLICATIONS

In treating bereaved parents, as in treating any bereaved person, there are two areas on which we should focus: grief and mourning. Often, in the literature, the terms have been used interchangeably, but they do have different meanings, processes, implications, and goals (Rando, 1988). *Grief* is the process of experiencing the psychological, social, and physical reactions to one's perception of loss. *Mourning* refers to the conscious and unconscious processes that gradually undo the psychological ties that had bound the mourner to the loved one; help the mourner to adapt to the loss; and help the mourner to learn how to live healthily in the new world without the deceased.

From these definitions, it can be seen that *grief is a reaction*. It expresses three things: (1) one's feelings about the loss; (2) one's protest at the loss and the wish to undo it and to prove it untrue; and (3) the effects one experiences from the assault on oneself caused by the loss.

For healthy grieving one must do the following (Rando, 1988): acknowledge the death, understand the death and have an explanation of its events, experience the pain, and react to the separation.

The ultimate goal of mourning, however, is to take mourners beyond the grief, the reactions to loss seen in acute mourning, and to assist them in adapting to it and accommodating to its changes. This process can go on forever, as the bereaved individual learns to go on healthily and adaptively in the new life without forgetting the old.

For healthy mourning, one must do the following (Rando, 1988): readjust to the world without the loved one, change emotional attachment and investment in the loved one, develop a new relationship with the deceased, learn how to keep the loved one "alive" appropriately, form a new identity, and reinvest emotional energy.

Mourning is, therefore, an active process that requires much work over time. In this regard it can be said that for some, there are aspects of mourning that never end. Grief is a part of mourning, but mourning is not necessarily a part of grief. Mourning goes beyond the acute reactions to loss in grief, and involves the mourner working actively to adapt to the loss and cope with it.

Rando (1984) has identified seven broad phases of general intervention for use with all mourners. These are:

1 Make contact and assess.
2 Maintain a therapeutic and realistic perspective.
3 Encourage verbalization of feelings and recollection of the deceased.
4 Help the mourner identify and resolve secondary losses and unfinished business.
5 Support the mourner in coping with the grief and mourning process.
6 At the appropriate time, help the mourner accommodate to the loss.
7 At the appropriate time, work with the mourner to reinvest in a new life.

To these, some specific suggestions must be added for intervention in parental bereavement (see Rando, 1984):

1   Clarify expectations for parental grief and mourning.
2   Help the mourner adjust the parental role.
3   Help the mourning couple adjust the marital relationship.
4   Teach coping skills.
5   Help parents understand the needs and mourning of surviving children.

For reasons outlined earlier in this chapter, many bereaved parents tend to have difficulty both with grief and with mourning. Since it is beyond the scope of this chapter to address the types of and treatments for complicated mourning in general, and in bereaved parents specifically, readers are referred to Rando (1984, 1986b, in press) for in-depth information.

A FINAL COMMENT

Although this chapter has been devoted to analyzing the unique difficulties of the parental loss of a child, it is imperative that readers remember one critical fact: Although this is the most complicated and painful of human losses, bereaved parents *can* and *do* survive. Research and clinical observation provide ample documentation, bearing testimony to the fact that parents can adapt to and live with the loss, unparalleled though it is. In our zeal to address the agony of this type of bereavement, we must not forget this fact. To do so would be to condemn bereaved parents to a future of unremitting pain, over and above that which they already must endure as a consequence of their loss.

REFERENCES

Gorer, G. (1965). *Death, grief, and mourning.* New York: Doubleday.

Jackson, E. N. (1977). Comments on "The Parents." In N. Linzer (Ed.), *Understanding bereavement and grief (pp. 187–190).* New York: Yeshiva University Press.

Klass, D. (1986–1987). Marriage and divorce among bereaved parents in a self-help group. *Omega, 17*(3), 237–249.

Lazare, A. (1979). Unresolved grief. In A. Lazare (Ed.), *Outpatient psychiatry: Diagnosis and treatment.* Baltimore: Williams & Wilkins.

Parkes, C., & Weiss, R. (1983). *Recovery from bereavement.* New York: Basic Books.

Rando, T. A. (1984). *Grief, dying, and death: Clinical interventions for caregivers.* Champaign, IL: Research Press.

Rando, T. A. (Ed.) (1986a). *Loss and anticipatory grief.* Lexington, MA: Lexington Books.

Rando, T. A. (Ed.) (1986b). *Parental loss of a child.* Champaign, IL: Research Press.

Rando, T. A. (1986c). Death of the adult child. In T. A. Rando (Ed.), *Parental loss of a child.* Champaign, IL: Research Press.

Rando, T. A. (1988). *Grieving: How to go on living when someone you love dies.* Lexington, MA: Lexington Books.

Rando, T. A. (in press). *Treatment of complicated mourning.* Champaign, IL: Research Press.

Raphael, B. (1983). *The anatomy of bereavement.* New York: Basic Books.

Worden, J. W. (1982). *Grief counseling and grief therapy: A handbook for the mental health practitioner.* New York: Springer.

Chapter 20

Grief Is an Individual Journey: Follow-up of Families Postdeath of a Child with Cancer

Ida M. Martinson

Parkes, in 1973, described grief as a process, not a state, which is more than a reaction to the loss of someone (Parkes, 1973). In this chapter, I present the results of a study on bereavement in families whose child died of cancer.

In Minnesota, in 1976, I began a research project called "Home Care for the Child with Cancer." More accurately, it was a study of the feasibility and desirability of home care for a child dying of cancer. During the first two years of the project, 58 children died, of whom 46 died at home (Martinson, Moldow, Armstrong, Henry, Nesbit & Kersey, 1986). We followed the grief process in these families by interviewing them at 1 month, 6 months, 12 months, 2 years, 7 years, and 9 years. I will summarize here they findings from this study, focusing on the results of the follow-up interviews with these families at 24 months.

The purpose of the study was to learn how families report the experience of

This research was supported in part by DHEW NCI CA 19490 ("Home Care for the Child with Cancer") and the American Cancer Society, California Division ("Impact on Childhood Cancer on American Families" and "A Longitudinal Study of Family Bereavement after Childhood Cancer").

bereavement, two years after their child had died of cancer (Martinson, Moldow & Henry, 1980). The main portion of this research was funded by the U.S. National Cancer Institute. Recently, the American Cancer Society funded revisitations of these same families seven to nine years after the death of a child with cancer.

From interviews with 49 families, parents, and siblings, we collected a large qualitative data set. Of the nine families that did not participate, seven declined, one had moved from the country, and one could not be located. We conducted 150 interviews with 46 mothers, 33 fathers and stepfathers, and 71 siblings. A total of 178 hours of audiotape was transcribed. From this qualitative data, we identified three types of grievers (McClowry, Davies, May, Kulenkamp & Martinson, 1987). Our main measurement tool was the Symptoms Check List (SCL-90) which was completed by 40 mothers and 26 fathers. Our data set is very large and we have not yet completed all possible analyses, however the changes over time, that we have so far identified in these families (Martinson, McClowry, Davies, & Kulenkamp, in press) will be presented.

FINDINGS FROM THE HOME CARE STUDY

The interviews with parents at 24 months after the child's death provided a considerable amount of information concerning the impact of the death on the family and the ways in which the family coped with the loss and the feelings engendered by the death of the child. Three of our questions concerned how often family members discussed the deceased child.

The first question asked about the length of time since the parents had last talked about the child. Almost $2/3$ of the parents reported that they either talked about the child "all the time" or that they had talked about the child within the previous 24 hours. The second question concerned the frequency with which the deceased child was mentioned by the family or by others; $1/4$ of the parents reported that it was difficult for some family members to talk about the child. Responses of 10 families specifically mentioned the father's difficulties. One father commented that he felt unable to talk about the child at work, and one mother remarked that her husband had mentioned the child only twice in the two years since the child had died. The third question asked parents whether their other children mentioned the deceased child; $1/2$ of the parents reported that their child talked about the deceased sibling whenever the surviving child was reminded of the sibling by an activity or by some occasion. About 14% reported that their children were having trouble talking about the deceased sibling.

Taken together, responses to the three questions suggest variability among families in the ability to talk about the deceased child. Although about $1/3$ of the parents and siblings were able to talk openly about the deceased child with some frequency, 15%–20% of both groups reported having difficulty two years after years after the death. Fathers, in particular, had difficulty in talking about the deceased child.

DURATION OF BEREAVEMENT

Two questions asked during the interviews at 24 months after the child's death provide information on the duration of the parents' sense of bereavement. First, we asked if they felt they had returned to their normal lifestyle. In all, 83% of the parents responded that they had returned to their normal lifestyle, while 17% stated they had not done so, but offered these comments:

> We're back to the routine but not to normal because your life is never the same again. you're not the same person because so much has happened.
>
> No, I don't think so. It's too deep in my soul and in myself. He had changed my whole life and my perspective in life.
>
> I don't think you ever do. There's always something kind of missing. I think you live more in the past than you ever did, because you want to think of things you did in the past.

Second, we asked parents to identify when the most intense time of their bereavement was over. Again responses to this question indicate wide variability among parents (Table 1).

Over $1/5$ of parents stated the most intense time of their bereavement was not yet over, 24 months after the child's death. About $1/4$ of parents stated the most intense time of their bereavement was not over until 12–18 months after the child's death. There were noticeable differences in responses between mothers and fathers. Four of 29 fathers, but only 5 of 46 mothers, stated that the

Table 1 Mothers' and Fathers' Responses 24 Months After the Child's Death to: When Was the Most Intensive Time of Your Bereavement Over?

	Mothers		Fathers		Total	
	N	%	*N*	%	*N*	%
First few weeks	5	9.8	4	23.8	9	11.3
1 month	2	3.9	5	17.2	7	8.8
3 months	6	11.8	4	13.8	10	12.5
6 months–1 year	7	13.7	0	—	7	8.8
1–1½ years	13	25.5	7	24.1	20	25.0
Not yet over	12	23.5	5	17.2	17	21.3
Unsure	6	11.8	4	13.8	10	12.5
Total	51	100.00	29	99.9	80	100.2

most intense time of their bereavement was over within a few weeks to one month after the child's death.

For a substantial portion, bereavement was a long-term process, it may have been intense and may have included disruption of the family's routine. Furthermore, fathers and mothers described their loss and their adjustment differently.

PARENTS' ADJUSTMENT TO THE LOSS OF A CHILD

Parents' Perceptions of the Adjustment

At 24 months after their child's death, 85% of the parents indicated they had adjusted fairly well, that they had accepted their child's death. The remaining 15% felt they had not adjusted well. Some of their comments were:

> We have a lot of trouble in making decisions about anything. We listen to our friends and end up doing something we don't like to do.
>
> It just seemed like it was never going to end and it's never going to get better, so I don't care. It's like you want to given in to it, and the heck with the whole world.
>
> I feel kind of an apathy for a lot of things I used to have more spirit for.

Parents were also asked to rate their level of coping with their grief, on a scale ranging from 10 (best coping) to 1 (complete distress). Table 2 shows some variation in how parents rated their coping, but ratings are generally on

Table 2 Parents' Rating of Level of Coping with Grief at 24 Months After Child's Death

	Mothers		Fathers		Total	
	N	%	N	%	N	%
10 (best coping)	8	18.2	8	27.6	16	21.9
9	11	25.0	4	13.8	15	20.5
8	13	29.5	8	27.6	21	28.8
7	5	11.4	6	20.7	11	15.1
6	2	4.5	3	10.3	5	6.8
5	4	9.1	0	—	4	5.5
4	0	—	0	—	0	—
3	1	2.3	0	—	1	1.7
2	0	—	0	—	0	—
1 (complete distress)	0	—	0	—	0	—
Total	44	100.0	29	100.0	73	100.0

the upper end of the scale. In all, 71 % of the parents rated their coping as 8, 9, or 10, and there is little variation between mothers' and fathers' ratings.

We then asked parents if there was anything they were unable to do, 24 months after the child's death. Fifty-five (67 %) of the parents reported there was nothing they were now unable to do. Four said they could not go to the hospital where their child had been treated; three mentioned they could not attend funerals (one specifically mentioned children's funerals); three said they could not cook or eat certain foods the deceased child had liked, and three reported they could not look at pictures of the child. One mother said it was difficult to visit the child's grave; another said she could not decide whether to have another baby or not. Two couples referred to difficulties in going out with other couples. One couple mentioned they could not go out with other couples because of conversation about children, another couple said they could go out only when other couples were present. Five other parents said they could not do specific things that were closely related to the deceased child; these ranged from caring for the child's horse to reading the diary kept during the child's illness.

These data give the impression of adequate coping by a large proportion of parents, but wide variability among the small group that expressed difficulties in coping.

General Reactions to Loss

During the interviews 24 months after the child's death, parents were asked whether their grief had interfered with their ability to function in their daily activities (i.e., their job or management of their home) during the 12 months preceding the 24-month interview.

A sizable proportion, 84 %, answered that their grief had not interfered in the past 12 months. There was a wide variation among the responses of the 16 % of parents who stated that grief had interfered. These include the following comments:

> I don't have an interest in anything anymore. Everything seems like it's such a hassle.
> We had trouble making decisions in our daily life. It was hard to manage our house or go to work.
> I'm not as good as a mother or housekeeper because I just don't feel like getting things done. I have all these feelings inside me.

To questions related to the effect of the parents' grief on their employment in the 12 months preceding the interview, only 7 % of parents said there had been days when they could not go to work. Of these, only one parent indicated he had missed more than one or two days because of his grief.

However, $1/3$ of the parents said there had been days when they went to work but did not get much done because of their grief. At 24 months after the child's death, we also asked parents whether they had changed employment in the preceding 12 months. Of the parents for whom data are available, 23 had changed employment, but no parents reported having had to stop working as a consequence of their grief. One father retired, and one mother quit work because she had a baby. All others changed jobs or entered the labor market for reasons other than grief. Ten mothers had begun new part- or full-time jobs in the previous 12 months.

A major concern in this study was the degree to which parents' grieving would be affected by the death of the child at home, the objective being to assess whether the child's death at home is related to any responses that might be characterized as "abnormal grief." As a result, we devoted considerable effort to characterizing "abnormal grief symptoms" as reported in the literature. Although a wide variety of models for the "normal" grieving process have been examined, comparatively little has been reported on "abnormal grief." On the basis of the literature, parents of children who received home care were rated by whether they were having no apparent difficulty with their grief or were having slight, moderate, or major difficulties, which were characterized as follows:

- *Slight difficulty* Few or no degrees of abnormal depressive symptoms; symptoms included depression, obsessive thoughts, hostility, guilt, delayed reaction, psychosomatic conditions, and alteration of social patterns (both minor at the time and those now resolved)
- *Moderate difficulty* Greater magnitude of few abnormal symptoms; symptoms included depression, guilt, psychosomatic conditions, and alteration of social patterns
- *Major difficulty* Either many abnormal symptoms of moderate severity or few abnormal symptoms of severe degree; symptoms included seeking psychiatric help for depression, delusions, absence of observable grief, depression, hostility, extreme guilt, delayed reaction, psychosomatic conditions, agitated depression, hostility against specific persons, and alterations of social patterns

Table 3 presents the results of these ratings. Although there was not a significant relationship between the various categories of difficulty and either the place of death or gender of the parents, the slight trend of evidence for place of death suggests that, if anything, parents of children who died at home may be less likely to experience difficulty with grief than parents of children who died in hospital.

Coping Strategies

Several questions in the interview with parents 24 months after the child's death provide some insight on how parents cope with grief. To the question, "Who/What do you feel was the key to your survival?" parents identified several

Table 3 Degree of Difficulty Parents Experienced in Dealing with Grief

| | Child Died at Home | | | | Child Died in Hospital | | | | | |
| | Mothers | | Fathers | | Mothers | | Fathers | | Total | |
	N	%	N	%	N	%	N	%	N	%
No apparent difficulty	24	53.3	20	55.6	4	33.3	2	33.3	50	50.5
Slight difficulty	10	22.2	6	16.7	4	33.3	2	33.3	22	22.2
Moderate difficulty	7	15.6	6	16.7	1	8.3	0	—	14	14.1
Major difficulty	4	8.9	4	11.1	3	25.0	2	33.3	13	13.1
Total	45	100.0	36	100.1	12	99.9	6	99.9	99	99.9

factors that were key to their survival. Table 4 shows that about 40% of the parents identified "close family ties" as a key to their survival and that more than 1/3 of the parents identified their faith as the key to their survival. The wide variety of responses included in these two categories and of the other responses shown in Table 4 again suggests individual approaches to handling grief among parents. Of importance is the recognition that parents derive support from many and varied internal and external sources.

Table 4 Survival Factors Identified by Parents 24 Months After Child's Death

Factor	N	% (of 81 responses)
Close family ties	33	40.7
Faith	29	35.8
Keeping busy	14	17.3
Determination	5	6.2
Close friends	5	6.2
Child's siblings	4	4.9
Being with the child at the time of death	2	2.5
Doing what is expected	2	2.5
Long-term goals	1	1.2
"My good nature"	1	1.2
Instinct	1	1.2

More specific questions about how parents handled grief concerned their use of psychosocial help and various aspects of their religious beliefs. Table 5 shows parents' responses to the question, "Did either of you seek any professional help to deal with your grief or other problems?" Most important, 71% responded that they did not seek any help in dealing with their grief. Among the parents who sought help, none used more than one of the types of help shown in Table 5. By far the most common form of help, used by 63% of those who sought help, was organized parent support groups (such as Candlelighters). Other sources of help were used less frequently.

Regarding religious beliefs, we asked parents whether their beliefs had affected the way they coped or dealt with the time between the child's original cancer diagnosis and the time of the interview 24 months after the child's death. There was essentially no difference between mothers' and fathers' responses. Of the 72 parents responding, 71% reported that their beliefs had affected the way they dealt with the time period in question. About ¼ of the parents replied that their religious beliefs had not affected the way they coped, and 4% of the parents were unsure. Of the 51 parents who responded affirmatively to this question, 45 also identified how their religious beliefs affected their coping. By far the predominant response in this group—cited by 33, or 73%, of the 45 parents—was that they had derived consolation and acceptance from their religious beliefs. Very few parents reported that their religious beliefs had had a negative effect on coping. Their comments indicated that they had stopped going to church or that they now had doubts about the power of prayer.

Parents were also asked whether their religious beliefs had changed in the 12 months preceding the 24-month interview. Of the 79 parents for whom data are available, 48 parents (61%) did not experience a change in their religious beliefs. Among the 31 parents (39%) who experienced a change, the beliefs of 20 (25% of all parents on whom data are available) grew stronger or more comforting, whereas the beliefs of 11 (14%) became weaker.

DISCUSSION

Only a few studies describe parents in a similar way to the parents under study in this research. Lindemann (1944) studied the relatives of persons who died in hospital. Miles (1985) studied emotional symptoms or bereaved parents. Cornwell, Nurcombe, and Stevens (1977) reported studies of parents of infants who died of sudden infant death syndrome. Rowe (1978) reported on parental reactions to perinatal deaths from various causes.

In general, these authors characterize as abnormal grief a variety of symptoms, such as seeking psychiatric help for depression, unbearable anxiety, delusions, as reported by Cornwell, Nurcombe, and Stevens (1977); absence of observable grief, severe somatic complaints, possible depression, phobias, obsessive thoughts, psychotic behavior, hostility and extreme guilt, as described

Table 5 Parents' Use of Professional Help to Deal with Grief or
Other Problems Within 24 Months After Child's Death

Source of help	N	% (of 24)
Organized parent support group	15	62.5
Priest/pastor	4	16.7
Marriage counselor	2	8.3
Personal physicians	1	4.2
Social worker at hospital	1	4.2
Psychologist	1	4.2

by Miles (1977); suicidal thoughts, acknowledged by Rowe (1978); delayed reaction, acquisition of symptoms of the deceased, psychosomatic conditions, agitated depression (characterized by tension, insomnia, agitation, feelings of worthlessness, bitter self-accusation, obvious need for punishment, suicidal ideation), hostility (against specific persons and inner struggle), alteration of social patterns, hyperactivity without sense of loss, and activities detrimental to the person's existence, as described by Lindemann (1944).

From the straightforward responses of the bereaved families and our rudimentary calculations, how are we to interpret the findings? There is no denying that grief after the loss of a child is an individual response. For a majority of the families, we have already reported elsewhere an assessment of their adjustment as late as seven to nine years after the child's death (McClowry et al., 1987) and concluded that grieving appears to have three patterns: "getting over it," "filling the emptiness," and "keeping the connection." These were families that underwent the long process of a child dying of cancer. We have scant comparison figures for families who lost a youngster through accidents or other diseases, although such an inquiry would be well worthwhile. We found considerable differences in assessment of the parents' own difficulties in coping with death. Our numbers are too small to draw any firm conclusions, but it is fair to say that the death of a child at home may reduce bereavement—that is, the grieving period and the complexities attendant to such a loss. It seems the process of "getting over it" is quicker, or that "filling the emptiness" or "keeping the connection" was already under way at the time of death. It is not clear, however, why the few parents who indicated major difficulty in dealing with grief were parents of children who died in hospital, since death in hospital is still within our cultural norm.

The Symptoms Check List (SCL-90) revealed that two years after the child's death, there was a significant difference between these parents and either the psychiatric patients (whose scores were elevated) and the nonclinical population, whose profiles were less elevated than the bereaved parents (Moore, Gillies & Martinson, 1988).

Looking at the depression scale of the SCL-90, seven years postdeath revealed no difference between parental depression at two and seven years. Over 22% of the variance in parental depression at seven years was accounted for by the depression at two years (Martinson, McClowry & Davies, 1989).

Finally, the loss of a child required individual intrapsychic reorganization and adjustment within the family system. Some changes were developmental in nature, and others, such as a sense of vulnerability, were experienced from the death of the child (Martinson, McClowry, Davies & Kulenkamp, in press).

Indeed, much of what we seem to see in our rudimentary calculations roughly confirms what is known. People do seek help in distress, in grief, in bereavement, and those who receive help benefit from it. Surprisingly, though, among the survival factors in grief identified by our parents, those parents whose child died at home attributed little value to the fact that the child died at home.

Although difficult to quantify, it is possible that parents may also have derived support from the interviews at 1, 6, and 12 months after the child's death. The interviewer who conducted the majority of these interviews is herself the mother of a child who died at home from cancer. At times, interview lasted more than 4 hours. A number of parents acknowledged the value of these interviews as a support mechanism and expressed disappointment when their schedule of interviews was finished.

This brings us to the question, what is bereavement? Is it a long period of grief? A time of reconciliation with a changed family configuration? Is bereavement a natural process or a cultural artifact? Would anticipating death—as the parents of the children who died of cancer had to do—make bereavement a more natural, shorter process? Would bereavement then have a more dignified, less guilt-ridden cloak?

Our study originally inquired into the feasibility of a child dying at home versus dying in hospital, and in the course of the inquiry we encountered many openings for future research. Bereavement study is one such topic. Naturally, we also studied cost effectiveness (Moldow, Armstrong, Henry & Martinson, 1982) for health care, that is nursing costs—alas, not the cost for families. For the health care system, death at home is cost effective, to be sure. For families, the cost should perhaps be called bereavement, a condition that affects all aspects of family life and can never be accounted for in financial terms.

REFERENCES

Cornwell, J., Nurcombe, B., & Stevens, L. (1977, April 30). Family response to loss of a child by sudden infant death syndrome. *The Medical Journal of Australia,* 656–658.

Lindemann, E. (1944). Symptomatology and management of acute grief. *American Journal of Psychiatry, 101*(2), 141–148.

Martinson, I. M. (1989). [Depression]. Unpublished raw data.

Martinson, I. M., McClowry, S. G., & Davies, B. (1989). *Parental depression following the death of a child.* Manuscript submitted for publication.

Martinson, I. M., McClowry, S. G., Davies, B., & Kulenkamp, E. J. (in press). Changes over time: Family bereavement following childhood cancer. *Research in Nursing & Health.*

Martinson, I. M., Moldow, D. G., Armstrong, G. D., Henry, W. F., Nesbit, M. E., & Kersey, J. H. (1986). Home care for children dying of cancer. *Research in Nursing & Health, 9,* 11–16.

Martinson, I. M., Moldow, D. G., & Henry W. F. (1980). *Home care for the child with cancer.* Final Report: Grant CA 19490, DHHS, National Cancer Institute. School of Nursing, University of Minnesota. Unpublished manuscript.

McClowry, S. G., Davies, E. G., May, K. A., Kulenkamp, E. J., & Martinson, I. M. (1987). The empty space phenomenon: The process of grief in the bereaved family. *Death Studies, 11,* 361–374.

Miles, M. S. (1985). Emotional symptoms and physical health in bereaved parents. *Nursing Research, 34,* 76–81.

Miles, M. S., Mattioli, L., & Diehl, A. M. (1977). Parent counseling: Psychological support of parents of children with critical heart disease. *Journal of the Kansas Medical Society, 78*(3), 134–151.

Moldow, D. G., Armstrong, G. D., Henry, W. F., & Martinson, I. M. (1982). The cost of home care for dying children. *Medical Care, XX*(11), 1114–1160.

Moore, I. M., Gilliss, C. L., & Martinson, I. M. (1988). Psychosomatic manifestations of bereavement in parents two years after the death of a child with cancer. *Nursing Research, 37*(2), 104–107.

Parkes, C. M. (1973). Anticipatory grief and widowhood. *British Journal of Psychiatry, 122*(570), 615.

Rowe, J., Clyman, R., Green, C., Mikkelsen, C., Haight, J., & Ataide, L. (1978). Follow-up of families who experience a perinatal death. *Pediatrics, 62*(2), 166–170.

Chapter 21

Marital Intimacy in Bereaved and Nonbereaved Couples: A Comparative Study

Ariella Lang and Laurie Gottlieb

Although infant mortality has declined dramatically in the last 60 years, in Canada, 8 out of every 1,000 infants die during the first year life following a live birth, with 8.7 out of 1,000 dying during the perinatal period (Statistics Canada, 1986).

There is suggestive evidence that a couple's marital relationship is affected by the death of their infant. However, the evidence is inconsistent concerning whether the relationship deteriorates or improves. For example, some investigators have reported a higher incidence of marital breakdown following infant death (Bergman, Pomeroy & Beckwith, 1969; Halpern, 1972). In contrast, others have reported that some couples felt that their marital relationship had improved and was strengthened by this experience (De Frain & Ernst, 1978; Giles, 1970; Helmrath & Steinitz, 1978). However, there is little empirical evidence to support either claim.

Researchers have merely speculated that one of the major causes of stress between parents may develop because the partners are experiencing grief at different times, expressing their grief in different ways, and/or coping with their grief differently (Miles, 1984). To date, evidence to link grief reactions to the couple's relationship has been based primarily on case study reports. For example, Videka-Sherman and Lieberman (1985) studied the psychosocial adjustment of parents following the death of their child and found that nearly 1/2 of parents mentioned marital problems.

To date, no study has examined the impact of an infant's death on a couple's marital intimacy. Although, some studies have examined how an infant's death affects certain intimate experiences, such as communication and sex, no study has examined the effects of such a loss on the entire "intimate relationship." According to Schaefer and Olson (1981) the "intimate relationship" is made up of emotional, social, sexual, intellectual, and recreational intimacy. Second, no study has included a comparative group of couples who have not experienced a loss, thus making it difficult to assess the extent of the disturbance on the couple's relationship following their infant's death. Furthermore, most studies have relied on women's reports and have failed to include men's evaluation of the impact of this event.

Therefore, the purpose of this study was twofold: First, we were interested in comparing how bereaved husbands and wives perceived their marital relationship. More specifically, we were interested in how bereaved husbands and wives perceived their present relationship, the change in their relationship since the loss, and the level of satisfaction with their relationship. Second, we were interested in understanding the relative impact of an infant's death on the marital relationship by examining how bereaved couples differed from nonbereaved couples in their ratings of their marital intimacy.

DESIGN AND SUBJECTS

To address these two issues, a comparative, correlational design was employed.* Data were collected from bereaved and nonbereaved husbands and wives in their homes. The sample consisted of 57 bereaved couples (wives and husbands) who had lost an infant (greater than 20 weeks gestation and less than 1 year of age) within 24 months of the home visit. These bereaved couples were compared with 55 nonbereaved couples who had never lost a child and who had not experienced the loss of a close family member or friend within 24 months of their home visit. To be eligible for the study couples had to read English, and be living together within a 100 km radius of Montreal.

During a 24-month period, 372 couples lost an infant (greater than 20 weeks gestation and less than 1 year of age) at one of the five Montreal University teaching hospitals. Of these couples, 147 (40%) did not meet the eligibility requirements for the study. Of the remaining 225 couples who had lost their baby, 110 (49%) were never contacted because the telephone number in the

*We thank Rhonda Amsel for her assistance and guidance with the statistical and computer analysis.

hospital records was no longer valid. A total of 57 of 115 eligible couples who were reached did agree to participate, resulting in an acceptance rate of 50%. The main reasons given for refusal were that couples did not wish to discuss their painful experience or anxiety about a subsequent pregnancy.

Bereaved couples had lost their infant approximately 12 months before the home visit (range: 1–24). Fourteen couples (24.6%) lost their baby before delivery, 24 couples (42.1%) within the neonatal period, and 19 couples (33.3%) at between 1 month and 1 year of age. Causes of death for these infants included complications during pregnancy and/or delivery ($n = 15$), prematurity ($n = 6$), genetic problems ($n = 4$), congenital malformations ($n = 20$), sudden infant death syndrome ($n = 7$), and unknown causes ($n = 5$).

Bereaved parents were predominantly Caucasian ($n = 102$, or 89%), ranged in age from 20 to 45 years (mothers' age: $M = 30.7$ yrs, fathers' age: $M = 33.4$), and had been married or living together from 2 to 19 years ($M = 7.7$ yrs). Nearly ½ the bereaved mothers were homemakers ($n = 26$), while 31 worked outside the home at the time of the home visit. Of the bereaved fathers, 17 (29.8%) held blue-collar jobs, 18 (31.6%) had clerical jobs, while 31 (54.4%) were employed in professional or managerial positions. Approximately 3/4 of the bereaved couples ($n = 42$) had other children at the time of the home visit, whose developmental stages ranged from infants to young adolescents.

With the exception of family income and fathers' occupation, the nonbereaved group was similar to the bereaved group on all major background variables (age, years together, years of education, number and developmental age of existing children). The bereaved group were in a slightly lower income bracket compared to the nonbereaved group ($M =$ approximately $45,000 vs. over $55,000, respectively) and had a lower percentage of husbands employed in managerial or professional positions (54.4% vs. 70.4%, respectively).

PROCEDURE AND INSTRUMENT

Names of bereaved families were obtained from five Montreal-area tertiary care settings with obstetrical and/or neonatal intensive care units. After the study received scientific and ethical approval from each institution, selected nurses from the five participating hospitals contacted potential bereaved couples to obtain their permission to release their name to the researcher. A letter of introduction describing the study was then mailed. Five days following the mailing, couples were telephoned to obtain their decision concerning their participation. Once verbal consent was secured, an appointment was made to visit the couple in their home, during which time both husband and wife completed the questionnaires independently. Before administration of the questionnaires, the spouses were each asked to sign a consent form advising them of their rights. A similar procedure was followed for the nonbereaved group, who were

recruited primarily through daycare centers, community clinics, and pediatricians' offices.

The couples' marital relationship was assessed using the Personal Assessment of Intimacy in Relationships, or PAIR (Schaefer & Olson, 1981). The
PAIR Inventory consists of 30 items, equally divided among the following subscales:

- *Emotional intimacy* (6 items), such as "My partner listens to me when I
need someone to talk to"
- *Social intimacy* (6 items), such as "My partner disapproves of some of
my friends"
- *Sexual intimacy* (6 items), such as "I am able to tell my partner when I
want sexual intercourse"
- *Intellectual intimacy* (6 items), such as "My partner helps me clarify my
thoughts"
- *Recreational intimacy* (6 items), such "I share in few of my partner's
interests"

A sixth subscale, namely Conventionality (6 items), was included to measure
social desirability. Couples were asked to rate their level of agreement on each
statement using a 5-point response format ranging 0–4. This extensively used
measure has been found to have high internal consistency for the items within
the subscale. Convergent validity was established using the Locke-Wallace
Marital Adjustment Scale (Locke & Wallace, 1959) and the Moos Family Environment Scale (Moos & Moos, 1976).

Both bereaved and nonbereaved couples completed two versions of the
PAIR. Each partner rated the items on the scale with reference to the past month
(*now*). They then completed the scale a second time, rating the items with
reference to how they would like their relationship to be (*ideal*). The bereaved
couples rated the items a third time with reference to how their relationship had
been before the death of their infant (*past*).

RESULTS

This study addressed two major issues: differences between bereaved husbands'
and wives' perception of their marital relationship, and differences between
bereaved couples and nonbereaved couples in the five areas of marital intimacy.
All analyses were conducted using the SPSS-X statistical program (SPSS, Inc.,
1988).

Are There Differences Between Bereaved Husbands'
and Wives' Perception of Their Marital Intimacy?

This section examines bereaved husbands' and wives' perception of marital
intimacy with reference to the way their marriage was during the previous
month, their level of satisfaction with their marriage, and changes in their

marriage at the present time compared to the way it was before their infant's death.

Marital intimacy was assessed by the PAIR, which comprised the five subscales mentioned above. Each subscale yielded a score with a theoretical range of 0–24.

The data from the five subscales of marital intimacy were subjected to a two-factor multivariate analysis of covariance (MANCOVA) with *spouse* (husband and wife) as the within-subject factor. Because the Conventionality subscale (social desirability) score was significantly correlated with the majority of the PAIR subscale scores, it was treated as a covariate. With a significant overall F on the MANCOVA, using Hotelling's T as the criteria, the data for each of the five subscales were then subjected to one-way univariate analysis of variance (ANOVA).

The data from the five subscales of marital intimacy that measured bereaved husbands' and wives' perception of their marriage at the present time were subjected to one-way MANCOVA. The analysis yielded a significant effect of *spouse* [F (5,51) = 3.03, p < .02], which was attributed to the subscales of emotional intimacy [F (1,55) = 4.75, p < 0.3], sexual intimacy [F (1,55 = 4.14, p < 0.5], and recreational intimacy [F (1,55) = 4.56, p < 0.4]. Husbands rated emotional intimacy higher than their wives did, and sexual and recreational intimacy lower than their wives did (Table 1).

We also assessed bereaved husbands' and wives' satisfaction with their marriage. A score of satisfaction with marital intimacy was computed for each

Table 1   Mean Scores of Bereaved Husbands' and Their Wives' Perceptions of Marital Intimacy (N = 114; 57 Husbands and 57 Wives)

Subscales	Husband	Wife	$F(1,55)$	p[a]
		Present Time[b]		
Emotional	17.9	17.0	4.75	*
Social	16.0	16.6	1.38	
Sexual	17.9	19.0	4.14	*
Intellectual	16.8	17.4	1.32	
Recreational	16.5	17.6	4.56	*
		Satisfaction[c]		
Emotional	− 3.3	− 5.2	8.58	* *
Social	− 1.7	− 1.8	.004	
Sexual	− 3.3	− 3.2	.27	
Intellectual	− 2.7	− 4.0	4.08	*
Recreational	− 2.8	− 2.4	1.78	

[a]* * = p < 0.1; * = p < 05.
[b]Theoretical range for present scores: 0–24.
[c]Higher negative score is less satisfaction.

spouse on each of the five subscales. This was done by subtracting spouses' subscale score during the past month (*now*) from their score on how they would like their relationship to be (*ideal*) (e.g., husband's rating of ideal score on emotional intimacy minus husband's rating of present emotional intimacy; wife's rating of ideal score on sexual intimacy minus wife's rating of present sexual intimacy). The data from each subscale were then subjected to a one-way MANCOVA, with Conventionality as the covariate, followed by one-way ANOVAs. The analyses yielded a significant overall main effect for *spouse* (F, $(5,51) = 2.89$, $p < .023$], which was attributed to the subscales of emotional intimacy [$F (1,55) = 8.58$, $p < .005$] and intellectual intimacy [$F (1,55) = 4.08$, $p < .05$]. Husbands were significantly more satisfied than their wives in the areas of emotional and intellectual intimacy (Table 1).

Finally, we considered how bereaved spouses' perception of their marriage had changed from before their infant's death to the present time. To examine this issue, the data from each of the five subscales were subjected to a 2×2 repeated measure ANOVA with *time* (past and present) and *spouse* (husband and wife) as the within-subject factors and the Conventionality score treated as the covariate. In these analyses we report only the main and interaction effects of *time*. The analysis yielded a marginally significant main effect of *time* only for the subscale of sexual intimacy [$F (1,55 = 3.45$, $p < 0.7$]. Couples reported less sexual intimacy after their infant's death (*now*) than before the death (*past*) (*M*: 18.45 and 18.85). There were no significant *spouse* x *time* interactions on any of the five subscales.

Is There a Difference Between Bereaved and Nonbereaved Couples' Perception of Marital Intimacy?

The second issue we addressed was whether bereaved couples differed from their nonbereaved counterparts in their ratings of marital intimacy. To address this issue, the data were subjected to 2 x 2 (MANCOVA) with *group* (bereaved vs. nonbereaved) as the between-subjects factor and *spouse* (husband and wife) as the within-subject factor. Again, the Conventionality score (social desirability) was treated as the covariate. (*Spouse* was included as a factor because in the previous set of analyses we found differences between bereaved husbands' and wives' perceptions of marital intimacy). With a significant overall MANCOVA F, the data for each subscale were then subjected to ANOVA.

The data for marital intimacy with reference to how their marriage was at present (*now*), revealed no significant main effect of *group* or interaction with *group*. In other words, bereaved couples did not differ from nonbereaved couples in their ratings of all five areas of marital intimacy (Table 2).

We also assessed bereaved and nonbereaved couples' satisfaction with their marriage, using the same approach to analysis. Scores on satisfaction of marital intimacy for the five subscales were computed as described above (i.e., *ideal*

Table 2   Mean Scores of Bereaved Couples' (N = 57) and Nonbereaved Couples' (N = 55) Perceptions of Marital Intimacy

Subscales	Bereaved	Nonbereaved	F(1,55)	p
		Present Time[a]		
Emotional	17.4	18.2	1.49	NS[b]
Social	16.3	16.9	.59	NS
Sexual	18.4	18.4	.07	NS
Intellectual	17.1	17.5	.20	NS
Recreational	17.1	17.2	.01	NS
		Satisfaction[c]		
Emotional	− 4.3	− 3.8	.003	NS
Social	− 1.7	− 1.9	.724	NS
Sexual	− 3.2	− 3.6	1.26	NS
Intellectual	− 3.3	− 3.1	.028	NS
Recreational	− 2.6	− 2.8	1.35	NS

[a]NS: Nonsignificant.
[b]Theoretical range for present scores: 0–24.
[c]Higher negative score is less satisfaction.

score minus *now* score). The analysis yielded no significant difference between bereaved and nonbereaved couples' level of marital satisfaction on any of the five subscales (Table 2). Thus, there was no difference between bereaved and nonbereaved couples' ratings of marital satisfaction.

DISCUSSION

Bereaved husbands and wives were found to differ on three of the five subscales when rating their perception of their marital intimacy at the present time (*now*). Husbands rated emotional intimacy higher than their wives, while wives rated sexual intimacy and recreational intimacy higher than their husbands.

These findings are consistent with other research on parental coping strategies when the aspects of marital intimacy are considered (Feeley & Gottlieb, 1988; Mandell, McNaulty & Reece, 1980; Helmrath & Steinitz, 1978). For example, emotional intimacy involves such experiences as the ability to share feelings openly; sexual intimacy includes physical closeness, such as sexual activity; recreational intimacy includes sharing of mutual interests (Schaefer & Olson, 1981). Indeed, past studies have reported that following an infant's death, wives' need to verbalize feelings may be greater than husbands'. It may be that wives turn to their spouse to satisfy this need to verbalize feelings. Because husbands' need to verbalize feelings may be less than their wives', it is not surprising that wives rated emotional intimacy lower than their husbands. This is not to say that husbands' need for closeness may be less than their wives' but that their need for closeness may take a different form. Husbands may express their need for closeness through sexual and recreational intimacy, whereas wives may seek their need for closeness through emotional forms of intimacy.

Bereaved Versus Nonbereaved Couples' Marital Intimacy

There have been contradictory findings in terms of how an infant's death affects the marital relationship. Several researchers have reported an increase in marital break-up following an infant's death (Bergman et al., 1969; Cornwell et al., 1977; Fish, 1986; Halpern, 1972), whereas other researchers have found that some marriages may be strengthened by this tragedy (De Frain & Ernst, 1978; Giles, 1970; Helmrath & Steinitz, 1978). We found that bereaved and nonbereaved couples did not differ on their ratings of marital intimacy, thus lending support to the latter set of research studies. However, we cannot unequivocally state that marital intimacy was not affected by an infant's death given the fact that 49% of all our couples could not be contacted and that of those who were contacted, 50% refused to participate. The couples who did not participate may have had stronger marriages to begin with or may have "weathered the storm" and decided to stay together. Indeed, we have some evidence that the death of an infant does put a strain on a marriage. We asked couples if they had thought of separating, and in 28% of bereaved couples, at least one of the partners had some separation ideation, compared to 7% of the nonbereaved group [chi-square $= 6.24 = p < .01$ (Yate's correction)]. Thus, those couples who decided to participate in our study may be those who have a stable marriage and/or who had already resolved or were in the process of resolving their marital difficulties.

Perhaps there are three different groups of couples. The first group may be couples whose marriage was not strong enough to survive the initial strain of their infant's death. These may be the couples we couldn't reach and/or those who refused to participate. The second group may be couples who have been able to help each other through this very difficult time. These may be the couples in our study. The third and final group may be those couples whose marriage may breakup further down the road.

CONCLUSION

Although this study provides us with some insight into the marital relationship of bereaved husbands and wives, it highlights the need for further longitudinal examination of the data as well as clear identification of different types of couples within the bereaved group.

REFERENCES

Bergman, A., Pomeroy, M., & Beckwith, B. (1969). The psychiatric toll of the Sudden Infant Death Syndrome. *General Practitioner, 19*, 26–31.

Cornwell, J., Nurcombe, B., & Stevens, L. (1977). Family response to loss of a child by Sudden Infant Death Syndrome. *Medical Journal of Australia, 1*, 656–658.

De Frain, J. D., & Ernst, L. (1978). The psychological effects of Sudden Infant Death Syndrome on surviving family members. *The Journal of Family Practice, 6*(5), 985–989.

Feeley, N., & Gottlieb, L. N. (1988). Parents' coping and communication following their infant's death. *Omega, 19*(1), 51–67.

Fish, W. V. (1986). Differences in grief experiences in bereaved parents. In T. A. Rando (Ed.), *Parental loss of a child* (pp. 415–428). Champaign, IL: Research Press Company.

Giles, P. F. (1970). Reactions of women to perinatal death. *Australian and New Zealand Journal of Obstetrics and Gynecology, 10*, 207–210.

Halpern, W. (1972). Some psychiatric sequelae to crib death. *American Journal of Psychiatry, 129*, 58–62.

Helmrath, T., & Steinitz, E. (1978). Death of an infant: Parental grieving and the failure of social support. *The Journal of Family Practice, 6*(4), 785–790.

Laroche, C., Lalinec-Michaud, M., Engelsmann, F., Fuller, N., Copp, M., McQuade-Soldatos, L., & Azima, R. (1984). Grief reactions to perinatal death—A follow-up study. *Canadian Journal of Psychiatry, 29*, 14–19.

Locke, H. J., & Wallace, K. M. (1959). Short marital adjustment and prediction tests: Their reliability and validity. *Marriage and Family Living, 21*, 251–255.

Mandell, F., McNaulty, E., & Reece, R. (1980). Observations of paternal response to sudden unanticipated infant death. *Pediatrics, 65*(2), 221–225.

Miles, M. S., (1984). Helping adults mourn the death of a child. In H. Wass & C. Corr (Eds.), *Childhood and death* (pp. 219–241). Washington, DC: Hemisphere Publishing Corporation.

Moos, R. H., & Moos, B. A. (1976). A typology of family social environments. *Family Process, 15*, 357–372.

Schaefer, M. T., & Olson, D. H. (1981). Assessing Intimacy: The PAIR Inventory. *Journal of Marital and Family Therapy, 7*, 47–60.

SPSS Inc. (1988). *SPSS-X user's guide.* Chicago: SPSS Inc.

Statistics Canada. (1986). *Births and deaths. Vital statistics Vol. 1, 1983.* (Catalogue 84-204). Ottawa: Ministry of Supply Services.

Videka-Sherman, L., & Lieberman, M. (1985). The effects of self-help and psychotherapy intervention on child loss: The limits of recovery. *American Journal of Orthopsychiatry, 55*(1), 70–82.

Chapter 22

Legitimate Grieving?: Working with Infertility

Sue Jennings

My task, in this chapter, is to illustrate the largely unrecognized suffering experienced by people who are unable to conceive children or who have difficulty conceiving children. Problems affecting fertility are present in 1 out of 10 of the population (some statistics suggest that the true figure could be 1 out of 6). Current developments in medical technology have a success rate of about 30%. Thus, at the present time, we are still unable to deal with the longings and unfulfillment of 70% of the people who suffer in this way.

The need for human beings to reproduce themselves is as ancient as civilization itself. Leah said to Jacob, "Give me sons or I shall die," an anguish expressed even earlier by Sarah to Abraham. Throughout history and throughout societies and cultures, fertility of human beings, as well as fertility in flora and fauna has been and still is a major preoccupation. Although medical science has made tremendous strides during the past decade to alleviate some of the

This chapter is presented on behalf of the Academic Unit of Obstetrics and Gynaecology, at the Royal London Hospital, Whitechapel, U.K. I am indebted to Prof. Gedis Grudzinkskas, without whose vision this program would never have started. I am grateful to Dr. Robert Silman, Ms Jean Campbell, and Sr. Prue Bakpa for their collaboration.

suffering of couples who would otherwise be childless, my contention, nevertheless, is that the true nature of this pain and the sometimes permanent emotional damage is in the main unseen and unacknowledged.

My work is placed within the Academic Unit of Obstetrics and Gynaecology of the London Hospital, which has a busy National Health Service Fertility Clinic. People attend the clinic with a variety of problems. Some of these, such as low sperm count or blocked fallopian tubes, can be diagnosed with appropriate medical exploration. Others yielded no easy medical diagnosis and are termed "unexplained infertility." The therapeutic service is available to all couples who attend the clinic and is seen as an integral part of their fertility treatment—a very courageous innovation for such a department.

All couples who attend the clinic also attend an initial counseling session and a follow-up session. In the counseling session, many complex issues are explored, concerning the possible choices people may have. For example, if there is a diagnosed medical condition, people then have to decide on the possible treatment that is appropriate. Does it conflict with their own ethical or religious beliefs? Are both partners equally sure about treatment? If it involves donor insemination or donor eggs, does this affect their attitudes and relationship? Is the infertility placing a stress on the relationship? Is adoption a possible choice?

These are some of the many themes that couples are able to explore and discuss in the nonjudgmental ambiance of a counseling session that is nondirective and emphasizes the patients' autonomy and right of choice. In the two sessions, people are also able to give vent to emotions that have built up over time—their rage, despair, frustration, fear, and sorrow. There is often guilt associated with the fertility problem—"it must be somebody's fault." Relatives often put pressure on couples to have children, as does society itself, since this is the "normal" thing to do. Therefore, by definition, couples who are unable to have children feel that they are not normal. They feel that they are failures.

Couples who have "unexplained infertility" experience the problem even more acutely. They want a diagnosis, a label, a reason. If there is no medical reason, then whose fault is it? Are they stopping themselves? Are they being punished? (The latter is a common feeling, especially for women who have had an abortion earlier in their lives or for men and women who feel they have been promiscuous.) Should they have waited so long? Should they have wanted a career first?

These couples torture themselves and try to "make sense" of their situation for which medical science has so far been unable to give an explanation. The counseling sessions are very important to allow them to express some of these feelings.

Some of the couples who attend the clinic are those for whom, because of medical reasons, having children is impossible. They need to come to terms with the feelings of hopelessness and try to discuss some possible choices they might have in their lives.

Another group of people, for whom specialist provision is necessary, is those who have "weight-related infertility," which means they are either too obese or too underweight to achieve regular ovulation. For most of these people the basic problem is an eating disorder, which frequently has an emotional cause.

We are now able to provide services to these four groups of people who may present: (1) a diagnosed medical problem that may respond to treatment, (2) an unexplained infertility, (3) an untreatable medical condition, or (4) a weight-related infertility.

After the two initial sessions, couples have the opportunity to join one of the therapeutic groups on a regular basis. There is no pressure on people to join these groups, but the groups are available as a service. However, if there is undue stress in a couple's lives, they are encouraged to attend. The staff team running these groups consists of a dramatherapist, a counselor, and an art therapist. Each group has its own characteristics and varies in its orientation. The following is a summary of the groups, which are organized around the four main types of problems already described.

PRETREATMENT GROUP

This is a group for couples who have chosen to have assisted conception, the usual medical procedure is GIFT (gamete intra-fallopian transfer). Couples join the group at least three months before treatment starts and if possible earlier. The main focus of the group is the anxiety about the operation and the fears that it may not work. Men often feel left out of the procedure, because once they have given their sperm, they have little further involvement. Couples are encouraged to express their doubts and fears and to give mutual support to each other; they are taught stress management exercises to maximize the efficacy of the treatment. However, the important subtext of this group is that only 30% of people who attempt it will achieve a pregnancy through assisted conception. It is important to address this issue from the outset. Many couples feel that they are bound to be among the 30% and refuse to consider the strong possibility that they will not achieve a pregnancy. It is important to address the realities in this group, so that the pregnancy does not stay as a "dream state." Early in the group there is often sudden shock, anger, and then a period of grieving when couples face up to the fact that they may not achieve a pregnancy. However, working through this time is important so that people are able to embark on the operation in a more philosophic mood, and have some resources to deal with the outcome. They are encouraged to continue to attend the group right through the operative time and then afterwards, whether the women are pregnant or not.

For those couples who have not achieved a pregnancy, the group acts in a supportive capacity, especially after the initial disappointment, when they are deciding whether to try again. Couples have the opportunity to have three attempts at the operation.

UNEXPLAINED INFERTILITY GROUP

This group is often the most volatile. Couples are angry because they do not know the reason for their infertility, angry with the doctors for not having an answer, angry with themselves for not producing a child. The common initial reaction in this group is either extreme flooding of tears followed by anger or the other way around. Couples are encouraged to express these feelings through dramatherapeutic methods—creating masks, for example, and then enacting scenes in which the masks can help them to articulate their feelings. Some people come to the group with the expectations that it will assist them to become pregnant—and indeed, some couples have achieved a pregnancy after relatively short attendance. It is important, however, that this does not become the raison d' être of attendance, because if it does, all the expectations on self and staff are continued. The purpose of the groups is to deal with feelings about the fertility problems, and if a baby happens to be an outcome, then it is a bonus.

The dramatherapy, like the art therapy, explores the dreams of people with fertility problems, which frequently contain very obvious related themes. In one group, a woman had a dream about her father; in the dream he was a bank manager, and she telephoned him to create a baby account.

The therapists work with people's body image; many people with fertility problems loathe their own bodies because they cannot make them do what they want. One woman, when painting a picture of herself, painted her womb black and said it was a garden where nothing would grow. She then described how she physically attacked herself every time she menstruated and showed us her abdomen, covered in bruises.

UNTREATABLE INFERTILITY GROUP

This group of people, who know that it is physiologically impossible for them to have children, need special consideration. This is where the grieving process is most evident and goes through all the stages experienced in bereavement. These couples are mourning for the child they have never had, and the feelings for this nonexistent child are as powerful as those for a child lost after months or years. They have to deal with the "no hope" position—that with all the technology in the world, they will not produce a baby together. Some relationships cannot sustain this trauma and break up; sometimes couples embark on a blaming procedure, if it appears to be one person's fault more than the other's. And, of course, we know that in some cultures divorce is permissible if there is barrenness. Other couples become entrenched in their own grief and believe that nothing can make life any better; for them, "What is the point of living if you can't have children" is a frequent statement. The importance of this group is to allow people the time and space to work through a normal grieving process, which may well take months, towards a point of reconciliation, when other decisions about their lives can be made. Maybe adoption is a choice after all, even though they initially refuted the idea that someone else's baby might bring them joy and fulfillment. The problem is exacerbated since the age limit for adoptive parents laid down by adoption agencies in the United Kingdom is getting lower, which means that by the time a couple are sure they cannot produce a child and decide to adopt, they may be too old. In addition, there are fewer babies available for adoption. One couple suddenly considered the idea of adopting an AIDS baby, feeling they could give her their love where no one else was prepared to give it.

WEIGHT-RELATED INFERTILITY GROUP

People in this group fall into a category of their own and are very complex to work with; the eating disorder itself may be a long-term condition that has not been diagnosed earlier. Anyone who has worked with anorexia and obesity knows how difficult therapists find it to bring about permanent change. For some people, the weight issue is connected with unresolved grieving from early in their lives, especially when it involved a parent. For others, a very high expectation has been put on them, and there is now a further expectation of having a baby. There are some women who consciously or unconsciously make use of extreme weight loss as a means of preventing pregnancy, which of course is a means of retaining control over their lives as well as their bodies.

DISCUSSION

The groups described above all share certain characteristics.

First of all, most people who come for treatment are frightened—frightened of the diagnosis and the treatment, but more than anything else they are frightened of failure.

Second, most couples with fertility problems are very lonely; they have often isolated themselves, particularly when siblings or friends have started families. They often give up hobbies and interests outside the home.

Third, together with the pain, depression, anger, and desperation, they nearly always feel very guilty.

Fourth, for many couples, the idea of a baby has taken on all the qualities of a "dream baby"; it has never had a reality associated with it, as happens with most couples during pregnancy and the early days after birth. Couples will therefore talk about the perfect child, who will be unblemished and well behaved.

Therapeutic intervention using art therapy and counseling enables many people to come to terms with these feelings and to have the opportunity to lead a life that at least can be fulfilling in some ways. This cannot happen unless the grieving process has been dealt with first.

A recent development in our program is the realization of the importance of joining art with medicine. Human beings express their fertility through art—myth, music, paintings, sculptures, drama. Being artistic and creative is one way of being fertile; it is also a way of expressing the human longing to be fertile. We have now appointed an artist-in-residence who is working with patients to transform the environment through sculptures and wall hangings. We now have open creative groups called "A Celebration of Living," to which patients and staff are invited. These open groups are not therapy groups but creative artistic groups, where participants can express their own creativity through a choice of all the art forms, both individually and as a group.

In many ways this is the most exciting and innovative development in this clinic. It is very courageous for a department of medicine to acknowledge the importance of art.

The department is also developing in other ways; for example, drama students from the Royal Academy of Dramatic Art attend regularly and work with medical students on dramatized case histories. Actors attend to role-model different doctor personas for the medical students. This is just the beginning of the rediscovery of art as a way to express things that cannot be expressed through verbal logic. By means of ritual and performance, art has always been a way that birth and death have been expressed. How appropriate that once again it can assist in the longings and mourning of those people who wish for children.

Part Six

Stress, Coping, and Needs of Professionals

Chapter 23

Working with Dying Children:
A Professional's Personal Journey

Danai Papadatou

I would never exchange the sorrows of my heart for the joys of the multitude.
And I would not have tears of sadness . . . turn into laughter.
I would, that my life remains a tear and a smile . . .
A tear to unite me with those of broken heart and a smile to be a sign of my joy in
existence.

Kahlil Gibran, "A Tear and a Smile"

Lito is a young Greek psychologist who has been working with seriously ill children for over 10 years. I know her well and would like to share some of her experiences and feelings as they were recorded in her personal diaries. Her journey is nothing out of the ordinary. Those who work with dying children may identify with her feelings, beliefs, or reactions. Yet her journey is also unique in the way Lito developed not only professionally but personally as well.

Her educational background was in clinical psychology and family counseling. Her interest in children who were confronted with death became more focused when she decided to study for her doctoral thesis the dynamics of families with children suffering from cancer. Based on her previous clinical experience with children having kidney failure, she started her professional journey filled with excitement and high expectations, along with some fears, expressed in her diary in the following lines:

> People react with astonishment and fear every time I tell them the topic of my dissertation. . . . Not that it doesn't scare me too. . . . The more I explore the issue of death, the more vulnerable I feel. Why have I chosen to work with families who face life-and-death issues?

The first year, after she returned from the United States and started working at the Children's Hospital in Athens, should have been a year of professional and personal preparation for Lito. But quite soon she was confronted with two deaths that affected her deeply and influenced her attitude in her daily work.

Yannis, a 15-year-old boy with kidney failure, affected by the recent loss of a young child in that unit, for the first time openly expressed his concerns and fears about death. He asked Lito, "Why do children die?" She felt helpless, powerless, unable to give any answer or explanation. "I don't know," she replied, but then spent the whole morning sharing with the boy his feelings and beliefs about death, discussing his priorities and values in life. When they parted he was relieved, and both were elated knowing they had "connected" somewhere deeply. "I'll see you tomorrow," he said with anticipation . . . but there was not tomorrow. Yannis died suddenly that night, and Lito was left with feelings of confusion, grief, and despair.

The same week, Katerina, a 15-year-old girl, was hospitalized after an attempted suicide by means of Gramoxon, a lethal dose of a toxic plant medication. The fourth night her condition suddenly deteriorated. Her shocked parents were totally unable to sit by her side. Medical interventions left them without hope. The young girl, who had developed a special bond with Lito a few days before, sought her presence. Lito spent that night alone with Katerina, attending to her. She spoke to her about the freedom of letting go, like a butterfly leaving its restricting cocoon. This was a story about death and dying she had heard Elisabeth Kübler-Ross use with her patients. It was the first time Lito was close to a child who was dying and discovered it could happen peacefully and in an atmosphere of dignity.

Those two experiences helped her confront her strengths and limitations, as well as her sense of contribution and helplessness. As time went by, she had to learn to accept and live with those contradictions and a variety of intense feelings.

Some times Lito felt sorrow, other times, anger and despair. She wrote in her diary:

If only I could cry today . . .
   I would find an outlet to my pain.
   But my pain is not sorrow . . . it is anger.
   I feel anger, as a storm that turns everything upside down in me and leaves
nothing intact. . . . Death seems so unfair!

Other times her emotional pain alternated with an overabundance of love
that was expressed in the following passage:

I am in love with life, with people around me! How foolish to think eternity is
numbered. . . . Each day is a treasure within eternity.

Accepting the death of a child was painful enough, but when death occurred under conditions that did not promote dignity, completing the process of
grief seemed harder. During those moments she tended to isolate herself and
seek refuge wherever there was life. She left the hospital and went to some
beautiful, quiet place where she could feel a healing energy in her contact with
nature, which seemed to ease her pain. There she found the precious quality of
being alone.

This spiritual isolation connected her with her own core, her own balance,
her own resources. However, in her search to isolate and reconnect with her
inner self, she discovered how close she felt to other people, and she understood that solitude alone was not the answer to the process of grief.

Solitude became for her the stage that allowed a creative force to come
forth and find ways of expression. For Lito, creativity developed in different
forms, such as writing, painting, and dancing. She quickly realized that the
more she allowed herself to express her feelings and to accept her grief, the
more she was able to invest energy and love in those children and families who
needed her.

As years went by, her relationships with children and families became
deeper and her interventions more effective. She noticed how some of these
children were trapped within a family system that was characterized by unhealthy dynamics. Was their disease an unconscious choice? At times, she was
convinced that it was, while other times she was left doubting.

Lito was present from the moment the diagnosis was made, and from then
on, she accompanied the whole family on its own difficult journey, through joy
and pain, through hope and frustration. But something in the depth of these
relationships was beyond her comprehension. At that time she wrote in her
diary:

What draws me towards the hospital in the middle of the night and takes me there
when I am most needed? Is it pure coincidence that I happen to be "there," close to

these children, during their very last moments, even when dying occurs quite unexpectedly?

She knew, though, that it was no coincidence. She had acquired a deeper intuition, which she learned to trust and respect, without trying to reason and understand. She regarded children's own intuition with the same trust and respect and quickly learned that they were not only aware of the seriousness of their condition but possessed an unconscious knowledge of their prognosis and ultimate outcome.

There was a little 7-year-old girl, Eleni, who soon after she was diagnosed with acute myeloblastic leukemia painted a story entitled "The Life of the Almond Tree." Her story begins with a seed, which grows, becomes a tree that blooms prematurely in spring and gives fruit in the summer. One day in autumn, a cloud appears and hides the sun. The sun bids good-bye to the almond tree, which fades and soon dies. Through this story Eleni expressed her own premature bloom in life and intuitive knowledge of death after the cycle of seasons was completed

A year after her diagnosis, one day as Eleni was waiting at the outpatient clinic for her regular treatment, she spontaneously sketched a little girl with a heavy cloud over her head. A few minutes later physicians confirmed the occurrence of a relapse. Within a few days Eleni's condition deteriorated dramatically. One day when Lito entered the child's room, she found Eleni in pain. Her

Figure 1 Paintings by a 7-year-old girl, Eleni, soon after she was diagnosed with acute myeloblastic leukemia. This is the beginning of her story, entitled "The Life of the Almond Tree."

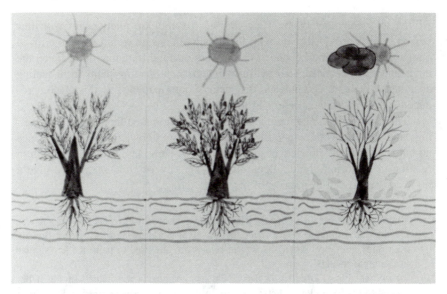

Figure 2 Continuation of the story of "The Life of the Almond Tree," expressing Eleni's intuitive knowledge of death after the cycle of seasons.

stomach was hurting due to internal bleeding. Lito asked if she could sit beside her and gently put her hands on Eleni's stomach. Then, they looked deep into each other's eyes for almost 10 minutes. Everybody around kept silent. A woman physician who entered the room to examine Eleni left without interrupting. She later said that there was something so powerful in the silent eye contact that it frightened her so that she decided to leave.

Lito and Eleni both knew that death was close and shared unspoken messages of courage, faith, and love. It was "okay" to let go. When the pain in Eleni's stomach disappeared, they said good-bye in joy! Lito cried not for Eleni's death, but for the love and communication they had shared, not in a relationship of possession, but in one allowing the soul to be freed and making death less frightening.

A question that preoccupied Lito was whether children could affect the course of their disease, and how. She believed that with appropriate help they could discover and use their inner resources and move toward a goal, whether this goal was to fight the disease, or to prolong life by enhancing everyday living, or even to prepare themselves and others for the coming death.

Lito realized that dying was a period of emotional fluctuations that seemed contradictory yet were part of the same process. While children expressed their awareness of dying, at other moments they seemed to deny it completely. With death approaching, they tended to withdraw and distance themselves from loved ones, yet at the same time they overinvested one person with intense feelings. She had noticed that children had a special sense in choosing a person able and willing to accompany them. They formed a symbiotic relationship with this person, which provided them with the illusion that they would carry the loved one along to death and beyond. This process of nondifferentiation between the other and self enhanced their sense of integrity, protecting them from feeling abandoned. It is no coincidence that many young patients, at this stage, produced stories and poems referring to birth.

Through symbolic communication children expressed their needs and feelings and sometimes their good-byes. They had no knowledge of death—since no human has such knowledge—but experienced emotions, beliefs, and faith in relation to death and dying. Regardless of age, every child seemed to give a mystical message of awareness of his or her dying.

Toula, a 4-year-old girl, gave the play therapist a good-bye present the day she was leaving the hospital to return home and die. It was a drawing of a field of flowers on a rainy cold day. When she was in remission, she used to paint for her similar but sunny drawings.

When dying, Dimitris, a 6-year-old boy, painted a red house, saying it belonged to his friend Peter. Peter used to draw similar houses before his death from the same disease.

Costas, a shy, quiet, very reserved 13-year-old boy, painted—just a day before his death—a volcano erupting in the dark night. Throughout the six years he lived with acute myeloblastic leukemia, this was the only drawing he volunteered to do when Lito suggested he painted his feelings.

The experience of dying was perceived and felt differently by Pavlos, a 14-year-old boy, who attempted to express his feelings by painting a peaceful sunset, only a few days before his death.

In one of her last drawings, Athena, a 14-year-old girl, painted a "Far Away Fantasy Land" where she perceived herself as a mermaid queen living between two worlds, earth and water, life and death. Her last drawing a few days before her death was that of a fish swimming in the deep waters of the ocean.

But how did this deep involvement with life and death affect Lito? Was it possible for her, or anybody else, to maintain a "detached concern" in those situations? Rather than *detached concern,* a term Lito never liked, she preferred to use the term *mature concern.* With mature concern she was able to identify with the pain of the other, but not with the other. She was able to understand their feelings, participate in their experience, and share their journey, knowing she would be affected by them. But never could she live their journey, their life, their death as if it were her own!

She learned that professionals must respect the ability of every human being, adult or child, to choose the way they want to live and die. She was convinced that our power as "experts" lies in our willingness to remain "students" and to learn from every child and family. However, she had noticed that sometimes, as a consequence of our own personal desires, we try to control the conditions of dying and deprive families of their right to decide how they want to go through the experience of dying. It is their dying, not ours. All we can do is to help them give meaning to their experience.

Then came a period for Lito during which she experienced an overload of deaths that—despite her attitude—influenced her effectiveness. She wrote:

> Only this month, six of my little friends died. . . .
> > I don't want to face any more deaths. Death is like a Sun:
> > It may bring light to deeper levels of awareness
> > and enhance the purpose of our life,
> > but it may hurt the eyes and blind the soul
> > when we are exposed to it for too long.

During these moments support seemed crucial for her. But who could provide this support? She turned to the people with whom she worked: her teammates. They were all faced with something in common: the threat of death. One would think that this alone would deepen their ties in the search for togetherness. Lito noticed, however, that when team members did not work out their personal feelings triggered by death, they were likely to project them upon others, thus creating consciously or unconsciously, various conflicts and tensions affecting the group's cohesion. But since nobody can afford to lose his or her group of reference, especially one's "professional family," defenses are developed to perpetuate the myth that the medical team is, and functions as, a "whole," a "group." Everybody acts "as if" this myth was real, and affirms it with behaviors, such as celebrations, get-togethers, or the exchange of gifts.

If, however, an event or a member of the team challenges the myth, the event or person is automatically rejected or becomes a scapegoat. In fact, finding a scapegoat may become the only method a group uses to maintain its unity. For members of the medical team to be confronted with a new threat that is more tangible and less painful than the threat of death is often an easy way of displacing the real problem and letting it remain unsolved. Sometimes a team's dysfunctioning is the reflection of a larger institution that avoids and denies death. Lito believed that the solution could only be found within ourselves, within our courage to explore how each one of us—and all together—are affected by death and dying. This is undoubtedly a painful process, but nonetheless very rewarding.

A medical team that seemed to Lito "stuck" in its own process of growth, and the experience of multiple deaths with no time for completing a grief process, led to such levels of stress that she started to somatize. After a long hesitation she decided to seek the help of a psychologist, who encouraged her to listen to and respect her deeper needs and to seek the distance that would allow a better understanding of her journey.

As she was slowly moving away from the hospital wards, she felt an intense need to reevaluate her experience in pediatric oncology. A pertinent question was bringing her back to the source, long before her journey had even begun: Why had she chosen to work with seriously ill and dying children, and why had she progressively developed a particular interest in dying adolescents?

She became aware that a circle was being completed. She was coming back to where she had started: to her own adolescence, an adolescence affected by her cousin's death in a car accident. At the age of 15 she had suddenly realized that she could die young, too, without having the chance to live her life. She then experienced a great deal of anxiety, which she tried to overcome by getting closer to other people. She consciously decided to leave the protective shell she had built around herself waiting for life to come to her. Getting closer to others, closer to life, was an "anti-thanatos" movement. It was the only way she felt she could fight her fear of death: with more communication, more depth in her relationships, more life! But wasn't that exactly what she was doing all along with dying children? Until their last breath, she considered them as living children, who needed to be recognized as nearing death, and who never stopped searching for a meaning in the midst of a difficult reality they were facing early in life. Without feeling sorry for them nor counting the time that was left, she focused on the time they were still living. This was the only way she knew to help children fight death. This was, in fact, Lito's victory over death.

Lito's professional journey is my own journey at the Children's Hospital, Aglaia Kyriakou, in Athens. Sharing some of my personal feelings, beliefs, and experiences with dying children was an attempt to answer a question I have been asked, by several people, through the years: "How can you do this job?" Answering that questions was never simple. But I know now that the answer is to be found within a long, difficult, and meaningful journey, which was mine and that of dying children and their families.

Chapter 24

Professional Stress: Creating a Context for Caring

Marcia Lattanzi-Licht

Music heard so deeply
That it is not heard at all, but you are the music
While the music lasts.

T. S. Eliot

Children represent a family's future, its hopes, its legacy to the world, the fruits of its efforts. They are a prized symbol of continuity of life. There is no threat that causes more crisis, dysfunction, and distress for a family than life-threatening illness or death of a child. Similarly, there are great challenges facing professionals involved in the care of seriously ill or dying children.

This chapter will focus on the unique nature of the stresses involved when a child is dying, and will refer to the ways professionals experience some measure of these same stresses. It will also explore the factors affecting how families and professionals respond in the face of death of a child, and the elements that help or hinder their coping abilities. Finally, it will examine the costs and impact of their work upon professionals.

It is important for us, as professionals, to consider why we have chosen to do this particular type of work, what influence it has upon the way we live our lives, and what it teaches us about human experience. In other words, is there some sense or meaning we can derive from witnessing the suffering of dying children and their families?

UNDERSTANDING THE DISTRESS

In an evolutionary context, families developed out of a need for safety and protection from dangers, such as predators. The desire to nurture and protect children became an instinctive element related to species survival. Much of the parents' and family's response to the serious illness or death of a child rises out of a situation that frustrates all of their basic ways of being, as well as their beliefs and assumptions about life. They are forced to confront tremendous feelings of helplessness and powerlessness.

Just as the ill or dying child experiences pain, distress, confusion, and uncertainty, parents and other family members experience similar feelings. It may often be observed that suffering is greater for the family members than for the one who is ill or dying. Many parents recount the wish that they could be the ill one, and with no hesitation would trade places with their child rather than watch the child suffer. The act of witnessing the serious illness and/or death of one's child causes unimaginable anguish for parents. In a parallel way, professionals involved in the care of these families taste the bitterness of this process. Dealing with seriously ill or dying children and their families involves work in situations with inherent and intensified distress.

In an earlier work (Lattanzi, 1985), I outlined the significant role-related and emotional stresses involved for professional caregivers in the terminal illness and death of a child. Part of the anguish experienced is due to the act of *witnessing suffering* and being reminded of our own vulnerability and insignificance (Lattanzi, 1985). This relates directly to our sense of *helplessness* and *powerlessness*. In spite of our best interventions, intentions, and efforts, we are unable to stop the dying process, or to prevent the pain of bereavement. Children have a way of decreasing adult defenses and bringing out our openness, and thereby increase the probability that we will become *overinvolved* with them and their families. As members of our own family and as parents, our fears for our own children can become distorted. *Identification* with a child or a specific parent may cause us to lose our boundaries and perspective. This happens more frequently when there are family conflicts or parental dysfunction. Finally, the most significant stress involved in the care of a dying child centers on the *grief* felt in the forced incompleteness of the relationships and the unfulfilled potential of the child's life. It is easy to expend significant energy on the care of a dying child and his or her family. When the child dies, the focus of that considerable energy is lost. Working with dying children creates a cumulative feeling of loss, in ways similar to wartime experiences. It is crucial for professionals caring for dying children and their families to remember the need for perspective: there are many healthy children who will grow to see old age.

PERSONAL REALITIES

After having worked in a hospice for nine years, I believed that I had significant empathy for and understanding of the pain and distress related to a serious illness and death of a child. It is with great humility that I say that I had no real idea of the pain parents experience. The sudden death of my 17-year-old daughter, Ellen, in 1985 at the hands of a drunken driver has left me with great sorrow and conflict. I am no longer just the professional talking about these issues; now I am also the grieving parent who knows the unimaginable grief in a profoundly personal way. The comments in this chapter will seek to bring together both of my realities and contexts surrounding the stresses the death of a child creates for all those involved.

A RESPONSE CONTINUUM

All families have their unique qualities and histories. Knapp (1986) believes that the structure and characteristics of families can either protect members from stress in the death of a child, or compound and intensify their distress.

Family characteristics relate on a continuum from "integrated" to "isolated," according to Knapp (1986). Integrated families possess the following characteristics:

- They are prepared and better equipped to handle stress.
- Stress evokes a family response.
- Channels of communication and cooperation are open.
- They trust other people.
- They engage in warm personal interrelationships with each other.
- They have confidence in friends and neighbors, and in themselves.
- They interact freely with the larger social system.
- They develop many relationships outside the community, which help strengthen the internal integrity of the family as a unit.

While most families do not exist at either pole of the continuum, families that are labeled "isolate" by Knapp (1986) have a limited ability to deal with the stress involved in the serious illness or death of their child. Isolate families are seen to respond with the following characteristics:

- Individual rather than family viewpoint
- Devastated by stress
- Isolated and lacking in family support mechanisms

- Having few resources to draw upon
- Internally separate
- Lacking in closeness
- Operating as closed systems (members do not interact in larger social environment)
- Having minimal social contacts both within and outside the immediate group.

Based on these attributes, most of the families Knapp studied fell somewhere between the isolate and integrated extremes. Besides the situational demands involved in the serious illness or death of a child, the family's resources and operational beliefs about life determine their response to the crisis.

PROFESSIONAL RESPONSES

In examining Knapp's characteristics, there is a direct application to the ways professionals respond to the stress of working with seriously ill or dying children and their families. These resources and definitions can be seen as a possible set of standards for professionals involved in care of families under this extreme stress. Professionals able to work effectively and "integrate" their experiences would possess distinguishable characteristics, such as:

- Open communication
- Ability to buffer and manage stress
- Ability to engage in warm interpersonal relationships, at work and at home
- Personal confidence, and confidence in others
- Ability to trust others
- Ability to function as a team member
- Ability to interact with resources in the community
- Tolerance of ambiguity and discomfort
- Sustaining beliefs.

In work that involves dealing with a family's definitions, hardships, and resources, professionals need to have great tolerance for stress-provoking events and circumstances. Perhaps the best way to approach this goal involves the selection of qualified professionals who have demonstrated competence in dealing with difficult situations. It may be useful for families to interact with professionals who represent appropriate models for ways of coping with distressing circumstances.

PROTECTIVE MECHANISMS

Rutter (1987) believes that it is possible to develop protective mechanisms against the psychological risks associated with stress and adversity. There can be a shift in focus from vulnerability to resilience. It may be useful to examine the "protective mechanisms" as they would apply to these most stressful situations. According to Garmezy's studies of stress-resistant children (1985), three sets of variables represent "protective factors": personal features, such as self-esteem; family cohesion and absence of discord; and, the availability of external support systems that encourage and reinforce a child's coping efforts.

This list represents the opposite of identified risk factors, such as low self-esteem or lack of family cohesion. It reflects several of the characteristics Knapp (1986) used to illuminate the adaptation of families. Resilience can be related to circumstances; yet, given the same difficult circumstances, there is always the powerful influence of the individual response to the situation.

Protection is reflected in the ways people deal with life challenges and in their response to stressful or disadvantageous circumstances. Providing support involves exploring ways to encourage, enhance, and channel a family's or a professional's mechanisms toward a more adaptive direction. In work with seriously ill or dying children and their families, it seems essential to keep our attention directed at those areas that will enhance the adaptation to a most difficult reality.

DEFINING THE ROLE OF PROFESSIONAL

Persons and families in crises often lose a process orientation and focus on details or small obstacles that seem overwhelming. During this period professionals can support families by expanding their view and reminding them of forgotten resources or strengths they can bring to the situation. Perhaps one of the most significant roles of professionals involved in the care of dying children and their families is to reflect the effectiveness of mechanisms that families are using, and to encourage the use of additional ones. The image of a stage production may be used in describing the process of supporting families. In the human drama involved in the life-threatening illness or death of a child, professional caregivers are the backstage crew. The family and the child are the important actors, and professionals do not step to the front stage and take on the important roles belonging to family. Rather, they arrange the lighting and props, have cue cards ready, and do all that is necessary and helpful to set the stage for the drama to proceed. In this sense, professionals provide technical assistance, moral support, and back-up services, while the family produces its own drama.

PROFESSIONAL CHALLENGES

It is possible to see how stress is created for caregivers when we lose sight of our appropriate role, or when we judge or disapprove of the family's performance. One of the most important lessons involved in work with seriously ill or dying children and their families centers on a clear definition of our role, and a distinct realization of our boundaries and personal limitations. Unrealistic self-expectations and grandiose feelings of indispensability are a prime source and symptom of distress. It is critical that we accept our limitations as caregivers, as well as the limitations of our efforts and interventions.

CONSEQUENCES OF THE LOSS OF BALANCE

When the high cost or personal impact of working with dying children and their families is not balanced by appropriate coping mechanisms and personal resources, consequences develop. A progressive cycle of symptoms and distress occurs when the efforts we make exceed our resources and abilities to cope. These symptoms of distress range from dissatisfaction to a diminished sense of self. I will discuss several of them briefly.

Dissatisfaction   A vague sense of discomfort leads to a growing unhappiness with situations and people at work and at home. The professional experiences an increase in exhaustion and physical complaints.

Distortion   Small concerns become obstacles, and the caregiver has an exaggerated sense of his or her own importance, or of the significance of certain incidents and events. This loss of perspective can involve seeing problems become too big to influence or change. It can also involve a minimization or denial or personal feelings.

Drama   Along with a distorted perspective, professionals may experience a heightened sense of emotionality surrounding events or circumstances. This response usually includes significant personalization, where professionals envision themselves to be the center of all critical events involving patients and families.

Decreased Tolerance   A heightened sense of vulnerability leads to an inability to function optimally. There is increased irritability, criticism, and complaining, along with a decreased productivity and inability to manage the workload effectively.

Distancing   A natural response to distress is withdrawal. A process of increased disinterest and detachment from both patients and peers begins.

Depersonalization   In an attempt to protect the self from further distress, the professional experiences a growing lack of concern for, or involvement with, parents, families, and coworkers. Others are seen as sources of additional demands.

Depression   In addition to a significant lack of energy and difficulty with decision making, disturbances in sleeping and eating pattern may be associated with the loss of balance. Often there is increased consumption of alcohol or other substances.

Diminished Sense of Self   Without intervention, the process of professional stress continues to the point where increasing distress brings about an erosion of self. Engagement and satisfaction with one's work are greatly diminished, which interferes with self-esteem and also with one's sense of self-worth. A growing sense of guilt over perceived failures, a sense of worthlessness, and, finally, feelings of despair may develop.

When professionals begin to lose balance in their abilities to cope with work-related demands, one of the ways they react is by attempting to work harder or run faster. In the flurry of activity and increased expenditure of energy, they actually accomplish less. Other consequences of distress involve increased frustration, fatigue, alcohol or drug dependence, and a growing sense of cynicism. Professionals can break under the strain of trying to give too much and exceeding their own boundaries. For some caregiving professionals, work becomes one way they attempt to meet their personal needs through the indirect route of receiving gratitude and admiration from others.

GUIDELINES FOR EFFECTIVE COPING

In addition to the demands and consequences of work with dying children and their families, the professional equation also contains the element of our responses to the stress and demands of the work. A critical distinction between the coping efforts of families and that of professionals is the reality that the illness and death of a child is not our entire world. We engage in different activities, which are separate and apart from our work-related concerns. Jaffee and Scott (1984) maintain that allocation of our energy should include all the areas of our life: work, play, relating to family and friends, and relating to self.

Typically, caregiving professionals spend most of their personal energy on work and relating to others. While an equal distribution of time and energy on these four areas is probably not realistic, paying attention to the importance of work, family, and personal needs is essential to a balanced life.

Another protective element in guarding against professional stress is the ability to balance energy between *intrinsic* and *extrinsic* demands (Jaffee & Scott, 1984). Extrinsic activities are the things we do because we feel some sense of responsibility or obligation ("shoulds and oughts"). Intrinsic activities include the things we do because we want to. In addition, Jaffee and Scott (1984) recommend balance between giving, the things we do to and for others, and receiving, the things that others do to and for us. Professionals typically enjoy the power involved in giving, and can sometimes be more interested in meeting extrinsic demands than intrinsic. In receiving, and in attending to our own needs, we acknowledge the parallel between caregiving and an image of accounting for financial resources. Often we overspend our resources, and operate in the "red." Not only do we pay interest on our overspending, but at some point, loans are called due. It is necessary to spend only those resources we are able to spend, and to allow for the restoration of our balance when we occasionally exceed our limits.

FAVORABLE OUTCOMES

There are ways to mediate the potentially damaging effects of work with the dying, and to enhance positive coping processes. In a study on hospice nurses, Chiriboga et al. (1983) found that the nurses who coped best with the difficulties inherent in their work did so by (1) expressing emotional responses to job-related stresses and (2) resorting to more cognitive and rational coping strategies.

This combination involves acknowledging our emotional experiences and putting them in a cognitive framework that allows us to live with them and continue doing the work. Chiriboga et al. (1983) also found that nurses persisted because of the emotional rewards involved in the work. Nurses who had experienced the loss of a loved one reported less work stress, in part because of personal reasons for being involved in a hospice setting. In addition, those nurses who found their spouses and the other staff to be supportive had the most favorable outcome. This seems to demonstrate again the need for balance and for a means for attending to our own needs outside of the work setting.

EFFECTIVE ACTIONS

Beyond the elements and factors that either predispose us to stress or enhance our coping efforts, there are actions professionals can take that have a sustaining influence. These actions help create a powerful approach to caregiving, which makes it possible to work in the most demanding and stressful of circumstances:

Develop an inner awareness/inner directedness In acknowledging our own needs and limitations, and by living up to our own internal standards, we function with greater levels of health and personal integrity.

Hold appropriate beliefs Beliefs sustain and allow us to endure difficult, painful situations by creating a context that helps us integrate our experiences.

Maintain physical health As a first line of defense, our body absorbs the effects of most of the stress we experience on the job. Regular exercise, a balanced diet, and adequate sleep are essential parts of the protection necessary to do this work.

Develop supportive relationships Both intimate relationships outside work and supportive work relationships are needed to help us maintain our morale and keep a balanced perspective. Encouraging relationships allow us to minimize the effects of the stress experienced when working with dying children and their families and to overcome difficult times.

Evaluate options and provide oneself with choices One of the best ways to manage stress is to adopt a problem-solving approach by identifying areas of difficulty and distress. By identifying the things we can do to improve the situation for patients, families, and professionals, we take a powerful, active orientation. Having choices and making appropriate changes enhance human functioning and self-esteem.

Play Perhaps the most significant lesson of working with dying children is the need to focus on life, and to adopt a light, playful attitude whenever possible. Children teach us to laugh and to maintain a balanced perspective. Dying children remind us how fragile life is and how short our time is—too short not to enjoy it.

REFLECTIONS ON CAREGIVING

Work with dying children and their families is both highly difficult and rewarding. Our own beliefs, values, and life experiences call us to do this work and act as filters against some of the distress involved. When I interviewed professional caregivers who work with the dying as part of my 1984 Winston Churchill Traveling Fellowship, a nurse in England told me, "There is no other kind of work I want to do." Another nurse in Canada found that "this work teaches you to make your stand and work to achieve your goals . . . to contribute." Others mentioned an awareness that "I must be at the front line, in the trenches." And one Canadian nurse found that work with the dying meant "refocusing my own life." Finally, a pediatric nurse I worked with for years at Boulder County Hospice believed that dealing with the dying was "nursing in its purest form."

There are important lessons surrounding work with dying children and their families. These lessons are as unique and individual as our own personal histories. Professional caregivers know that dying can be hard, and that nothing is harder than the death of a child. We are awed by the strength, courage, and understandable struggles of families we work with. Almost universally, witnessing suffering helps us to feel grateful for our own blessings.

INFLUENCING THE WAY WE LIVE

Caring for others has a way of clarifying and ordering our own values. We have the opportunity to develop a sense of patience that allows people room to live and die in their own way. There can also be a growing sense of humility at our lack of control in situations, coupled with a sense of honesty toward our own limits and struggles. And work with dying children and their families helps us develop a sense of trust in the ways families deal with difficulties and distress, handling problems together the best way they can.

Finally, this work is worthy of our commitment and investment because it is mutual, and our gain encompasses lessons that show us a great deal about the meaning of human experience. In the process of caring for dying children and their families, we merge the understanding of our own experiences with those of the people we care for, enriching our vision of all that is difficult, and all that is worthwhile, in life.

As I reflect upon the integration of my own experiences surrounding the death of my daughter, Ellen, with my professional experiences, there is remarkable congruence. Our experiences with people, particularly people we love, leave permanent imprints upon our lives. Ellen's death, along with my work, reminds me again of the preciousness of time, and of each individual person's value. There is never enough time when you love someone, and people we love are irreplaceable. All my life, I will remember Ellen's energy and love, and the way she believed in me, challenged, and sustained me. As my grandmother wisely told me just a few days after Ellen's death, "Never make Steve (my son) feel bad that he is still alive." This wise advice still reminds me that the most important thing is to care for and to love those people who are available to us.

REFERENCES

Chiriboga, D. A., Jenkins, G. & Bailey, J. (1983). Stress and coping among hospice nurses: Test of an analytic model. *Nursing Research, 32*(5).

Garmezy, N. (1985). Stress resistant children: The search for protective factors. In J. Stevenson (Ed.), *Recent research in developmental psychopathology.* Oxford: Pergamon.

Jaffee, D. T., & Scott, C. D. (1984). *Self-renewal.* New York: Fireside.

Knapp, R. (1986). *Beyond endurance: When a child dies.* New York: Schocken.

Lattanzi, M. E. (1985). An approach to caring: Caregiver concerns. In C. A. Corr & D. M. Corr (Eds.), *Hospice approaches to pediatric care.* New York: Springer.

Rutter, M. (1987, July). Psychosocial resilience and protective mechanisms. *American Journal of Orthopsychiatry, 57*(3).

Chapter 25

Achievement in Failure: Working with Staff in Dangerous Situations

Derek Steinberg

Dangerous is a heavy word, and one I hesitated to include in the title of this chapter. In day-to-day work in clinical psychiatry, psychology, psychotherapy, social work, and related fields, we tend to use euphemisms. We say that a patient or a situation or a problem is "very difficult" or "challenging." We may say we are anxious or worried about something. It is of interest, moreover, that in recent years, a new word has crept into our professional vocabulary, in England at least; people do not talk about their fears or worries, they talk about their "concerns." I think these are all words and phrases we use to avoid scaring ourselves, our colleagues, and our patients in what indeed are often quite frightening situations.

Isobel Menzies (1970), in what has become a classic paper entitled "The Functioning of Social Systems as a Defense Against Anxiety," described how a large general hospital managed its staff in such a way that anxiety and distress were avoided, at least in theory. For example, nursing staff was discouraged

The workshop on which this paper is based was developed from a presentation first made at the Tavistock Clinic, London, in August 1987, at a symposium on the theme *The Supervision of Staff Working in Dangerous Situations*.

from becoming "too involved" with patients who were critically ill or dying, or with their relatives, because it was taken for granted that the nurses would not be able to cope with their feelings, or with those of the patient, when death or the fear of death had to be faced. Instead, being confident and optimistic became all-important. Under those circumstances, patients were expected to face something really frightening or genuinely threatening—such as a diagnosis of cancer, news that they would have to undergo a major surgical operation, or prognosis of death—with no real help at all. I will refer to four points I consider relevant to this kind of situation.

First, groups and organization develop these defenses not only because it is so hard to cope with the pain of our patients and their relatives, but also because staff, particularly senior staff, do not want the task of handling the pain of their colleagues. The fear is that if we, as teams or working groups or professionals, tried to face what *our patients* have to face, we would be in danger of becoming as much in need of help as the patients themselves. And this is quite a threatening thought. In the psychiatric field, there are special fears associated with experiencing the way our patients feel. What would happen if the therapist, or the colleagues of the therapist, felt the same despair, the same fear, or the same insanity as the patient? So my first point is that the problem is not only our own feelings, or our relationship with the patient; it also concerns our working relationships with one another.

Second, there is a set of fears among professionals that is only indirectly connected with the clinical issue. One is the fear of failure. I believe this fear goes very deep; deep enough, I would say, to be associated with whatever made people like us decide to train and work in the caring and therapeutic professions in the first place. I am sure such motivations are mixed, and they vary for different individuals. I am also quite certain that such motives as rescuing people from dangerous situations—that is, *succeeding* in doing so—and being in control of complex, fundamental phenomena and feelings related to life, death, and sex are common among professionals. With the wish to avoid failure (if *wish* is a strong enough word, *need* being a better one) goes the fear of failure.

In the film by Ingmar Bergman, *Wild Strawberries,* made in 1957, an old physician, the night before he is due to receive an academic honor, has a dream, or rather, a nightmare, in which he finds himself in an examination and unable to answer the examiner's question: "What is a doctor's first duty?" The examiner tells him that "a doctor's first duty is to ask forgiveness." He also informs him that he has been "found guilty; guilty of guilt." This is art, not science, but it draws attention to the depth of feelings we see every day in our work, if we are honest and perceptive.

In a number of studies I have conducted with others on the working relationships between staff of therapeutic and child care organizations, there are a number of recurring themes (Steinberg & Yule, 1985; Steinberg & Hughes, 1987; Steinberg, 1989). Some of these themes have to do with the anxiety about the uncertainty and unpredictability of the work, the difficulty in getting a grip on things for which, nonetheless, people are held personally responsible, and the experience of conflicts among staff members who each manage such impossible situations in different ways. All these cause fear and distress, and make working very hard. So hard, in fact, that not only does people's competence suffer, but they often think of giving up the job, rather than expecting any help with such feelings within the job; and often they do leave.

So my second general point is that there is often an idealism and a conscientiousness about people in these fields that generate potential anxiety, quite apart from the anxieties directly due to the clinical and therapeutic problems of the patient. Related to this point, therefore, are the professional's feelings, which are indeed feelings of danger.

My third point is easy to state but not easy to substantiate. That is, that those of us who work in broadly psychotherapeutically oriented fields of work tend to find it only too easy to criticize other people, whether they are the general medical and surgical staff of Menzies's study (1970) or workers who have had more training and experience in psychological and social aspects of work. There is often a generally critical atmosphere, even in the most psychotherapeutically or socially sophisticated circles where efforts are made to handle painful feelings and where there is training and supervision. Even then, failure or a sense of failure is never very far away. The task is not so much to feel competent and confident about handling pain and danger and death; rather, it is to learn how to be realistic, yet positive, in situations where the worker does indeed feel incompetent, helpless, impotent, and lacking in confidence. Bennett (1979, 1987), in two helpful books, has dealt with this theme.

The last point I would like to make grows from the earlier points. It refers to the great range and variety of threats and dangers in our work, some of which are described in the following paragraphs.

The threat of physical violence is seldom far away. A common example is that of the young patient whose history and emotional state suggest a need for therapeutic intervention (e.g., psychotherapy or admission to a therapeutic milieu), but whose dangerous behavior seems controllable only in a physically secure place. This may seem like a prison; in some cases it may actually be a prison. In the field of adolescent care and adolescent psychiatry, there are many young people who need both the therapeutic approach *and* physical containment. In adolescent and other psychiatric services there are many patients on this borderline, whom we try to help. Individuals get hurt, sometimes seriously hurt; occasionally professionals, particularly in the nursing and social work professions, have been killed.

The danger of patients at risk of killing themselves causes great anxiety among staff who feel, and are often made to feel, that any step they take may cause death. Confronting a patient—in an attempt to try to stop a dangerous pattern of behavior—may itself cause dangerous behavior. How do you help a patient who has been suicidal, or how do you help a parent who has behaved dangerously to a child, to begin taking again the responsibility for self or for the child, without taking risks? When do you let people at risk out of hospital, or decide against admitting them to hospital? The community, your colleagues, and your own conscience will not treat a mistake lightly.

The problem of professional responsibility without proper acceptance of professional authority in the wider community is a very real one. In England it is common for social workers to be accused of intervening too quickly if a child is thought to be at risk from physical or sexual abuse; equally, they have been accused with as much force for intervening too slowly. They often feel they "cannot win" whatever they do. The use of the phrase being "unable to win" demonstrates that it does indeed feel like a battle.

There are so many other dangerous situations. There are the dangers of prescribing drugs, because of their side-effects, and the danger of *not* prescribing them; or the threat of the therapist's self-esteem when the adolescent challenges the professional, in a way that only the adolescent can, so vividly described by Winnicott (1971). There is the threat of legal action when things go wrong, more prevalent in some countries than others; there is the threat of breakdown in supportive relationships when colleagues disagree, as is bound to happen at times (Steinberg, 1986), there is the problem of handling the bitterness and anger of the parents of chronically disturbed or handicapped children, characteristically aimed at the very people who most try to help (Steinberg, 1983, 1987); and, of course, there are the "inside" threats, related to the feelings that workers in these fields experience about themselves and their colleagues. For example, although it is difficult enough to deal with the tragedy of unavoidable death when everything possible has been done to avoid it, I suggest that there is an ever greater threat and anxiety when, especially in the psychiatric field, there is a disagreement about what "should" have been done or "might" have been done, as in the case of death by suicide. I believe that such feelings, and fear of such feelings, cause a special pain, and that their origins and effects are profound and complex.

SOME CONCLUSIONS

All this may sound profoundly pessimistic. Fortunately for us, and for our clientele, there are things we can do. I will mention a few of them briefly.

First, my experience in my own unit (Steinberg, 1986) and in consultative work to other agencies (Steinberg & Hughes, 1987; Steinberg, 1989) is that even to acknowledge that the feelings described actually exist, and thereby to give permission to have such feelings, provides relief, reassurance, and support. This can be provided systematically in groups for staff, preferably led by a consultant from outside that working team (Foskett, 1986).

Second, proper supervision of professionals' work and in-service training are often in short supply. They tend to get lower priority than "providing the service" when, in my view, they are *integral* to the service. Good training is inseparable from good practice; it is at least as important as providing "support" and probably better.

Third, although it is essential to deal with professionals' feelings, one sometimes gets the impression that the pendulum can swing too far in that direction; good, systematic teaching; intellectual, rational understanding; and the provision of practical information and advice (e.g., what do you actually do if someone attacks you?) are all equally important. Time, space, and resources for these and other needs are so often inadequate. We have to be imaginative in making time, and this means we sometimes have to do things that do not come easily in these fields, such as—in the face of some expectations and demands—having to say no.

Finally, we must recognize that we do not have to force things to run smoothly in order to "succeed." It is better to accept that we are working in turbulent, chaotic, and unpredictable fields. Managing this as best we can and riding out the storms is what we should be competent at doing, not having the vanity to think we can avoid them. What we do need to avoid is the illusion that work with irrational feelings, crazy behavior, and incurable illness could ever be easy and somehow smoothed out. This realization is in itself a success of sorts.

REFERENCES

Bennett, G. (1979). *Patients and their doctors.* London: Bailliere Tindall.

Bennett, G. (1987). *The wound and the doctor.* London: Secker and Warburg.

Foskett, J. (1986). The staff group. In D. Steinberg, *The adolescent unit.* Chichester: Wiley.

Menzies, I. (1970). *The functioning of social systems as a defence against anxiety.* Pamphlet 3. London: Tavistock Institute.

Steinberg, D. (1983). *The clinical psychiatry of adolescence.* Chichester: Wiley.

Steinberg, D. (1986). *The adolescent unit.* Chichester: Wiley.

Steinberg, D. (1987). *Basic adolescent psychiatry.* Oxford: Blackwell Scientific.

Steinberg, D. (1989). *Inter-professional consultation.* Oxford: Blackwell Scientific.

Steinberg, D., & Hughes, L. (1987). The emergence of work-centered issues in consultative work. *Journal of Adolescence, 10,* 309–316.

Steinberg, D., & Yule, W. (1985). Consultative work. In M. Rutter & L. Hersov (Eds.), *Child & adolescent psychiatry: Modern approaches.* Oxford: Blackwell Scientific.

Winnicott, D. (1971). Contemporary concepts of adolescent development and their implications for higher education. In D. Winicott (Ed.), *Playing and reality.* London: Tavistock.

Conclusion

Chapter 26

Children and Death:
Insights, Hindsights,
and Illuminations

Sandra L. Bertman

My charge in preparing this chapter was to weave together some themes of death, dying, and bereavement as they relate to children and their families. The literary and visual arts and the world of popular culture express the concerns, fears, and fantasies of children—and of those of us who interact with them. The art works I have chosen to discuss here been used in educational and therapeutic settings, with children and adults—teachers, counselors, and parents—some of whose responses are cited. My intention is to illustrate the dynamics of grief, and to show how the arts offer creative ways of addressing the pain and facilitating grief work, for youngsters and for ourselves.

INTRODUCING THE SUBJECT
FROM A SAFE DISTANCE

It has been observed that we cannot talk to children until we can talk to ourselves. Two frames of a popular cartoon strip, "The Smith Family," illustrate this dilemma. In the first frame a father, glancing at the fish floating inert on the water in a fishbowl, says to his young daughter, "One thing you should know

Copyright 1991 by Sandra L. Bertman. All rights reserved.

about goldfish . . .'' In the second frame the sentence is completed: ''They don't take naps.'' The cartoonists have called attention to our adult discomfort with death, and its logical consequence, awkwardness when we talk about death with our children. Furthermore, they have provided us with a classic example of the well-meaning explanations and phraseology that can lead to misunderstanding and anxiety on the part of the child.

Equating sleep—the nap being an exceptionally short sleep—with death does imply that the dead goldfish will return to life. We note that the father carefully avoids using the word death, further intimating that the subject itself is just too horrible to mention. With merely a shift in word choice, the cartoonists could vary for us the all too familiar scenarios: telling the child the goldfish (flushed down the toilet) took a long journey, or went to be with God in Fish Heaven. When the child comes to realize that things are not as the seem—i.e., that the goldfish's nap is not a brief rest but a permanent and irreversible state— it would not be beyond the realm of possibility to predict that she might have difficulty at bedtime, lest she too share the goldfish's fate. How can we be surprised at youngsters who show anxiety when parents pack their bags for the next holiday trip? Or who try to attend religious school less often, given that the reward of living the good life is being with one's Maker in His heavenly abode? This charming cartoon, a simple tool for death education, is innocuous. Comics, cartoons, and children's literature, calling upon nature, pets, or animals rather than the death of a grandparent, friend, parent, or sibling to introduce the subject of death can be a first and early introduction from afar.

In the classroom or home setting, a number of picture books concerning the death of an animal offer appropriate distance. Margaret Wise Brown's book, *The Dead Bird* (1965) fits the bill perfectly and outlines for us as well an ideal grief trajectory. In picture and text we accompany a group of youngsters as they discover and bury a dead bird. They express their curiosity and fascination with its stiff, inert body. They articulate their sadness. Creating a mound and epitaph, they mimic the adult ritual of burial and commemoration. The last four pictures are preceded by the commentary: ''and everyday until they forgot they went and sang to their little dead bird and put fresh flowers on his grave.'' This final sequence of pictures shows the boys and girls laying flowers at the gravesite, then playing ball, the grave receding further and further into the woods. In the last picture, the gravesite is not even visible.

Teachable moments occur continually in our daily lives and also provide appropriate distance. One of Alexander Tsiaras's photographs captures some village children gazing down from the graveyard wall as a group of rural Greek women perform a ritual five-year exhumation of remains (Figure 1). Children are present in several of these extraordinary photographs, witnessing the adults engaging in religious rituals familiar to the village. The children's presence and their participation—facing the reality of the death in the midst of community, particularly if it is not the death of one's own relative or close

Figure 1 Photography by Alexander Tsiaras captures some village children gazing down from the graveyard wall as a group of rural Greek women perform a ritual five-year exhumation of remains. Used by permission of author.

friend—is a more serious, sobering, but excellent vantage point for an initial initiation (Figures 2 and 3).

UNIVERSAL QUESTIONS AND THE "IDEAL" GRIEF TRAJECTORY

Whether goldfish, bird, or the material remains of an exhumed villager, three questions confront child and adult: (1) What is dead? (2) What makes one dead? Or, why does one die? (3) Where is the dead one now?

The picture book *The Dead Bird* and the photographs of Alexander Tsiaras quite nicely define for us the process of grief, which seems to have a universal cross-cultural, cross-generational application. In both these works (book and series of photographs)

- The reality of the event is acknowledged: the dead body is touched or viewed
- The emotions as well as the intellect are attended to
- Participation in both the burial rites and commemoration is assumed prerequisite to a healthy "moving on."

What is a healthy "moving on"? The phrase "until they forgot," the last commentary in *The Dead Bird,* does require some thought, and in the classroom or living room, some discussion. Its intention is to give permission to forget, and to demonstrate that one will "pull through." One will not remain forever in a state of sadness. One does walk *through* the Valley of the Shadow. I would like to have seen another picture or commentary acknowledging the

Figure 2 Second photograph by Alexander Tsiaras of ritual five-year exhumation of remains. Used by permission of photographer.

solace and joy of memory. A children's book by Andrea Clardy (1984), which deals directly with the death of a friend, addresses this point beautifully in words:

> I think of him when I see someone who has a space between his front teeth or when I hear the knock-knock jokes he taught me. . . . I think he matters more to me now than he did when he was alive. Dusty was my friend and I am glad that he was.

Figure 3 Third photograph by Alexander Tsiaras of ritual five-year exhumation of remains. Used by permission of photographer.

DEVELOPMENTAL PLATEAUS
AND THE PRESCHOOLER IN ALL OF US

Clearly, developmental level is a predictable interference with a child's under-standing of death. The research (Nagy, 1948; Piaget, 1965; Fox, 1985) identi-fies three sequential levels. First, for the very young, the preschoolers, death is reversible, simply ongoing life elsewhere, though perhaps in a diminished state. Documenting animism is apparent in youngsters' drawings and explanations. The body is often shown sleeping (Figure 4). We might find a ladder drawn in some of these pictures, allowing for eventual return, or we may view the dead in their box-like houses visiting one another, or playing cards (Figure 5). If in

Figure 4   This drawing shows how a young child documents animism. The body is often shown sleeping. Bertman collection.

Figure 5 This drawing shows a child's understanding of life after death. The dead are playing cards. Bertman collection.

heaven, the dead are often depicted as happy, armed with wings, halos, and smiles.

The second level of understanding adds an ominous note, as death becomes personified. The deathman or bogeyman snatches the living either for whim or punishment. If one is quick, clever, and good, it is possible to evade him. As Sandra Fox (1985) found in her research, he catches the old, the disabled, and the "klutzes," those who cannot run fast enough to escape death when it comes for them. The third plateau—the one at which we have arrived by virtue of our years—maturity, is marked by the knowledge that death is irreversible, inevitable, irrevocable, and personal.

What, then, is dead?

Dead is when the body functions, as we know them, stop. One does not breathe, sneeze, eat, talk, or sleep anymore. We are told one does not feel heat or cold, joy or pain. Goldfish don't "nap" and, floating on the water, could care less who changes it. In time, the body rots. Worms crawl in and out of fish, bird, man, and woman. Though exhumed remains can be brought back to the land of the living, as in Tsiaras's photographs, the process of decomposition cannot be reversed. Five years after death, individualizing human markers of hair and skin no longer exist. Only the skull and bones are retrievable. The Greek women kiss and pray over the skull (Figure 6). Carefully passing it around in a white handkerchief, they welcome it back to their world from its long "journey." The priest washes the exhumed bones and skull in wine, and recites the *Trisayio* prayer as the bones and skull are ceremoniously transported to the village ossuary for their final "resting" place. Have we not just been told *not* to confuse youngsters by correlating images of "sleep" and "journey" with death? Isn't it curious how the adults in this Greek culture, as in so many others, have long used these metaphors themselves in order to come to terms with the most profound loss of all.

The arts in any culture and in every era speak to these developmental phases, which may not in fact be age limited. Perhaps, even in maturity and old age, all three levels not only exist, but exist simultaneously. The child in all of us keeps us company until—and even after—we leave the land of the living.

In Greek art we have depictions of the deathman. He is hooknosed Thanatos, who with his brother Hypnos (sleep), carries off the living. How many Greek myths have as their subject the gods killing mortals! In just as many, whim and punishment are the justification (Figure 7). Let us review what we know of how Boreas, Zeus, Apollo, Poseidon, and Eos spent their days—and nights.

What do the dead do? Not only the preschoolers depict afterdeath as ongoing functioning in life as we know it—sleeping, keeping company, playing cards. In Greek mythology (as in Egyptian) we have numerous representations

Figure 6 Photograph by Alexander Tsiaras of women holding a skull, part of the five-year exhumation ritual. Used by permission of photographer.

of the dead playing at the gaming boards,[1] receiving gifts and libations from the living (Figure 8) and engaging in far less innocuous activities. Take, for example, Eos carrying off young boys to try them out as lovers, and Zeus, not even waiting to get back to his heavenly abode before impregnating lovely young maidens (wooing Leda in the guise of a swan, and Danae in a showering of gold seed.) In an early fifth-century frieze at the Museum of Fine Arts, Boston, figures are following a large round.[2] It is not a hula-hoop or game of croquet

---

[1]Winged daimons with magic staffs at a gaming board, Attic black-figured cup, sixth century B.C., Danish National Museum, Copenhagen; funerary relief, men at gaming board, Museum of Fine Arts, Boston.

[2]Zeus rapes Ganymede from Troy: Attic red-figured kantharos, early fifth century B.C., Museum of Fine Arts, Boston.

Figure 7 Boreas carrying off Orithyia. Artist unknown.

that is being played by god and mortal; rather, Zeus's rape of Ganymede is prefaced by the courting gesture of gifts of hoops (Vermeule, 1979).

As for irreversibility, in the British Museum in London is a cup on which is recorded the story of Glaukos, a young Greek boy who died and was brought back to life. This particular scene shows the seer Polyidos, who was shut up with the youth's body in the tomb, killing a snake with his spear. Observing that a fellow snake revived the dead one with an herb, Polyidos attempts to do the

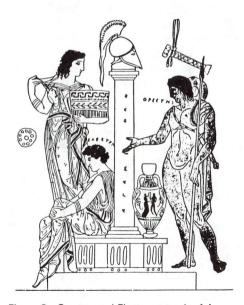

Figure 8 Orestes and Electra at tomb of Agamemnon. Artist unknown.

same for Glaukos. The scene immortalized on the cup is of the boy watching the prelude to his own revival.

We are all well aware of the traditional depictions of heaven, particularly the religious ones. The kingdom of heaven is a place of ongoing life. But, for the purposes of studying children's concepts as revealed in their drawings, we find amazing parallels in thought and imagery not only with Greek mythology but with the personal folklore of many contemporary artists. In the painting, *Evocation: Burial of Casagemaus,*[3] we would be hesitant to call the artist, Picasso, the most precocious of preschoolers, yet is not his portrayal of afterlife blatant animism? One might speculate that the young man, whose body is being mourned in the lower half of the painting, is resurrected into a brothel-like heaven, where angels, wingless and stockinged, are suggestive more of ladies of the night than of haloed cherubim. A psychiatric interpretation imputed to this painting claims that Casagemaus, nude, riding the horse, is fulfilling his unrequited sexual fantasies in this far better world. Could the horse be yet another one of Zeus's whimsical seductive guises?

DEATH AND GRIEF IN THE FAMILY: SEVERAL TAKES ON *THE TRAGEDY*

Initial bereavement is a time of contraries, of numbness, disbelief and preoccupation. It is a time of feeling separate and unconnected. In another of Picasso's paintings, we can see and feel the withdrawal from the outside world (Figure 9). Notice how the figures use their own bodies as consolation. In their agony, each person is alone.

The toneless mood and monochromatic coloring of the painting, all in blues, could be viewed in light of Claus Bahnson's point that not only the terminal child but the entire family is sick. The choice of words is troublesome; *sick,* doesn't feel quite right. The connotation is too pejorative. But the concept that a terminal illness or loss is a family affair is apparent in the painting and documented in the clinical literature.

Let us assume that missing from this family grouping is a dying child. Myra Bluebond-Langner's work (1989) shows that the well siblings of terminally ill children live in houses of chronic sorrow. Whether the sorrow is spoken of or not, the sibling sees the tears, hears the hushed conversations, and experiences the physical and emotional unavailability of the parents. In the painting, the boy's hand tentatively reaches out to his father's thigh. What is the meaning of this gesture? Is the child to be the consoler? Caretaker to the parent? Is he about to tug at his father's clothing for the attention and support he needs? Is the child a personification of what Irving Goffman calls "non-persons," who are there but not there. In this scenario, though absent from it, one might

[3]Pablo Picasso, *Evocation: Burial of Casagemaus,* 1901, Paris, Musée d'Art Moderne.

Figure 9 Picasso, *The Tragedy*, 1903. Washington, DC. National Gallery of Art, Chester Dale Collection. Used by permission.

conclude that the terminally ill (or deceased) child is decidedly the subject of the painting.

Taking liberties with the arts, thus engaging them in dialogue, can be enlightening. Remove the mother from the picture and we are confronted with the impossibility of one parent assuming the other's role. As a matter of fact, it is doubtful that the remaining parent can fulfill his own parental role at this time. Being father must conflict with being husband: a bereaved man needs to grieve for his wife. We become acutely aware of a new terror for a bereft child: the loss of one parent, and the symbolic or temporary loss—the unavailability—of the other makes the actual loss of the lone surviving parent a threatening reality.

Who will take care of me now . . . and later? becomes the alarming question for a youngster.

The painting underscores Therese Rando's point that parents need to mourn their *separate* relationships with the child. We can appreciate the conflicting demands both to let go of the parent role (in the case of the child who died) and, at the same time, to continue to be parent to the remaining sibling. Furthermore, parents are losing not only their child, and their roles in terms of family, they are losing their planned-for future: their hopes, dreams, expectations, fantasies, wishes. Ida Martinson has us consider how families deal with the empty space left behind by the death of a child. Literally remove the youngster from this group of three in Figure 9 and continue to speculate.

Utilizing this Picasso painting in a workshop setting, one health care professional placed this family by the grave of a 2-year-old daughter/sister. He explains that the mother is infected with HIV. He attributes a mixture of emotions to the father/husband: fear ("My wife is going to die; I'll be alone to raise our son"), helplessness ("How could this have happened? These things aren't supposed to happen"), anger ("It's not fair! She's leaving me. If I'd been in another relationship this wouldn't have happened"), and sadness ("I love her. I loved my daughter. I miss my child. It's hard to live on knowing the pain the future will bring"). In his commentary, the group role-plays, and in the ensuing discussion of the painting in this context, ethical and existential questions are addressed: "Is the way the mother became infected important? What values do we express/feel when we hear how someone contracted the virus? Was the child an 'innocent' victim? Does that mean that some people with the virus are 'guilty' victims? If so, guilty of what?"

Assume for a moment, that the youngster in Figure 9 is a Holden Caulfield, an adolescent whose younger brother Allie died of leukemia, in the classic American novel by J. D. Salinger, *The Catcher in the Rye* (1964). In the novel, we could understand Holden's behavior as a sibling's acting out. The night Allie died, Holden physically attacks their garage, and hurts himself so badly that he ends up in the hospital. As he tells it, he broke "all the goddam windows with [his] fist just for the hell of it."

> I even tried to break all the windows on the station wagon we had that summer, but my hand was already broken and everything by the time, and I couldn't do it. It was a very stupid thing to do, I'll admit, but I hardly didn't even know I was doing it, and you didn't know Allie.

Holden's behavior could be interpreted in a number of ways: rage against a father who was powerless to save his brother Allie, rage turned inward emerging as guilt at himself for still being alive, a desperate plea for attention and concern from parents who neglected him due to the demands of a brother's illness, anger at God and the universe for his own painful loneliness and grief, or all of these. A broken fist demands attention. Juxtaposing the painting in

Figure 9 with this section from the Salinger novel, a gesture as tentative as reaching for a father's thigh cannot go unnoticed. Both gestures are poignant manifestations of grief.

Intense preoccupation, yearning, and pining for the return of a dead family member could also be seen as the subject of the painting in Figure 9. The implicit tragedy of the title may not be solely the death of another, perhaps a sibling. It may be the unavailability of grieving family members to support one another at such a tender time, since each is so locked into personal worlds of pain and preoccupation.

SHOCKING EMOTIONAL EXPLOSIVES

When the pain of reality of the loss sets in, with the realization that the inconceivable has happened, the bereaved enter another realm or phrase. A mother whose daughter died at age 16 in a car accident tells us what happens when the suspended limbo-like state wears off:

> My child has died! My heart is torn to shreds. My body is screaming. My mind is crazed! . . . The question is always present on my mind. Why? How could this possibly have happened. The anger is ever so deep, so strong, so frightening. Will I ever let go of it?

This phase of grief defined by Parkes (1970) as acute distress, by Bowlby (1966) as despair, is characterized by such intense emotional turmoil. Changes in eating or sleeping behaviors (as reported to us in letters to bereaved parents, edited by Carlson [1989]), indulging in drugs or sex, seeking solace in sensation (see films such as *Ikiru, Husbands*) are all manifestations of the onslaught and are also invoked to avoid or block the pain of loss.

A provocative way of distancing or acting out might be the use of black or gallows humor. After President Lincoln was assassinated at Ford's Theater in Washington, the joke going around was: "Other than that, Mrs. Lincoln, how did you like the play?" Predictably, in any country, in any era, bizarre humor follows in the wake of tragedy. Reported to me by Irene Renzenbrink after the Hoddle Street shootings on September 8, 1987, in Australia were the following examples:

> *Question:* What's the quickest way to get to Clifton Hill?
> *Answer:* Just shoot up Hoddle Street.

> *Question:* They're opening a new supermarket in Clifton Hill. Guess what it's called?
> *Answer:* TARGET [a popular supermarket chain].

And in the United States after the space shuttle *Challenger* disaster of January 28, 1986:

Question: What's worse than glass in baby food?
Answer: Astronauts in water.

Question: What were Christa McAuliffe's last words to her husband?
Answer: I'll feed the fish, you feed the dogs.

Even if behaviors are as bizarre or distasteful as indulging in this type of gross humor, they offer instantaneous relief, albeit temporary. And they are seen by some bereaved as more tolerable than giving in to the quicksands of despair. In the vocabulary of popular culture, the Australian artist Mike Brown[3] captures for us this profound fear of children and adults with his marvelous poster, *Gloom* (1962). A close-up portrait of a young boy with one tear falling from an eye is centered between two captions, "7 lonely days" and "1 lonely week." The overriding terror for so many of us is that the sadness will be totally preoccupying and will ultimately envelop us in its tentacles. It will be overwhelming in the *now* and will last forever. One will *never* feel peace of be happy again. A bereaved mother in her letter to other bereaved parents concurs: "You're able to cry, and cry, and cry. . . . You do this for a long time, crying yourself a river, wondering if it can or ever will stop."

In classroom and counseling sessions, a before–after technique inviting participants to focus on change over a period of time is revealing. In a telling pair of drawings, a youngster sketches a physician pronouncing a boy dead. The dead boy's body lies inert on the stretcher or bed, but his essence or spirit-self is drawn leaving his corpse and entering his parents' heads. He depicts the parents totally preoccupied with their dead child, crying quantities of tears—so many, in fact, that they accumulate in a puddle at their feet (Figure 10). In the second drawing, supposedly three months later, the youngster foresees the par-

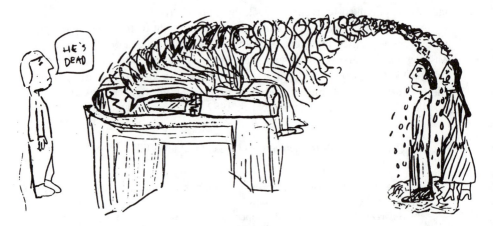

Figure 10 Drawing by a youngster showing parents grieving over the death of child. Physician is on the left. From collection of student work. In Sandra Bertman, *Death: A Primer for All Ages* (New York: Center for Thanatology Research and Education, 1990).

ents still totally immersed in the sadness of their grief (Figure 11). Even their occupation is related; they are now "making sad balloons." They have enormous circles under their eyes and, as he explains, have gained a great deal of weight because they are eating to fill up the emptiness. We can thank this youngster for expressing so graphically such a grown-up reality of despair.

HEALING MILESTONES: FUNERAL, BURIAL, AND MEMORIALIZATION

The final phase of grief is defined as recovery. But what Bowlby (1966) calls detachment, and Parkes (1970) reintegration, is not recovery in the medical sense of the word. One does not revert to normalcy. A bereaved parent tells us, "Family, friends and people around you think that after a certain amount of time you should be back to your old self again. Not so! For me, my old self died with my child. . . . It's like learning to walk all over again, only this time in a different direction." The adjustment or acceptance implicit in this phase is more a repatterning, an acclimation.

Critical, perhaps prerequisite to viable reinvestment in life are the activities or rituals of commemoration and memorialization. Participation in the rites of funeral and burial is more than a gesture of respect and tribute to the dead person. These rites are cathartic and a balm not only for the grieving family but for the community as well. Alexander Tsiaras's photographs are a profound illustration of a village burying one of its own. Conducting memorial services, letting children decide how to commemorate a death, composing and sending letters and pictures to the families in grief are restorative activities and a fine antidote to helplessness and anxiety. As we can see in the drawings elementary school youngsters sent to the families of the *Challenger* astronauts, black humor was not the only response to tragedies such as the space shuttle disaster (Figure 12).

COMMON THREADS

Let us end with a series of paintings from a remarkable contemporary Australian artist whose paintings and sketches recording her father's illness and death could be viewed as a paradigm, a visual roadmap for the trajectory of grief. Davida Allen painted a number of works in which she concerns herself with her father's physical death. She sketches him in his sickness, before his death, and as she imagines him inside the coffin (Figure 13). After his death her preoccupation persists. Only now she adds to the renderings the words, "My father is dead. I weep for him." Eventually she includes a portrait of herself in grief in the visual details. These words and her father's physical presence continue to be concrete images in all the drawings, even as her pregnancy and the idea of new life appearing in her world takes shape (Figure 14). She places herself between

BUSNESS: MAKING SAD BALLOONS

Figure 11 A second drawing, supposedly three months later, showing parents still immersed in the sadness of their grief. From collection of student work. In Sandra Bertman, *Death: A Primer for All Ages.* (New York: Center for Thanatology Research and Education, 1990).

Figure 12 Elementary school child's drawing sent to families of the *Challenger* astronauts. Bertman collection.

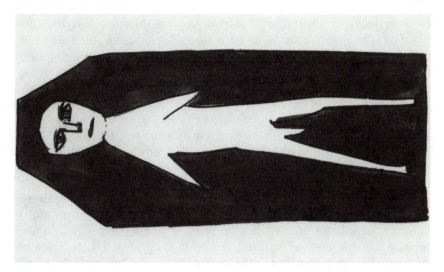

Figure 13 Artist Davida Allen's sketch of her sick father, before his death, as she imagines him in his coffin. Sketches: ''Death of My Father,'' 1983. Courtesy Ray Hughes Gallery, Australia.

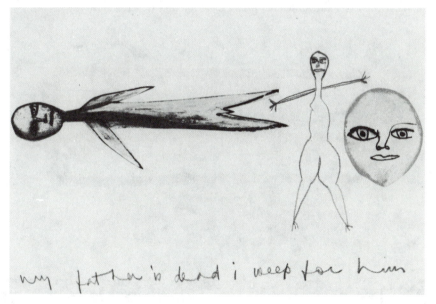

Figure 14 Davida Allen's sketch of her dead father, herself, and her unborn child. Sketches: ''Death of My Father,'' 1983. Courtesy Ray Hughes Gallery, Australia.

her father and the symbol of new life, pulled in both directions, caught in the middle as if at a crossroads. Quite some time after his death, her father still remains an acknowledged presence; missed, dead, and yet symbolically, eternally alive; a memory to be drawn upon for strength and renewal. One of the most moving sketches is of her newborn daughter and father joining hands through the boundary of the coffin (Figure 15). Her adaptation to ongoing life is signaled by what she is now omitting from her work. Her grief is no longer so painfully central as to need literal depiction in the painting. Her father is dead. There is no question of ever forgetting. She still weeps for him. But his presence is and will always be felt, incorporated in both bittersweet and joyous ways in the continuation of her family's life cycle.

Artists are lucky. The very tools of their craft assist them in the recovery process. Some of these—Picasso's *Evocation: Burial of Casagemaus* or Kathe Kollwitz's magnificent paintings on the death of a child, for example[4]—like Davida Allen's sketches on the death of her father, might well be instances of artists working our their personal grief as they focus on it, giving it shape and color. Their grief is given a place in the world, a healthy permanence. For the artist, the painting insures against belittling or forgetting the event or the indi-

[4]Pablo Picasso, *Evocation: Burial of Casagemaus,* 1901, Paris, Musée d'Art Moderne; Kathe Kollwitz, *Pieta, Death Seizes a Woman,* and *the Children Die,* private collection.

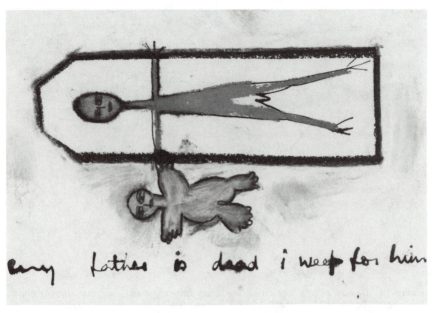

Figure 15 Davida Allen's sketch of her dead father and her newborn daughter joining hands through the boundary of the coffin. Sketches: "Death of My Father," 1983. Courtesy Ray Hughes Gallery, Australia.

viduals involved. One has, after all, a concrete memorial—the finished painting itself. Ultimately, the pain and meaning expunged from within, committed to canvas or print, is to be drawn upon forever for affirmation, solace, and renewal.

Artists, then, invite us to take notice, to pause at telling details, to share their confusion and pain and by so doing to get in touch with our own. As we have seen, the commemorative statement of a painting, cartoon, or story becomes a shorthand to our own unique experience. We bring our particular queries, values, and memories as we the viewers and readers conjure up our own images and read our own messages between the lines. Thus art is a visual or verbal language, constructed not only by the artist but by the onlooker. As such, it transcends barriers of tongue, culture, age, and time connecting us all with the threads of pain and possibly in the never-ending human tapestry of grief.

BIBLIOGRAPHY

Bluebond-Langner, Myra (1989). Worlds of dying children and their well siblings. *Death Studies, 13*, 1–16.

Bowlby, John (1966). Processes of mourning. *International Journal of Psychoanalysis, 42*, 418–438.

Brown, Margaret Wise. (1965). *The dead bird.* Reading MA: Addison-Wesley.

Carlson, Paula. (1989). *Dear parents—Letters to bereaved parents.* Omaha NE: Centering.

Clardy, Andrea (1984). *Dusty was my friend.* New York: Human Science Press.

Fox, Sandra Sutherland. (1985). Good grief: Helping groups of adolescents when a friend dies. *Forum for Death Education and Counseling Newsletter, 8*(8).

Nagy, M. (1948). The child's theories concerning death. *Journal of Genetic Psychology, 73*, 3–27.

Parkes, Colin Murray. (1970). The first year of bereavement: A longitudinal study of the reaction of London widows to the death of their husbands. *Psychiatry, 33* 444–467.

Piaget, J. (1965). *The child's conceptions of the world.* C. K. Ogden (Ed.) Totowa, NJ: Littlefield, Adams.

Raphael, Beverly (1983). *The anatomy of bereavement.* New York: Basic Books.

Salinger, J. D. (1964). *The catcher in the rye.* New York: Bantam Books.

Vermeule, Emily. (1979). *Aspects of death in early Greek art and poetry.* Berkeley: University of California Press.

Worden, William. (1983). *Grief counselling and grief therapy.* London: Tavistock.

Epilogue

Chapter 27

Before Adolescence and Coming of Age

Byron Samios and Nassia Varveri-Sofra

If you have the flower of youth,
you have the utmost vigor

Homer

There are just a few words, a hymn to youth, a verse by Homer, the blind bard from Chios. It is a testimony stemming from the dawn of our Greek history and refers to the dynamic and promising role of the child in society, and society's dependence on the child. The verse was not written by grammarians for the scholars of the time, but was sung wherever people gathered, accompanied by the sweet-toned lyre, which was a gift of Apollo, the god of music.

We believe that what is expressed about death and children in Greek art, over its 3,000 year history, constitutes a valid way of discovering the status of the child within ancient Greek society.

The authors extend their gratitude to the National Numismatic Museum, in particular Ms. M. Oikonomidou and Ms. Galani, and to the National Archaeological Museum, in particular Ms. Morati.

Never was Greek society indifferent to, nor did it ever come to terms with, the idea of children dying. No other activity, concern, or necessity of life could hide or minimize the significance of children who die "before they grow up and come of age," and "before their parents' death," as testified for centuries by the inscriptions on the graves of the Greek children.

FROM GREEK MYTHOLOGY

The mythology of a culture fills the gaps in its history. Mythology does not deal with facts but rather summarizes the glories and beliefs of the people who created it, thus forming the "historicity" of myth.

Theogenic Swallowing of Children

> From these Muses of Helikon let us begin the song . . . They taught Hesiod, he tells us, the beautiful song when he was minding the sheep on sacred Helikon: First of all, chaos was created and then, the broad-bosomed earth. And the earth generated above all, the star-scattered sky, equal to itself.

The ancient Greek world was born onto a superb poetic stage on which Love and Death ruled together. The premature death of newborn creatures was often considered not final; the idea of putting children to death was suppressed because it did not contribute to the generation of mankind. Moreover, folk imagination abhorred and rejected the death of its newborn preternatural ancestors, considering it senseless and inconceivable.

This is seen in the early myths of Uranus, who buried the children he spawned by his wife, Ge (Earth) in the depths of their mother's womb. As a result, the mother was suffering from a strange reversal of pregnancy. However, she decided not to give in and conceived a fiendish and effective plan, which could only be executed by her last child, the devious Cronus. Brandishing a sharp sickle, Cronus cut off the genitalia of his father Uranus. The child defeated his deadly sire by reversing his father's intentions and making him the creator of new life. Blood drops fell to the earth and gave birth to giants and nymphs, while others fell into the sea from which came the Nereids or sea-nymphs. Finally, Cronus did not allow a drop of fertile sperm to go to waste; he threw his father's bleeding organs into the sea, thus giving birth (the first extracorporeal fertilization) to Aphrodite, goddess of love, symbol of the magnificent and unquenchable passion that would maintain and reproduce life over the ages.

The passion for power then led Cronus to destroy his offspring. To ensure his own safety, he swallowed his children, "so that none but immortals could know royal glory."

When his wife gave birth to Zeus, she deceived Cronus by giving him a swaddled rock to swallow, then hid the newborn Zeus in the cave of Ida. Once again life triumphed overwhelmingly, since the rock caused Cronus to vomit all the children he had swallowed.

This myth emphasizes that killing of one's children is not permitted; it is considered evil and senseless.

Medea: Child-slayer from Colchis

Ah! Would to Heaven the good ship Argo ne'er had sped its course to the Colchian land through the misty blue Symplegades . . . on its way to fetch the golden fleece for Pelias.

These are the words of the nurse of Medea's children. She was terrified by her lady's implacable desire to murder her two children, thus taking revenge on her husband, Jason, who had betrayed her love.

Euripides, in the tragedy *Medea,* has the double murder committed in the palace, but offstage. According to the Chorus's song, infanticide is considered as a far more serious matter than the natural death of two children. It underlies an attitude of life, according to which one can kill superstitions, deplore errone-ous ideologies, as well as revitalize values that have begun to dim. The Chorus speaks thus (sixth scene):

O earth, O sun whose beam illumines all, look, look upon this lost woman, ere she stretch forth her murderous hand upon her sons for blood; for lo! these are the scions of thy own golden seed, and the blood of gods is in danger of being shed by man. O light, from Zeus proceeding, stay, hold her hand. . . .

O hopeless mother, surely thou hast a heart of stone or steel to slay the off-spring of thy womb by such a murderous doom. Of all the wives of yore I know but one who laid her hand upon her children dear, even Ino, whom the gods did madden on the day the wife of Zeus drove her wandering from her home. But she, poor sufferer, flung herself into the sea because of the foul murder of her children, leaping o'er the wave-beat cliff, and in her death was she united to her children twain. Can there be any deed of horror left to follow this?

Medea was implacable. She had slyly arranged and ensured a safe refuge in Athens with the unsuspecting Aigaias, a childless man, precisely at the moment he was praying to the gods to make him a father. The poet deliberately juxta-poses a lover of children with a child-murderer. Here the Chorus comments on the city that will provide refuge to the wicked mother:

Sons of Erechtheus, happy heroes of yore, children of the blessed gods, fed on wisdom's glorious food in a holy land ne'er pillaged by its foes, ye who move with sprightly step through a climate ever bright and clear, where, as legend tells, the muses nine, Pieria's holy maids, were brought to birth by Harmonia with the golden hair.

And poets sing how Cypris, drawing water from the streams of hair-flowing

Cephissus, breathes o'er the land a gentle breeze of balmy winds, and even as she crowns her tresses with a garland of sweet rose-buds, sends forth the Loves to sit by wisdom's side, to take apart in every excellence.

How then shall the city of sacred streams, the land which welcomes those it loves, receive thee, the murderess of thy children? Nay, by thy knees, one and all, we implore thee, slay not thy babes. . . .

Thou canst not, when they fall at thy feet for mercy, steel thy heart and in their blood dip thy hand.

Here's how Jason confronts Medea after her crime:

. . . this hast thou done and still dost gaze upon the sun and earth after this deed most impious. . . . I now perceive what I, then, missed the day I brought thee, fraught with doom, from thy home in a barbarian land to dwell in Hellas, traitress to thy sire and to the land that nurtured thee. On me the gods have hurled the curse that dogged thy steps, for thou didst slay thy brother at his hearth ere thou cam'st aboard our fair ship, Argo. Such was the outset of thy life of crime, then didst thou wed with me, and having borne me sons to glut thy passion's lust, thou now has slain them. Not one amongst the wives of Hellas e'er had dared this deed; yet before them all I chose thee for my wife, wedding a foe to be my doom, no woman, but a lioness fiercer in nature than Tyrrhene Scylla.

ANCIENT GREECE

There has been no historical verification of the theory that in ancient Sparta, newborns with serious defects, who could not have survived under any circumstances given the treatment available then, were "put into" the Kaiadas, chasm of Taygetos. Recent excavations in the chasm have brought to light adult skeletons and the skeleton of just one child of about 10 years old. The laws of Solon provided a series of measures for the eugenic training of young men and women and a premarital test for those planning to be married.

Although the Kaiadas theory has now been disputed, there are accounts of cruel, group training of small children through deprivations and floggings. These actions, which were considered unacceptable, were imposed by a small minority of local rulers who had acquired power in Sparta. Sparta, according to Pericles' description in "Epitaphio," was considered oligarchic and despotic compared to the democracy of Athens.

Child and Coinage

Children held a special place in ancient Greek society, and one way this becomes evident is through the representations of children on coins. Coins are instruments of exchange, but the Greeks quickly discovered their unique value in communication. In the numismatic microsculpture of the age, the child occupies an important position. It is the child of the Greek myths, the myths composed to codify morality and ethics in the city-state. The micro-sculptural perfection of these coins has been compared with the works of the great sculptor Pheidias. Their subject matter, with due attention paid to se-mantics and symbolism, represents the child as the hope of the present and the strength of the future, who nevertheless requires unceasing care as well as respect.

There are Corinthian coins representing Melicertes Palaemon riding on a dolphin. In Greek mythology, Melicertes was the son of Ino. According to the myth, his mother went mad and committed suicide, taking along to death her two children, Learchos and Melicertes (these are the children referred to by the Chorus in *Medea,* cited above). According to a variation of the myth, Meli-certes Palaemon was the divine child of the sea; he was considered the protector of sailors, and the Isthmian games were instituted in his honor.

Several coins from Corinth and Achaia show scenes from the myth of Opheltes Archemoros. According to legend, the Nemean games were estab-lished to honor another child, Opheltes, who was brought up by Hypsipyle, queen of Lemnos. His nurse had strict orders not to put Opheltes on the ground before he could walk, because the oracle had said that he would be eaten by a dragon. In the valley of Nemea, Hypsipyle and the nurse encountered the ex-hausted soldiers of the seven armies marching towards Thebes, who sought water. The nurse, in her panic, left the baby on the ground and ran to lead them to the spring. In the meantime, a snake devoured Opheltes. According to the myth the soldiers killed the snake, buried the child, and in his honor founded the Nemean funeral games. Since then, the spring has been called *Adrasteia* [i.e., the negative prefix *a* and the verb *dratto* (hold)] and the child has been called *Archemoros* (the beginning of death). From then onwards, the spring's babbling waters would recount the disaster that occurred because of the nurse's failure to heed the oracle.

Hercules, the wonder child, is also represented on coins. According to the myth Alcmene, the mother of the newborn Hercules, left the door of his room open, and two snakes sent by the goddess Hera glided through it. Little Hercu-les immediately strangled them, before the horrified eyes of his nurses and guards who heard the noise and ran to help. The death of a child had been averted, and the prophet Tiresias predicted that Hercules would slay a number of wild beasts on earth and in sea. This myth stressed the message of childhood as the power of tomorrow, the only power able to fight and reverse the suffer-ings previous generations had been unable to deal with.

Coins figuring a god carrying a child represent Greek respect for the child as well as the child's need for superhuman protection. The god Hermes, in the celebrated statue by Praxiteles, is carrying the little Dionysos on his left wrist.

Child Deaths: Testimony from the Tombs
(500 B.C.–A.D. 600)

Why, thoughtless Charon did you so hastily seize our newborn? (152)*

Three years old and unready he left this life
His mother's name I here repeat:
Aristoneike, whom he made to suffer so. (170)

These are poetic epitaphs from the ancient Greek world. They constitute a silent testimony to the special place held by the child in the ancient Greek community, in the family, and in the hearts of the parents.

Passerby, I am a mute rock, but with these inscriptions I speak that you may learn who hides within me. (94)

I, Eros herein, under this gravestone, as you see, am sleeping.
They spirited me away illegally like a spring rose. (40)
[*Protest of a 4-year-old child for being "seized unlawfully"; verse of an anonymous poet*]

A piece of marble found around the temple of Zeus in Athens had engraved on it the ideas by which Athenians brought up their children:

I am Eutychianos. I was born out of the womb of my mother Eutychida. Stay a while, traveller, and hear the wisdom which I believed I would learn and the joys I would have brought to my mother and father. But fate took me away unholy at eleven years old. (58)

Anne Marie Verilhac in her two-volume work entitled *Paedes Aoroi: Poésie Funéraire* (1978) presents information about 201 epitaphs she collected from 100 places in Greece, covering the era between 500 B.C. and A.D. 600. We will quote several examples in the remainder of this chapter.

Death did not grieve us since it was your written fate
but its swift arrival did, before your youth could bloom.
Impatient death grabbed the child.
The good father Zotikos and Domna,
the mother of the dead child,
erected an immortal monument
to virtue. (126)

*The numbers in parentheses refer to funeral inscriptions as cited in Verilhac (1978).

The epitaph verses express the grief at the "unholy" snatching away of the child and the lost hopes of the parents and the city.

> As a flower that had just sprouted and started growing
> with the sweet water of the breast,
> lovely budding rose, gorgeous flower of love,
> for such was my son whose body is now covered by the earth,
> Zotikos [a name meaning "Alive"] was just eight years old. (39)

Unbearable pain and sorrow find consolation in the refined, the pleasant, and the superlative.

> Eternal tears accompany the tender little girl
> who lies here, stranger.
> Her breath honey, sweet pollen,
> a triple flower with noble features. (140)

Virtues and Praises

Although babies, children, and even the young who died, had no time to develop and prove all their virtues, we frequently find them praised on epitaphs.

> Unfair Klotho,
> Where did the sweet strength of knowledge go?
> What happened to my service under the Pierides Muses?
> I was just twelve years old and now I am lying
> under the depths of the earth in cruel Hades. (76)

> The immortals gave me gifts
> that I might excel in arts and sports. (51)

> Here lies Syntrophion
> in this holy grave
> cherished for four years
> and as many months.
> You were Eros,
> noble
> and in feats,
> even more noble. (44)

Contrasts

Frequently epitaphs stress the contrast between the child's tender age and the significant events in life.

> Instead of blessed bridal songs
> I am a tomb and stele and hated earth. (76)

> Fate spirited me off to the halls of Persephone . . .
> as soon as my youth began to bloom. (77)

Laments of Mothers

The suffering of the mother offers fertile ground for exaggeration and tears. The poets, however, prefer to bow before her with lyric simplicity worthy of her deep pain.

> The mother, the wretched one, wails in the house,
> her grief surpassing the mourning of the nightingale. (164)

> More than the sorrowing halcyon, the woman wept. (164)

Love and Death

Reference to love (Eros) in epitaphs for dead children takes the form of praise, since Eros is a god: "Flower of the good, Eros"; "This virtuous Eros"; "Name and shape Eros gave him"; "He whom Eros arrayed with passion."

Closeness to God

> Do not grieve too much,
> as some have said.
> Every young person who pleases the gods
> find early death. (62)

> Aethera, at eight years old,
> your glance reigns in the sky,
> shines among the stars,
> close to the horn of Capricorn. (200)

Hades

> Insatiable Hades, why did you take me,
> baby that I am.
> Why were you in such a hurry
> to deprive me of life?
> Is it not you who determines us? (223)

Destiny

Destiny—in the form of the Fates, the Devil, Luck, or Klotho—is present in epitaph poetry and accompanied by surprise, protest, and irony.

Moira's threads of unhappiness
he failed to escape and
met his bitter fate. (25)

Shameless Fate,
you seized Aristona from the light of dawn
when he was seven years old.
Tear-drenched Pluto,
do not all mortal souls belong to you?
Why then do you harvest the unripe youths? (154)

Philosophical Reflections

Parents, poets, and philosophers have recourse to philosophical reflection as an antidote to the pain of a child's death.

Why do you weep for me, father?
Among mortals immortality is difficult.
Live, then, and forget me,
never more shall I be of use to you.
Geminos Geminiou, thirteen years old. (182)

Here lies Xenophon, still seven years old
he who lived so little and without sorrow. (19)

Here my parents have laid me, a newborn
and my soul sent to the kingdom of the pious. (193)

Earth brought you to light, Sibyrtios,
and now the earth covers you.
The air, as it gave you breath, took it away.
You left at seven years old, filling
your parents with grief, taken by need. (195)

Night keep the light of my life. The sleep-giver who in my body's sweet sleep
dissolved the pains of illness . . .
By command of Moira, they brought me the gift of forgetfulness . . .
As Hermes announced, the favor of Zeus brought me among the immortal gods.

He led me to heaven holding me by the hand and honored me with bright glory that I might dwell in the heavens among the blessed and sit like an intimate on golden thrones.

And when, near the tripod and the tables heavy with divine ambrosia, I enjoy the pleasure of the table, friendly glances come my way. When I fill the glasses of the blessed with nectar, on their divine faces a smile blooms. (199)

The flesh and bones of a charming child are possessed by the earth.
But his soul is in the halls of the Gods. (194)

Causes of Death

And what did I die of? Of Fever. And how old?
Thirteen, therefore uneducated. (63)

We are frequently taken aback by the realism that sometimes permeates the lyric verse of the epitaphs and may remind us of a medical case history.

Travelers, this is my grave, even though I am small. Perhaps you too will shed a tear when you read on the stone stele what I suffered during my short life. As soon as the Hours brought me to light through the pains of my mother, my father, overjoyed, lifted me from the ground, washed the blood off me, wrapped me in swaddling clothes and begged the immortal gods for all that will now never happen to me because the Moires had already decided on my fortune. I grew up as a beautiful flower loved by all. A little later, the signs of Fate marked me, striking me with a serious illness of the testicles.

My unhappy father managed to cure me of this terrible illness and believed that with practical treatment he could save me from my predestined fate. But another illness found me, worse than the first, and it caused an incurable wound in the bones of my left foot. My father's friends cleaned out the rotting bones with an operation, and this caused horror and vomiting for my parents, but I was cured of the disease as before. Despite all this, my cruel Fate was not satisfied, and once again sent me another disease which made my entrails swell and my body begin to disintegrate, up to the point when I drew my last breath in the arms of my mother. (106)

To the gods I offered sacrifices and feasts because I was happy, I was enjoying your first birthday, when a pain in the gums, in the roots of your teeth, my child, plunged me into tear-drenched lamentation because you died in three days, little Theogene, and scattered the great hope of your parents. (104)

Other causes of death included crime, fire, earthquake, injuries, and drowning, as seen in the following examples.

I died a babe at the lawless hands of killers. (86)

Instead of bridal chambers the grave followed All fire and ashes destroyed them. (171)

I died amid pains from fire and ashes. (172)

When he was seven years old, Moira took his sweet light in an earthquake. (90)

You, cruel Charon, who in the reed-filled lake row your boat toward Hades, taking the dead to the end of their torments, give a hand to welcome the son of Kinyros who was killed trying to climb a stair. His sandals threw him down and that is why he is afraid to step barefoot on the sands of the lake's edge. (187)

Hit by a large rock . . . in Hades now I find myself with a severe wound. (36)

A swift-footed horse took away my beloved light. Heleios is my name, and only seven turnings of the sun did I see, and having died young, amid lamentation I went to Hades. (94)

He loved learning, was charming, friendly and honest, lived eleven years, fell from a tree and broke his spine, his head falling into father's arms. (61)

Down a little step the baby . . . fell and mortally broke his neck. (89)

Here am I buried, a five-year-old child dead in the fish-bearing sea. (97)

The steps of little Kleodemos, the suckling, led him to the edge of the boat, and a real Thracian north wind threw him into the wild sea, and a wave extinguished his baby soul. (98)

The Evros, deceived, was bound by the winter's ice. The young boy's legs slipping, broke the ice. As the current dragged him along, a sharp piece of ice protruding from the river Vistonio cut his throat and his body was carried away in the whirlpool. Thus, his mother at his grave buried only his head which had floated to the surface. (99)

After eating, I came with my aunt to wash my hair, and immediately my Fates placed me at that well. I was undressing when it dragged me in. My aunt ran, tearing her chiton, my mother ran, beating her breast. With no time to lose, my aunt fell at Alexander's knees and he, seeing her desperation, lost no time, and jumped into the well. As soon as he found me sunk in the water he took me out in a basket. My aunt immediately seized me as I was, to see if I had some hope of life. Thus, ill-fated, before I had time to go to school, my evil Fate sent me to Hades at three years old. (101)

What certainly moved poets to engrave so many details on the gravestones of dead children was the fact that any early death caused both parents and the city to lament. The name of the city was often included in the epitaph verse, indicating once again the important position held by the child in the society of the time. The same society that deified Death, called Death "a thief" and considered it unjust when Death touched a baby, a child, a youth, or even a young man. Children and young people were the pride of any city.

The sarcophagus of 13-year-old Parmenion confirms this and considers the child a hero:

> He enjoyed studying because it made him happy to do what was wise and good. He was the pride of his father, grandfather and his country. This tender offspring, taken away abruptly by all-conquering destiny was honored by the Council and the People.

There are also several testimonies of "ceaseless mourning" by people who experienced the death of a child as the destruction of life at its roots, an incomprehensible and unjust deed by Fates and Demons.

A boy from Mysia, in Asia Minor, expresses his astonishment for dying at the age of thirteen and gives in few words the reply to why the death of children was incomprehensible to the ancient Greeks:

> Did I die uneducated, coarse, unrefined? How can this be possible?

EPILOGUE

Prose, verse, and sculpture attempt to immortalize the child who dies before his or her time, "before growing up and coming of age," and "before its parents' [death]." The artist, obeying the mandate of ancient Greek society, attempts in every way to present the death of a child as being incomprehensible and senseless, the cutting off of life at the moment it should be bearing fruit, the extinguishing of hope at its dawn.

BIBLIOGRAPHY

Ariés. (1973). *L'enfant et la vie familiale sous l'Ancien Régime.* Paris: Editions du Seuil.

Coloboba, K. M., & Ozeretskaia, E. L. (1988). *Everyday life in Ancient Greece.* Athens: Papademas.

Euripides. *Medea.* Athens: Papyrus.

Head, Barclay. (1959). *Guide to the principal coins of the Greeks from circa 700 B.C. to 270 A.D.* London.

Hesiod. *Theogony.* Athens: Papyrus.

Macris, N. (1988). *Study of death.* Athens: Dodoni.

Rudhardt, J. (1987). *Eros and Venus in cosmogonic systems of the Ancient Greeks.* Athens: Kardamitsas.

Verilhac, A. M. (1978). *Pedes Aori: Poésie Funéraire.* Athens: Academy of Athens.

Index